Resisting Barriers
to Belonging

Resisting Barriers to Belonging

Conceptual Critique and Critical Applications

Edited by
Beverly S. Faircloth, Laura M. Gonzalez,
and Katherine Ramos

LEXINGTON BOOKS
Lanham • Boulder • New York • London

Published by Lexington Books
An imprint of The Rowman & Littlefield Publishing Group, Inc.
4501 Forbes Boulevard, Suite 200, Lanham, Maryland 20706
www.rowman.com

86-90 Paul Street, London EC2A 4NE

British Library Cataloguing in Publication Information Available

Library of Congress Cataloging-in-Publication Data Available

ISBN: 978-1-7936-3213-5 (cloth)
ISBN: 978-1-7936-3215-9 (pbk.)
ISBN: 978-1-7936-3214-2 (electronic)

Contents

List of Figures and Tables

Preface

Resisting Cultural Barriers to Belonging— Conceptual Critique, Critical Applications

Laura I. Rendón

As this book's cultural auditor, I begin by emphasizing that belonging is a basic, self-evident human right that constitutes the very foundation for our authentic existence as a part of the earth's family. Relationship-centered philosophical viewpoints are a key part of Indigenous and spiritual traditions across the world. In Indigenous cultures we exist in relationship and share a common humanity. Human beings have a relationship to nature and a responsibility to protect the environment. A Tao teaching reminds us that all of us seek belonging and that this union should always be open to all of us. In lak'ech, associated with the Mayan culture, posits the notion that you and I exist in relationship to each other; in essence, I am another you. The Lakota phrase Mitakuye Oyasin (all my relations) addresses the interconnectedness of our existence. In a similar way, the Zulu term ubuntu, umuntu ngumuntu ngabantu is an expression of oneness and common humanity—I am because you are and my sense of being is intertwined with your humanity. In the Islamic tradition Alamaeia is a remembrance that we are never alone and that divine presence is always with us both as individuals and as members of the collective. Alamaeia illuminates the fascinating concept of *withness* with those who we love. Taken together all of these relational philosophical perspectives highlight universal truths that are often not acknowledged in today's society. These truths are ways of knowing and being which emphasize that we all belong to the great family of the world, and it is *withness*, the ultimate form of belonging, that brings forth our authenticity and our ability to walk in the world attuned to nature while understanding that we exist not just as individuals but also as a part of the greater social collective (Rendón, 2009).

As the authors of this volume note, there is extensive research on importance of sense of belonging, relationships, and validation as foundational to healthy human development and to student success (Felton & Lambert, 2020; Rendón, 1994; Rendón-Linares & Munoz, 2011). Nonetheless, far too many institutions and organizations operate in opposition to ancestral traditions of relationality, belonging, and the unity of existence. These institutions have stolen what Beverly S. Faircloth in this volume terms "rightful presence" from the very individuals who could benefit most from experiencing a strong sense of belonging: low-income people, students of color, immigrants, refugees, as well as undocumented and LGBTQ+ populations. The end result is unhealthy, even toxic environments for those who experience the trauma of being otherized, marginalized, racialized, and/or excluded.

As a scholar who studies the experiences of low-income, first-generation college students, I have learned that there are diverse forms of cultural assaults that can make students feel unwelcome, unsafe, and unsure of their ability to attain academic success. For instance, students can encounter devaluing experiences such as bullying, racism, homophobia, and early labeling as "problem students" requiring disciplinary actions and/or special education classes. In some cases, faculty, staff, and artifacts of the institution do not reflect the diverse community of students. With these kinds of macro- and micro-aggressions students get overt and covert messages that they are not good enough or that they can't succeed. Therefore, it is not surprising that such students privately question: Do I really belong here? Does anyone care about me? Am I good enough? Should I drop out? The perpetuation of lack of belonging, especially for our most vulnerable students, is a gross form of educational neglect and academic injustice (Conchas & Acevedo, 2020; Valenzuela, 1999).

The need to belong, have presence, feel validated and worthwhile are basic human needs yet remain not fully attainable for those that suffer from inequitable and unjust structures in American society. I write as a person who has grappled over the course of her life with multiple, intersecting marginalized identities (Chicana/Latina/Indigenous, Mexican American, first-generation college student, queer scholar of color), all of which I embrace and some which put me at a significant disadvantage depending on cultural context. I have lived the racist, exclusionary history of the United States—being born in poverty, attending segregated, poorly resourced schools, as well as being considered at risk, inferior and unlikely to succeed (Rendón, 2020a). Yes, I succeeded against the odds, but so many others did not succeed because entrenched, unfavorable odds stacked against us made sure only a few would rise to the top. Among detrimental odds students often face are those that create a sense of isolation and otherness, for example, lack of access to faculty and staff of color and the exclusion of our culture, voices, perspectives, histories, and contributions to the nation. Consequently, it becomes imperative to get a deep, critically informed understanding of why lack of belonging remains so pervasive and what can be done to foster a greater sense of inclusion.

To understand belonging involves the examination of race and class inequalities, as well as oppressive structures which have a long history of racist practices such as exclusion, segregation, and marginalization of people of color. The educational arena provides a prime example of how students' exposure to race and class inequalities can result in them virtually being shut out of first-rate schooling and ultimate participation in the nation's democratic structures. Today, the nation has an exceedingly high level of wealth inequality, virtually assuring that a mostly White, elite ruling-class endures across generations, while limiting (if not ending) the hope of social mobility and policy influence for the poor. In an undemocratic system, low-income people of color have become a large part of the wealth underclass with little to no assets that can be transferred from families to children. These children are largely doomed to a scenario where they will (1) likely attend poorly resourced, racially segregated schools, (2) have virtually no access to elite institutions of higher education, (3) assume mostly low-level careers, and (4) have very limited policy-making power and access to high-level leadership roles over their lifetime. The only sense of belonging low-income people will likely have is with other individuals in similar situations. It is not surprising that even when low-income students access college they find it difficult to get full membership in a higher education context that has not been set up for students whose cultures do not represent the dominant White culture (Rendon, 2020b). Some suffer anxiety, stress, and lack of confidence related to what has been termed "imposter syndrome," a feeling one is a fraud and does not belong in college (Clance & Imes, 1978; Vaughn, Taasoobshirazi, & Johnson, 2019). Belonging and connectedness require both individual and institutional responsibility, and the role of institutions in merging the student world and the culture of schools and colleges cannot be overstated (Rendon, Jalomo & Nora, 2000).

We now know that wealthy students have a significant head-start on life and benefit from resource-rich school systems where everything is set up for them not only to find belonging but also to access the academic and social support needed to attain their educational goals. The nonprofit EdBuild has noted that "nonwhite school districts get 23 billion dollars less than white districts despite serving the same number of students" (2019, p. 1). It is not surprising that well-funded schools typically operate with credentialed teachers, state-of-the-art textbooks and curricular materials, as well as laboratories and technology tools which can facilitate college preparedness, access to well-paying jobs and to the most selective colleges and universities. In fact, children from the top 1 percent of the income distribution are almost always assured that they will attend Ivy League schools (Reeves, 2017; Hobbes,

2019; Rendon, 2020b). In short, our highly unequal social structures are set up to confer significant advantages to access wealth, first-rate education, high-level leadership positions, policy influence, and social belonging to those who are already privileged.

This extraordinary book fills a void in the literature about sense of belonging in two major areas. In the first part of the book the authors provide examples of nuances associated with belonging, as well as what it means to lack equitable presence especially for members of oppressed student groups, those at the margins of our society and for adult populations such as teachers and adults in palliative care. The authors provide missing links in the research and practice literature about fostering inclusivity and offer a critically informed view of belonging. The second part of the book takes us to critical applications or practices to support belonging. Among the authors' most important contributions include the following:

- Diverse theories and frameworks are employed to address how issues of belonging are intertwined with power, equity, justice, and agency (i.e., rightful presence, critical race theory, structural belonging, critical humanism, authentic belonging, and critical validation).
- Belonging requires the transformation of educational institutions and social organizations. Teachers, administrators, and clinicians can play a significant role in fostering equitable, inclusive, and validating contexts where individuals from diverse cultures and linguistic backgrounds can optimize intellectual, social, emotional, and inner-life skills through a humanized educational praxis. Ways and means to support belonging and foster critical consciousness may include: safe learning spaces such as ethnic studies, anti-racist and culturally responsive pedagogies, Spanish language programs, summer writing and art-based camps, and validating practices that honor and value student identities.
- To theorize belonging we must consider not only its characteristics and sociocultural manifestations. As Kathy Ramos in this volume reminds us, belonging can be both experienced and felt. Consequently, we must also consider what it means to *feel* to have equitable presence, as well as what it *feels* to not have a sense of belonging. In this view a person's sense of belonging becomes what Cherrie Moraga (2015) calls "a theory in the flesh." Theorizing belonging can involve critical analyses of *feeling* "what it means to be 'the other,' to live with contradictions, embody diverse social identities and struggle with invisibility and marginalization" (Chang & Rendón, 2018, p. 8).
- Lack of belonging is a product of the long-lasting racist features of US history and perpetuated by entrenched, unchallenged narratives that privilege the already-privileged such as the myth of meritocracy and colorblindness.

The authors also contend that lack of belonging is a failure not of the individual, but of institutions, governing boards, and policymakers. Along these lines, Laura M. Gonzalez in this volume presents a critical humanist view of belonging that includes both individual agency and structures of power. The idea is to eradicate unjust, unneeded barriers to rightful presence and to attend to the agency of individuals in a way that allows them to self-actualize and live up to their full potential.

This is an important book that not only unpacks the notion of belonging but that also lifts the knowledge base of healthy human development through a critical, equitable, and culturally sustaining perspective. Through its careful centering of experiences and voices of marginalized groups, the book moves away from anchoring its frameworks and applications associated with dominant, mainly White, perspectives. In the past these flawed yet prevailing views advocated the idea that to fully belong, the onus was on outsiders to assimilate while institutions remained unchanged (Rendón, Jalomo & Nora, 2000).

I urge educators, community/organizational leaders, and policymakers to read this book and remind themselves of what our ancestors knew in their hearts and minds to be true. We all belong. Belonging is a universal quality we owe to each other. In fact, to even insinuate that one is not worthy of belonging is to renounce the notion of withness and of attending to the helplessness of those in our communities who have been cast aside. The book's authors understand that there is nothing wrong with low-income and other marginalized populations. We are not imposters, frauds, or mentally incompetent. Beyond our hopes and dreams we have gathered brilliant strengths from our culture to help us succeed such family work ethic, perseverance, resistance, navigational competence, curiosity, and giving back (Rendón, Nora & Kanagala, 2014; Rendón, Nora, Bledsoe & Kanagala, 2020; Salis-Reyes, 2018; Yosso, 2005).

I trust that this book can bring educators, policymakers, and organizational leaders to work with what the book's authors strongly advocate. Belonging is a human right, not a gift or a privilege. Therefore, restoring the stolen right of belonging for our most vulnerable populations is a most important restorative justice imperative facing educational systems and social organizations. This book represents a giant leap forward to ensure that no individuals from marginalized groups will ever again wonder about their belongingness, but instead enthusiastically affirm: I feel valued, and yes, I really belong here.

Laura I. Rendón, author of *Sentipensante Pedagogy: Educating for Wholeness, Social Justice and Liberation.* Sterling, VA: Stylus Press.

REFERENCES

Chang, L.C. & Rendon, L.I. (2018). Educating for wholeness in the intersections. *Diversity & Democracy, 21*(1), 8–12.

Clance, P.R. & Imes, S. (1978, Fall). The imposter phenomenon in high achieving women: Dynamics and therapeutic intervention. *Psychotherapy Theory, Research and Practice, 15*(3), 1–8.

Conchas, G. & Acevedo (2020). *The Chicana/o/x Dream. Hope, Resistance, and Educational Success.* Cambridge, MA: Harvard University Press.

EdBuild (2019). Nonwhite school districts get $23 billion less than white districts despite serving the same number of students. https://edbuild.org/content/23-billion#CA.

Felten, P. & Lambert, L.M. (2020). *Relationship-rich Education.* Baltimore, MD: John Hopkins University Press.

Hobbes, M. (2019). The "Glass Floor" is keeping America's richest idiots at the top. https://www.huffpost.com/entry/the-glass-floor-is-keeping-americas-richest-idiots -at-the-top_n_5d9fb1c9e4b06ddfc516e076?guccounter=1

Moraga, C. (2015). Entering the lives of others. Theory in the flesh. In C. Moraga and G. Anzaldúa (eds.). *This Bridge Called My Back. Writings by Radical Women of Color.* Fourth edition. Albany, NY: State University of New York Press, 19.

Reeves, R.V. (2017). *Dream Hoarders: How the American Upper Middle Class Is Leaving Everyone Else in the Dust, Why That Is a Problem, and What to Do About It.* Washington, DC: Brookings Institution Press.

Rendón, L.I. (1994). Validating culturally diverse students: Toward a new model of learning and student development. *Innovative Higher Education, 19*(1), 33–51.

Rendón, L.I. (2009). *Sentipensante Pedagogy: Educating for Wholeness, Social Justice and Liberation.* Sterling, VA: Stylus Press.

Rendón, L.I. (2020a). A First-Generation Scholar's Camino de Conocimiento. In L.W. Perna (Ed.), *Higher Education: Handbook of Theory and Research: Volume 35* (pp. 1–47). Springer International Publishing. https://doi. org/10.1007/978-3-030-11743-6_1-1.

Rendón, L.I. (2020b). Unrelenting inequality at the intersection of race and class. *Change. The Magazine for Higher Learning, 32*(2), 32–35.

Rendón, L.I., Jalomo, R. & Nora, A. (2000). Theoretical considerations in the study of minority student retention. In J. Braxton (ed.). *Rethinking the Student Departure Puzzle: New Theory and Research on College Student Retention*, 127–156. Nashville, TN: Vanderbilt University Press.

Rendón, L.I., Nora, A., Bledsoe, R., & Kanagala, V. (2020). Científicos Latinxs: Uncovering the counter-story of success in STEM. In S.J. Paik, S.M. Kula, J.J. González and V. González (eds.). *High-Achieving Latino Students. Successful Pathways Toward College and Beyond*, 159–178. Charlotte, NC. Information Age Publishing.

Rendón, L.I., Nora, A., & Kanagala, V. (2014). *Ventajas/assets y Conocimientos/ Knowledge: Leveraging Latin@ Strengths to Foster Student Success.* San Antonio, TX: Center for Research and Policy in Education, The University of Texas at San Antonio.

Rendón-Linares, L.I., & Muñoz, S.M. (2011). Revisiting validation theory: Theoretical foundations, applications, and extensions. *Enrollment Management Journal, 5*(2), 12–33.

Salis-Reyes, N. (2018). *What Am I Doing to Be a Good Ancestor? An Indigenized Phenomenology of Giving Back Among Native College Students.* Unpublished doctoral dissertation. University of Texas-San Antonio.

Valenzuela, A. (1999). *Subtractive Schooling: US-Mexican Youth and the Politics of Caring.* Albany, NY: State University of New York Press.

Vaughn, A.R., Taasoobshirazi, G., & Johnson, M.L. (2019). Imposter phenomenon and motivation: *Women in Higher Education. Studies in Higher Education.* Advance online publication. doi:10.1080/03075079.2019.1568976

Yosso, T.J. (2005). Whose culture has capital? A critical race theory discussion of community cultural wealth. *Race Ethnicity and Education, 8*(1), 69–91. doi: 10.1080/1361332052000341006

Acknowledgments

It goes without saying that serving as coeditors during a global pandemic came with a unique and unprecedented set of challenges. Our collective ability to come together, cheer each other on, and show grace has made the experience of getting this book to the finish-line far more rewarding than we knew possible. To that end, we want to extend our deepest and sincere thanks to all the contributing authors that made this book possible. Your scholarship and insights to the construct of *belonging* have surpassed all our expectations, hopes, and ambitions for this text.

A very special thanks goes out to Dr. Laura I. Rendón for her thoughtful contribution as captured in the Preface. It is an honor having you review a text we feel so privileged to be part of and that we now get to share with a larger audience. We also owe an enormous debt of appreciation to Holly Buchanan and everyone on the publishing team. This book wouldn't have been possible without everyone's generous guidance and understanding.

To our colleagues both past and present who have helped our careers, contributed to our knowledge, and inspired the work we love doing every day: Thank You. To the future readers of this book, who will have a key role to play in reimagining and enacting what belonging means: Thank you as well.

Our deepest gratitude goes out to our family and friends in supporting this brainchild that came from our respective experiences of understanding our own belonging. Thank you for your unwavering patience when we are gone for hours on end writing, and for always greeting us with a smile and great warmth when we resurface for air.

Introduction

Framing Sense of Belonging for Our Time

Beverly S. Faircloth, Laura M. Gonzalez, and Katherine Ramos

INTRODUCTION

The vast body of work created by worldwide efforts to understand and support positive human development leaves little question about the urgent and complex need to understand and support positive human development, not just for some, but for all. As insights have been gathered from parents, teachers, youth, counselors, doctors, psychologists, social workers, community organizers, and advocates, the concept of sense of belonging has emerged as pivotal to our well-being. The human need for belonging, in its many forms, has been well-established in theory, research, and practice as an essential and foundational aspect of how we come to understand and engage with ourselves and the world around us. As such, work that pushes the field of belonging forward to a more holistic, global, and critical understanding is a worthwhile endeavor.

Over the previous three decades, a large body of work from multiple fields has demonstrated that experiencing an enduring positive, authentic, and meaningful sense that one belongs within the contexts one inhabits serves as a nonnegotiable underlying element of positive development. Early on, in his hierarchy of basic human needs Maslow laid the cornerstone (1943, 1999), articulating the universal and essential nature of the need to belong. The seminal conceptual foundation for belonging research published by Baumeister and Leary in 1995 also identified belonging as central among human needs, fundamental to our well-being and motivation. Aligned with this lens, Gray et al. (2018) described belonging as a kind of psychological hub that facilitates important outcomes—from motivation and achievement to health and well-being. Indeed research has consistently demonstrated that individuals have salient psychological needs—such as belonging—that they are driven to fulfill within their various contexts, with significant results (e.g., Eccles & Roeser, 2011).

Sense of belonging has recently been referred to as one of the premier social issues of our time (Allen & Boyle, 2016). Specifically, there is ample evidence that belonging is essential to motivation, engagement, and learning in school settings (Faircloth, 2006; Benner et al., 2008; Goodenow, 1993; Gray et al., 2011) and holds formative implications for both psychological and physical health across the life span. For example, Slaten et al. (2016) provide a helpful rendering of the psychological benefits of belonging—including well-being, increased self-esteem, positive mood, improved memory, positive life transitions, and reduced stress—as well as physical benefits— including reduced risk of stroke, lowered disease risk, and reduced mortality. Importantly, the benefits associated with belonging—whether it be to a group, organization, school, or community—have also been found to have lasting effects (Walton & Cohen, 2011; Walton et al., 2012; Wong et al., 2003). The cost of a lack of belonging is evident in many reports of the essential contribution of belonging to positive development, engagement, and school achievement (Anderman & Anderman, 1999; Benner et al., 2008; Faircloth, 2008; Knifsend et al., 2018). Despite growth in this field, answers to the challenges to belonging among diverse groups and contexts remain especially elusive (Faircloth, 2019; Gonzalez et al., 2014). For decades, this work was anchored primarily in dominant, whitestream lenses and contexts, despite the fact that communities, schools, and organizations increasingly represent complex intersectionalities of identities, cultures, and perspectives. Even as attention has turned in this direction, much more is needed. Not only are diverse perspectives not drawn on frequently, marginalized communities often find themselves blamed for their lack of belonging and the onus is put on them to assimilate. We attempt here to highlight the responsibilities of systems—and those who wield power in them—to intentionally make space for belonging for all, by supporting the inclusion and preservation of culture, identity, and agency, and drawing on the strengths of all.

MOVING FORWARD

As we start to pick up the pieces from the devastation of the year 2020, at least one lesson we need to carry forward is the enduring importance of belonging. In the aftermath of the COVID-19 pandemic and the clarion call to address racial injustice, we have seen and heard stories about disconnection and connection; about the moral imperative to say that one's life, agency, and voice matter and deserve to be heard; and about the futility of an us versus them framing to lead us anywhere constructive. We have seen images of teachers driving by the houses of their students, reaching past the quarantine to provide support and a message of belonging. We have heard the songs being sung from balconies to remind us of the ways that life and living in community are precious and valuable things. Violence against Black and Brown lives, pushback toward the Black Lives Matter movement, as well as hate crime atrocities to Asian Americans and Pacific Islanders (AAPI) have highlighted the inherent attack on belonging by not valuing their worth or recognizing that they too belong. However, we have seen waves of peaceful protesters calling for accountability, asserting the worthiness of their lives and their right to membership in the just community that we are still working to achieve. At our very core, we have wrestled with this deep understanding that belonging is critical to our well-being and is simultaneously vulnerable to attack. If we, the editors and authors of this book, could hold up anything for our collective memory from the past year, we would borrow the words poet Amanda Gorman spoke at her 2021 inauguration presentation, "We are striving to forge a union with purpose, to compose a country committed to all cultures, colors, characters and conditions of man" (which we would amend to "conditions of all").

For the purposes of this book, we start with a working definition of belonging that pushes back on some of the more traditional roots of belonging in scholarly literature. We move into creating this definition with a type of community bricolage that helps us explore the contours of belonging with greater nuance and from many perspectives. Authors in this book engage with the idea of belonging by naming the realities of power and marginalization, identifying relevant structural barriers that make belonging more complicated for some populations than for others. We reflect on the dynamics of belonging in a variety of settings—schools, universities, work, home, hospice, professional development sites, summer camp, clubs, counseling groups, and the public square. This is important because a power-aware analysis of belonging must examine these structures, systems, and contexts. We ask readers to consider a "both/and" approach where individual potential for self-actualization and agency are encouraged, while at the same time, systems that have been inequitable are interrogated for their role in denying space for belonging.

However, we do not stop with the barriers—our title is *Resisting Barriers to Belonging*, after all. This community of scholars identifies culture, identity, voice, and agency—active forms of engaging and reshaping belonging. Together we share descriptions of counterspaces for belonging and the critical consciousness to see the need for those spaces. We call out to leaders to take responsibility and create spaces where belonging is possible—not to just wait for individuals to find their way. We identify the ways that belonging goes beyond simple connection to an invitation to show up in fully authentic ways and make contributions. This genuine, rightful presence must be grounded in a space where respect and accountability are also present, however. As will be discussed in the next chapter, the "hospitality" model, wherein people are invited into a space but still marked as outsiders and constrained in their actions, is not what we are after. To borrow a metaphor, we are not asking just to enter the room as guests but to have the right to move the furniture around and make it our own (Watt, 2015).

Moreover, we draw on insights from multiple fields—education, psychology, sociology, counseling, higher education, teacher education, cultural foundations, community organizing, advocacy, policy, peace and conflict studies, women and gender studies, Black/African American and African diaspora studies, each with essential contributions to this work. We do not anchor our work, nor ask contributors to anchor theirs, in particular or traditional models of belonging. Rather, we draw heavily on conceptual models that purposefully highlight issues of power, inequity, social justice, and agency in this struggle (e.g., "rightful presence"). Regardless of the particular lens adopted, it is undeniable that considering belonging through a critical, equitable, culturally sustaining perspective, while simultaneously identifying settings where more attention to barriers to belonging is crucial, is a nonnegotiable element of moving the work of positive human development forward.

THE CURRENT BOOK

In an attempt to address this salient need, our book is composed of two complementary halves of this conversation. In broad strokes, the first six chapters of this book initially focuses on conceptual critique, eliciting deeper and more nuanced understandings of belonging, and framing the ways that marginalized voices have expereinced barriers to belonging. To set the stage for the remaining work, Faircloth draws on a criticality framework to address the concept of *the right to belong*, naming the struggles and historicized injustices that shape belonging for many individuals and groups. After tracing the trajectory of belonging research and theory from its initial social underpinnings, through the addition of sociocultural insights, this chapter suggests criticality as an essential addition to belonging work, especially against the backdrop of the huge proportion of the world's population being made *invisible* or *missing* by societies' and systems' clinging to dominant cultural perspectives. This viewpoint then invites the sociopolitical work of dismantling oppressive systems and structures that contribute to marginalization to *make present* or *visible* those who had formerly been made invisible, in order to forge new possibilities of belonging.

Hope, Smith, Griffin, and Briggs utilize critical race theory to focus on schools as systems that can do more to actively promote and create spaces where belonging is possible for Black students, an especially important endeavor as Black students are far too often overlooked and positioned on the margins of classrooms, schools, and educational opportunities. Acknowledging the contemporary and historic systems that undermine Black students' capacity to belong in schools, the chapter shifts the burden of responsibility from students (to feel like they belong) to educators and policymakers (to create spaces where belonging is possible). Focusing on instructional and institutional opportunities for belonging, the authors describe how educators can develop critical race consciousness and use antiracist pedagogy to support the belongingness needs of Black school students.

The chapter by Antonicci, Killion, and Johnson considers the campus-based structures that often serve as barriers to belonging for members of the LGBTQ+ community (lesbian, gay, bisexual, transgender, queer, and other identities). As individuals whose rights (e.g., the right to exist, the right to safety, the right to accurately self-identify, the right to belong) are often challenged, attacked, or ridiculed, members of this group face multiple obstacles to their safety and well-being, much less their sense of belonging. The college campuses they inhabit are not exempt from these barriers. The authors of this chapter quote Gannon (2020) to powerfully illuminate such oppression:

> higher education proclaims itself to be the arena of opportunity and the engine driving the changes necessary to create a better world. . . . But institutional and educational practices that exclude students—that push them to the margins, figuratively or literally—render those pronouncements nothing more than a cruel joke. (p. 56)

These authors skillfully identify strategies for gauging and building campus cultures with LGBTQ+ students' belonging in mind. Moreover they argue that it is incumbent upon all of us to be the change agents to disrupt the patterns through which so many are marginalized.

In the next chapter, Gonzalez uses the lens of critical humanism to ask the question, "Does a piece of paper confer belonging?" The chapter addresses the difficult situation of young adults with Deferred Action for Childhood Arrivals (DACA) or without documented status who feel in their hearts that they belong in the United States but are told repeatedly in the public discourse that they do not. Through the lens of critical humanism, she unpacks the tangle of legal terms, statuses, and the tide of discrimination, scapegoating, and backlash experienced by immigrant youth advocating for their right to belong in the United States. Her skillful exploration of these issues suggests the need for a higher ethical standard, not one based on paper, but one based on lived experiences in our communities. Pulling from a variety of social science and health-related fields, she reviews the following constructs for their potential to change the ways we think about legal status and belonging: (1) shifting and persisting, (2) mattering, (3) coping and healing ethno-racial trauma, (4) substantive membership, (5) civic engagement, (6) critical validation, and (7) advocacy *with.*

In chapter 5, Wilson, Baucom, Hare, Wonsavage, Duggan, Webb, McCulloch, Stephan, Mawhinney, and Schwartz (a group of mathematics education leaders in their state) wrestled with dimensions of belonging and community as they struggled to establish a sense of community across a state-wide professional learning initiative. In collaboration with state and district mathematics leaders, three iterations of an attempt to develop a statewide learning community had been enacted, with mixed results regarding teacher enthusiasm or engagement. Committed to the belief that teachers hold an essential key to, and voice in, powerful professional development and essential progress in mathematics education, they retrospectively examined their work with a focus on belonging. In their chapter, they suggest key insights for both mathematics education and professional development when belonging is leveraged to position teachers as central agents, rather than recipients of developments in these fields. Specifically, they highlight the differences between designing for a sense of community levied on teachers (a common pattern in traditional professional development models tackling huge systemic complexities) versus designing for a sense of belonging actually authored by teachers. They conclude that, when designing for community, one is also assuming the mantle of designing for self-authored, authentic, and meaningful belonging.

In a particularly self-reflective chapter, Ramos offers an informative counterpoint in her lens on belonging. She reflects on her own experience as *in-betweener:* a Latinx woman, from a poor, underprivileged background, first-generation student, first-generation faculty member, mental health clinician, and academic in palliative and hospice care at a prestigious and historically White institution. In this poignant narrative, she deftly traces her experience of, and supports the readers' negotiation of, a nuanced fluid and determinedly authentic sense of belonging across the multiple spaces we inhabit. She harnesses these intimate insights as she "comes to see the role of in-betweener as a source of strength" to help those who she treats, as she bears witness to their struggles with mortality and what it means to exist in the face of impending death. The chapter concludes with imminently practical suggestions for performing, engaging, and participating in the act of belonging.

In the second part of the book, we provide examples of critical applications that support belonging for individuals from marginalized communities. This section begins with a reflection by Harris, Ingram, Hockaday, and Gonzalez on a school-based College and Career Readiness (CCR) group for Black girls, described from the perspective of the young girls who participated, the graduate student who led the group, and the faculty member who cocreated the group. These Black women's voices together tell the story of constructing counterspaces for safety, belonging, and educational aspirations, which they genuinely learned from each other. The students not only constructed their own counterspaces for belonging within the CCR group but also catalyzed a new understanding of belonging, one that cannot be bestowed—but must be genuinely co-constructed within and across spaces of community. The authors explain that the potential ripple effects go backward, forward, and sideways, especially for this particular minority group who are often ignored in K–12 literature.

The next chapter wrestles with the reality that despite growing diversity in US public schools, curricula persistently cling to whitestream norms, treating learning as a colorblind experience, thereby often yielding detrimental consequences for nondominant youth whose cultural backgrounds are marginalized. In a yearlong, after-school club for sixth-grade students at a diverse, urban middle school, Faircloth, Barrett, and McClanahan employed the practice of *ethnic studies* to support critical consciousness, and therefore belonging, among middle-grade students, highlighting the potential of beginning such meaningful work as early as middle school. These students' stories reflect their own growing belonging, their insights about belonging, and their commitment to the belonging of their schoolmates—as they grew into allies, advocates, and agents of change for their classroom and school.

Hinman, He, Wilson, Paschal, and Nelson's chapter reporting on a *Heritage Language Academy* (HLA) is based on the idea that students who are building on their home language as a base can generate a greater sense of belonging in school, which can translate into achievement in many ways. In particular, HLA programs bridge the gap between the schools and immigrant families, who are often marginalized in academic spaces. Explaining that it is critical to consider heritage language learners' cultural and linguistic assets when constructing learning spaces that support the development of students' sense of belonging, the chapter describes a Spanish Heritage Language Program that does just that. The HLA engages teachers, students, and families in an alternative learning space that promotes four specific dimensions of students' lives: learners' positive emotions, positive social relations, involvement, and harmonization. The chapter shares lessons learned about constructing spaces of belonging for culturally and linguistically diverse families observed across 10 years of program implementation.

The learning needs of newly resettled members of our communities (i.e., immigrants and refugees) present important and urgent issues that deserve careful attention. Their needs are complex by any measure but are made particularly problematic in the US society by a history of assimilationist and

nationalist thought and practice that pervades attempts in US society to make
sense of this situation. In chapter 10, Faircloth, Hinman, Marhatta, McDaniels,
Vetter, and Zoch illustrate the belonging experiences of immigrant and refugee youth who participated in a Community Voices summer writing camp
for sixth- to twelfth-grade English learners. The camp attempted to support
belonging by anchoring summer camp writing experiences in youth culture,
identity, voice, language, and background, and by encouraging students to
represent their literacy abilities in nontraditional forms (e.g., art work, hip-
hop poetry, identity maps, and their heritage language if desired). Drawing on
the youths' own stories (written and otherwise), the authors illustrate important ways that these youth effectively employed four resources—cultural
capital, relational capital, linguistic capital, and voice/agency—to understand
and construct their experiences of belonging in camp and beyond.

In Chapter 11 of this book, Chang, Baimaganbetova, Yang, Cheung,
Pun, and Yip valuably draw our attention beyond the boundaries and
assumptions of the United States, to a very different culture and prospect
for belonging in Hong Kong. After decades of being known as one of the
world's great metropolises, more recently, Hong Kong has experienced
massive long-term protests for democracy and socioeconomic justice while
under de facto rule by mainland China. Following the protests, heightened
sociopolitical repression was brought down upon students, other activists,
and mainstream society. Under such conditions, it is understandable that
students and teachers struggled to develop a sense of agency, belonging,
and community. Against that backdrop, the authors discuss the Project for
Critical Research, Pedagogy and Praxis' efforts to use sociocultural learning
and critical pedagogy, to address equity issues in a teacher education pipeline that serves primarily working-class students and those who are the first
in their family to attend college. Adapting social-justice-oriented theories
originally developed in the Global North, this chapter presents insights for
teacher education and educational pipeline work in Asia, and how they can
be sustained as spaces of greater agency, belonging, and community abroad.
This much-needed pivot from a dominant Western and predominantly individualistic lens provides an essential prism for our understanding of the
work of belonging.

We are aware that we have not, and indeed cannot, address all salient
social identities and life experiences within one book. Here we specifically
acknowledge our own positionalities as a way to help readers draw their own
conclusions about this book's ability to speak to their circumstances, needs,
or concerns. Biographical information about each chapter author is also made
available in the pages of this book. The first editor (pronouns: she/hers; cisgender female) is White, Western, and middle-class. While this positioning
bestows considerable privilege, a childhood shaped by long-term poverty

and abuse carved an indelible awareness of, and determination concerning, issues such as marginalization and othering. Dr. Faircloth's work in education, from classroom teacher to professor, has been rich with opportunities, role models, and challenges to recognize her own privilege and attempt to stand against the systems of power and inequity rampant in US society today. Her work, *Resisting Barriers to Belonging*, especially among nondominant youth, emerges from that background. The second editor (pronouns: she/hers; cisgender female) identifies as a fifth- or sixth-generation Scots-Irish-German American who is married to a first-generation Panamanian American. Although Dr. Gonzalez (previously McLaughlin) grew up in a small, homogeneously White and middle-class town, she has recognized the deep limitations of that background and has actively tried to spend time learning with and from people with other backgrounds (in terms of race-ethnicity, nationality, religion, gender identity, sexual orientation, socioeconomic class, etc.). She has acquired Spanish as a second language as a way to hear more directly from Latinx immigrant families in their own voices, and continues to position herself as a learner. The third editor is a first-generation multiracial, cisgender woman, who grew up mostly lower class. Dr. Ramos (pronouns: she/hers) is a first-generation student, graduate, and now faculty member at Duke University. She acknowledges her own lived experience and her privilege of having the opportunity to secure an education, live a life with good mental health, and secure a career afforded by her education. She is fluent in Spanish and has developed a line of work that advocates for good mental health for all with an anchor in equity, self-care, and compassion.

Due to the limitations of our social positions and in order to reflectively guide this manuscript, mitigate any blind spots, and augment the perspectives available to address these issues, we have invited Dr. Laura Rendón, a nationally recognized educational theorist, scholar, and activist to serve as *cultural auditor* for the volume. As such, we have asked her to mentor our efforts and to introduce the volume with a preface that sets the stage for the importance of this conversation, highlighting powerful threads of theory and practice that emerge in the work. We are deeply grateful for her contributions.

We identify our positionalities and invite critique and conversation about them because identifying our cultures and naming where we belong are exercises in power. Who gets the right to name or be named? Whose stories are honored in a name? Whose are erased? We wish to offer an acknowledgment of the stories lifted up in this volume and the stories that are missing. The act of acknowledgment of traditional land, for example, is a public statement of the rightful presence of Native inhabitants of a place. However, acknowledgment by itself is an initial gesture. It becomes meaningful when coupled with authentic relationships and informed by action. However, this small step of acknowledgment can be an opening to greater public consciousness of Native sovereignty and cultural rights, a step toward equitable relationships and reconciliation. Because many of the authors of this volume have a connection to North Carolina, we would like to honor and respect the diverse Indigenous peoples connected to this territory in which we live and work.

North Carolina has been home to many Indigenous peoples at various points in time, including the tribes/nations of: Bear River/Bay River, Cape Fear, Catawba, Chowanoke, Coree/Coranine, Creek, Croatan, Eno, Hatteras, Keyauwee, Machapunga, Moratoc, Natchez, Neusiok, Pamlico, Shakori, Sara/Cheraw, Sissipahaw, Sugeree, Wateree, Weapemeoc, Woccon, Yadkin, and Yeopim. Today, NC recognizes 8 tribes: Coharie, Lumbee, Meherrin, Occaneechi, Saponi, Haliwa Saponi, Waccamaw Siouan, Sappony, and the Eastern Band Cherokee. (Our thanks to Brad Johnson for sharing this land acknowledgment, drawn from https://libconf.uncg.edu/land-acknowledgment/)

By acknowledging our debt to those who came before us, inviting a critique by a cultural auditor, and bringing together the wide range of perspectives and strategies included in this volume, we invite a broad scope of readers, researchers, practitioners, and theorists to be—and feel—included in this conversation, to ask their own questions about belonging. As such, we hope that all will find a home in this work, as we learn, question, contribute, and fight for our own—and others'—right to belong, and that we may actually work together to do something about the current national crisis of barriers to belonging. It is only fair to foreshadow the final chapter of this book where all will be invited to consider action related to belonging. That is because noticing and naming barriers to belonging is not nearly enough; it is imperative that we also interrupt those barriers and work to ensure a right to belong for all. It is our hope that readers of this book will hear in its pages refrains that call them to this work. For, together we rise, but only when we cherish a shared sense of equitable community and stake our future to our shared right to belong.

NOTE

1. Please note that chapter-related articles or book references mentioned in this Introduction are cited in the reference list for that respective chapter.

REFERENCES

Allen, K. & Boyle, C. (2016). Pathways to school belonging. *The Educational and Developmental Psychologist, 33*(1), ii–iv.

Baumeister, R.F. & Leary, M.R. (1995). The need to belonging: Desire for inter-personal attachment as a fundamental human motivation. *Psychological Bulletin, 117*(3), 497–530.

Benner, A., Graham, S. & Mistry, R. (2016). Discerning direct and mediated effects of ecological structures and processes on adolescents' educational outcomes. *Developmental Psychology, 44*(3), 840–854.

Eccles, J. S. & Roeser, R. W. (2011). Schools as developmental contexts during adolescence. *Journal of Research on Adolescence, 21*(1), 225–241. doi:10.1111/j.1532-7795.2010.00725.x

"Rightful Presence" vs. Getting "Lost in the Sauce": Understanding Belonging using "Hanging Out" Research Methodology. Invited Paper Presentation at Special Session (Delving Deeper into Phenomena: Case Study as a Methodology for Investigating Motivation). To be presented at the 2019 Annual Convention of the American Psychological Association in Chicago, IL.

Gannon, K. (2020). *Radical Hope: A Teaching Manifesto.* West Virginia University Press.

Gonzalez, L. M., Stein, G. L., Kiang, L. & Cupito, A. M. (2014). The influence of support and discrimination on developmental competencies in Latino adolescents. *Journal of Latina/o Psychology, 2*, 79–91.

Goodenow, C. (1993). Classroom belonging among early adolescent students: Relationships to motivation and achievement. *Journal of Early Adolescence, 13*, 21–43.

Gorman, A. *The Hill We Climb.* January 6, 2021.

Gray, D.L., Hope, E.C. & Matthews, J.S. (2018). What opportunities do Black adolescents have to belong at school? A case for cultural distinctiveness and citizenship as instructional and institutional opportunity structures. *Educational Psychologist, 53*(2), 97–113. doi:10.1080/00461520.2017.1421466

Knifsend, C.A., Camacho-Thompson, D.E., Juvonen, J. & Graham, S. (2018). Friends in activities, school-related affect, and academic outcomes in diverse middle schools. *Journal of Youth Adolescence, 47*(6), 1208–1220. doi:10.1007/s10964-018-0817-6.

Maslow, A.H. (1943). A theory of human motivation. *Psychological Review, 50*(4), 370.

Maslow, A. (1999). *Toward a Psychology of Being,* 3rd edition. Princeton, NJ: Van Nostrand.

Poulton, R., Caspi, A. & Milne, B.J. (2002). Association between children's experience of socioeconomic disadvantage and adult health: A life-course study. *Lancet, 360*, 1640–1645. doi:10.1016/S0140-6736(02)11602-3

Slaten, C., Ferguson. J., Allen, K., Brodrick, D. & Waters, L. (2016). School belonging: A review of the story, current trends, and future directions. *The Educational and Developmental Psychologist, 33*(1), 1–15.

Wadsworth, M.E., Thomsen, A.H., Saltzman, H., Connor-Smith, J.K. & Compas, B.E. (2001). Coping with stress during childhood and adolescence: Problems, progress, and potential in theory and research. *Psychological Bulletin, 127*, 87–127. doi:10.1037/0033-2909.127.1.87

Walton, G.M. & Cohen, G.L. (2011). A brief social-belonging intervention improves academic and health outcomes of minority students. *Science Journal, 331*, 1447–1451. doi:10.1126/science.1198364

Walton, G.M., Cohen, G.L., Cwir, D. & Spencer, S.J. (2012). Mere belonging: The power of social connections. *Journal of Personality and Social Psychology, 102*, 513–532. doi:10.1037/a0025731

Watt, S. (2015). *Designing Transformative Multicultural Initiatives: Theoretical Foundations, Practical Applications and Facilitator Considerations.* Stylus Publishing.

Wong, C., Eccles, J. & Sameroff, A. (2003). The influence of ethnic discrimination and ethnic identification on African American adolescents' school and socioemotional adjustment. *Journal of Personality, 71*(6), 1197–1232.

Chapter 1

The Right to Belong

A Critical Stance

Beverly S. Faircloth

Reflecting on events like the rampage that erupted in Los Angeles after police brutality against Rodney King, Ronald Takaki penned these compelling lines to urgently call for Americans to learn to see one another in a "different mirror," one that genuinely recognizes and honors our varied narratives:

> What happens . . . when someone with the authority of a teacher describes our society, and you are not in it? Such an experience can be disorienting—a moment of psychic disequilibrium, as if you looked into a mirror and saw nothing.

With these words (Takaki, 1993, p. 16), Takaki highlighted the invisibility and dispossession that threaten to rob so many minorized individuals and groups of a sense that they belong in our schools, organizations, institutions, and communities, and identified the profound toll such invisibility and dispossession take. Nearly three decades on, given the events of the year 2020–21 as our witness, the goal of recognizing and honoring our varied narratives appears doggedly elusive in the United States. Disparities and power differentials with regard to race, ethnicity, nationality, gender, sexual orientation, gender identity, ability/disability, socioeconomic status, English language proficiency, or religion/spirituality remain deeply entrenched, marginalizing and oppressing many individuals and groups. One particularly poignant example—the current Black Lives Matter movement—brings into sharp relief the urgency of these issues in our society today from rampant institutional violence against marginalized people to their unjust murders at the hands of those who are sworn to protect them. Enduring "messages of inadequacy and undesirability in media and society" persistently foster and justify such brutalities (Johnston, D'Andrea Montalbano & Kirkland, 2017, p. 18). Long-standing inequities

13

have also been highlighted by the COVID-19 pandemic of 2020–2021, in the form of (for example) inequitable access to health care, and differing access to devices and high-speed Internet when those technologies become necessary for education during a pandemic. Moreover, demeaning and restrictive policies, as well as negative media coverage regarding new arrivals to many US communities (i.e., immigrants and refugees), erect additional, seemingly insurmountable barriers. Indeed, the stereotypes and negative connotations associated with the mere use of the term "immigrant," generated by current harsh political and policy positions, compound these obstacles (Bondy, 2015) not to mention the knotty obstructions faced by undocumented individuals or those with temporary status (Gonzalez, chapter 4, this volume). These barriers are mirrored in debates addressing whether, when, where, and how a LGBTQ+ person can count on legal protection, a situation that inherently (but shamefully) suggests that "the value and humanity of some people are *debatable*" (Antonicci, Killion, and Johnson, chapter 3, this volume). These collective events have served as catalysts for nondominant peoples and their allies and advocates to rightfully demand permanent change. Clearly, we are miles from seeing one another through a different mirror that recognizes and honors our varied narratives. Although Takaki specifically calls out teachers as complicit in this devastation, the reality is far more encompassing. The time is long overdue, and all individuals, systems, and institutions in our country are called to address this issue.

While we may be miles from equity and justice, every journey begins with first steps. Among such efforts, a sense of belonging has come to be depended upon to remedy the struggles and consequences of the invisibility or dispossession experienced by so many. As delineated in our Introductory chapter, over the previous three decades, work from multiple fields has demonstrated that experiencing an enduring, authentic, and meaningful sense that one belongs within one's primary contexts serves as an essential element of positive development, engagement, and agency within those contexts. This body of work has drawn from a variety of lenses that frame belonging in different ways, providing multiple approaches to understanding its primary elements and mechanisms. This has driven the work of belonging along different—sometimes contradictory—paths, offering differing notions of what belonging is, how it operates, and what makes it possible. Research on cultural frames explains how some contrasting practices and perspectives are perceived as normative in relation to others, delimiting understandings and applications beyond that lens. Moreover, the dynamics of frames (i.e., whose frames get taken up, under what conditions, how a frame supports or constrains other frames, and how they might be contested) can make particular frames difficult to dislodge (Hand et al., 2013). For example, traditional school frames are largely invisible to the teachers and students who construct them because of their entrenchment in the educational system (Varenne & McDermott, 1998) and alignment with predominant social, cultural, and institutional discourses (Erickson, 1987; Gutiérrez et al., 1999). This shapes our understanding of what belonging means in those settings, how it is supported and what purpose it serves, and with what could be vastly different results. It is the goal of this chapter to unpack three overarching frames: Frame 1. Belonging as Relationship, Frame 2. A Sociocultural Renaissance in Belonging. Frame 3. Critical Models of Belonging (i.e., the Right to Belong). These lenses have shaped differentially (and potentially limited) the work of belonging. It is our hope that this understanding will help us see our way through to belonging's most powerful enactments, in order to challenge chronic experiences of invisibility or dispossession.

FRAME 1: BELONGING AS RELATIONSHIP (AND ITS SHORTCOMINGS)

Traditionally the concept of belonging has been firmly anchored in interpersonal relationships and participatory experiences (Faircloth, 2006, 2009, 2011; Anderman & Freeman, 2004; Finn, 1989; Goodenow, 1993; Osterman, 2000; Wetzel, 1997, 1998, 1999). In-depth reviews of theoretical and research literature (e.g., Juvonen, 2006; Marlsbury, 2012; Slaten et al., 2016) have highlighted the role of perceptions of interpersonal support, respect, and care, as well as participation-identification, as positively associated with sense of belonging, fostering positive affect, motivation, and engagement. This is a conceptualization that works for some who benefit from the expectation of societal support and have access to opportunities to participate. Unfortunately, with the escalating invisibility and dispossession inflicted on large swaths of our nation, such connections that support belonging can be hard to come by for groups with less access.

Critical theorists have long argued that the discursive practices, forms of reasoning, and social relations that proliferate in most US contexts mirror those of the dominant culture, which lift up some but not all, and leave the processes of history, power, and privilege that marginalize many invisible or unmarked (Darder, 1991; Gee, 1990; Giroux & McLaren, 1989). True to this lens, historically, the United States has followed an assimilationist model for incorporation of culturally diverse individuals into a standardized American mainstream with its prescribed cultural norms, all too frequently treating the cultural and discursive practices of non-whitestream groups as oppositional to an American ideal (Urrieta, 2009; Warikoo & Carter, 2009). Even Black and Brown citizens with immigrant backgrounds may be subjected to xenophobic foreigner objectification as assumptions are made about their belongingness in the United States (Kiang et al., 2018). Regrettably, such "whitestream" experiences (Urrieta, 2009, p. 47) can signal that the perspectives, philosophies, and histories of Eurocentric racial-ethnic groups are more important than those of other groups (Cammorata, 2015; de los Rios et al., 2014; Dee & Penner, 2017; Gray, et al., 2018; Paris & Alim, 2017). All too often, this reproduces hierarchies that reinforce dominant codes, artifacts, language, practices, and styles, as well as allocating resources based on the degree to which students possess dominant cultural capital (Bourdieu & Passeron, 1990; Farkas et al., 1990; Paris & Alim, 2017; Stanton-Salazar, 1997). Each of these perspectives can erect significant barriers to belonging.

FRAME 2: A SOCIOCULTURAL RENAISSANCE IN BELONGING

The awareness that individuals, contexts, communities, and cultures are repositories of heritable legacies that help make a feeling of belonging within one's group possible but which may stand in conflict with others' legacies, thereby potentially erecting barriers to belonging, has helped push the study of belonging beyond traditional views (Clarke, 1994; Gray, et al.; 2011; King, 2006). It is therefore essential to recognize how the framing, construction, and design of environments carry explicit and implicit racialized and gendered notions of who does and does not belong (Hand et al., 2013; Nasir et al., 2013). For example, a significant body of work highlights the ways that learning and motivation are inherently cultural, fundamentally tied to one's culturally rooted perception of the context and one's positioning as having (or not having) valid knowledge in settings like schools (Bang & Medin, 2010; Berman, 1989; Gaines et al., 1997; Gutiérrez & Rogoff, 2003; Lee, 2007; Majors, 2003; Nasir, 2002; Taylor, 2009; Triandis, 1999). As noted by Nasir et al. (2013), such a sociocultural lens is typically built upon a Vygotskian framework and illustrates that

> learning takes place in culturally and socially organized settings, occurs in relation to social others, and is guided by culturally defined goals and norms and is therefore tied to the learners' culturally rooted perceptions of the learning settings and one's cultural relation to the content and the process. (p. 295)

This lens suggests the potential need to draw attention to individuals' values, beliefs, styles, symbols, stories, rituals, worldviews, speech styles, language, physical interactions, tastes in music, clothing, and food, and other ethnic cues (Gans, 1979; Swidler, 1986; Warikoo & Carter, 2009). Any of these wide-ranging perspectives can shape whether, how, and by whom belonging is experienced and what belonging actually means (Borrero et al., 2012, Gray et al., 2012).

Research built on such a sociocultural lens has consistently demonstrated that a strong connection with one's heritage culture, coupled with a meaningful connection with a host culture (i.e., an integrationist rather than an assimilationist model), consistently promotes well-being (Berry et al., 2006; Urdan, 2011; Vedder & Horencyzk, 2006). For example, both Garcia Coll and colleagues' "integrative model" of development among minority youth (1996, p. 1891) and the model of "biculturalism" set forth by LaFromboise et al. (1993, p. 395) advocate for sociocultural supports that form bridges between an individual's culture of heritage and the host culture (see also Valenzuela, 2015). Indeed, an integrative model, in which individuals are able to develop a meaningful sense of place within a host community or country while maintaining strong connections to their cultural heritage (without necessarily assimilating into some form of unity or sameness), appears to offer the most adaptive behavioral, motivational, and psychological profile (Garcia Coll et al., 1996; LaFromboise et al., 1993; Liebkind, 2001; Phelan Davidson & Cao, 1991).

For example, teachers, administrators, and peers at K–12 schools that value the cultural assets of youth (e.g., their heritage legacies, bilingualism, their transnational ties, their worldview, or value systems) and worked to build "confianza," or trust, contribute to diverse students' sense of belonging (DeMartino, 2021, p. 246; see also Bartlett & García, 2011). This resonates with Etzioni's (1996) concept of "responsive communities," (p. 1) a set of methods by which a community mediates how individuals can belong. He writes, "responsiveness is the cardinal feature of authentic communities. If the values the community fosters do not reflect its members' needs, or only reflect the needs of some, the community's order will be ipso facto instead of truly supported" (1996, p. 2). Fearing a fundamental contradiction between the needs of community members and the common good, Etzioni suggests that it is the task of every community to find ways in which responsiveness can be enhanced. This is mirrored in substantial research, for example, validating the need for minority college students to retain and nurture connections to their cultural heritage, and the well-documented benefits of connecting with people outside the university system who share the student's cultural heritage (Guiffrida, 2006). Results of qualitative studies investigating the experiences of Latino (Rosas & Hamrick, 2002), Chicano (Gonzalez, 2006), Chicana (Delgado Bernal, 2002), Navajo (Jackson & Smith, 2001), and African American (Guiffrida, 2005) college students have found that students perceived their families and members of their home communities as providing essential cultural connections and nourishment that helped them deal with racism, cultural isolation, and other adversities at college.

The Ghanian notion of "Sankofa" provides a particularly suitable meta-phor for this multilayered work of laminating aspects of culture, language, identity, and community to support a sense of belonging (Knight & Watson, 2014, p. 551). Sankofa is a metaphorical symbol, generally depicted as a bird with its head turned backward taking an egg from its back. It expresses the importance of reaching back to knowledge gained in the past and bringing it into the present in order to move forward in meaningful and authentic ways. This reminds us to reach back and leverage these multiple resources in order to support forward movement. As an example, the Afrocentric praxis of "Teaching for Freedom" (King & Swartz, 2015, p. 1) uses academic content and pedagogical techniques to emphasize belonging at school by exposing Black students to the cultural legacies and traditions of the African diaspora. This culturally relevant pedagogy functions as an instructional opportunity for belonging that reaffirms Black students in their racial identity. Black students in culturally affirming classrooms thus have opportunities to explore their racial identity in a context that legitimizes their culture, thereby allow-ing them to see commonalities and take pride in their connection to people who look like them. This suggests that curriculum and instruction can serve as linchpins in this quest. The reclamation of cultural heritage captured in the notion of Sankofa is an apt metaphor suggesting a conscious effort to recover the cultural aspect of the self or the community, thus experiencing "belonging in continuity with their ancestral heritage" (King & Swartz, 2015, p. 18). Sankofa is not, however, just for minoritized peoples. Black history is American history and lessons from this example of Afrocentric praxis can be amplified by considering its impact on all students, not just those whose histories, cultures, and realities have been marginalized.

All of these insights point out an essential distinction regarding looking beyond traditional whitestream models of belonging. That is, a well-devel-oped sociocultural perspective on belonging positions positive develop-ment as at least a two-dimensional process, including preservation of one's heritage culture (as well as any self-selected adaptations to the host culture), rather than being a linear process of change requiring giving up one's culture of origin and assimilating into a new one (Berry, 1990, 1997; Alim & Paris, 2017; Urrieta, 2009).

FRAME 3: CRITICAL MODELS OF BELONGING

Even given the most socioculturally aware notions of belonging, the harsh reality of abuse against minoritized individuals rampant in the US society (invisibility and dispossession of every description) argues for continued sharpening of our tools for the most powerful enactments of belonging as well as the dismantling of barriers to belonging. Borrowing from the notion of critical reflection advocated by Schön (1983), reconsideration of the most fundamental assumptions underlying belonging (including challenges to epistemological, critical, political, or policy positions consciously or unconsciously inherent in our models) can be considered a worthwhile step. One central issue that arises to suggest a valuable paradigm shift is the need for a *criticality* that is sometimes absent, or often only emerging, in this field. Criticality suggests an agentic ability to identify, reflect on, critique, and act against systemic racism and other forms of marginalization (Dee & Penner, 2017; de los Rios et al., 2014; Jay, 2003). In this case, this would position belonging as a right to be self-authored, rather than a gift to be received, thus inviting disruption of the status quo as it relates to belonging,

Even the most generous sociocultural framings of belonging (e.g., "biculturalism" [LaFromboise et al., 1993, p. 395] or an "integrative model" [Garcia Coll et al., 1996, p. 1891]) can inadvertently depict belonging as an experience that is bestowed by those at the top of cultural and critical hierarchies. That is, it is possible for even those with an understanding of the vital sociocultural nature of belonging to frame belonging as something generously and insightfully conferred, like a gift of hospitality or welcome, rather than a self-evident, self-authored right. Unfortunately, belonging that is authored by another, instead of by self, can easily fail to fully grasp—across multiple dimensions—the perspective or needs of the individual, potentially serving the giver more than the gifted. For example, Derrida (2000) highlights the problematic contradiction in the very word hospitality, which he points out is a generosity rather than a right (p. 3). "Dependent on a host"—whether citizen, community, nation, or state—the *term* itself therefore automatically introduces conditionality, simultaneously giving *and* taking (p. 7), which could end abruptly once conditions for hosting are no longer favorable (e.g., "too many" asylum seekers, running out of money, etc.). Through a lens of hospitality, individuals therefore do not necessarily have total freedom to choose who they want to be in every instance. Rather, as they participate in everyday activity, individuals are constantly being 'hailed' into particular subjective positionings, some forms made more available while access to others is curtailed (Nasir et al., 2013, p. 293). For example, people of color with financial privilege, or very light skin (who can "pass" for White, Crothers & K'Meyer, 2007, p. 24), may be invited into more privileged positions than others. In addition, there are trends in scholarship, education, social sciences, humanities, and the law to analyze groups through singularized identities that reinforce dominant discourses and lack global, intersectional, transcultural, or transnational focus (Glick-Schiller et al., 1992; Sólorzano & Yosso, 2001). For example, Black women are too often depicted in monolithic, negative, stereotypical terms (e.g., "angry Black women"), and immigrant and refugee youth are too often positioned in disparaging terms, ignoring the richness of their global, transcultural resilience, insights, and language skills. These tendencies flatten identities, failing to see their intersectional richness, which may dismiss many realities of people's lives from a genuine opportunity to belong.

Moreover, notions of belonging bestowed by group members who may place a premium on group unity can inadvertently invoke notions of sameness, likeness, or unity useful to the group. For example, culture is too often understood as part of an identity that is common to members of a group and maintained because of its presumed foundation in their shared experiences. Individual differences within the group are acknowledged, but culture is made knowable by privileging the experiences that are common to everyone, asserting these common experiences as the core of cultural identity (Williams, 2006). Again, the tendency to treat Black women as a singular category dismisses the realities and complexities of the diverse sociocultural spaces from which their identities, potentialities, and belonging can (or cannot) arise (Dillard, 2006; Wallace et al., 2020; Wilder, 2013). These limitations are cautioned against by Bettez's (2011) concern that such unifying perspectives can exclude as much as they include and Gray's (2017) warning against conceiving of belonging as merely a function of "fitting in" (p. 103). Likewise, Furman (1998) and Noddings (1996) argue against conceptions of community based on sameness among members, noting the tendency of conceptions of community to be exclusionary, and insisting on breaking down binaries between community differences. Even in his concept of responsive communities, Etzioni claimed that it is not desirable to "absorb fully members' identities, energies, and commitments into the social realm" (1996, p. 15), an act that can diminish the idiosyncratic aspect of individual selves that enable the development of new social patterns. Instead, Etzioni envisioned responsiveness as including desirable conflict between individuals and their social embeddedness, to the betterment of all community members.

Lastly, as made clear by Tedesco and Bagelman (2017), being an outsider means more than not having one's experiences, knowledge, or practices valued in the learning community. When students are positioned as outsiders because of who they are and which cultural assets they bring to learning, they are made invisible, that is, they are made "missing" (Edkins, 2011, p. 15; Tedesco & Bagelman, 2017; see also the example provided by Calabrese Barton & Tan, 2018). As such, they are continually dehumanized and positioned without important forms of power and authority. This significantly limits or completely denies them opportunities to be important contributing members of the learning community in ways that support their own growth and development, that of others, and that of the social context in which learning takes place. Similarly, Vrasti and Dayal (2016) differentiate between a sense of citizenship in a community or a polity based on status (a set of rights) by which persons are afforded entry, entitlement, and protection by the group versus one based on capacity for agency within the group, which they argue serves a much greater value as a cornerstone for genuine democracy (p. 995).

A critical theory paradigm helps us unpack critical elements of the relationship between criticality and a sense of belonging. As laid out by Williams (2006, pp. 214–215), recognizing that reality is produced through historically based social and political processes and structures that serve the purposes of the powerful (Guba & Lincoln, 1998) requires that we view culture as the outcome of oppressive processes that constrain potential cultural expression. Therefore, engagement with culture requires engagement with the structures that have contributed, *and served as barriers,* to formulations of ethnic or cultural identity, group status, and opportunities for individuals. Vakil and colleagues (2016) refer to this layer as "moving from sociocultural to sociopolitical analyses of learning" (p. 207), connecting our work to issues of power, hierarchy and inequity, and the roots of those issues (Booker et al., 2014, p. 1), that is, a critical sociopolitical lens as a core feature of democratic education and positive human development (including belonging, Kirshner et al., 2015; see also Nasir & McKinnery de Royston, 2013). Thus, a criticality approach to belonging requires the availability of appropriate learning experiences, pathways for advocacy, and time and space for culturally authentic and agentic practices. For example, culturally responsive and sustaining practices in education (Ladson Billlings, 2014; Paris & Alim, 2017) harness critical theory practices to provide students and teachers with the opportunity to dismantle barriers generated by educational models that have traditionally been predominantly "whitestream" (Urrieta, 2009), by "pushing students to consider critical perspectives on policies and practices that may have direct impact on their lives and communities" (Ladson Billings, 2014, p. 78). As explained by Paris and Alim (2016):

> We cannot continue to act as if the White middle-class linguistic, literate, and cultural skills and ways of being that were seen as the sole gatekeepers to the opportunity structures over a quarter-century ago have remained so or will remain so as our society changes. (p. 6)

Examples of critical theory efforts to resist and dismantle such erroneous thinking include *First Wave*, a spoken word and hip-hop arts program sponsored by the University of Wisconsin-Madison, designed to change the way students think, learn, perceive, and perform the world, and attempt to give back to their community (Ladson Billings, 2014) and the *Summer Scholars Program* at Michigan State University which allows high school students to explore issues of power and privilege, with the goal of resisting the curricularization of racism (Paris, 2017).

From this critical theory perspective, belonging requires the ability to foster positive cultural identity, empower individuals and groups to negotiate oppressive social structures, and promote social change by altering institutional processes that contribute to marginalization. It is this agency that lies at the heart of the criticality that must now undergird our considerations of belonging. Taking up this need for criticality that dislodges older, traditional models driving our understanding of belonging, Wenger (1998) argues for a social justice mission for communities, embracing space for cultural knowledge, socio-familial histories, language, values, and agency to resist a dominant status quo. He writes, for example,

> Building our identity consists of negotiating the meaning of our experience of membership in social communities. . . . This frames identity as the locus of social selfhood and social power, that is, the power to belong, to be a certain person, to claim a self-authored place with the legitimacy of membership. (p. 145)

Wenger distances himself, however, from thinkers who see the individual and the collective at odds, refusing to negate or minimize either the individual, or the community. As explained in his work on communities of practice, a community is a project where culture, learning, and personal identity are organized in ways that involve the interaction of multiple convergent and divergent trajectories (Wenger, 1998, p. 154), contributing to both the social development of the group and the development of the individual, opening new possibilities for all. Even peripheral membership can be a place of strength and contribution, pushing the practice of members to change and develop. As such, "the inclusion of new members can create a ripple of new opportunities for mutual engagement which can translate into a renegotiation of the enterprise, producing a whole generation of new elements in the repertoire" (p. 97). Such critical participation shapes the democratic potential of communities, introducing the potential of social justice and power, thus "forging new potential modes of belongingness" (Wenger, 1998, p. 151). That is, as narratives, categories, roles, positions, norms are worked out in communities of practice, power derives from exercising control over what we belong to (p. 207). Wenger refers to such negotiations as "cultural brokering, that is, translating, coordinating and aligning between perspectives, addressing conflicting interests . . . purposefully introducing elements of the other . . . enabling new possibilities for meaning" (p. 109). Through such self-authored, agentic participation, brokers have choice around how they locate themselves in the social landscape, engage their energies, and steer their trajectories, hence, potentially authoring new, transformative and powerful modes of belonging.

It is important to note that it is not the claim here that all who adopt a sociocultural lens when unpacking belonging omit such criticality that can forge new modes of belonging; many do not, or do so inadvertently. It is however the suggestion here that attention to the criticality undergirding such experiences is essential and must have its due. While belonging that results from hospitality remains a goodwill act, dependent upon the willingness and the ability of the host to welcome guests, critical participation shapes the democratic potential of communities, creating space for the disruption of the status quo, and for the work of social justice. Hooks refers to such negotiated spaces as cracks in the world which can serve as essential spaces of empowerment (hooks, 2003). The point here is that intentionally taking up such spaces defines a powerful new frontier for belonging.

Rightful Presence: Metaphor for the Right to Belong

In search for a cultural tool (i.e., a metaphor or model [Vygotsky, 1978]) with which to better grasp and employ criticality as a tool for belonging, the framework of "rightful presence" emerged (Squires & Darling, 2013, p. 59). As an alternative to a model based on hospitality, Squire and Darling's work proposed a politics of "rightful presence" that questions the statist division between insiders and outsiders, legitimate and tolerated, and extends "the right to have rights" to all (Arendt 1951). Rightful presence is not about pursuing inclusion into an already established order; rather, it seeks to assert a new measure of justice even if that means undoing the order we currently exist in and benefit from (Vrasti & Dayal, 2016, p. 999). Drawn from critical justice studies of borderland and refugee communities in welcoming host countries, rightful presence provides an alternative when a lens of hospitality does not always capture the ongoing social and political struggles for legitimacy by guests in these host settings. Thus, it challenges normative guest/host relationships, calling for the disruption of established power hierarchies and for reconfiguring what it means to belong as more than having the borders of practice opened to newcomers (Calabrese Barton & Tan 2018 p. 619; see also Barnett, 2005).

Highlighting the invisibility created by a lack of rightful presence, Tedesco and Bagelman (2017) cite Edkins (2011) to challenge the guest/host, settler-colonial model in which certain bodies, communities, or cultures are treated as "missing"—or worse, "unmissed"—to the dominant cultural eye. Edkins describes,

> Those who are invisible to a Western imagination in the first place . . . with its focus on the world as seen from a particular perspective, as if that were the only one. Their absence from your consideration and discussions is . . . so

fundamental that we don't even realize they are missing from our parochial picture of the world . . . assuming a singular, universal space in which all that is apparent from a dominant perspective is all that is acknowledged as being politically present. (pp. 5–6)

Recognizing that the politically missing have been rendered as such by processes of colonization, hierarchical ordering, and segregation, Edkins (2011) observes that

> [w]e have not counted [as missing] those that are invisible to our (post)colonial gaze, or those whose appearance renders them invisible to our sight even when they are in plain view, thus dismantling any existing structures of belonging. (p. 6)

Such lack of rightful presence, exacerbated by the lack of any opportunity to demand it, easily erodes opportunities for belonging, as illustrated by Ahmed's notion of "atmospheric walls" (2014, para. 24). Looking for ways to understand the circulation of privilege and exclusion, Ahmed derived the notion of atmospheric walls as techniques which serve as subtle gatekeeping devices by "making space available to some more than to others" (para. 9). For example, a context that designates one individual as worthy of full membership can exclude others who, by virtue of their social origin, have a hard time living up to the normative standards set by the dominant culture. The mood becomes so uncomfortable that some decide to leave without anyone forcing them to, or they do not dare even enter the space. Such barriers can be both invisible and selective: visible and real to those they are meant to keep out, while imperceptible to those with the right of access. For Ahmed, this becomes a crucial instrument for talking about racial exclusion in particular.

> I think whiteness is often experienced as an atmosphere. You walk into a room and you encounter it like a wall that is at once palpable and tangible but also hard to grasp or to reach. It is something, it is quite something, but it is difficult to put your finger on it. When you walk into the room, it can be like a door slams in your face, the tightening of bodies: the sealing of space. The discomfort when you encounter something that does not receive you. (para. 12)

Such barriers slice through belonging, causing individuals to be restricted, guarded, or reluctant in their participation within particular contexts. Without the strong anchors provided by both culturally and critically informed practices, the ability to construct meaningful connections that animate engagement collapses. De-walling such situations requires making transparent, and interrupting, the atmospheric barriers enforced by cultural and institutional conventions that reflect and invite the movement of some bodies more so than others.

A criticality lens borrowed from the notion of rightful presence and its complement, atmospheric walls, is therefore an ideal and powerful frame for understanding how to move forward with belonging, lending it a much-needed power and agency. That is, such a lens can be employed to break down binaries between those that do and those that do not belong by asserting a new measure of belonging, "facilitating movements and exchanges that were not there before," opening up moments of possible rightful presence (Vrasti and Dayal, 2016, p. 999). However, activism and advocacy required for this work can look like luxury items to people who see themselves as dealing with issues of survival (Williams, 2006, p. 214). Just how this can be done is a vital next step in this conversation.

"Making Present" Practices

The compelling barrier to belonging outlined in the opening paragraphs of this chapter, and attacked head-on by criticality and rightful presence, is the invisibility generated by systems whose treatment of certain groups and individuals position them as "missing," or worse, "unmissed." Tedesco and Bagelman (2017) combat this practice with what is referred to as "making present practices, modes for making present" those who have been made missing (invisible) by forms of racialization and colonization that manifest in schooling (Squire & Darling, 2013, p. 59; Nasir & Vakil, 2017). According to Vrasti and Dayal (2016, p. 999), making present practices comprise a struggle to have one's life and lived experiences legitimized, disrupting binaries between outsider/insider and novice/expert. Such practices can take many forms but share the goal of "bringing to bear" lives lived, into new spaces in ways that may disrupt those spaces (Squire & Darling, 2013, p. 62), as opposed (as stated earlier) to pursuing inclusion into an already established system (Vrasti & Dayal, 2016). Squire and Darling (2013) suggest the importance of naming and addressing concrete injustices from the past and present. This would include, for example, acknowledging the injustices nondominant groups have experienced historically and working to interrupt those oppressive patterns and experiences.

In an exemplar of rightful presence and making present practice work in the field of science education, Calabrese Barton and Tan (2019) proffer specific pedagogical moves as ways to design for rightful presence. Addressing the fact that minority youth have been historically marginalized in both science and schooling, even if positioned as a welcomed guest, the authors adopted a critical justice view of rightful presence as a powerful frame for understanding equity-oriented teaching efforts in school science. Laying out their problem space in STEM education, they explain:

Students from historically marginalized communities have cultural knowledge and experience that are highly relevant to doing STEM. However, the way in which STEM is often taught . . . does not always encourage and support students in leveraging their powerful expertise toward empowered learning in STEM. When students are expected to engage in STEM through power-mediated cultural norms, some people (e.g., boys, White students, monolingual English speakers) are unfairly privileged, while others (e.g., girls, students of color, emerging bilinguals) may be positioned as outsiders, which creates barriers to meaningful engagement and participation. . . . When students are positioned as outsiders because of who they are and the cultural assets they bring to learning, they are made invisible—they are made missing (Tedesco & Bagelman, 2017). . . . We refer to this as being denied a rightful presence in their learning community. (p. 619)

Calabrese Barton and Tan (2017) set about to co-construct a cluster of opportunities for students to first (a) model ethnographic data through iterative observations, interviews, and discourse (at school/in neighborhoods) that allowed them to name and make visible concerns or social issues faced by themselves and others. Following that, the students were encouraged to (b) reperform injustices in science education by using *Making* to innovate in ways that would actually allow them to address their concerns. While it is not the goal of this chapter to review their work in detail that enterprise is highly recommended as it models a skilled understanding and application of these issues.

Recognizing the challenges and significance of these issues, and approaching it from multiple angles, a substantial body of research and theory invoking criticality has begun to address how race, culture, and power play into processes specifically within teaching, learning, and learning contexts (e.g., Esmonde & Langer-Osuna, 2013; Gutiérrez et al., 1999; Lee, 2008; Nasir & Shah, 2011; Nasir & Hand, 2006; Nasir & de Royston, 2013). This scholarship, which resonates with rightful presence, or the right to belong, has been instrumental in advancing equity-oriented educational research committed to not only studying but also working to transform unjust educational practices and systems. This work is often manifested in the theory and design of learning environments that build directly on the cultural practices and strengths of learners (Bell et al., 2012; Ladson- Billings, 2009; Lee, 2007) and that are rooted in antiracist and decolonizing pedagogies (Duncan-Andrade & Morrell, 2008; Freire, 2000; Gutstein, 2003; hooks, 1989; Paris, 2012).

In addition to educational practices and spaces, other disciplines have taken up this call to authentic presence and belonging. The field of Social Work, as an example, is a profoundly client-centered enterprise, but has often found itself mired in the positive empiricism from which the profession emerged (Schön, 1983), often leading to a technical rationality with regard to practice that denied the confusing complexities of clients' lives. However, recent work in the field has confronted this perennial problem, focusing on reflexivity and critical perspectives, thus freeing social work practice from being a prescriptive set of rules of the profession. This also invites analyses of power, discourse, language and narrative, identity and difference, as well as a commitment to social change and social justice previously missing from social work, thus promoting sustainable, appropriate, and politically informed modes of practice (Fook, 2006; Healy, 2000). A simultaneously emerging focus on more "personal" practice models has also begun to allow social workers and clients to work together to notice and understand relevant complex and idiosyncratic elements of clients' lives and to consider potentially novel paths forward (Reisch & Andrews, 2002). Together these new lenses have moved the field of social work forward toward addressing the authentic and complex barriers to clients' growth and belonging.

NOTICING, NAMING, AND INTERRUPTING

Borrowing lessons learned from "making present practices" suggests a model framework for empowering a right to belong (although they rarely self-identify in this way). It appears that an essential first step is *noticing* the barriers to belonging that shape the contexts we inhabit. We may need to remove our own blinders to actually recognize the invisibility and dispossession described by Takaki in the opening paragraphs of this chapter, noticing the insidious ways that these oppressions are woven into the very systems in which we live and work everyday. This will likely require reflecting deeply enough to notice the barriers to belonging that we (un)intentionally contribute, even simply by not being aware of the impact of the privilege we enjoy. Whether by not listening or seeing, gatekeeping, defaulting to dominant whitestream norms, or simply forgetting to question our own assumptions in these areas, barriers to belonging begin with us, and so does the responsibility to notice them. The next step in this process is acknowledging these issues for what they are, that is, accurately *naming* them, from messages (spoken and unspoken) of inadequacy and undesirability to concrete injustices from the past and present and to rampant institutionalized violence. With that comes the opportunity (some would say the responsibility) to *interrupt* such realities. From acknowledging that it is injustice we are facing, to bringing to bear the value of lives lived and honoring the right to be present, to legitimizing others' perspectives or stepping back to allow other voices to be lifted up, to advancing educational reform or antiracist and decolonizing pedagogies, all are needed, all are welcome. The use of the term *interrupt* is purposeful.

Although not as forceful as a term such as *disrupt*, it is meant to remind us that we all need different entry points. Small bridges built and intimate lessons learned are every bit as worthy as those that make the front page news; we all have a home in this task. In all their derivative forms, *noticing*, *naming*, and *interrupting* offer us a wealth of ways to envision, and contribute to, resisting barriers to belonging.

An important caution is required here; although a slight adjustment, it may be a defining step in understanding the radical potential of belonging as a right. In order to fuel the hoped-for potency of engaging in *rightful* belonging, making present practices such as Noticing, Naming, and Interrupting must guard against allowing a hospitality model to infiltrate this work, positioning such practices as something that nonmarginalized individuals enable for marginalized. Again, this is just a caution that while making present practices typically (and perhaps essentially) include working in partnership with allies, the genuineness of partnership (i.e., working "with" and not "for") is paramount. That is, even the transformative notion of making present must be careful to avoid connotations that could be seen to imply an opportunity that is opened or gifted by another. Complicated by the fact that we all do have a role in this important work, we must not lose the thread that each individual has the right to perform as an origin, rather than a pawn, in our systems and relations. We must conduct ourselves in a manner that rightly positions us not as benefactors, but as parallel, side-by-side occupants of this territory, carefully working in tandem. Again—while only a slight distinction—it is vital that making present practices consciously, explicitly embrace "making *oneself* present."

In the account given here, these strategies are divided into those that focus primarily on opportunities to Notice/Name inequities with the goal of "bringing to bear" the narratives of the "missing" and those that invoke pressure for change, striving to directly interrupt inequities. Although this binary is somewhat arbitrary—indeed many strategies exist at the intersection of these domains—this organization is designed to provide a helpful conceptual map to these proceedings.

Strategies for Noticing and Naming

Counternarrative

Addressing the reality that culturally and socially organized systems and settings in US society often define available and allowable experiences by another's perspectives, norms and goals, research on culture and learning suggests recrafting whose knowledge or perspectives counts as valid (Ryu & Tuvilla, 2018; Delgado, 1998; Nasir Snyder et al., 2013; Solorzano & Yosso,

2001). Along this line, Anzaldua (1990) argues that the very fact that certain groups or individuals are often disqualified or excluded from certain discourses (e.g., certain professions, academia), as though there were forbidden territory, makes it vital for those precise people to "occupy," and potentially transform those spaces (p. xxv). Drawing on a tradition found in social sciences, humanities, and the law, counternarratives (also referred to as counter storytelling) serve as a method with which to tell stories that are not often told (because they exist on the margins of society) and to notice, name, and interrupt stories grounded in and limited to the dominant discourse, by which individuals and groups are often marginalized (Delgado, 1989, 1993; Solorzano 2001). In ordinary, everyday discourse we employ narratives in the attempt to make sense and signal this sense-making to others, often including how we craft a sense of self and identity. These efforts take place against the backdrop of existing master or metanarratives—preexistent sociocultural forms—that attempt to delineate how narrators are allowed to position themselves within their story (Bramberg, 2004). Encouraging youth to agentively author their identities in more empowering ways by challenging dominant narratives and constructing new narratives for and about themselves, through *counternarratives* (Nasir Snyder et al., 2013) challenging these preexisting sociocultural forms. As such, Bramberg (2004) argues, while telling stories, narrators position themselves against dominant narratives circulating in the society, explicitly constructing what kinds of person they actually are, or are attempting to be. As an example, working with a group of refugee youth, Ryu and Tuvilla (2018) observed that the youth recognized marginalized positions imposed on them in the United States because of their limited English proficiency, ethnicity/race, and refugee status. They, however, authored narratives of themselves that contested such marginalizing narratives by providing stories of refugees that differed from dominant ones. This positioned them as valuable members of local communities and as change agents for a more equitable society. That is, even though they recognized that they were victims of oppression, they positioned themselves as active pursuers of better life. Thus, while they were impacted by the existing social structure (could notice and name it), they also challenged it (a move toward interrupting it) by authoring their own stories. Reflecting on Ryu and Tuvilla's project, Bamberg (2004) goes on to describe how the participants had thus developed a keen awareness of inequity, empathy for people who suffer from inequity, and critical minds for injustice.

The youths cared about topics that are relevant to [their culture] and others who are disadvantaged and who had suffered inequity and injustice, and they were concerned about how local and global inequity can shape an individual's life quality. The youths started seeing themselves as agents of change. We note that various equity issues that humanity is facing are closely related to school topics, such as water shortage, public health, and climate change, which all impact people differently depending on individuals' and their communities' socioeconomic status. There are ample possibilities where such topic areas can meaningfully engage refugee youths and develop the youths' critical literacy. (pp. 555–556)

Even while master narratives attempt to constrain and delineate the agency of subjects, seemingly reducing the range of their actions, through counternarratives, these youth accomplished what Bamberg refers to as "doing 'being critical,'" countering and even being directly subversive within the fabric of our daily interactions (p. 36). Such counternarrativity is often guided by concern with power and hegemony, and might theoretically and materially connect the cultural, political, and personal contents of narratives, surfacing silenced, forgotten, or marginalized life experiences. Thus, Solorzano and Yosso (2001) identified many functions served by counternarratives: (1) building community, (2) challenging taken-for-granted dominant narrative, (3) opening new potential realities for marginalized peoples, and (4) demonstrating that by infusing what is taken to be current reality with a new story, understanding or perspective, we can construct another world that is richer than either perspective alone. Such criticality and rightful presence opens up a whole new world of possibilities regarding belonging.

Ethnography

Similar to counternarratives, ethnography is well situated to the task of noticing and naming. Rooted in the belief that inequalities associated with social structures and labeling devices (i.e., gender, race, and class) are consequential and fundamental dimensions of all lived experiences, critical ethnography strives to push back against such inequalities by exposing, critiquing, and invoking strategies to transform them. Identifying and challenging in this way can serve as an effective making present practice against injustice (Tedesco & Bagelman, 2017). Calabrese Barton and Tan (2019) drew heavily on a version of ethnography deeply rooted in their STEM community—community ethnography—as a pedagogy toward increasing the possibilities for enacting making present practices as a part of teaching and learning STEM. They embedded this practice by supporting teachers and students to incorporate extensive community dialogue throughout their learning and design processes, including observations, surveys and informal conversations, and multiple feedback cycles with different community constituents. As mentioned earlier, this enabled students to name and make visible challenges or social issues faced by themselves and others—some of which they found oppressive—and to discuss (and enact) ideas they had for addressing those challenges. This served as an essential avenue to making present practices in their work also expanding social networks among community members, which increased opportunities to broker for rightful presence.

Black female autoethnography (BFA) also serves as an example of ethnographic work that highlights intersectionalities and oppression, in this case, among Black women against dominant discourses, giving insight to the unique ways they make meaning of and address oppression. It offers a narrative means for Black women to highlight struggles common to Black womanhood without erasing the diversity among Black women. Dillard (2006) explains,

> Advocating for one's own authentic self-presentation and actively practicing self-care may not seem like a revolutionary act, but for many Black women, the ability to advocate for themselves is radical. When it comes to Black women and their ability to advocate for themselves, the dominant narrative is that they are unable to advocate for themselves in ways legible to their white counterparts, (p. 15)

BFA addresses this gap. A BFA by Wallace and colleagues (Wallace et al., 2020) describes their unique stories as Black female scholars in the academy (i.e., higher education). Higher education centers the White, cismale experience (Wilder, 2013) and as Black women, these scholars occupy two marginalized identities that challenge this norm. For them, BFA challenges the dominant discourse within the academy and creates space for their voices, allowing them to think about how to better navigate their institutions. Together, community ethnography and BFA provide models for noticing/naming, thereby making sense of intersectionalities and oppression, situating knowledge and action in the cultural spaces out of which they arise, and serving as a platform from which to survive, resist, and envision new possibilities regarding belonging and beyond.

Strategies for Interrupting

Hybridity

A growing line of research, on the border of noticing/naming, and interrupting, investigates the connection between dominant discourses with marginalized ones, such that they signal the celebration of *hybridity*, with its possibilities for new meanings and interpretations for diverse individuals and groups (Gutiérrez et al., 1995; Wortham, 2006). That is, hybridity offers a productive response to the reality that most settings—learning environments, for example—are sites where diversities of culture, language, histories, practices, norms, and values can collide. Some communities try to ignore, resist, and suppress such differences while others embrace them as opportunities for potential learning. For example, appreciating the additional perspectives, insights and skills (multilingual, global, transnational) brought to the classroom by new arrivals to our country, is celebrating hybridity. Hybridity encompasses the moments where such differences are negotiated or harnessed, offering new opportunities for growth or learning (e.g., highlighting and valuing the global perspective introduced to the classroom by refugee youth) (Gutierrez et al., 2000). This has also been referred to as a "third space," a zone of proximal development where participants draw on tools, social arrangements, and sociocritical literacies that "privilege and [are] contingent upon students' socio-historical lives" (Gutiérrez, 2008, p. 149). This disrupts traditional schooling scripts with counter-scripts and alternative (and often collaborative) discourse structures within authorized classroom space.

One example within classrooms is that a teacher can adopt a coaching frame rather than a didactic teaching frame, locating students from nondominant backgrounds within a task or setting in which they were presumed to be competent instead of labeling them as struggling or behind. Research suggests that such layering or laminating of such new possible practices or positionings onto an existing one can disrupt the hegemony of predominant cultural frames (Jurow, 2005; Leander, 2001). In a second example, looking to disrupt the traditional, rote, "doing school" frame, so deeply entrenched in our educational system, Hand, Penuel, and Gutierrez (2013) found that the lamination of a new classroom practice frame of "productive disciplinary engagement" (p. 255) (e.g., invoking the coaching model of teaching rather than a didactic one, Engle & Conant, 2002) served to rearrange classroom social arrangements and hierarchies in ways that stabilized this new frame. That is, by putting a coaching frame into play as the teacher did—using her positional authority within the dominant hierarchies of schooling to do so—the teacher laminated, or reframed, learning experiences, in an attempt to destabilize the larger, rote, "doing school" frame (p. 259). In a similar vein, Leander [2001] illustrated how layering a civil rights frame onto the traditional school-standards frame allowed for hybridization of discourse structures such that individual and collective identities were remediated in important ways, empowered by students' embracing a civil rights lens when considering their school experiences.

Gutierrez and her colleagues (Gutiérrez et al., 1999) describe an exemplar of hybridity and third space in their after-school club, *Las Redes*, in which educational activities are organized around several dimensions of play in a lively after-school computer club. They describe a sample activity that highlights the interrupting possible in hybridity and third space:

A multi-purposed writing activity that utilizes mixed genres, i.e., letters and narratives, and mixed discourses, including problem-solving, narrative, and academic discourse . . . because no one single language or register is privileged, the larger linguistic repertoires of participants become tools for meaning making. Such language practices certainly challenge current English-only policies that privilege one particular language and minimize learning. In a Bakhtinian (1981) sense, hybridity increases the possibility of dialogue—and, thus, the possibility of collaborating and learning. We have referred to these productive spaces for learning as the third space. (p. 89)

Side-by-Side Research

The notion of conducting research alongside and with, rather than on and for, has deep roots in critical approaches to educational research and reform (Cammarota & Fine, 2008). Erickson, for example, refers to collaborative action ethnography in which researchers, education professionals, students, and parents inquire together on meaningful issues that they define mutually, as studying "side by side" (p. 237). Gutierrez and Vossoughi (2010) articulate a radical application of such designs, the "social design experiment," that maintains interest in learning by individual participants by anchoring research in their lives and lived experiences, while harnessing the insight that "change in the individual involves change in the social situation itself" (p. 101). Tightly tied to Erickson's (2006) notion of side-by-side research, social design experiments engage in the design of new social practices that aim to change relations among theory, practice, and institutional actors.

Cammerota and Fine's (2008) edited volume *Revolutionizing Education* provides a particularly exemplary model of side-by-side research, *Youth Participatory Action Research* (YPAR), conducted "with" rather than "on" youth, around the issues they find most important to their lives. Grounded in the belief that research should be participatory, should embrace student/ community knowledge and realities, and should contribute to creating a better world, YPAR provides young people with opportunities to study social problems affecting their lives and then determine actions to rectify these problems, thus situating an individual's learning in his or her own sociohistorical context (p. 7). An essential component of YPAR is that such work only proceeds in concert with adult allies, hence, side by side. Through these experiences youth

> learn through research about complex power relations, histories of struggle, and the consequences of oppression. They begin to re-vision and de-naturalize the realities of their social worlds and then undertake forms of collective challenge based on the knowledge garnered through their critical inquiries. (p. 2)

Youth, with adult allies, have written policy briefs, engaged sticker campaigns, performed critical productions, coordinated public testimonials, and more—all dedicated to speaking back and challenging conditions of injustice, enabling oppressed youth to name, understand, challenge, and transcend their own oppression (i.e., noticing/naming and interrupting).

In remediating school structures and hierarchies that perpetuate race- and power-based school failure, these side-by-side strategies transform learning environments in ways that ultimately expand our notions of learning and developing, and simultaneously, our conceptions of nondominant communities and their members. Moreover, this collaborative, side-by-side work serves as an ideal opportunity for nondominant youth (indeed all youth) to make themselves present around issues resonant with their lives and lived experiences, both noticing/naming, and interrupting, in ways that claim and establish their own right to belong.

Ethnic Studies

Another practice based on criticality, with direct application to the right to belong, is ethnic studies. Traced back to the push for multicultural education during the civil rights movement, when people who had been historically marginalized by systemic inequalities in US education demanded curricula that were less dominated by Euro-American histories, perspectives, and experiences (Banks, 2012; Dee & Penner, 2017; de los Rios et al., 2014; Sleeter 2011; Tintiangco-Cubales et al., 2015), ethnic studies is clearly a struggle in the fight for the right to belong. It insists on countering literal invisibilities by affirming and including multiple voices, perspectives, and artifacts within the corpus of sanctioned knowledge (de los Rios et al., 2014), connecting education to the lived experiences of youth (de los Rios et al., 2014), and challenging (from within the curriculum itself) the dominant discourses and paradigms that drive traditional academic disciplines (Cabrera et al., 2014). Drawing on reflection, community involvement, advocacy, organizing, and activism (Cammarota & Aguilera, 2012; de los Rios et al., 2014; Sleeter, 2011; Tintiangco-Cubales et al., 2015), ethnic studies attempts to provide students with tools for identifying, reflecting on, critiquing, and acting against systemic racism and other forms of marginalization (Dee & Penner, 2017; de los Rios et al., 2014; Jay, 2003) with clear parallels to making oneself present, noticing and naming, and interrupting conscious and dysconscious marginalization. Importantly, recent research (Cabrera et al., 2014; Dee & Penner, 2016) has demonstrated that traditionally marginalized students have more success (increased attendance, grade point average, and credits earned, as well as increased academic confidence in writing, identity development, and critical literacies) when provided with tools for identifying, reflecting on, critiquing, and acting against systemic racism and other forms of marginalization. (See Faircloth, Barrett and McClanahan, this volume for a more expansive treatment of ethnic studies.)

CODA

This chapter is purposefully positioned against the backdrop of an alarming historic and contemporary reality in which a huge proportion of the US population is made "invisible," that is, made "missing" by society's clinging to dominant perspectives (Edkins, 2011, pp. 5–6; Tedesco & Bagelman, 2017). Worse, Edkins describes, many are completely overlooked, that is, "unmissed," by a dominant cultural eye unable to see beyond its own assumptions. This chapter contends that it is only with this understanding in mind that an unpacking or harnessing of belonging appropriate for this moment in history can occur. This reality demands pushing the boundaries of current models when we set out to explore whether, how, and by whom belonging is experienced and what belonging actually means. Traditional concerns such as these are important: What is belonging? How does it operate? What makes it possible? However, we must look beyond traditional frameworks to challenge ourselves: What are we missing? What mistakes are we making? What assumptions are hidden in our lenses that limit the potential of belonging, including dangerous assumptions of generalizability across cultures, communities, and even countries? Embracing such criticality in our work with belonging, we are able to ask, What MORE can Belonging be?

After tracing the trajectory of belonging research and theory through the terrains of its established social underpinnings and the empowerment provided by sociocultural insights, this chapter goes one step further by overlaying a stronger lens of criticality on our belonging work. The implications of this critical perspective require reconsideration of the most fundamental assumptions underlying our work, including recognizing what is hidden in the very language we use. By exploring the crossroads between belonging and the burgeoning notion of rightful presence, the chapter introduces the concept of having a right to belong, and all that it offers. For example, models of belonging as a gift or bestowed, or that insinuate an act of generosity, acceptance, or hospitality on the part of a *host*, unravel the self-evident, self-authored right to belong suggested by this chapter. Moreover, it would be a travesty to champion a right to belong—however, free from the notion of hospitality—based on great insights and good intentions, without insisting on parallel sociopolitical work of dismantling inescapable, intractable, laminated oppressive social structures, altering institutional and systemic processes that contribute to marginalization (Williams, 2006) to "make visible" those who had formerly been invisible or missed (Vakil et al., 2016, p. 196; Tedesco & Bagelman, 2017; Vrasti & Dayal, 2016).

The model suggested within this chapter for considering and addressing barriers to belonging involves a framework of Noticing/Naming and then

Interrupting such barriers. It is not the only possible model but is offered as a starting place for such thought, discourse, and action. Strategies proffered here to support Noticing/Naming include Counternarratives and Ethnography, each a respected body of knowledge and work in its own right. Likewise, those suggested as supports for Interrupting include hybridity, side-by-side research such as YPAR, and ethnic studies. It is important to point out that—not only do each of these perspectives come with their own rich and empowering bodies of work that cannot be fully addressed here, there are also many more possibilities that many people would add to this list. That raises an essential point with regard to the need to work together to advocate for a right to belong: we are in this battle together and moving forward will require powerful, wide-ranging partnerships as well as extensive, authentic discourse.

The scholar hooks refers to such acts as negotiating cracks in the world which can serve as essential new spaces of empowerment (2003). As explained by Wenger, such critical participation shapes the potential of social justice and power, thus "forging new potential modes of belongingness" (1998, p. 151). It is the contention of this chapter that such new potential and new spaces of empowerment are central to what belonging needs to be. This chapter is meant as an invitation for us all to join hands to dismantle existing barriers to belonging as well as barriers to our understanding of the experience, and, as well, to forge a new frontier of belonging befitting a nation and a world desperately in need of, and deserving of, a right to belong.

REFERENCES

Anderman, L. H., & Freeman, T. (2004). Students' sense of belonging in school. In M. L. Maehr & P. R. Pintrich (eds.), *Advances in Motivation and Achievement*, Vol. 13. *Motivating Students, Improving Schools: The Legacy of Carol Midgley* (pp. 27–63). Greenwich, CT: Elsevier.

Anzaldua, G. (1990). Haciendo caras, una entrada. In G. Anzaldua (ed.), *Borderlands/ La frontera: the new mestiza* (pp. xv–xxviii). San Francisco, CA: Aunt Lute Books.

Arendt, H. (1951). *The Origins of Totalitarianism*. New York: Harcourt Brace.

Bang, M., & Medin, D. (2010). Cultural processes in science education: Supporting the navigation of multiple epistemologies. *Science Education*, *94*(6), 1008–1026.

Banks, J. A. (2012). Ethnic studies, citizenship education, and the public good. *Intercultural Education*, *23*(6), 467–473.

Barnett, C. (2005). Ways of relating: Hospitality and the acknowledgement of otherness. *Progress in Human Geography*, *29*(1), 5–21. doi:10.1191/0309132505ph535oa

Bartlett, L., & Garcia, O. (2011). *Additive Schooling in Subtractive Times: Bilingual Education and Dominican Immigrant Youth in the Heights*. Nashville, TN: Vanderbilt University Press.

Baumeister, R. F., & Leary, M. R. (1995). The need to belonging: Desire for inter-personal attachment as a fundamental human motivation. *Psychological Bulletin, 117*(3), 497–530.

Bell, Philip & Tzou, Carrie, Bricker, Leah, & Baines, Annmarie. (2012). Learning in diversities of structures of social practice: Accounting for how, why and where people learn science. *Human Development, 55*, 269–284. doi:0.1159/000345315

Berman, J. (1989). *Cross-Cultural Perspectives*. Nebraska Symposium on Motivation, 1989, Volume 37.

Berry, J. (1990). Psychology of acculturation: Understanding individuals moving between cultures. In R.W. Brislin (ed.), *Applied Cross Cultural Psychology* (pp. 232–253). Sage.

DOI:http://dx.doi.org/10.4135/9781483325392Berry, J. W. (1997). Immigration, acculturation and adaptation. *Applied Psychology: An International Review, 46*, 5–68.

Berry, J., Phinney, J., Sam, D., & Vedder, P. (2006). Immigrant youth: Acculturation, identity, and adaptation. *Applied Psychology, 55(3),* 303–332.

Bettez, S. (2011). Critical community building. *Educational Foundations, 25*, 3–19.

Borrero, N., Yeh, C., Cruz, C., & Suda, J. (2012). School as a context for "othering" youth and promoting cultural assets. *Teachers College Record, 114*(2), 1–37.

Bourdieu, P., & Passeron, J.-C. (1990). *Theory, Culture & Society. Reproduction in Education, Society and Culture*, 2nd edition (R. Nice, Trans.). London: Sage Publications, Inc.

Bamberg, M. (2004). Talk, small stories, and adolescent identities. *Human Development, 47*, 366–369.

Cabrera, N. L., Milem, J. F., Jaquette, O., & Marx, R. W. (2014). Missing the (student achievement) forest for all the (political) trees: Empiricism and the Mexican American studies controversy in Tucson. *American Educational Research Journal, 51*(6), 1084–1118.

Calabrese Barton, A., & Tan, E. (2019). Designing for rightful presence in STEM: The role of making present practices, *Journal of the Learning Sciences, 28*, 4–5, 616–658. doi:10.1080/10508406.2019.1591411

Cammarota, J. (2015). The praxis of ethnic studies: Transforming second sight into CC. *Race Ethnicity and Education, 19*(2), 233–251.

Cammarota, J., & Fine, M. (2008). Youth Participatory Action Research *Pedagogy for Transformational Resistance* (pp. 1–11)/Revolutionizing Education: Youth Participatory Action Research in Motion, Revolutionizing Education. New York: Routledge.

Crenshaw, K. (1993). Mapping the margins: Intersectionality, identity politics, and the violence against women of color. *Stanford Law Review, 43*, 1241–1299.

Crothers, A. G., & K'Meyer, T. E. (2007). "I was black when it suited me; I was white when it suited me": Racial identity in the biracial life of Marguerite Davis Stewart. *Journal of American Ethnic History, 26*(4), 24–49.

Darder, A. (1991). *Culture and Power in the Classroom: A Critical Foundation for Bicultural Education*. New York: Bergin & Garvey.

de los Rios, C. V., Lopez, J., & Morrell, E. (2014). Toward a critical pedagogy of race: ES and literacies of power in high school classrooms. *Race and Social Problems, 7*(1), 84–96.

DeMartino, L. (2021). De-centering the deficit framework: Courageous refugee mentors in educational spaces. *Urban Review, 53*, 243–263. doi:10.1007/s11256-020-00579-7

Dee, T. S., & Penner, E. K. (2017). The causal effects of cultural relevance: Evidence from an Ethnic Studies curriculum. *American Educational Research Journal, 54*(1), 127–166.

Delgado, Richard. (1989). Storytelling for oppositionists and others: A plea for narrative. *Michigan Law Review, 87*, 2411–2441.

Delgado, Richard. (1992). The imperial scholar revisited: How to marginalize outsider writing, ten years later. *University of Pennsylvania Law Review, 140*, 1349–1372.

Delgado Bernal, D. (2002). Learning and living: Pedagogies of the home. *International Journal of Qualitative Studies in Education, 14*(5), 623–639.

de Royston, Maxine McKinney. (2013). Power, identity, and mathematical practices outside and inside school. *Journal for Research in Mathematics Education, 44*(1), 264–287. doi:10.5951/jresematheduc.44.1.0264

Derrida, J. (2000). *Of Hospitality.* Stanford, CA: Stanford University Press.

Dillard, C. B. (2000). The substance of things hoped for, the evidence of things not seen: Examining an endarkened feminist epistemology in educational research and leadership. *International Journal of Qualitative Studies in Education, 13*(6), 661–681. doi:10.1080/09518390050211565

Duncan-Andrade, J. M. R., & Morrell. E. (2008). *The Art of Critical Pedagogy: Possibilities for Moving from Theory to Practice in Urban Schools.* New York: Peter Lang.

Edkins, J. (2011). *Missing: Persons and Politics.* New York: Cornell University Press.

Engle, R. A., & Conant, F. R. (2002). Guiding principles for fostering productive disciplinary engagement: Explaining an emergent argument in a community of learners classroom. *Cognition and Instruction, 20*, 399–483.

Erickson, F. (2006). Studying side by side: Collaborative action ethnography in educational research. In G. Spindler & L. Hammond (eds.), *Innovations in Educational Ethnography: Theory, Methods and Results* (pp. 235–257). Lawrence Erlbaum.

Esmonde, I., & Langer-Osuna, J. (2013). Power in numbers: Student participation in mathematical discussions in heterogeneous spaces. *Journal for Research in Mathematics Education, 44*(1), 288–315. doi:10.5951/jresematheduc.44.1.0288

Etzioni, A. (1996). *Presidential Address: The Responsive Community: A Communitarian Perspective.* Paper presented at the American Sociological!Association.

Etzioni, A. (2000). Creating good communities and good societies. *Contemporary Sociology, 29*(1), 188–195.

Faircloth, B. S. (2009). Making the most of adolescence: Harnessing the search for identity to understand classroom belonging. *Journal of Adolescent Research, 24*(3), 321–348.

Faircloth, B. S. (2012). "Wearing a mask" vs. connecting identity with learning. *Contemporary Educational Psychology, 37,* 1–9.

Faircloth, B., McClanahan, J., & Barrett, K. (2018). *"Rightful Presence" – The Heart of Belonging.* Paper presented at the 2018 annual convention of the American Psychological Association, in San Francisco, CA.

Faircloth, B. S., & Hamm, J. V. (2005). Sense of belonging among high school students representing four ethnic groups. *Journal of Youth & Adolescence, 34*(4), 293–309.

Farkas, G., Grobe, R. P., Sheehan, D., & Shuan, Y. (1990). Cultural resources and school success: Gender, ethnicity, and poverty groups within an urban school district. *American Sociological Review, 55*(1), 127–142. doi:10.2307/2095708

Finn, J. (1989). Withdrawing from school. *Review of Educational Research, 59*(2), 117–142.

Finn, J. D. (1992, April). *Participation among eighth-grade students at risk.* Paper presented at the annual meetings of American Educational Research Association, San Francisco, CA.

Fook, Jan Oz. (2002). *Social Work: Critical Theory and Practice.* London: Sage Publications.

Freire, P. (2000). *Pedagogy of the Oppressed.* New York: Continuum International Publishing Group.

Furman, G. (1998). Postmodernism and community in schools: Unraveling the paradox. *Educational Administration Quarterly, 34*(3), 298–328.

Gans, H. J. (1992). Second-generation decline: Scenarios for the economic and ethnic futures of the post--1965 American immigrants. *Ethnic & Racial Studies, 15*(2), 173.

García Coll, C., Lamberty, G., Jenkins, R., McAdoo, H., Crnic, K., Wasik, B. & Vázquez García, H. (1996). An integrative model for the study of developmental competencies in minority children. *Child Development, 67*(5), 1891–1914.

Gee, J. P. (1990). *Social Linguistics and Literacies: Ideology in Discourse,* 1st edition. New York: The Falmer Press.

Giroux, H. A., & McLaren, P. L. (eds.) (1989). *Critical Pedagogy, the State, and Cultural Struggle.* Albany, NY: State University of New York Press.

Glick Schiller, N., Basch, L., & Blanc-Szanton, C. (1992). Towards a definition of transnationalism. *Annals of the New York Academy of Sciences, 645*(1), ix–xiv.

Gonzalez, K. P. (2000).Campus culture and the experiences of Chicano students in a predominantly White university. *Urban Education, 37*(2) 193–218.

Goodenow, C. (1993b). Classroom belonging among early adolescent students: Relationships to motivation and achievement. *Journal of Early Adolescence, 13,* 21–43.

Gray, D. L. (2017). Is psychological membership in the classroom a function of standing out while fitting in? Implications for achievement motivation and emotions. *Journal of School Psychology, 61,* 103–121. doi:10.1016/j.jsp.2017.02.001

Gray, D. L., Hope, E. C., & Matthews, J. S. (2018). What opportunities do Black adolescents have to belong at school? A case for cultural distinctiveness and citizenship as instructional and institutional opportunity structures. *Educational Psychologist, 53*(2), 97–113. doi:10.1080/00461520.2017.1421466

Guba, E. G., & Lincoln, Y. S. (1998). Competing paradigms in qualitative research. In N. K. Denzin & Y. S. Lincoln (eds.), *The Landscape of Qualitative Research* (pp. 195–220). Thousand Oaks, CA: Sage Publications.

Guiffrida, D. (2006). Toward a cultural advancement of Tinto's theory. *The Review of Higher Education, 29*(4), 451–472.

Gutiérrez, K. D. (2008). Developing a sociocritical literacy in the third space. *Reading Research Quarterly, 43*, 148–164.

Gutiérrez, Kris D., Baquedano-López, Patricia, & Tejeda, Carlos. (1999). Rethinking diversity: Hybridity and hybrid language practices in the third space. *Mind, Culture, and Activity, 6*(4), 286–303. doi:10.1080/10749039909524733

Gutiérrez, K., Baquedano-López, P., Alvarez, H. H., & Chiu, M. M. (1999). Building a culture of collaboration through hybrid language practices. *Theory into Practice, 38*, 87–93.

Gutiérrez, K., Rymes, B., & Larson, J. (1995). Script, counterscript, and underlife in the classroom: James Brown versus 'Brown v. Board of Education.' *Harvard Educational Review, 65*, 445–471.

Gutiérrez, K., & Rogoff, B. (2003). Cultural ways of learning: Individual traits or repertoires of practice. *Educational Researcher, 32*(5), 19–25.

Gutiérrez, K., & Vossoughi, S. (2010). Lifting off the ground to return anew: Mediated praxis, transformative learning, and social design experiments. *Journal of Teacher Education, 61*, 100–117.

Gutstein, E. (2003). Teaching and learning mathematics for social justice in an urban, Latino school. *Journal for Research in Mathematics Education, 34*(1), 37–73.

Hamm, J. V. & Faircloth, B. S. (2005). Peer context of mathematics classroom belonging in early adolescence. *Journal of Early Adolescence, 25*(3), 345–366.

Hand, V., Penuel, W. R., & Gutiérrez, K. D. (2013). (Re) framing educational possibility: Attending to power and equity in shaping access to and within learning opportunities. *Human Development, 55*(5–6), 250–268.

Healy, K. (2000). *Social Work Practices: Contemporary Perspectives on Change.* London: Sage Publications.

hooks, B. (2003). *Teaching Community: A Pedagogy of Hope.* New York: Routlege.

Jackson, A. P., & Smith, S. A. (2001). Postsecondary transitions among Navajo Indians. *Journal of American Indian Education, 40*(2), 28–47.

Jay, M. (2003). Critical race theory, multicultural education, and the hidden curriculum of hegemony. *Multicultural Perspectives, 5*(4), 3–9.

Johnston, E., D'Andrea Montalbano, P., & Kirkland, D. E. (2017). *Culturally Responsive Education: A Primer for Policy and Practice.* New York: Metropolitan Center for Research on Equity and the Transformation of Schools, New York University.

Jurow, S. (2005). Shifting engagements in figured worlds: Middle school mathematics students'participation in an architectural design project. *Journal of the Learning Sciences, 14*, 35–67.

Juvonen, J. (2006). Sense of Belonging, social bonds, & school functioning. In Alexander, P. & Winne, P. (eds.), *Handbook of Educational Psychology,* 2nd edition (pp. 655–424). Mahweh, NJ: Lawrence Erlbaum.

Kia-Keating, M., & Ellis, B. (2007). Belonging and connection to school in resettlement: Young refugees, school belonging, and psychosocial adjustment. *Clinical Child Psychology and Psychiatry, 12*, 29043.

Kiang, L., Broome, M., Chan, M., Stein, G. L., Gonzalez, L. M., & Supple, A. J. (2019). Foreigner objectification, English proficiency, and adjustment among youth and mothers from Latinx American backgrounds. *Cultural Diversity and Ethnic Minority Psychology, 25*(4), 461.

King, J. E. (2006). "If justice is our objective": Diaspora literacy, heritage knowledge, and the praxis of critical studyin' for human freedom. Year- book of the National Society for the Study of Education, *105*, 337–360. doi:10.111 1/j.1744-7984.2006.00089.

King, J. E., & Swartz, E. E. (2015). *Afrocentric Praxis of Teaching for Freedom: Connecting Culture to Learning.* New York: Routledge.

Knifsend, C. A., Camacho – Thompson, D. E., Juvonen, J., & Graham, S. (2018). Friends in activities, school – related affect, and academic outcomes in diverse middle schools. *Journal of Youth Adolescence, 47*(6), 1208–1220. doi:10.1007/ s10964-018-0817-6.

Knight, M. G., & Watson, V. W. M. (2014). Toward participatory communal citizenship: Rendering visible the civic teaching, learning, and actions of African immigrant youth and young adults. *American Educational Research Journal, 51*, 539–566.

Ladson-Billings, G. (2014). Culturally relevant pedagogy 2.0: A.k.a The remix. *Harvard Educational Review, 84*(1), 74–84.

Ladson-Billings, G., & Tate, W. (1995). Toward a critical race theory of education. The *Teachers College Record, 97*(1), 47–68.

LaFromboise, T., Coleman, H. L. K., & Gerton, J. E. (1993). Psychological impact of biculturalism. *Psychological Bulletin, 114*(3), 395–341.

Leander, K. M. (2001). 'This is our freedom bus going home right now': Producing and hybridizing space-time contexts in pedagogical discourse. *Journal of Literacy Research, 33,* 637–679.

Lee, C. (2007). *Culture, Literacy, and Learning.* New York: Teachers' College Press.

Majors, Y. (2003). Shoptalk: Teaching and learning in an African American hair salon. *Mind, Culture and Activity, 10*(4), 289–310.

Marlsbary, C. B. (2012). The pedagogy of belonging: The social, cultural, and academic lives of recently-arrived immigrant youth in a multiethnic, multilingual high school. *UCLA.* ProQuest ID: Malsbary_ucla_0031D_10342. Merritt ID: ark:/13030/m58k8q2b. Retrieved from https://escholarship.org/uc/item/5sp7r6fg

Mullen, E. J. (1983). 'Personal practice models.' In A. Rosenblatt and D. Waldfogel (eds.), *Handbook of Clinical Social Work* (pp. 623–649). San Francisco, CA: Jossey-Bass.

Nasir, N. (2002). Identity, goals, and learning: Mathematics in cultural practice. In N. Nasir & P. Cobb (eds.), *Mathematical Thinking and Learning*, Special issue on Diversity, Equity, and Mathematics Learning, 4(2 & 3), 211–247.

Nasir, N., & Hand, V. (2006). Exploring sociocultural perspectives on race, culture, and learning. *Review of Educational Research, 76*, 449–475.

Nasir, N. S., & Shah, N. (2011). On defense: African American males making sense of racialized narratives in mathematics education. *Journal of African American Males in Education, 2,* 24–45.

Nasir, N., Snyder, C. R., Shah, N., & Ross, K. M. (2013). Racial story-lines and implications for learning. *Human Development, 55*(5–6), 285–301. doi:10.1159/000345318

Nasir, N. I. S., & Vakil, S. (2017). STEM-focused academies in urban schools: Tensions and possibilities. *Journal of the Learning Sciences, 26*(3), 376–406. doi: 10.1080/10508406.2017.1314215

Noddings, N. (1996). On community. *Educational Theory, 46*(3), 245–267.

Osterman, K. (2020). Students' need for belonging in the school community. *Review of Educational Research, 70*(3), 323–367.

Paris, D., & Alim, H. S. (2017). What is culturally sustaining pedagogy and why does it matter? In D. Paris & H. S. Alim (eds.), *Culturally Sustaining Pedagogies: Teaching and Learning for Justice in a Changing World* (pp. 1–21). New York: Teachers College Press.

Phelen, P., Davidson, A. L., & Cao, H. T. (1991). Students' multiple worlds: Negotiating the boundariesof family, peer, and school cultures. *Anthropology and Education Quarterly, 22,* 224–250.

Reisch, M., & Andrews, J. (2002). *The Road not Taken: A History of Radical Social Work in the United States.* New York: Brunner-Routledge.

Rosas, M., & Hamrick, F. A. (2002). Postsecondary enrollment and academic decision making: Family influences on women college students of Mexican descent. *Equity and Excellence in Education, 35*(1), 59–69.

Ryu, M., & Tuvilla M. (2018). Resettled refugee youths' stories of migration, schooling, and future: Challenging dominant narratives about refugees. *The Urban Review, 50,* 539–558.

Schön, D. A. (1983). *The Reflective Practitioner: How Professionals Think in Action.* New York: Basic Books.

Slaten, C., Ferguson. J., Allen, K., Brodrick, D., & Waters, L. (2016). School belonging: A review of the history, current trends, and future directions. *The Educational and Developmental Psychologist, 33*(1), 1–15.

Sleeter, C. E. (2011). *The Academic and Social Value of Ethnic Studies: A Research Review.* National Education Association Research Department.

Solorzano, Daniel. (1998). Critical race theory, racial and gender microaggressions, and the experiences of Chicana and Chicano scholars. *International Journal of Qualitative Studies in Education, 11,* 121–136.

Solórzano, Daniel G., & Delgado-Bernal, Dolores. (2001). Examining transformational resistance through a critical race and Latcrit theory framework: Chicana and Chicano students in an urban context. *Urban Education, 36*(3), 308–342.

Sólorzano, D. G., & Yosso, T. J. (2001). Critical race and LatCrit theory and method: Counter-storytelling. *Qualitative Studies in Education, 14*(4), 71–95.

Squire, V., & Darling, J. (2013). The "minor" politics of rightful presence: Justice and relationality in city of sanctuary. *International Political Sociology, 7*(1), 59–74. doi:10.1111/ips.2013.7.issue-1.

Swidler, A. (1986). Culture in action: Symbols and strategies. *American Sociological Review, 51*(2), 273–286.

Takaki, R. (1993). *A Different Mirror: A History of Multicultural America.* Boston, MA: Back Bay Books.

Tan, E., & Calabrese Barton, A. (2017). Designing for rightful presence in STEM-rich making: Community ethnography as pedagogy. *Proceedings of FabLearn17.* doi:10.1145/3141798.3141807

Taylor, E. (2009). The purchasing practice of low-income students: The relationship to mathematical development. *Journal of the Learning Sciences, 18*(3), 370–415.

Tedesco, D., & Bagelman, J. (2017). The 'missing' politics of whiteness and rightful presence in the settler colonial city. *Millennium: Journal of International Studies, 45*(3), 380–402.

Tintiangco-Cubales, A., Kohli, R., Sacramento, J., Henning, N., Agarwal-Rangnath, R., & Sleeter, C. (2015). Toward an ethnic studies pedagogy: Implications for K–12 schools from the research. *The Urban Review, 47*(1), 104–125.

Triandis, H. C. (1990). Cross-cultural studies of individualism and collectivism. In J. J. Berman (ed.), *Nebraska Symposium on Motivation, 1989: Cross-Cultural Perspectives* (Vol. 37, pp. 41–133). Lincoln, NE: University of Nebraska Press.

Urdan, T. (2011). Factors affecting the motivation and achievement of immigrant students. APA educational psychology handbook, Vol 2: Individual differences and cultural and contextual factors. 293–313.

Urrieta, L. (2009). *Working from Within: Chicana and Chicano Activist Educators in Whitestream Schools.* Tucson, AZ: University of Arizona Press.

Valenzuela, A. (1999). *Subtractive Schooling: U.S. Mexican Youth and the Politics of Caring.* Albany, NY: State University of New York Press.

Vedder, P. H., & Horenczyk, G. (2006). Acculturation and the school. In D. L. Sam & J. W. Berry (eds.), *The Cambridge Handbook of Acculturation Psychology* (pp. 419–438). Cambridge, MA: Cambridge University Press. https://doi-org.libproxy.uncg.edu/10.1017/CBO9780511489891.031

Vrasti, W., & Dayal, S. (2016). Cityzenship: Rightful presence and the urban commons. *Citizenship Studies, 20*(8), 994–1011. doi:10.1080/13621025.2016.1229196

Vygotsky, L. S. (1978). *Mind in Society: The Development of Higher Psychological Processes.* Cambridge, MA: Harvard University Press.

Wallace, Erica R., Adams, J'nai D., Fullwood, Carla Cadet, Horhn, Erica-Brittany, Loritts, Camaron, Propst, Brandy S., & Walker, Coretta Roseboro (2020). "The black feminist mixtape: A collective black feminist autoethnography of black women's existence in the academy." *Journal of Critical Scholarship on Higher Education and Student Affairs, 5*(3), Article 7.

Warikoo, Natasha, & Carter, Prudence. (2009). Cultural explanations for racial and ethnic stratification in academic achievement: A call for a new and improved theory. *Review of Educational Research, 79*(1), 366–394.

Wenger, E. (1998). *Communities of Practice: Learning, Meaning, and Identity.* Cambridge, MA: Cambridge University Press.

Wentzel, K. R. (1997). Social motivational processes and interpersonal relation-
ships: Implications for understanding motivation at school. *Journal of Educational Psychology, 91*(1), 76–97.

Wentzel, K. R. (1998). Social relationships and motivation in middle school: The role of parents, teachers, and peers. *Journal of Educational Psychology, 90*, 202–209.

Wentzel, K. R. (1999). Social influences on school adjustment. *Educational Psychologist, 99*(34), 59–70.

Wilder, C. S. (2013). *Ebony and Ivy: Race, Slavery, and the Troubled History of America's Universities.* New York: New Bloomsbury Publishing.

Williams, C. C. (2006). The epistemology of cultural competence. *Families in Society: The Journal of Contemporary Human Services, 87*(2), 209–220. doi:10.1606/1044-3894.3514

Wortham, S. (2006). *Learning Identity: The Joint Emergence of Social Identification and Academic Learning.* New York: Cambridge University Press.

Chapter 2

Centering Antiracism in Schools to Support Belonging for Black Students

Elan C. Hope, Chauncey D. Smith, Charity Brown Griffin, and Alexis S. Briggs

Goodenow (1993) defines school belonging as how well an adolescent "fits" within the school environment with regard to support, relatedness, and acceptance from teachers and peers. As such, belonging is an important psychological need that can contribute to positive academic outcomes for adolescents (Freeman et al., 2007; Matthews et al., 2014; McMahon & Wernsman, 2009). For Black students, research consistently shows that when Black students feel like they belong in school, they have better academic and psychological outcomes (Butler-Barnes & Inniss-Thompson, 2020; Leath & Chavous, 2018; Murphy & Zirkel, 2015). For instance, among African American middle-school students, greater sense of belonging in schools was associated with higher educational goals (e.g., college degree attainment) and efficacy (Murphy & Zirkel, 2015). Among Caribbean Black adolescent girls, greater school belonging was related to less school discipline (e.g., suspension; Butler-Barnes & Inniss-Thompson, 2020).

This is particularly important given the history of public education for Black students in the United States. Public schools were intentionally created and maintained to provide inadequate education for Black students and these historical roots are maintained in present-day educational policy and practice (O'Connor, 2016). Despite attempts to redress the resulting educational disparities, Black students are still relegated to seeking public education within a system that was never intended to make Black students feel like they belong as students, scholars, and high achievers. In fact, researchers find that Black students, via stereotypes and persistent stigma, receive messages that they do not belong in schools or as students of academic promise (Cook et al., 2012; Hope et al., 2015; Walton & Cohen, 2007). Public schools in the United States were designed to isolate Black students and communicate that Black students do not belong in academic and school settings, and, therefore, are second-class citizens.

Given this racist history of public education, scholars have expanded our conceptual definition of school belonging to shift from a focus on how individual students perceive their own belonging or "fit" within an educational space to include how instructional practice and institutional policies support or negate the belongingness needs of Black students (Gray et al., 2018). Belongingness is not just a need that manifests within the individual; schools have an obligation to purposefully meet the belongingness needs of Black students through opportunity structures that exist through interpersonal interactions, instructional practice, and institutional policies (Gray et al., 2018). Interpersonal opportunity structures are the connections between Black students, their peers, and their teachers. Instructional opportunity structures are the pedagogical and classroom activities that reinforce belongingness for Black students and dismantle racist practices and embedded stigmas. Institutional opportunity structures exist within the structural makeup of school policies and practices.

One method of engaging the belongingness needs of Black students is by taking an antiracist approach. The fundamental assumptions of antiracism are that (1) racial groups are equal, (2) racist policies make up the legal foundation of society, and (3) active measures should be taken to remove racist policies (Kendi, 2019). In this chapter, we extend belongingness research to explore how antiracism pedagogy, rooted in culturally relevant pedagogy and Critical Race Theory (CRT), can support the belongingness needs of Black students, via institutional opportunity structures in schools.

BLACK STUDENTS' EXPERIENCES IN SCHOOLS

Research on Black students' experiences in schools documents the struggles they endure in their matriculation across school contexts (Fisher et al., 2019; Griffin et al., 2020; Leath et al., 2019; Sondel et al., 2019; Smith & Hope, 2020). These struggles are defined by a broader context of structural racism in the United States. As a key component of the cultural DNA of the United States, racism permeates every corner of the human experience (Ladson-Billings & Tate, 1995); the school context is no exception. For Black students in school contexts, structural racism is realized through a series of structural insufficiencies that they learn to navigate.

For decades, scholars have narrated the manifestations of structural racism in the experiences of Black students with the examination of two notable disparities in metrics of academic success across racial groups: the achievement gap and the discipline gap (Gregory et al., 2010). The achievement gap, largely examined between Black and White students, was one prominent trend in scholarly literature and popular media. Researchers tracked racial group differences in reading and math-standardized test scores from elementary through high school, often finding that Black students' scores were lower, on average, than White students' scores (Braun et al., 2010; Chatterji, 2006; Rumberger & Willms, 1992). A failure of only discussing achievement gaps is that it centers responsibility on children and their families without holding schools and their governing bodies accountable for creating safe and effective learning environments for Black students.

Another example of disproportionality, which contributes to the isolation that Black students experience in schools, is a discipline gap. After controlling for individual characteristics, Black students are targeted for disciplinary referrals at higher rates than their White peers (Bradshaw et al., 2010). Increasing in degrees of severity, these disciplinary referrals lead to after-school detention, in-school suspension, and out-of-school suspension (Kinsler, 2011; Leath et al., 2019). These punishments address undesired student behavior by demanding more of students' time, withdrawing them from the classroom, or removing them from the school altogether. According to Civil Rights Data Collection by the US Department of Education, Black students are three times more likely to be suspended than White students; this was even evident in the disproportionate suspension of Black preschoolers when compared to their White schoolmates (US Department of Education Office for Civil Rights, 2014). Given the role teachers play in referring students for disciplinary action, scholars point to teacher training that confronts racial bias and promotes equitable practices as a lever to disrupt this trend (Gregory & Roberts, 2017; Gregory et al., 2016).

As structural racism is the soil where anti-Black school governance practices are planted, racial discrimination is a fertilizer. In concert with the gaps in achievement and disciplinary action, Black students throughout the pipeline report experiences of racial discrimination from their administrators, teachers, and peers (Butler-Barnes et al., 2018; Chavous et al., 2017; Leath et al., 2019). Beyond the negative effect on academic outcomes, school-based discrimination is linked with psychological distress among Black students (Benner et al., 2018). Taken together, there are long-standing threats to Black students' belonging in schools. From being told that they do not and cannot achieve to being kicked out of classrooms and schools at disproportionate rates, all while facing discrimination from multiple directions—that message is clear (Bottiani et al., 2016; Hope et al., 2015). Still, there are some pathways from threats to belonging to hope and community for Black students *within schools*. These pathways are not defined by working around or avoiding the racial injustice that Black students face in school, but rather facing it and co-constructing antiracist and justice-oriented possibilities in instructional and institutional standards.

ANTIRACISM: ROOTS IN CULTURALLY RELEVANT PEDAGOGY AND CRITICAL RACE THEORY

Given the recent increase in diversity within the student population of public schools in the United States, considerable attention has been given to the need to use culturally responsive and culturally relevant teaching practices. Coined by Ladson-Billings (1995; 2014), *culturally relevant pedagogy* focuses on teacher methods and practice that engage individual students in academically rigorous curriculum and learning while affirming their racial identities and experiences. Culturally relevant pedagogy rests on three fundamental pillars that work in tandem with another: (1) academic achievement (educators holding high academic expectations and teaching content based on who their students are as people and as learners); (2) cultural competence (educators interrogating one's own identity and culture to strengthen instructional practice, using students' culture as the basis for learning, and intentionally creating opportunities for students to learn more about the lived experiences of others); and (3) sociopolitical consciousness (educators actively thinking about and educating students on how to act in ways that challenge inequality; Ladson-Billings, 2006). Similarly, Gay (2000) defined *culturally responsive* teaching as "using the cultural knowledge, prior experiences, frames of reference, and performance styles of ethnically diverse students to make learning encounters more relevant to and effective for them" (p. 31). Thus, at the heart of culturally relevant and responsive teaching there is a bridging of students' home and school worlds, and social justice is centered in a way that makes true belonging possible.

While those seeking to engage in culturally relevant and responsive practices honor difference, celebrate diversity, and show care for addressing individual student needs, at the same time, many educators endorsing this pedagogical stance discount the significance of race and the ways that racism and racist systems impact schooling experiences (Whipp, 2013). In Ladson-Billings' (2014) recent reflection of culturally relevant pedagogy, she argued that even amid its growing popularity, educators tend to omit its critical and sociopolitical aspects. Without explicitly naming and talking about race, educators risk engaging in colorblind or color-evasive practices (Carter et al., 2017; Dowd & Bensimon, 2015; Galloway et al., 2020). This omission further ostracizes Black students, and does not contribute to the interpersonal, instructional, or institutional opportunities for belonging in schools.

The interrogation of race and racism can also be found in CRT and its application to education. CRT was designed to address societal inequities through a framework of race, racism, and power (Crenshaw et al., 1995). CRT was first conceptualized by law practitioners and academics to address the sociohistorical origins and functions of White supremacy and its byproducts (i.e., the continued oppression of people of color) with the intention to dismantle structural racism (Bell, 2008; Crenshaw et al., 1995). This theory and its mission have applied across fields, and has been thought about in education in interesting ways that contribute to strategies of promoting equitable learning environments for Black youth. Scholars addressing the application of CRT to the field of education (1) acknowledge the social construction, structural mechanisms, and endemic nature of racism, (2) center intersectionality (see Collins, 2015), and (3) reject dominant ideologies forged by White supremacy to center the narratives of folks of color (Solórzano & Yosso, 2000; Yosso, 2002; Carbado, 2011; Ladson-Billings & Tate, 2016). Insidious practices (e.g., disparate discipline practices; inadequate funding), when examined critically, are evidence of how structural racism is present and prevalent in public schools and are indicative of inequities in the education system.

Dominant ideologies that sustain White supremacy, such as meritocracy and racial color blindness (Ladson-Billings & Tate, 2016) provide palatable explanations for a structurally unequal system that thrives off of hierarchy and furthermore are harmful to people of color (Carbado, 2011). The myth of meritocracy poses that resources, specifically wealth and income, are distributed according to the merit of individuals (McNamee & Miller, 2009), and racial color-evasiveness insists that sociohistorical anti-Blackness is in the past and that we have moved beyond issues of race and racism (Frankenberg, 1993). CRT aims to challenge and expose dominant ideologies by centering those who are marginalized by them. A way in which this is achieved in education using a CRT framework is via the act of counter-storytelling, which looks to the experiences of people of color as a primary source of knowledge (Delgado, 1989; Yosso, 2002; Ladson-Billings & Tate, 2016).

Indeed, a major challenge in education is the difficulty educators have in engaging constructively around issues of race and the open refusal to recognize connections between race, White privilege, and White supremacy (Dei & Linton, 2019; Dowd & Bensimon, 2015). Ideologies promoting merit, hard work, individual responsibility, and freedom of choice have limited dialogue about institutional responsibility and complicity in the creation of racial inequities (Dei & Linton, 2019). As a result, educators may fail to see how racism and White supremacy are embedded within education as a set of ideas and practices that dominate and script everyday experiences in classrooms and schools (Carter et al., 2017). Because of these existing politics in education, scholars argue that educators must engage in antiracist practices which place explicit focus on naming power, acknowledging the maintenance and reproduction of White privilege, and identifying how individuals can resist the status quo (Welton et al., 2019; Yong & Laible, 2000).

Antiracism pedagogy is explicitly race-conscious and compels teachers and students to explore notions of race by exposing the role White racial dominance plays in producing and sustaining inequity (Brooks & Witherspoon Arnold, 2013; Welton et al., 2019; Young & Laible, 2000). In this way, antiracism pedagogy challenges the essential underpinnings of the education system, which has been historically grounded in whiteness, and seeks to deconstruct White dominance couched in "objectivity" and "universality" (Wagner, 2005). Consequently, antiracism work in educational spaces requires that teachers and administrators challenge previously unquestioned "truths," reconsider what is valued, and center voices previously silenced. Through this approach, the belongingness needs of Black students can be adequately addressed in structural ways that decenter the responsibility of belonging within each individual student and places the responsibility of creating environments that support belonging at the school and school district level.

ANTIRACISM AND SCHOOL BELONGING: OPPORTUNITIES FOR INSTITUTIONAL CHANGE

Antiracism pedagogy and practice can facilitate the school belongingness needs of Black children and youth. This is imperative so that Black students are not just physically present in schools, but feel wholly and completely included as equal participants in the broader educational process. Scholars have identified strategies for researchers and practitioners to consider when assessing and implementing instructional and institutional opportunities for school belonging, particularly in relation to the experiences of Black students (Gray et al., 2018, 2020). Here, we describe several opportunities for institutional and instructional change that schools can adopt to meet the belongingness needs of Black students. We provide examples of these strategies from the empirical research and educational practice. In many instances, we describe exceptions to the typical rules of public education. We present these exceptions in the hopes that they will become the standard for educating Black students and meeting their needs of belonging in structural and systematic ways.

Diversify the Educator Workforce

Gray et al. (2018) describe several institutional opportunities for policy and practice that can enhance the opportunities for belonging among Black students. One strategy is to consider *how existing school policies might undermine or enhance belonging* for Black students. From an antiracism perspective, this would include considering policies that exist that limit the possibility for success among Black students. This would also include imagining or reimagining policies that expand opportunities for Black students in schools. One such institutional policy for schools and school districts to examine is teacher recruitment and hiring practices in relation to the racial-ethnic composition of their teacher and administrator workforce.

According to the National Center for Education Statistics (de Bray et al., 2019), 80 percent of teachers are White. With regard to the student population, 49 percent of students are White. Specific to the Black population, only 9 percent of teachers are Black while 15 percent of students nationwide are Black. Further, while the teacher workforce is becoming more diverse nationwide, the student population is becoming even more diverse at a much faster rate (US Department of Education, 2016). Racial-ethnic diversity and representation among teachers and administrators is not just important from a statistical equity standpoint. Researchers across several recent studies have found that Black students have better schooling outcomes when they have teachers and administrators that share their racial-ethnic background and heritage (e.g., Dee, 2004; Ouazad, 2014; Redding, 2019). Although these studies were not framed explicitly from a belonging point of view, the relevance for sense of belonging and seeing oneself in the classroom is obvious.

For instance, using data from a large experimental study of public schools in Tennessee, Dee (2004) found that Black kindergarteners who had a Black teacher had significantly higher mathematics and reading scores than their Black peers who had a White teacher. Further, in that study, White students were more than twice as likely to have a teacher of their own race (94 percent) than Black students (45 percent; Dee, 2004). Using data from the Early Childhood Longitudinal Study, Kindergarten cohort of 1998, Ouazad (2014) found that students are assessed more positively by teachers of the same race. These effects start in kindergarten and continue throughout the elementary school grades (Ouazad, 2014). Further, Black children receive worse behavioral assessments by White teachers than Black teachers (Bates & Glick, 2013). In a review of 37 studies, Redding (2019) found that Black teachers rated Black students more favorably in terms of both positive and negative classroom behavior. In terms of teacher ratings of academic performance, Black teachers rate Black students highly and Black students reported more favorable test scores when they have a Black teacher (Redding, 2019). These results are more pronounced in elementary school, as compared to secondary school. Finally, researchers found that Black students perceive their Black teachers more positively than their White teachers, especially with regard to holding high academic standards and clear explanations of content (Cherng &

Halpin, 2016). Altogether, this research suggests that we can support belong-ingness and related academic success for Black students by diversifying our teacher and administrator workforce to include more Black educators.

While the data from recent studies provides evidence to support recruiting, hiring, and retaining a more diverse teacher workforce, there are several bar-riers to implementation that schools and school districts must contend with. One such barrier is entry into the teaching profession. Researchers have found that White college students are twice as likely than Black students to graduate with a bachelor's degree in education and White graduates are more likely to enter the teaching workforce after graduation than Black graduates (Redding & Baker, 2019). This suggests that in order to increase recruitment, hiring, and retention of Black teachers, there needs to be a multifold approach. First, teacher training programs should consider how to better reach and retain promising future Black educators. Second, schools and school districts should consider recruitment strategies to attract the existing Black students who major in education into the teaching profession. This might include direct outreach through universities and related student organizations at universi-ties. Third, schools and school districts might consider competitive offers and retention packages that incentivize Black teachers to come to and remain in their particular district. Finally, schools and school districts should consider broader policies and expectations to maintain a positive work environment for Black professionals, wherein colleagues and supervisors are trained in antiracist practices that support Black teachers having a positive and racial discrimination-free environment to engage in teaching.

Antiracism Policy Audits

Another way to understand how school policy promotes or deters institutional opportunities for belonging for Black students is through antiracism policy audits. Gray et al. (2018) recommend a policy audit where educators examine the intended and unintended consequences for school policies in relation to the belongingness needs of Black students. For instance, a common policy that at the outset seems to be neutral and is enforced inequitably are school discipline policies. According to the US Department of Education Office for Civil Rights, compared to White girls, Black girls are over three times more likely to receive in-school suspension, over seven times more likely to receive out-of-school suspension, and almost four times more likely to be arrested in school (Inniss-Thompson, 2017). Further, in the southern United States, Black students make up only 24 percent of public school students and yet are 48 percent of all suspended students and 49 percent of all expelled stu-dents (Smith & Harper, 2015). School leaders should first disaggregate their own disciplinary data to determine whether their school is disproportionately punishing Black students, and thus threatening their sense of belonging in schools. If disparities are found, it is next important to audit disciplinary policies and practices and determine alignment with current best practices in the field. Respected scholars in education have repeatedly called for the removal of zero-tolerance disciplinary policies (American Psychological Association (APA), 2008; Fabelo et al., 2011; Smith & Harper, 2015). To replace outdated zero-tolerance discipline methods, scholars recommend multitiered disciplinary strategies that include large-scale primary prevention efforts, targeted behavioral interventions, graduated systems that adjust consequences based on the severity of the infraction, and training for educators regarding alternative disciplinary strategies and consistent application (APA, 2008; Morgan et al., 2014).

Empirical research supports this idea. In a randomized control trial with 86 classrooms, Gregory et al. (2016) evaluated the effectiveness of the My Teaching Partner Secondary (MTP-S) teacher coaching program. In the MTP-S program, coaches observed teachers and provided feedback regarding teacher–student interactions and how teachers can create, maintain, and improve emotionally positive and cognitively challenging classrooms. They found that teachers in the intervention condition did not discipline Black students at higher rates than their peers, while racial disparities remained for teachers who did not receive the intervention. Even more, the year after the coaching program ended, teachers who had received the intervention did not discipline Black students more harshly, while teachers in the control condition continued to exhibit racial bias against Black students in their disciplinary practice (Gregory et al., 2016). It is important to note that this intervention did not directly target student behavior but sought to change the norms and expectations of the classroom culture to facilitate positive and trusting relationships between teachers and students (Gregory et al., 2016). Similar antiracism audits can be performed to examine other policies, including, but not limited to, placement into gifted and Advanced Placement (AP) courses, content of dress codes and student codes of conduct, and placement into special education classes. With the assumption that racism is a baseline in the educational system, efforts to work against it must be proactive, vigorous, and ongoing.

Understand Your School Racial Climate

Another recommendation from Gray et al. (2018) is to interrogate the messages that Black students receive in school about opportunities to develop their cultural and heritage knowledge (via instructional content, bulletin boards, communal spaces, extracurricular offerings, etc.). Broadly, racial socialization generally refers to the verbal or nonverbal messages transmitted to youth about race and ethnicity (Hughes et al., 2016). While parents are primary socialization agents for cultural practices and norms (Hughes et al., 2016), schools also function as an important place where Black students learn about race and ethnicity and the ideological values that schools and society place on members of their racial group (Aldana & Byrd, 2015; Byrd & Hope, 2020). This suggests that schools and educators should purposefully attend to the direct and indirect messages that their practices and policies send to students about race and belongingness. According to over two decades of research, Black students have a positive sense of belonging in schools that promote the cultural values that reflect students' home and community life (Boykin & Ellison, 1995; Dotterer et al., 2009; Rouland et al., 2014). In practice, the examination of opportunities for students to develop their cultural heritage should include an assessment of the school racial climate.

School racial climate focuses on how students experience interpersonal interactions and socialization with regard to race and culture in schools (Byrd, 2015; Byrd 2017). Experiences of interpersonal interactions include how often interactions across racial groups occur, the positive or negative nature of those interactions, how fairly different groups are treated, whether schools support intergroup interactions, and whether one's group is treated according to stereotypical beliefs (Byrd, 2015). In empirical work among high school students, higher school belonging was related to higher quality intergroup interactions, more frequent intergroup interactions, greater perceptions of equal status, greater support for positive intergroup interactions, and less stereotyping (Byrd, 2017). Students feel a greater sense of belonging in schools where they have more opportunities to engage with peers from other racial backgrounds and have positive interactions that promote equal status and minimize stereotyping with the support of teachers and administrators. As such, schools can assess how students experience their interactions at school and determine whether trainings and cultural norms in the school should be revisited to promote positive interpersonal interactions. Importantly, the onus and responsibility for generating greater engagement should not lie with the students, but with the leaders and systems of the school.

Racial socialization in schools includes what students learn about their own culture, what students learn about mainstream US norms and values, what students learn about the cultures and traditions of other groups, what students learn that promotes a colorblind approach that ignores the importance of race, and what students learn with regard to historical and contemporary manifestations of differential power and privilege across racial groups (Byrd, 2015). Students across racial groups who experienced more promotion of cultural competence and more socialization of their own culture in schools also reported greater feelings of belonging (Byrd, 2017). This was similar to students who reported more experiences of socialization of mainstream values and socialization of the historic and contemporary manifestations of systemic oppression also reported greater feelings of belonging in schools (Byrd, 2017). Surprisingly, students who reported experiencing more color-blind socialization that deemphasizes the importance of race also reported greater sense of school belonging (Byrd, 2017). It is possible greater feelings of school belonging are related to colorblind socialization overall, but that these relationships differ by racial/ethnic group or racial composition of the school, which was not a part of the original analyses. Further, culturally relevant pedagogy was positively associated with cultural socialization and critical consciousness socialization; students who reported high levels of socialization about their own culture and the realities of racial oppression were likely to have teachers who implemented culturally relevant pedagogical approaches (Byrd, 2017).

As with interpersonal interactions, teachers and administrators can assess how their own students experience the racial socialization practices of the school. With data in hand, educators can adjust school standards and participate in relevant professional development to increase culturally relevant pedagogy in support of socialization practices that increase belonging. Specifically, practices that increase cultural socialization, critical consciousness socialization, and cultural competence, while decreasing colorblind ideology will benefit the academic and belongingness needs of Black students.

Privilege Student Voice and Perspective

In addition to examining the intended and unintended consequences of school policies for Black students and evaluating the racial climate of the school, Gray et al. (2018) recommend that schools consider whether the voices and perspectives of Black students are represented within existing policies and practices. Research suggests that Black students' perspectives are not generally reflected in school practices and policies (Fine et al., 2004; Hope et al., 2015). Likewise, there is a growing body of research that suggests that when student voice is included there are benefits for students, educators, and school (e.g., Lenzi et al., 2014; Mitra & Serriere, 2012; Voight, 2014). Specific to belongingness, when Black students feel their perspectives are considered and reflected in institutional policy and instructional practice, they are more engaged in learning and feeling a greater sense of belonging in schools (Mirra et al., 2013; Taines, 2012). Further, the employment of critical pedagogies in language, literature, and social studies classes reinforce critical analysis skills taught while promoting the principles of social justice (Duncan-Andrade & Morrell, 2008). Finally, when student voices are not heard clearly, there is a legacy of empowerment from students who restore their own hope through activism that challenges schools to care for them—with or without permission of adult school leaders (Kirshner, 2015). This advocacy and agency are important skills that are a part of civic development (Malin et al., 2015) but is also a responsibility that is better placed with the school leaders in conversation and collaboration with students, and not on the shoulders of the students alone.

In one example from an urban middle school, Voight (2014) found that student voice has a positive influence on school climate in three unique ways. First, participant-driven and researched-focused interventions, such as Youth Participatory Action Research (YPAR), help students identify and vocalize barriers they face in schools, analyze the root causes of those barriers, and propose solutions that involve policy change at the school and classroom levels. Second, youth-focused interventions can strengthen student–educator relationships, which has a direct impact on how Black students interpret their "fit" within the school context. Third, YPAR interventions promote civic competencies among study participants, which can further permeate the broader prosocial culture of the school. Other scholars have found similar success with YPAR interventions as a viable option to promote critical thinking and social justice among Black youth in school settings (Smith & Hope, 2020). When coupled with an antiracist pedagogical approach, YPAR can serve as an avenue for students to have an active role in antiracist structural changes in schools. This combined approach will have benefits of increasing sense of belonging among Black students via the YPAR project and adding institutional opportunity structures to support belongingness among Black students, even beyond the students who participate in the YPAR experience.

CONCLUSION

Traditionally, in the achievement motivation literature, belongingness is situated within the individual (Goodenow, 1993). We contend that the school belongingness needs of Black students can and should be supported through structural changes in instructional practice and institutional policy (Gray et al., 2018, 2020). Given the historic roots of racism in education, we cannot contend with adequately addressing belonging in schools without contending with racism. As such, an antiracist approach that acknowledges the roots of racism in education policy and actively seeks to redress those policies provides a framework to reconsider belonging in school. Belongingness research and practice, particularly when considering Black students in schools, cannot move forward without actively fighting against racism in schools and implementing antiracist pedagogy and philosophy within the structures of our education system. We provide just four places to begin to implement antiracist approaches in support of belonging for Black students: diversifying the educator workforce; conducting antiracism audits of school policies; assessing the school racial climate; and prioritizing Black student voices in policy and practice decisions. We see from the existing research and practice that when we take these approaches, Black students belong in schools and thrive as academicians and scholars. When the structure of school provides an opportunity to belong, Black students are empowered to reach their optimal development in the classroom and beyond.

REFERENCES

Aldana, A., & Byrd, C. M. (2015). School ethnic-racial socialization: Learning about race and ethnicity among African American students. *The Urban Review, 47*(3), 563–576. doi:10.1007/s11256-014-0319-0

American Psychological Association Zero Tolerance Task Force. (2008). Are zero tolerance policies effective in the schools? An evidentiary review and recommendations. *American Psychologist, 63*(9), 852–862.

Bates, L. A., & Glick, J. E. (2013). Does it matter if teachers and schools match the student? Racial and ethnic disparities in problem behaviors. *Social Science Research, 42,* 1180–1190. doi:10.1016/j.ssresearch.2013.04.005

Bell, D. (2008). *Race, Racism, and American Law* (6th edition). Aspen Publishers.

Benner, A. D., Wang, Y., Shen, Y., Boyle, A. E., Polk, R., & Cheng, Y.-P. (2018). Racial/ethnic discrimination and well-being during adolescence: A meta-analytic review. *American Psychologist, 73*(7), 855–883. doi:10.1037/amp0000204.supp

Bottiani, J. H., Bradshaw, C. P., & Mendelson, T. (2016). Inequality in Black and White high school students' perceptions of school support: An examination of race in context. *Journal of Youth and Adolescence, 45*(6), 1176–1191. doi:10.1007/s10964-015-0411-0

Boykin, A. W., & Ellison, C. M. (1995). The multiple ecologies of Black youth socialization: An afrographic analysis. In R. L. Taylor (ed.), *African American Youth: Their Social and Economic Status in the United States* (pp. 93–128). Praeger.

Bradshaw, C. P., Mitchell, M. M., O'Brennan, L. M., & Leaf, P. J. (2010). Multilevel exploration of factors contributing to the overrepresentation of Black students in office disciplinary referrals. *Journal of Educational Psychology, 102*(2), 508–520. doi:10.1037/a0018450

Braun, H., Chapman, L., & Vezzu, S. (2010). The Black-White achievement gap revisited. *Education Policy Analysis Archives, 18,* 21. doi:10.14507/epaa.v18n21.2010

Brooks, J. S., & Witherspoon Arnold, N. (2013). *Antiracist School Leadership: Toward Equity in Education for America's Students.* Information Age Publishing.

Butler-Barnes, S. T., & Inniss-Thompson, M.N. (2020). "My teacher doesn't like me": Perceptions of teacher discrimination and school discipline among African-American and Caribbean Black adolescent girls. *Education Sciences, 10*(2), 1–14. doi:10.3390/educsci10020044

Butler-Barnes, S. T., Richardson, B. L., Chavous, T. M., & Zhu, J. (2018). The importance of racial socialization: School-based racial discrimination and racial identity among African American adolescent boys and girls. *Journal of Research on Adolescence, 34*(1), 493–417. doi:10.1111/jora.12383

Byrd, C. M. (2015). The associations of intergroup interactions and school racial socialization with academic motivation. *The Journal of Educational Research, 108*(1), 10–21. doi:10.1080/00220671.2013.831803

Byrd, C. M. (2017). The complexity of school racial climate: Reliability and validity of a new measure for secondary students. *British Journal of Educational Psychology, 87*(4), 700–721. doi:10.1111/bjep.12179

Byrd, C. M., & Hope, E. C. (2020). Black students' perceptions of school ethnic-racial socialization practices in a predominately Black school. *Journal of Adolescent Research, 35*(3), 1–26. doi:10.1177/0743558419897386

Carbado, D. (2011). Critical what what? *Connecticut Law Review, 43*(5), 1593–1643.

Carter, P. L., Skiba, R., Arredondo, M. I., & Pollock, M. (2017). You can't fix what you don't look at: Acknowledging race in addressing racial discipline disparities. *Urban Education, 52*(2), 207–235. doi:10.1177/0042085916660350

Chatterji, M. (2006). Reading achievement gaps, correlates, and moderators of early reading achievement: Evidence from the Early Childhood Longitudinal Study (ECLS) kindergarten to first grade sample. *Journal of Educational Psychology, 98*(3), 489–507. doi:10.1037/0022-0663.98.3.489

Chavous, T. M., Richardson, B. L., Webb, F. R., Fonseca-Bolorin, G., & Leath, S. (2017). Shifting contexts and shifting identities: Campus race-related experiences, racial identity, and academic motivation among Black students during the transition to college. *Race and Social Problems, 10*(1), 1–18. doi:10.1007/s12552-017-9218-9

Cherng, H. S., & Halpin, P. F. (2016). The importance of minority teachers: Student perceptions of minority versus white teachers. *Educational Researcher, 45*(7), 407–420. doi:10/3102/0013189X16671718

Collins, P. H. (2015). Intersectionality's definitional dilemmas. *Annual Review of Sociology, 41*, 1–20.

Cook, J. E., Purdie-Vaughns, V., Garcia, J., & Cohen, G. L. (2012). Chronic threat and contingent belonging: Protective benefits of values affirmation on identity development. *Journal of Personality and Social Psychology, 102*, 479–496. doi:10.1037/a0026312

Crenshaw, K., Gotanda, N., Peller, G., & Thomas, K. (1995). *Critical Race Theory: The Key Writings that Formed the Movement.* New Press.

de Brey, C., Musu, L., McFarland, J., Wilkinson-Flicker, S., Diliberti, M., Zhang, A., et al. (2019). *Status and Trends in the Education of Racial and Ethnic Groups 2018* (NCES 2019-038). National Center for Education Statistics.

Dee, T. S. (2004). Teachers, race, and student achievement in a randomized experiment. *The Review of Economics and Statistics, 86*(1), 195–210. doi:10.1162/003465304323023750

Dei, G. J. S., & Linton, R. (2019). Racism in schools and classrooms: Towards an anti-racist pedagogy of power and systemic privilege. In A. Jule (ed.), *The*

Compassionate Educator: Understanding Social Issues and the Ethics of Care in Canadian schools (271). Canadian Scholars.

Delgado, R. (1989). Storytelling for oppositionists and others: A plea for narrative. *Michigan Law Review, 87*(8), 2411–2441.

Dotterer, A. M., McHale, S. M., & Crouter, A. C. (2009). Sociocultural factors and school engagement among African American youth: The roles of racial discrimination, racial socialization, and ethnic identity. *Applied Developmental Science, 13*(2), 61–73. doi:10.1080/ 10888690902801442

Dowd, A. C., & Bensimon, E. M. (2015). *Engaging the "Race Question": Accountability and Equity in US Higher Education.* Teachers College Press.

Duncan-Andrade, J. M. R., & Morrell, E. (2008). *The Art of Critical Pedagogy: Possibilities for Moving from Theory to Practice in Urban Schools* (Vol. 285). Peter Lang.

Fine, M., Burns, A., Payne, Y., & Torre, M. (2004). Civic lessons: The color and class of betrayal. *Teachers College Record, 106,* 2193–2223.

Fisher, A. E., Fisher, S., Arsenault, C., Jacob, R., & Barnes-Najor, J. (2020). The moderating role of ethnic identity on the relationship between school climate and self-esteem for African American adolescents. *School Psychology Review, Advance Online Publication.* doi:10.1080/2372966X.2020.1760690

Frankenberg, R. (1993). *White Women, Race Matters: The Social Construction of Whiteness.* University of Minnesota Press.

Freeman, T. M., Anderman, L. H., & Jensen, J. M. (2007). Sense of belonging in college freshmen at the classroom and campus levels. *The Journal of Experimental Education, 75*(3), 203–220. doi:10.3200/JEXE.75.3.203-220

Galloway, M. K., Callin, P., James, S., Vimegnon, H., & McCall, L. (2020). Culturally responsive, antiracist, or anti-oppressive? How language matters for school change efforts. *Equity & Excellence in Education, 52,* 485–501. doi:10.108 0/10665684.2019.1691959

Gay, G. (2000). *Culturally Responsive Teaching: Theory, Research, and Practice.* Teachers College Press.

Gray, D. L., Hope, E. C., & Byrd, C. M. (2020). Why Black adolescents are vulnerable at school and how schools can provide opportunities to belong to fix it. *Policy Insights from the Behavioral and Brain Sciences, 7*(1), 3–9. doi:10.1177/2372732219868744

Gray, D. L., Hope, E. C., & Matthews, J. S. (2018). Black and belonging at school: A case for interpersonal, instructional, and institutional opportunity structures. *Educational Psychologist, 114*(2), 1–17. doi:10.1080/00461520.2017.1421466

Gregory, A., Hafen, C. A., Ruzek, E., Mikami, A. Y., Allen, J. P., & Pianta, R. C. (2016). Closing the racial discipline gap in classrooms by changing teacher practice. *School Psychology Review, 45*(2), 171–191. doi:10.17105/SPR45-2.171-191

Gregory, A., & Roberts, G. (2017). Teacher beliefs and the overrepresentation of Black students in classroom discipline. *Theory Into Practice, 56*(3), 187–194. doi: 10.1080/00405841.2017.1336035

Gregory, A., Skiba, R. J., & Noguera, P. A. (2010). The achievement gap and the discipline gap. *Educational Researcher, 39*(1), 59–68. doi:10.3102/0013189X09357621

Griffin, C. B., Stitt, R. L., & Henderson, D. X. (2020). Investigating school racial climate and private racial regard as risk and protector factors for Black high school students' school engagement. *Journal of Black Psychology, Advanced Online Publication, 46*(6–7), 514–549. doi:10.1177/0095798420946895

Hope, E. C., Skoog, A. B., & Jagers, R. J. (2015). "It'll never be the white kids, it'll always be us": Black high school students' evolving critical analysis of racial discrimination and inequity in schools. *Journal of Adolescent Research, 30*(1), 83–112. doi:10.1177/0743558414550688

Hughes, D. L., Watford, J. A., & Del Toro, J. (2016). A transactional/ecological perspective on ethnic–racial identity, socialization, and discrimination. In *Advances in Child Development and Behavior* (Vol. 51, pp. 1–41). JAI.

Inniss-Thompson, M. N. (2017). *Summary of Discipline Data for Girls in U.S. Public Schools: An Analysis from the 2013—14 U.S. Department of Education* Office *for Civil Rights Data Collection*; National Women's Justice Institute: Berkeley, CA; Available online: https://www.acsa.org/application/files/5215/0532/2372/NBWJI_Fact_Sheet_090917FINAL.pdf (accessed on 27 May 2020).

Kendi, I. X. (2019). *How to be an Antiracist*. One World/Ballantine.

Kinsler, J. (2011). Understanding the black-white school discipline gap. *Economics of Education Review, 30*(6), 1370–1383. doi:10.1016/j.econedurev.2011.07.004

Kirshner, B. (2015). *Youth Activism in An Era of Education Inequality*. NYU Press.

Ladson-Billings, G. (1995). Toward a theory of culturally relevant pedagogy. *American Educational Research Journal, 32*(3), 465–491.

Ladson-Billings, G. (2006). Yes, but how do we do it? Practicing culturally relevant pedagogy. In J. Landsman & C. W. Lewis (eds.), *White Teachers/Diverse Classrooms: A Guide to Building Inclusive Schools, Promoting High Expectations and Eliminating Racism* (pp. 29–42). Stylus Publishers.

Ladson-Billings, G. (2014). Culturally relevant pedagogy 2.0: aka the remix. *Harvard Educational Review, 84*(1), 74–84.

Ladson-Billings, G., & Tate, W. F. (1995). Toward a critical race theory of education. *Teachers College Record, 97*(1), 47–68.

Ladson-Billings, G., & Tate, W. F. (2016). Toward a critical race theory of education. In *Critical Race Theory in Education* (pp. 10–31). Routledge.

Leath, S., & Chavous, T. (2018). Black women's experiences of campus racial climate and stigma at predominately white institutions: Insights from a comparative and within-group approach for STEM and Non-STEM majors. *The Journal of Negro Education, 87*(2), 125–139.

Leath, S., Mathews, C., Harrison, A., & Chavous, T. (2019). Racial identity, racial discrimination, and classroom engagement outcomes among Black girls and boys in predominantly Black and predominantly white school districts. *American Educational Research Journal, 56*(4), 1318–1352. doi:10.3102/0002831218816955

Lenzi, M., Vieno, A., Sharkey, J., Mayworm, A., Scacchi, L., Pastore, M., & Santinello, M. (2014). How school can teach civic engagement besides civic education: The role of democratic school climate. *American Journal of Community Psychology, 54*(3–4), 251–261.

Malin, H., Ballard, P. J., & Damon, W. (2015). Civic purpose: An integrated construct for understanding civic development in adolescence. *Human Development, 58*(2), 103–130. doi:10.1159/000381655

Matthews, J. S., Banerjee, M., & Lauermann, F. (2014). Academic identity formation and motivation among ethnic minority adolescents: The role of the "self" between internal and external perceptions of identity. *Child Development, 85*(6), 2355–2373. doi:10.1111/cdev.12318

McMahon, S. D., & Wernsman, J. (2009). The relation of classroom environment and school belonging to academic self-efficacy among urban fourth- and fifth-grade students. *The Elementary School Journal, 109*(3), 267–281. doi:10.1086/592307

McNamee, S. J., & Miller, R. K. (2009). *The Meritocracy Myth.* Rowman & Littlefield.

Mirra, N., Morrell, E. D., Cain, E., Scorza, D. A., & Ford, A. (2013). Educating for a critical democracy: Civic participation reimagined in the Council of Youth Research. *Democracy and Education, 21*(1), 1–10.

Mitra, D. L., & Serriere, S. C. (2012). Student voice in elementary school reform: Examining youth development in fifth graders. *American Educational Research Journal, 49*(4), 743–774. doi:10.3102/0002831212443079

Morgan, E., Salomon, N., Plotkin, M., & Cohen, R. (2014). *The School Discipline Consensus Report: Strategies from the Field to Keep Students Engaged in School and Out of the Juvenile Justice System.* The Council of State Governments Justice Center.

Murphy, M. C., & Zirkel, S. (2015). Race and belonging in school: How anticipated and experienced belonging affect choice, persistence, and performance. *Teachers College Record, 117*, 1–40.

O'Connor, C. (2016). Black agency and the ongoing struggle for Black educational opportunity. *Du Bois Review-Social Science Research on Race, 13*, 413–4242. doi:10/1017/s1742058x16000254

Ouazad, A. (2014). Assessed by a teacher like me: Race and teacher assessments. *Education Finance and Policy, 9*(3), 334–372.

Redding, C. (2019). A teacher like me: A review of the effect of student-teacher racial/ethnic matching on teacher perceptions of students and student academic and behavioral outcomes. *Review of Educational Research, 89*(4), 499–535. doi:10.3102/0034654319853545

Redding, C., & Baker, D. J. (2019). Understanding racial/ethnic diversity gaps among early career teachers. *AERA Open, 5*(2), 1–17. doi:10.1177/2332858419848440

Rights, U. S. D. O. E. O. F. C. (2014). Civil Rights Data Collection "Data Snapshot: School Discipline" (PDF), 1–24.

Rouland, K. K., Matthews, J. S., Meyer, R. L., Byrd, C., & Rowley, S. J. (2014). Culture clash? Interactions between Afro-cultural and main- stream cultural styles in classrooms serving African-American students. *Interdisciplinary Journal of Teaching and Learning, 4*, 186–202.

Rumberger, R. W., & Willms, J. D. (1992). The impact of racial and ethnic segregation on the achievement gap in California high schools. *Educational Evaluation and Policy Analysis, 14*(4), 377–336.

Smith, C. D., & Hope, E. C. (2020). "We just want to break the stereotype": Tensions in Black boys' critical social analysis of their suburban school experiences. *Journal of Educational Psychology, 112*(3), 551–566. doi:10.1037/edu0000435

Smith, E. J., & Harper, S. R. (2015). *Disproportionate Impact of K–12 School Suspension and Expulsion on Black Students in Southern States.* Philadelphia, PA: University of Pennsylvania, Center for the Study of Race and Equity in Education.

Solórzano, D. & Yosso, T. (2000). Maintaining social justice hopes within academic realities: A Freirean approach to critical race/LatCrit pedagogy. *Denver University Law Review, 78*, 595–621.

Taines, C. (2012). Intervening in alienation: The outcomes for urban youth of participating in school activism. *American Educational Research Journal, 49*, 53–86. doi:10.3102/0002831211411079

US Department of Education, Office of Planning, Evaluation and Policy Development, Policy and Program Studies Service. (2016). *The State of Racial Diversity in the Educator Workforce.* Washington, D.C.

Voight, A. M. (2014). Student voice for school-climate improvement: A case study of an urban middle school. *Journal of Community & Applied Social Psychology, 25*(4), 310–326. doi:10.1002/casp.2216

Wagner, A. E. (2005). Unsettling the academy: Working through the challenges of anti-racist pedagogy. *Race Ethnicity and Education, 8*(3), 261–275.

Walton, G. M., & Cohen, G. L. (2007). A question of belonging: Race, social fit, and achievement. *Journal of Personality and Social Psychology, 92,* 82–96. doi:10.1037/0022-3514.92.1.82

Welton, A., Diem, S., & Carpenter, B. W. (2019). Negotiating the politics of antiracist leadership: The challenges of leading under the predominance of whiteness. *Urban Education, 54*(5), 627–630.

Whipp, J. L. (2013). Developing socially just teachers: The interaction of experiences before, during, and after teacher preparation in beginning urban teachers. *Journal of Teacher Education, 64*(5), 454–467.

Yosso, T. J. (2002). Toward a critical race curriculum. *Equity & Excellence in Education, 35*(2), 93–107.

Young, M. D., & Laible, J. (2000). White racism, anti-racism, and school leadership preparation. *Journal of School Leadership, 10*, 374–415.

Chapter 3

Out and About

LGBTQ+ Students' Journey to Belong

Nicholas Antonicci, Louis Killion, and R. Bradley Johnson

Human beings are social creatures; people innately want to belong. This desire to belong is called "sense of belonging" and is important for overall human development. Although much research has been conducted around sense of belonging and the factors affecting it (e.g., Anderman & Freeman, 2004; Hagerty et al., 1992; Hausmann et al., 2007; Rhee, 2008; Tovar & Simon, 2010), we are utilizing Strayhorn's (2019) definition of sense of belonging to frame this chapter, which he describes as

> a basic human need, a fundamental motivation, sufficient to drive behaviors and perceptions. Its satisfaction leads to positive gains such as happiness, elation, wellbeing, achievement, and optimal functioning. Given its significance in various social contexts, as well as its consistent association with positive health, and social and psychological outcomes, I think its importance cannot be stressed enough. (p. 9)

As it relates more specifically to the higher education environment and climate, Strayhorn (2019) states that sense of belonging refers to

> students' perceived social support on campus, a feeling or sensation of connectedness, and the experience of mattering or feeling cared about, accepted, respected, valued by, and important to the campus community or other on campus such as faculty, staff, and peers. (p. 4)

He further states that a sense of belonging is important not only for college students but important for all of us, "although it may take on heightened importance for college students given where they are generally in their personal development—traditionally at the crux of identity exploration and vulnerable to peer influence" (p. 28). For those working in higher education institutions whose responsibilities center around student success (recruitment, retention, persistence, and graduation), there is a stated need for campus professionals to value the environmental climates and policies just as much as "predictive analytics, intrusive advising, curricular alignment, and early alert systems" (Strayhorn, 2019, p. 2).

Yet in the pursuit of our overall desire to belong and develop a sense of belonging, individuals can sometimes be met with obstacles making this process more challenging. These obstacles can range from the individual (personal interactions with others) to larger, more systemic issues (law and legal procedures, educational policies, workplace and business norms, and healthcare access). For individuals from marginalized populations, the effects of these obstacles can be compounded and have detrimental effects upon their well-being. As one such marginalized population found on our campuses, LGBTQ+ (lesbian, gay, bisexual, transgender, queer, and other identities) individuals face challenges to their daily lives and sense of belonging in the areas mentioned earlier (e.g., Blackmon, 2018; Johnson, 2009; Rankin et al., 2010) on the basis of their sexual or romantic orientation and/or gender identity. LGBTQ+ students are not monolithic in their experiences. For students who face additional marginalization related to their racial or ethnic identity, religious or spiritual identity, ability, socioeconomic status, and, more, the journey toward a sense of belonging becomes increasingly more complex and difficult.

Within this chapter, we explore and examine the concept of sense of belonging specifically related to LGBTQ+ students with respect to structural or institutional barriers (law and policy, health and wellness, and physical and virtual spaces) as well as overall campus climate (classrooms, residence halls, athletics, and fraternity and sorority life). Our goal is to encourage campus professionals to proactively create space which facilitates LGBTQ+ students' journey toward belonging.

STRUCTURAL AND INSTITUTIONAL BARRIERS TO SENSE OF BELONGING

Although LGBTQ+ college students may or may not experience social challenges to their sense of belonging, they all experience the effects of systemic inequality. LGBTQ+ college students contend with macro-level national barriers as well as policies and circumstances specific to higher education (Renn, 2017). We define structural belonging here as the degree to which people fit into the tangible constructions of society. As Burns (2011) explains in an article about structural discrimination, "In any given institution there are established organizing principles, rules and regulations, procedures, role definitions and so on, which discriminate against individuals and groups that do not 'belong' to majority society" (p. 1). In our discussion of structural belonging, our conception of "structures" includes law, policy, public services, and public spaces. As important as it is to discuss barriers in these structures, the landscape of structural belonging also includes protections and resilience strategies.

Some structural influences impact the LGBTQ+ community as a whole while others speak specifically to sexual orientation or gender identity. Systemic protections more frequently extend to LGBQ (lesbian, gay, bisexual, queer) identities. Structural discrimination against trans-spectrum (students with nonnormative gender identities and gender expressions) people reveals a legal system that is entrenched in the idea of binary gender. Most public higher education institutions protect sexual identity minorities in their antidiscrimination statements, but there is room for improvement in their protections for trans students. For example, the Board of Governors for the public institutions in North Carolina's State University system voted in 2013 to ban gender-neutral housing plans from all 16 schools in the system (Equality North Carolina, 2013). A private college not beholden to a state governing body could have avoided such an obstacle and implemented affirming policies and procedures for LGBTQ+ students.

Private institutions receive far more legal latitude, depending on circumstance, to discriminate against students on the basis of LGBTQ+ identities, so structural discrimination against sexual and romantic minorities may still be observed there. This is particularly true of religious, private colleges that may legally refuse to admit gay students (Gjelten, 2015). At the same time, private institutions may also use that same latitude to better serve LGBTQ+ populations, for example, by virtue of the fact that they can create gender-inclusive housing options with less oversight.

Law and Policy

Because issues at institutions of higher education exist within a broader social context, we will begin by discussing nationwide systemic forces that impact LGBTQ+ students. For LGBTQ+ students, federal law seldom protects against sexual and romantic identity or gender identity discrimination explicitly; the responsibility of protecting LGBTQ+ students is largely left up to states or institutions (Renn, 2017). The positive aspect of this system is that the minimum of federal antidiscrimination law is not a limit, which means that institutions may go beyond legal minimums to achieve human rights minimums. The negative aspect is that practitioners and offices may not extend themselves beyond the minimums required. Therefore, ensuring rights for marginalized populations often requires raising the minimum protections set by the federal government. For this reason, we will discuss federal laws that protect or hinder LGBTQ+ people and provide some examples of implications for LGBTQ+ students.

The Supreme Court ruled on June 15, 2020, that "an employer who fires an individual merely for being gay or transgender violates Title VII" (Bostock v. Clayton County, 2020, "Syllabus," p. 1). This case set a fascinating precedent; it did not offer protections directly for a gay or transgender person, but rather it used the protected class under Title VII of "sex" to argue for antidiscrimination in the workplace. "Sex" as discussed in Title VII does not have a written definition and is also not differentiated from gender, a practice that is exclusionary toward gender-diverse people (Civil Rights Act, 1964). The Supreme Court's decision on employment discrimination avoided defining "sex" as stated in Title VII. As noted in the court's decision, the lack of explicit reference to sexuality and gender identity underneath sex did not amount to exclusion of people of transgender or "homosexual" status from the broad protections of the law. In the words of the Court's opinion,

> An employer who fires an individual for being homosexual or transgender fires that person for traits or actions it would not have questioned in members of a different sex. Sex plays a necessary and undisguisable role in the decision, exactly what Title VII forbids. (*Bostock v. Clayton County*, 2020, "Opinion of the Court," p. 2)

The manner in which the Court used "sex" to secure protections for LGBTQ+ people may trickle into other protections moving forward, given the ubiquity of antidiscrimination law in the United States on the basis of sex. But still, private institutions have more room to discriminate if they do not accept federal funding. And even if they do accept federal funding, a private school that is sectarian or controlled by a religious organization is exempt from portions of Title IX that conflict with the religious tenets of the institution (Office for Civil Rights, 2020).

It is worth noting that while these laws can be viewed through the perspective of what outcomes they engender for LGBTQ+ people, structural belonging is more than just what civil rights a population is or is not granted. The fact that cases debate when, where, and how a LGBTQ+ person can count on legal protection inherently communicates a lack of belonging. Whenever a population's rights become a subject of argument, the underlying message is that the value and humanity of some people are debatable. The hypothetical absence of homophobia and transphobia in law does not guarantee the unbiased application of justice. "Justice" may refer to the rulings of judges in court or the ways in which employees of institutions interpret policy and law.

As an example of the social and legal context influencing belonging, one of the authors was denied service at the Department of Motor Vehicles (DMV). The DMV would not issue an updated driver's license in terms of address, name, or gender because they disputed the validity of his physician's letter describing his gender transition. The DMV employee cited a policy that required original documentation, but in practice she evaluated the presented documentation by the higher standards of self-authentication (Legal Information Institute, n.d.-a, n.d.-b). This denial could have been interpreted as an honest mistake were it not for her rude commentary referencing the author's genitals and her limited efforts at seeking a solution. The requirement that transgender people undergo surgery before being allowed to legally change their gender is, in itself, concerning. But even when that standard is met, it can be challenged because of an interpretation of that standard.

For gender and name change policies at institutions of higher education that require doctor's letters, there is a scenario where approval can be left to the discretion of the university employee receiving a student's documentation. Modeling university policies on the precedents in state and federal law risks repeating the same flaws. Namely, laws pertaining to trans rights requiring an "original, signed letter from a physician" allow institutions to interpret that language harshly or impose templates for letter structure that disregard the fact that trans-related health care is barely standardized. These requirements can be difficult and expensive to meet. So for trans students to get their needs met, there are two layers to sift through: gatekeeping, in the form of the person or entity in charge of interfacing with the student interpreting policy in favor of the student, and privilege, in that the institution would need to eliminate the inherent bias toward trans students with economic and social privilege.

Health and Wellness

The institutionalized gender binary is not the only structural system impacting LGBTQ+ students. The long history of pathologizing LGBTQ+ people in Western, White tradition has permeated medical services for this population (Benedetti, 2015). Most student health and counseling centers in the United States name and offer programing around the needs of LGBTQ+ students, so there is progress. In a survey dating from 2010 to 2012, researchers found room for improvement in psychotherapy services for sexual and romantic minorities, or LGBQ people (Quiñones et al., 2017). Clients appreciated providers addressing sexual orientation and displaying competence around sexual minority culture, but excessive focus on the subject could "take the form of stereotyping, microaggressions, and failures to see clients as unique individuals" (Quiñones et al., 2017, "Preventing and Alleviating Minority Stress," para. 2). An example of the microaggressions offered in the study was, "I had one therapist that laughed at me and told me I was not queer and that she didn't 'buy' bisexuality." Another participant recalled an unhelpful therapist saying that she "needed to cut [her] hair in order to be a lesbian and didn't really believe [she] was gay" (Quiñones et al., 2017, "Theme C," para. 2). Therefore, mental health service providers may need additional or extended opportunities to build trust with LGBTQ+ students on campus to prevent such experiences.

On the medical side of student health, medical insurance companies may choose to disregard their policies at will to deny coverage; moreover, policies written around trans health care intentionally complicate access. For example, hormone replacement therapy forms may require none or up to one form of proof for cisgender patients, but approximately 17 criteria for gender identity dysphoria (GID) patients (BlueCross BlueShield of North Carolina, 2017). In addition to the challenges of medical policy, there are financial obstacles in obtaining care and treatment. As with many other minoritized identities, LGBTQ+ people experience higher rates of poverty (Badgett et al., 2019). Therefore, student health centers must evaluate the cost of services and consider the number of students wishing to use health-care benefits. For universities to create structural change in health-care outcomes for LGBTQ+ students, they need to carefully consider their choice of student insurance provider. If no insurance company that covers LGBTQ+ care exists, then the larger issue becomes the existence of medical insurance companies that exclude people with uncommon needs to ensure the highest profits with the least public pushback. The policies that raise the burden of proof for LGBTQ+ students seeking care through extensive lists of requirements take the responsibility for access away from insurance and pharmaceutical companies and place it onto the shoulders of marginalized people in a way that further challenges their belonging.

Physical and Virtual Spaces

Ultimately, higher education is tasked with figuring out how to include LGBTQ+ students in a context not designed for them in a way that reduces the harm inherent in a schism between self and structure. For trans-spectrum students, bathroom access highlights the barriers of building codes and existing structures as well as social anxieties. Bathroom access affects any gender-nonconforming student, not just trans-identified students. Cisgender students in the LGBQ community whose gender presentation challenges social norms also risk harassment when using public facilities. According to the principles of universal design (Burgstahler, 2015), gender-inclusive bathroom options allow for use by a much greater range of students, even beyond gender-nonconforming and trans-spectrum students. Students with disabilities who have other-gender caretakers, student parents with other-gender children, and women students wanting to save time by not staying in queue for a women's bathroom all would benefit. The bathroom debates ignore other experiences too. They often discuss sex in a way that excludes intersex people, or people whose physical sex does not match social models of "male" or "female" (Rolker, 2016). Some arguments in favor of retaining sex-segregated bathrooms also note the needs of religious women whose beliefs mandate against sharing facilities with any other genders, or the needs of women who may not feel able to wash menstrual cups at shared sinks because of stigma (Anonymous, n.d.). The last point ignores that not all people who menstruate are women.

Like other debates around LGBTQ+ belonging, the bathroom debates sometimes arrive at a contrived dichotomy between LGBTQ+ people and religious people or between LGBTQ+ people and cisnormative people. There is an assumption that the needs of these populations are mutually exclusive, where belonging becomes a zero-sum game. Although no simple solution exists in discussions of public bathrooms and universal design, higher education practitioners can come back to prioritizing choice and agency. When there are multiple bathroom types available then a person has agency to choose which type of bathroom best suits their needs. For the most part, existing binaried bathroom options remove agency from the individual because of the way cissexism has been institutionalized.

Residence halls, bathrooms, and building entrances all communicate that White, straight, cisgender, thin, able-bodied people are the expected users. Expanding the accessibility of facilities means expensive and time-consuming remodeling; it also means confronting the limitations of building codes and legal protections. In some states, building codes mandate the required number of gendered bathrooms per building, so even single-stall restrooms physically suitable for gender-inclusive use must retain gendered labels (Spula, 2017). The more embodied a structure is, the more slowly it changes. A good example of this comes from a 2016 study by Goldberg et al. (2019) of mostly US-based, trans and gender-nonconforming students in higher education who answered an online survey about their experiences on campus. The top desired campus change was gender-inclusive bathrooms, although only 45 percent of students at public, four-year institutions reported gender-inclusive bathrooms in most campus buildings. By contrast, 93 percent of these students reported a university-recognized student organization for LGBTQ+ people and allies (Goldberg et al., 2019).

This study shows that malleable, peripheral accommodations like student organizations come into being far more easily than implanted structural considerations like gender-inclusive bathrooms. And conversely, malleable factors such as personal bias are the easiest way to discriminate despite structural protections. Does this mean that structural elements do not matter and that discrimination or support will take place within our structures no matter the intent? Is structural inclusion the first step in pressuring our cultural norms to catch up? Or do social prejudices need to change first to get structural inclusion to follow? Changing the most permanent aspects of our environment represents an enormous commitment to social equity in terms of time and money, but it also secures the most permanent protections in the event of fluctuating intangibles. At an even higher level, changes in building code law, though intangible, could change the course of new construction and therefore our physical world.

In an increasingly digital world, institutional IT systems play a significant role in virtual structural belonging for LGBTQ+ students. Some student record systems at institutions of higher education do not allow for students to change their displayed name, especially not without legal name change documentation (Beemyn, 2005). Even fewer systems include pronouns as a standard form of identification. Students who go by a name other than their legal name for gender affirmation face the task of outing themselves to professors and potentially their classmates for every class, every term, as long as their system name matches their legal name. The IT systems that house official student records represent a virtual "building": slow to remodel. Fortunately, staff and faculty at many institutions have begun to normalize the inclusion of their pronouns in email signatures, staff biographies, and videoconferencing apps. These virtual behaviors signal a cultural support of LGBTQ+ students that may influence the development of future IT systems. LGBTQ+ resilience strategies stand in the face of virtual discrimination, such as through apps developed by LGBTQ+ people. An app called "The Validation Station" sent affirming messages to trans-spectrum people in unwelcoming homes during the COVID-19 lockdown (Parsons, 2020). "Refuge Restrooms" is an app that identifies safe bathrooms on a map for gender-diverse people to use (Nichols, 2015). These community-led efforts create a virtual space of belonging that offers a healing counterpoint to structural inequities.

BELONGING ON CAMPUS AS LGBTQ+ PEOPLE

In this chapter, we have explored and examined structural and institutional barriers which impact and influence LGBTQ+ students' sense of belonging. Bronfenbrenner's theory of developmental ecological systems offers an important reminder that the development of a person is impacted by the many contexts in which they are situated (Bronfrenbrenner, 1994). Those contexts range from the most proximal (e.g., peers, family, daily contacts) to the most distal (media, policies, cultural norms). As we have illustrated in our discussion of structural and institutional barriers, those distal macrosystems and exosystems can be slow to change. However, campus professionals can look to their microsystems to see what is within their control to shift, and how more positive interactions within those microsystems can improve sense of belonging. Next, we explore LGBTQ+ students' journey toward belonging through campus climate in the specific context of classrooms, residence halls, athletics, and fraternity and sorority life to better understand the impacts of these microsystems.

Climate

The climate of a campus significantly impacts, either positively or negatively, the experiences of LGBTQ+ students. Climate may be thought of as the "attitudes, behaviors, and standards of practices of employees and students of an institution" (Rankin & Reason, 2008, p. 264). Rankin and Reason (2008) critique common conceptualizations of climate, asserting that climate is too often defined with anthropomorphic descriptors such as "friendliness, hostility, or accepting" (p. 264). This point serves as an important reminder that while campuses are comprised of policies, practices, and people, it is the people with whom students interact that implement and enact those policies. In their *Transformational Tapestry Model* of climate, Rankin and Reason (2008) offer that campus climate is influenced by the following areas: (1) access and retention, (2) research/scholarship, (3) inter- and intragroup relations, (4) curriculum and pedagogy, (5) university policies and practices, and (6) external relations. Within each of these areas are multiple possibilities for facilitating a sense of belonging for LGBTQ+ students on campus.

Despite national and institutional progress, campus climate remains hostile for LGBTQ+ students (Garvey et al., 2015). Queer-spectrum (students with nonnormative sexual and romantic orientations) students who experience a positive and more welcoming campus climate are more likely to rate their academic success as higher (Garvey et al., 2018). In their study *2010 State of Higher Education for Lesbian, Gay, Bisexual, and Transgender People*, Blumenfeld et al. (2015) surveyed 5,149 students, staff, faculty, and administrators from institutions of higher education from all across the United States and found that 30 percent of the participants "experienced a difficult or hostile campus" (p. 6) and 21 percent of the participants expressed they had been harassed in connection to their identity as an LGBTQ+ person. Campus climate may also be experienced differently by those within LGBTQ+ communities. For example, trans-spectrum folks, when compared to queer-spectrum folks, hid their identities at higher rates to avoid intimidation while on campus; those rates are 63 percent and 43 percent, respectively (Blumenfeld et al., 2016). It is difficult to imagine a space for belonging in which your relevant identities must be disguised.

Classroom

Academic faculty play an integral role in ensuring their institution is inclusive and affirming for LGBTQ+ students, especially within the classroom and other academic spaces such as research laboratories. Transgender students who experience lack of inclusion in the classroom may not participate as much in discussions or may withdraw from class entirely (Pryor, 2015). Yet, faculty regularly lack the knowledge, support, and resources needed to create classrooms where students of all sexual orientations, romantic orientations, gender identities, and gender expressions have a sense of belonging and feel safe (e.g., Broadhurst et al., 2018; Garvey & Rankin, 2015), so this is one action step that universities could commit to. One author, in his role as the director of a university LGBTQ Center, regularly speaks with faculty members who desire to create inclusive spaces but feel ill-equipped to turn their hopes into action.

For many LGBTQ+ students, one important step toward belonging in the classroom is being able to come out safely if they choose. LGBTQ+ students who are "more out" report higher levels of active and collaborative learning (Rankin et al., 2010). Some students may feel reluctant to come out in the classroom due to the relative authority of the professor and the fear of being more harshly graded (Furrow, 2012). The burden of remaining in the closet in the classroom can be mentally and emotionally exhausting, contributing to an increased cognitive load that is in conflict with learning course material (Cooper & Brownell, 2016). In some classrooms where writing from a personal perspective may be emphasized, students are encouraged to write about topics where describing their experiences may require disclosure of their identity (Furrow, 2012). Each time the course or assignments veer toward a student's personal life, the student must make mental calculations to possibly come out or perhaps change key components of their story in an effort to conceal their identity. A student might change the pronouns of the person they are dating to appear heterosexual or perhaps make subtle changes in describing their interests to appear more "masculine" or more "feminine." A sense of belonging is not supported when safe expression of self is not possible.

Students also may perceive different academic departments as being more or less inclusive (Pryor, 2015). Comfort in the classroom may be linked to academic major, indicating differential experiences based on department (Furrows, 2012). In their study of 17 lesbian, gay, and bisexual students enrolled in an engineering department at a major institution of higher education in the United States, Cech and Waidzunas (2011) found that engineering students were subjected to heteronormative environments, experienced a unique type of LGBQ exclusion specific to engineering, and were subjected to the existence of a social/technical dichotomy which deemed issues and experiences related to identity as irrelevant to engineering. This was echoed by Cooper and Brownell (2011) whose participants discussed similar sentiments: disclosure of LGBTQIA+ identity was seen as inappropriate within science communities. For example, faculty members teaching statistics may say the following when discussing statistical analysis in which there are only two variables: "For this statistical method, only two variables are used. Let's use gender since there are only two variables: male and female." For many trans-spectrum students, the assertion that only two genders exist (e.g., male and female, which are actually sex terms) feels exclusionary. During an anatomy class, a professor may make generalizations such as "when women menstruate" which fails to acknowledge transmasculine people who menstruate and will leave students wondering if conversations about trans men menstruating are welcome in the classroom. Faculty in science, technology, engineering, and math fields are not exempt from ensuring their classrooms and the curriculum is inclusive and affirming for LGBTQ+ students.

Heteronormative and cisnormative environments (ones where it is assumed that everyone is heterosexual and/or cisgender) are not unique to STEM fields. For example, within some social sciences, research may exist that cites differences between "men and women." Faculty may create more inclusive classrooms for transgender students by encouraging students to question how these differences may be attributed to the ways girls and boys are socialized differently, rather than assuming innate differences. Similarly, faculty must ensure the literature and scholarship from which they draw is current and relevant, otherwise they risk perpetuating harmful narratives about transgender people (Wentling et al., 2008). In theater programs, trans-spectrum students should be afforded agency to decide which roles they would like to audition for, and ultimately play. When LGBTQ+ students enter the classroom, they bring their entire selves including their identities and experiences. Faculty must avoid relegating issues and experiences of identity to other parts of campus in order to create learning environments where everyone feels safe to be themselves. How might a faculty member who feels the experiences of transgender students have no place in the classroom respond when one of their students feels they've been ignored or mistreated by their classmates? Whether it is adding a statement of inclusion in the syllabus, incorporating pronouns in the classroom, and/or including LGBTQ+ authors of color in the curriculum, there are many options available to faculty wishing to create inclusive classrooms that generate a sense of belonging for LGBTQ+ students.

Residence Halls

For many college students, residence halls are more than just the rooms and buildings they live and sleep in during their time enrolled at a university. Within these on-campus buildings, there exists great potential for students to find thriving communities which will sustain and support them through-out their time as a student. The "safety, security, and comfort" a residence hall provides, especially those with inclusive housing options, is especially important to LGBTQ+ students (Garvey et al., 2018, p. 11). Safety, security, and comfort go far beyond physical safety and include emotional well-being and a sense of belonging.

The physical structure of residence halls, including bathrooms and how floors or buildings are gendered, pose considerable challenges for many LGBTQ+ students and their sense of belonging. For many students, being forced into a binary space is an act of violence that limits a student's sense of belonging. Trans-spectrum students regularly report not being allowed to live in residential housing that affirms their identity due to their assigned sex (Seelman, 2014). Similarly, they are regularly prevented from using the bath-room that affirms their identity (Seelman, 2014). Trans-spectrum students must have access to housing and bathroom options which affirm their gender and must not be limited to assignments based on their assigned sex. One such way is through the implementation of gender-inclusive housing which allows students of different genders to share a living space (Taub et al., 2016). Notably, LGBQ students are also better served in gender-inclusive housing because it allays fears they may have about needing to perform in more mas-culine or feminine ways to meet strict gender expectations.

As of this writing, approximately 272 colleges and universities now have some variant of gender-inclusive housing (Beemyn, 2020). These changes represent a concerted effort on the part of many institutions to address a need that is salient to the LGBTQ+ community, but the impact of this effort depends on the details. For example, Southern Illinois University at Edwardsville only offers gender-inclusive accommodations for upper-class students and defines gender-inclusive housing as "housing in which members of the opposite gender live together in a living unit/apartment" (Southern Illinois University Edwardsville, 2020, "Gender-Inclusive Housing"). This characterization of gender-inclusive housing imposes a binary gender standard and reduces the significance of the accommodation. As another example, The Ohio State University offers all-gender rooms and bathrooms in a gender-inclusive residence hall, which also happens to be one of the most expensive on-campus housing options (Ohio State University, 2020a, b). This is one of the unfortunate side effects of a world not structured for LGBTQ+ needs: opportunities to live in affirming and inclusive environments are often more expensive. Additionally, housing models that integrate gender-inclusive assignments among other rooms in any residence hall remove the "separate but equal" impact of distinct gender-inclusive communities. This allows equitable access for LGBTQ+, particularly trans-spectrum, to participate in the traditional college experience of on-campus life, regardless of where they live. At the same time, integrating gender-inclusive assignments could raise safety concerns for LGBTQ+ students who may be placed among potentially unfriendly peers or for administrators fearful of drawing attention to an often marginalized and vulnerable population.

For many LGBTQ+ students, one of their primary concerns upon entering a residential university is related to their potential roommate(s) and hall-mates. Students may ask themselves: "Will my roommate be accepting of a queer person?" "What if I am the first transgender person my roommate has met?" "What happens if my roommate holds strong negative beliefs about queer and/or transgender people?" For asexual students, they may question, "Will I be pressured to have sex or subjected to endless talk about sex and hookups?" These questions are particularly salient for LGBTQ+ students without access to gender-inclusive housing.

The residential staff's role in creating safe and affirming residence halls for students cannot be understated. Resident Assistants (RAs) require training to understand the unique needs that LGBTQ+ students face living in residential spaces. Training of RAs must encompass not only techniques for helping students work through marginalizing experiences but also proactive ways to ensure residence halls are affirming and that marginalizing experiences do not occur in the first place (Mollet et al., 2020). Since many RAs are responsible for hosting social and educational programming with their residents, it is critical they learn ways to make their programs inclusive and affirming. For example, an RA of a single-sex floor may feel compelled to host a social with the RA of another floor whose residents are of another sex in hopes of promoting across-gender socializing and to encourage dating. They may even go as far as announcing to their residents "We're hosting a Valentine's Day mixer with the girls' floor above us! You might meet your future girlfriend!" Proper training of residential staff will help to ensure heteronormative and cisnormative language is reduced to a minimum, thus creating more safe and affirming spaces for LGBTQ+ students.

Athletics

For many student athletes, participation in sports yields much support and encouragement from teammates, coaches, and community. LGBTQ+ college students who wish to pursue a collegiate athletic career may experience difficulty in achieving a sense of belonging within their team. Within collegiate athletic environments, LGBTQ+ students regularly experience hostility, exclusion, and discrimination (Atteberry-Ash et al., 2018). In the *Out in the Fields* Report, which surveyed 9,494 athletes (including 7,000 lesbian, gay, and bisexual athletes) across the world, Worthen (2014) found that 82 percent of LGBQ participants have witnessed or experienced homophobia in sports, including social barriers that include expectations to conform to hypermasculinity on men's teams or misperceptions that women who participate in sports are masculine and therefore lesbian.

In addition to the social barriers faced by LGBTQ+ students, there are a number of structural and institutional barriers faced by LGBTQ+ student athletes. Institutional barriers may include lack of policies protecting LGBTQ+ student athletes from discrimination, or lack of policies which explicitly state transgender students' right to access to sex-segregated sports and the binaried nature of (male–female) locker rooms, changing rooms, and sports facilities. Despite the NCAA release of *NCAA Inclusion of Transgender Student-Athletes* Handbook in 2011, which provides guidance for transgender athletes who wish to participate in NCAA sports, most institutions lack clear policies for club and intramural sports. Furthermore, while some policies, including the NCAA policy, create access for transgender athletes, they may be experienced by some trans-spectrum students as restrictive and in contradiction in its consideration of the diversity of transgender identity and experience.

To address these social and institutional barriers, athletic departments may combat homophobia and transphobia inherent to athletic culture by implementing protective policies to ensure LGBTQ students to access sports without facing hostility (Atteberry-Ash et al., 2018). Athletic departments may also elect to explicitly outline policies to encourage transgender student participation in all sports, including club and intramural sports. Training (e.g., LGBT SportSafe Inclusion Program, http://lbgtsportsafe.com) must be provided for administrators, coaches, and teams on how to create teams devoid of anti-LGBTQ+ culture. Athletic departments must also ensure the creation of gender-inclusive locker rooms, restrooms, and changing rooms to provide LGBTQ+ students safe and comfortable facilities. Lastly, organizations such as Athlete Ally (www.athleteally.org) exist both nationally and on many individual campuses to provide students with a space to simultaneously envision sports without homophobia and transphobia while encouraging them to engage in advocacy to work toward that vision.

Fraternity and Sorority Life

For some LGBTQ+ students, the opportunity to develop close relationships and a tight-knit community within fraternities and sororities offer great promise. For many LGBTQ+ students, however, the explicit binary structure for fraternities and sororities, and the attitudes, beliefs, and behaviors of members present a challenge for experiencing a sense of belonging. Within fraternities, members may be subjected to strict expectations to conform to hegemonic masculinity where members distance themselves from LGBTQ+ people by engaging in homophobic behaviors (Worthen, 2014). Neumann et al. (2013) explored attitudes and beliefs of heterosexual sorority women toward lesbian and bisexual members. While the women viewed themselves as accepting of lesbian and bisexual women, they simultaneously expressed a desire for their members to "dress/act like a girl/woman" (Neuman et al., 2013, p. 5). While sororities and fraternities may be open to membership of LGBTQ+ students and welcome their participation, they may likely hold LGBTQ+ students to expectations that are inherently exclusionary. LGBTQ+ students may feel marginalized and excluded in fraternity and sorority spaces when mixers, date parties, or other social events are held with the expectation that members hook up (Evans et al., 2017). When the majority of events and programs held by a chapter are done so in hopes of encouraging heterosexual dating, queer students may become isolated from other members or may then perform in ways that are not authentic to their identities (Neumann et al., 2013). Expectations to have sex at parties present challenges to lesbian, gay, and bisexual students who are not yet out and for asexual students who do not experience sexual attraction.

Within LGBTQ+ communities, both experiences and perceptions may be mixed. With some fraternities and sororities enacting inclusive and affirming practices, some LGBQ students may feel welcomed and affirmed. Transgender students, however, face additional barriers for entry, membership, and affirmation. For example, a national chapter for a fraternity or sorority may deny access to transgender students whose legal names and sex are not in alignment with organizational policies. Despite the positive intentions for creating inclusive organizations, transgender students on campuses may be subjected to exclusionary policies or practices from national chapter organizations. While some students hope to reform these organizations, increasingly, others view the inherent exclusiveness of fraternities and sororities as irreconcilable with inclusion and are calling for the complete dissolution of fraternity and sorority life.

Implications

We have examined a wide range of areas on campus that LGBTQ+ students must navigate under potentially hostile conditions. It is important for those of us working in higher education with the power, authority, and influence to effect change to do so on behalf of our marginalized LGBTQ+ student populations to ensure they get the most out of their educational experience as possible during their time with us. We therefore have developed some considerations, recommendations, and questions based on our discussion to assist practitioners with gauging their campus' progress with meeting the needs of their LGBTQ+ students:

- *Education:* Are faculty, staff, and administrators (health-care providers, RA staff, student organization leadership, IT personnel, student affairs and academic affairs staff, athletics, registrar staff, etc.) receiving education on the unique needs of LGBTQ+ students on their campus in order to better position themselves to be able to support these students?
- *Policies and Procedures:* How easy is it for LGBTQ+ students to navigate areas like name changes within the institution's main database, indicating one's sexual orientation or gender identity, or indicating the pronouns that one wishes to use? Does the Residence Life/Housing office have procedures in place by which LGBTQ+ students can be matched with roommates who will affirm their identities? Does the health insurance offered to students cover things like hormone replacement therapy, which is often vital to trans students' well-being?
- *Facilities:* When new facilities are being constructed, are there automatically plans for/considerations for things like single-use/gender-inclusive bathroom facilities?
- *Forms and Administration:* Do essential forms and administrative processes establish an inclusive and welcoming environment for our students (e.g., asking about things like preferred name, pronouns, gender identity, etc.)?

It is our responsibility as professionals working in institutions of higher education to provide as inclusive and welcoming environments as possible for all our students to form a healthy sense of belonging and connection, no matter what identities, backgrounds, or lived experiences they may bring to our campuses. Kevin Gannon (2020) in *Radical Hope: A Teaching Manifesto* provides a very clear charge to us: "If we want to say to each one of our students, *you are welcome here, and you can succeed,* then it's incumbent upon us to create inclusive learning spaces" (p. 57). Gannon (2020) goes on to state:

> Higher education proclaims itself to be the arena of opportunity and the engine driving the changes necessary to create a better world. We say the education we offer possesses urgent importance and relevance. We claim institutions of higher education are an inherent good for our society and polity. But institutional and educational practices that exclude students—that push them to the margins, figuratively or literally—render those pronouncements nothing more than a cruel joke. (p. 56)

As practitioners and professionals in higher education, it is incumbent upon us to be the change agents that we know we need on our campuses, especially for LGBTQ+ students who so often are marginalized in many aspects of their educational journey. When grappling with structural inequality for LGBTQ+ people in higher education, we inevitably end at broad questions aimed at our social and cultural conventions: Do we accept disparities in belonging among students? Do we feel motivated to change, or to stay the same, and what are our reasons for either? Do our macro systems as we know them—economics, law, and medicine—allow for the creation of an equitable world? Where do we have agency and authority in the microsystems to generate a climate that supports belonging for LGBTQ+ people? What aspects of a transition to a more equitable world frighten us, possibly inspire us?

In answering these questions, we can listen to the wisdom of LGBTQ+ students themselves. People with LGBTQ+ identities—diverse sexual and romantic identities, gender identities, or both—often experience powerful transitions in their journeys to self-ownership or internal sense of belonging. Dismantling heteronormative, genderist systems occurs first within LGBTQ+ people every time they affirm themselves and create space for belonging. Student-led support groups and organizations provide community and advocacy. Peer mentors can share valuable experience in navigating a sometimes harsh world. Campus leaders must follow their leads. If we aim to transform the structures of our physical, virtual, and social environments to create belonging for LGBTQ+ people, we might begin with harnessing the wisdom of their journeys, healing the trauma of their experiences, and turning our focus to the roots of the barriers to their inclusion.

REFERENCES

Anderman, L. H., & Freeman, T. M. (2004). Students' sense of belonging in school. In M. L. Maehr & P. R. Pintrich (eds.), *Advances in Motivation and Achievement*, Vol. 13. *Motivating Students, Improving Schools: The Legacy of Carol Midgley* (pp. 27–63). Elsevier.

Anonymous. (n.d.). Gender neutral toilets don't work for women. Women's Place UK. https://womansplaceuk.org/gender-neutral-toilets-dont-work-for-women-2/

Atteberry-Ash, B., Woodford, M. R., & Center, S. (2018). Support for policy protecting LGBT student athletes among heterosexual students participating in club and intercollegiate sports. *Sexuality Research and Social Policy*, *15*(2), 151–162.

Badgett, M. V. L., Choi, S. K., & Wilson, B. D. M. (2019). LGBT poverty in the United States. UCLA School of Law: Williams Institute. https://williamsinstitute.law.ucla.edu/publications/lgbt-poverty-us/

Beemyn, B. G. (2005). Making campuses more inclusive of transgender students. *Journal of Gay & Lesbian Issues in Education, 3*(1), 77–87. doi:10.1300/ J367v03n01_08

Beemyn, G. (2020). Colleges and universities that provide gender-inclusive housing. Campus Pride. https://www.campuspride.org/tpc/gender-inclusive-h ousing/

Benedetti, R. (2015). Belonging: Ontogeny of a gay psychoanalytic candidate. *International Journal of Psychoanalytic Self Psychology, 10*(4), 398–407. doi:10. 1080/15551024.2015.1074002

Blackmon, Z. R. (2018). Microaggressions, sense of belonging, and sexual identity development among LGBQ students: A moderation analysis (10936203). [Doctoral dissertation, UNC Greensboro]. ProQuest Dissertations Publishing. https://search. proquest.com/docview/2173250308

BlueCross BlueShield of North Carolina. (2017, October). Androgens: Prior review/ certification faxback form. Blue Cross and Blue Shield Association. https://ww w.bluecrossnc.com/sites/default/files/document/attachment/services/public/pdfs/f ormulary/Androgens_standard_fax.pdf

Blumenfeld, W. J., Weber, G. N., & Rankin, S. (2016). In our own voice: Campus climate as a mediating factor in the persistence of LGBT people in higher education. Queering classrooms: Personal narratives and educational practices to support LGBTQ youth in schools, 1–20.

Bostock v. Clayton County, GA, 590 U.S. _____ (2020) https://www.supremecourt. gov/opinions/19pdf/17-1618_hfci.pdf

Broadhurst, C., Martin, G., Hoffshire, M., & Takewell, W. (2018). "Bumpin' up against people and their beliefs": Narratives of student affairs administrators creating change for LGBTQ students in the South. *Journal of Diversity in Higher Education 11*(4), 385–401.

Bronfenbrenner, U. (1994). Ecological models of human development. *Readings on the Development of Children, 2*(1), 37–43.

Burgstahler, S. (2015). Universal design: Process, principles, and applications. Disabilities, Opportunities, Internetworking, and Technology. https://www.was hington.edu/doit/universal-design-process-principles-and-applications

Burns, T. (2011). Towards a theory of structural discrimination: Cultural, institutional and interactional mechanisms of the 'european dilemma.' In G. Delanty, R. Wodak, & P. Jones (eds.), *Identity, Belonging and Migration* (pp. 152–172). Liverpool University Press. doi:10.5949/UPO9781846314537.009

Cech, E. A., & Waidzunas, T. J. (2011). Navigating the heteronormativity of engineering: The experiences of lesbian, gay, and bisexual students. *Engineering Studies, 3*(1), 1–24.

Civil Rights Act of 1964, Pub. L. No. 88-352, 42 U.S.C. § 2000e *et seq.* (1964) https ://www.eeoc.gov/statutes/title-vii-civil-rights-act-1964#

Cooper, K. M., & Brownell, S. E. (2016). Coming out in class: Challenges and benefits of active learning in a biology classroom for LGBTQIA students. *CBE—Life Sciences Education, 15*(3), ar37.

Equality North Carolina. (2013, August 9). UNC board of governors ban gender neutral housing. Equality North Carolina. https://equalitync.org/news/UNC_boa rd_of_governors_ban_gender_neutral_housing/

Furrow, H. (2012). LGBT students in the college composition classroom. *Journal of Ethnographic & Qualitative Research, 6*(3).

Gannon, K. (2020). *Radical Hope: A Teaching Manifesto.* West Virginia University Press.

Garvey, J. C., & Rankin, S. R. (2015). Making the grade? Classroom climate for LGBTQ students across gender conformity. *Journal of Student Affairs Research and Practice 52*(2), 190–203. doi:10.1080/19496591.2015.1019764

Garvey, J. C., Squire, D. D., Stachler, B., & Rankin, S. (2018). The impact of campus climate on queer-spectrum student academic success. *Journal of LGBT Youth, 15*(2), 89–105.

Garvey, J. C., Taylor, J. L., & Rankin, S. (2015). An examination of campus climate for LGBTQ community college students. *Community College Journal of Research and Practice, 39*(6), 527–541.

Garvey, J. C., Taylor, J. L., & Rankin, S. (2015). An examination of campus climate for LGBTQ community college students. *Community College Journal of Research and Practice, 39*(6), 527–541.

Gjelten, E. A. (2015, April 9). Can private schools discriminate against students? Lawyers.com. https://www.lawyers.com/legal-info/research/education-law/can-pri vate-schools-discriminate-against-students.html

Goldberg, A. E., Beemyn, G., & Smith, J. Z. (2019). What is needed, what is valued: Trans students' perspectives on trans-inclusive policies and practices in higher education. *Journal of Educational & Psychological Consultation, 29*(1), 27–67. do i:10.1080/10474412.2018.1480376

Gortmaker, V. J., & Brown, R. D. (2006). Out of the college closet: Differences in perceptions and experiences among out and closeted lesbian and gay students. *College Student Journal, 40*(3), 606–620.

Griffin, P., & Carroll, H. (2011). *NCAA Inclusion of Transgender Student-Athletes.* Indianapolis, IN: National Collegiate Athletics Association.

Hagerty, B. M. K., Williams, R. A., & Oe, H. (2002). Childhood antecedents of adult sense of belonging. *Journal of Clinical Psychology, 58*, 793–801.

Hausmann, L. R. M., Schofield, J. W., & Woods, R. L. (2007). Sense of belonging as a predictor of intentions to persist among African American and White first-year college students. *Research in Higher Education, 48*(7), 803–839.

Johnson, R. B. (2009). Workplace climate, degree of outness, and job satisfaction of gay and lesbian professional staff in higher education (3387599). [Doctoral dissertation, UNC Greensboro]. ProQuest Dissertations Publishing. https://search.proqu est.com/docview/304964846

Kogan, T. S. (2007). Sex-separation in public restrooms: Law, architecture, and gender. *Michigan Journal of Gender and Law, 14*(1). https://repository.law.umich .edu/cgi/viewcontent.cgi?referer=https://duckduckgo.com/&httpsredir=1&article= 1067&context=mjgl

Legal Information Institute. (n.d.-a). *Federal rules of evidence rule 902: Evidence that is self-authenticating*. Cornell Law School. https://www.law.cornell.edu/rules/fre/rule_902

Legal Information Institute. (n.d.-b). *Federal rules of evidence rule 1001: Definitions that apply to this article*. Cornell Law School. https://www.law.cornell.edu/rules/fre/rule_1001

Masterpiece Cakeshop, Ltd., et al. v. Colorado Civil Rights Commission et al., 584 U.S. ____ (2018) https://www.supremecourt.gov/opinions/17pdf/16-111_new2_22p3.pdf

Mollet, A., Weaver, K. E., Holmes, J. M., Linley, J. L., Hurley, E., & Renn, K. A. (2020). Queer in residence: Exploring the on-campus housing experiences of queer college students. *Journal of Student Affairs Research and Practice, 58*(1), 1–14.

Neumann, D. C., Kretovics, M. A., & Roccoforte, E. C. (2013). Attitudes and beliefs of heterosexual sorority women twoard lesbian and bisexual chapter members. *Oracle: The Research Journal of the Association of Fraternity/Sorority Advisors, 8*(1), 1–5.

Nichols, J. M. (2015, April 10). Refuge restrooms launches mobile app to help users locate gender neutral bathrooms. Queer voices. https://www.huffpost.com/entry/refuge-restrooms-app_n_7042448

Office for Civil Rights. (2020, January 15). *Exemptions from Title IX*. U.S. Department of Education. https://www2.ed.gov/about/offices/list/ocr/docs/t9-rel-exempt/index.html

Parsons, V. (2020, March 25). First non-binary BBC presenter launches validation station for trans people stuck at home during coronavirus lockdown. PinkNews. https://www.pinknews.co.uk/2020/03/25/the-validation-station-non-binary-bbc-presenter-trans-people-self-isolation-coronavirus-lockdown/

Pryor, J. T. (2015). Out in the classroom: Transgender student experiences at a large public university. *Journal of College Student Development, 56*(5), 440–455.

Quiñones, T. J., Woodward, E. N., & Pantalone, D. W. (2017). Sexual minority reflections on their psychotherapy experiences. *Psychotherapy Research, 27*(2), 189–200. doi:10.1080/10503307.2015.1090035

RAINN. (n.d.). *Perpetrators of sexual violence: Statistics*. Rape, Abuse & Incest National Network. https://www.rainn.org/statistics/perpetrators-sexual-violence

Rankin, S., & Reason, R. (2008). Transformational tapestry model: A comprehensive approach to transforming campus climate. *Journal of Diversity in Higher Education, 1*(4), 262.

Rankin, S., Blumenfeld, W. J., Weber, G. N., & Frazer, S. (2010). *State of Higher Education for LGBT People*. Charlotte, NC: Campus Pride.

Renn, K. (2017, April 10). LGBTQ students on campus: Issues and opportunities for higher education leaders. Higher Education Today, American Council on Education. https://www.higheredtoday.org/2017/04/10/lgbtq-students-higher-education/

Rhee, B. (2008). Institutional climate and student departure: A multinomial multilevel modeling approach. *Review of Higher Education, 31*(2), 161–183.

Rolker, C. (2016, May 30). Bathroom bill, bogus biology, and intersex. Männlich-weiblich-zwischen. https://intersex.hypotheses.org/3600

Seelman, K. L. (2014). Transgender individuals' access to college housing and bathrooms: Findings from the National Transgender Discrimination Survey. *Journal of Gay & Lesbian Social Services, 26*(2), 186–206.

Southern Illinois University Edwardsville. (2020). *Housing Options.* University Housing. https://www.siue.edu/housing/options/special-living-accommodations.shtml

Spula, I. (2017, September 30). An unexpected ally of gender-neutral restrooms: Building codes. The Journal of the American Institute of Architects. https://www.architectmagazine.com/practice/an-unexpected-ally-in-gender-neutral-restrooms-building-codes_o

Stuart, K., Stuart, D. B. (2019). Behind closed doors: Public restrooms and the fight for women's equality. *Texas Review of Law & Politics, 24*(1), 1–39.

Taub, D. J., Johnson, R. B., & Reynolds, T. (2016). The implementation of gender-neutral housing: A mixed-methods study across ACUHO-I member institutions. *Journal of College & University Student Housing, 42*(2).

The Ohio State University. (2020a). Gender-inclusive housing. LGBTQ at Ohio State. https://lgbtq.osu.edu/community/gender-inclusive-housing

The Ohio State University. (2020b). Graduate, professional and non-traditional housing. University Housing. https://housing.osu.edu/living-on-campus/graduate-professional-and-non-traditional-housing/

The University of North Carolina at Greensboro. (n.d.). Changes to personal information. University Registrar's Office. https://reg.uncg.edu/policies/changes-to-personal-information/

Tovar, E., & Simon, M. A. (2010). Factorial structure and invariance analysis of the sense of belonging scales. *Measurement and Evaluation in Counseling and Development, 43*, 199–217.

U.S. Department of Education Press Office. (2017, February 22). U.S. secretary of education Betsy DeVos issues statement on new Title IX guidance. U.S. Department of Education. https://www.ed.gov/news/press-releases/us-secretary-education-betsy-devos-issues-statement-new-title-ix-guidance

Wentling, T., Windsor, E., Schilt, K., & Lucal, B. (2008). Teaching transgender. *Teaching Sociology, 36*(1), 49–57.

Worthen, M. G. (2014). Blaming the jocks and the Greeks? Exploring collegiate athletes' and fraternity/sorority members' attitudes toward LGBT individuals. *Journal of College Student Development, 55*(2), 168–195.

Chapter 4

Legal Status and Belonging

A Critical Humanist Perspective

Laura M. Gonzalez

In this chapter I would like to explore and question the nuances of belonging for immigrants without permanent legal status, which is a contested and often misconstrued topic. Is it a piece of paper that confers belonging, or is it human agency and experience?

HOLISTIC SENSE OF BELONGING

The tension between a holistic sense of belonging and experiences of bias or rejection is played out in the lives of immigrants across the United States. The word "holistic" is important, as it connotes a broad and inclusive view of belonging across aspects of our identities and characteristics of our environments. Sense of belonging may be experienced differently in many spaces across a person's life (e.g., school, work, neighborhood or community, peer group, family, nation) and should be considered across those contexts (Abrego & Gonzales, 2010; Suarez-Orozco et al., 2011). We may receive conflicting messages about our belonging in each of those spaces, some affirming and some hostile. Does belonging then reside with the power of an individual to construct it and claim it, or with the power of a system to negate it?

How shall we define belonging? At the individual level, sense of belonging resonates across all aspects of the holistic self, affecting our thoughts/beliefs, feelings, and responses or behaviors in a particular sociocultural context (Walton & Brady, 2020). If I do experience a sense of belonging, I have thoughts that center me as a part of my context (e.g., "I am an American"), feelings that bolster my connection to the context (e.g., "I am welcomed and appreciated here for who I am"), and thus I can behave in a way that reinforces my implicit membership in the context (e.g., I can vote, I can participate, I can apply for school or work, I can speak my ideas freely). If I do not experience a sense of belonging, or if I have uncertainty about my belonging in a context, my thoughts/beliefs, feelings, and behavior reflect isolation, disconnection, and otherness (Walton & Brady, 2020).

Individuals without documented status also may experience structural discrimination, pervasive negative stereotypes, systemic oppression, and a hostile receiving context (Hernandez et al., 2010; McWhirter et al., 2013; Portes & Rumbaut, 2001). By taking an ecological view of belonging, we are directed to interrogate power, privilege, and systems as they weigh in on the belonging of an individual to a context (e.g., Abrego & Gonzales, 2010). The current chapter argues that we must hold in tension both the individual human being's sense of belonging and the structures that may attempt to support it or undercut it. In particular, how do people without permanent legal status generate a sustained sense of belonging in the United States against a backdrop of unmet basic needs and hostile social reception? This is the central question being taken up by this chapter.

Dueñas and Gloria (2020) suggest a psychosociocultural analysis, wherein any person's experiences include an individual motivational dimension, a collective social dimension, and the degree of congruity between those two. Psychologically, individuals must ascertain their motivation to belong in a given context, and often must be ready to generate an intrinsic sense of belonging if the biases and inequities in the context mean that an extrinsic sense of belonging is not available to them. In the case of immigrants, motivation is often a strong contributory factor for making the journey from the country of origin to the United States. This motivation can be associated with basic health and safety of self and family, opportunity to thrive in education or occupation, and escape from poverty, persecution, and danger (Portes & Rumbaut, 2001). Over time, when immigrants are more familiar with the US context, they can set their motivation to belong within specific local environments more precisely, with a greater understanding of the ways in which the system may or may not welcome them.

In sociological terms, individuals or groups may need to create spaces of belonging within their communities (Murdock-Perriera et al., 2019) that offer shelter from stigma and discrimination, an opportunity to set aside the emotional labor that comes with vigilance against threats, and life-giving connection with similar peers. Although this might be understood as a retreat, it can also be seen as a purposeful effort to push back on isolation by funneling into spaces where one can see similar peers and feel validated (Strayhorn, 2018). Finally, in terms of the balance of congruency between individuals and systems, having an experience of belonging means one's own cultural values, norms, and beliefs and those that are predominant in the context can coexist or grow together to make something new. For example, light-skinned

European immigrants were scapegoated in their time, but were eventually accepted into the Euro-American cultural milieu. This gradual inclusion as a form of belonging (also called "segmented assimilation," per Portes & Rumbaut, 2001) is something that darker skinned immigrants may not experience (Chung et al., 2008), and is thus conditional.

Part of the belonging dilemma that faces immigrants in the United States is the xenophobic sociopolitical climate that ebbs, flows, and changes over time, but has never gone away (Yakushko, 2009). Thus, even with a positive motivation to belong at the individual level and welcoming enclaves of belonging at the community level, there are still larger systems and structures that may make belonging more or less accessible, depending on racism, classism, xenophobia, etc. (Portes & Rumbaut, 2001). Understanding and addressing sense of belonging for immigrants to the United States demand careful attention to power structures and these attendant costly psychological, social, and cultural realities.

CITIZENSHIP PRIVILEGE

Social privileges can accrue in several forms that we are accustomed to interrogating in educational or developmental spaces—socioeconomic class, skin color, gender identity and sexual orientation, physical or mental ability, and so on. However, our discourse does not often encompass the privilege of having (or being assumed to have) citizenship status (Gee et al., 2016). This privilege, like many others, operates within intersectional systems of power (Crenshaw, 1989). There are many things that can be taken for granted when one has long-standing unearned privilege (as in this author, whose European immigrant ancestors who arrived in the United States five to six generations ago under a different set of rules and procedures). In the case of white-skinned or economically privileged citizens, in particular, they can apply for benefits if they are needed, make claims and complaints if they are wronged, receive education and training when desired. On the community level, white-skinned citizens can find spaces where their identities are recognized, supported, and welcomed. As individuals, they can move forward from childhood to adolescence and into emerging adulthood with the expectation that they will pass certain milestones of development and be able to make a contribution or leave a meaningful legacy. In this way, a sense of belonging in one's environment or context can be understood as a "hub" which promotes positive outcomes along a variety of spokes (Baumeister & Leary, 1995).

However, our neighbors who do not have citizenship privilege are in a very different space (Gee et al., 2016). Young children may be taken away from extended family, friends, or school if the threat of deportation is leveled against a parent or guardian (Suarez-Orozco et al., 2011). Illness may not be treated, if there is no health insurance to offset the costs. Abusive labor practices are tolerated, with little recourse to legal action. Even a simple pleasure like turning 16 and applying for a driver's license is impossible without a social security number, which generates cascading difficulties with transportation, employment, and earning enough for one's daily needs (Gonzales, 2010). Higher education represents a mirage-like dream that shimmers with possibility but requires enormous sacrifices to reach (Perez & Rodriguez, 2012). Permanent legal status is a key that may open many doors, but is a complex and moving target. These intersecting systems of power can create barriers to belonging which are challenging, but can be overcome with advocacy and resistance.

(RE)DEFINING LEGAL STATUS

Public discourse regarding legal status is awash in half-accurate statements and heightened emotions (Turner & Figueroa, 2019). The idea of legal status first must be clarified in order to have a nuanced discussion of its implications, as there are inaccurate perceptions of the pathways to legal belonging that are and are not available to immigrants. Individuals may enter the United States with a temporary visa to work, study, or visit, but would lose their initial legal status if they overstayed the dates of the visa (American Immigration Council, n.d.). Obtaining a visa from the US consulate in one's home country confers eligibility to seek entry to the United States, but does not guarantee that entry will be granted. Administrations can interpret immigration priorities as they please, emphasizing "high-skilled" workers, seasonal agricultural workers, or exchange students in only certain academic disciplines. In addition, there is a cap on how many individuals will be granted entry from any given country in any given year, so even if a person has a reasonable claim (such as reunifying with family members who are already living in the United States), they might have to wait up to 20 years if they are coming from a highly immigrant sending country such as Mexico or the Philippines (American Immigration Council, n.d.).

It is not uncommon for members of the same immigrant family to have differing statuses, if younger children were born in the United States and older siblings were born elsewhere and brought here at a younger age (Turner & Figueroa, 2019). These mixed-status families may include adults without legal status or with temporary status, individuals who have sought humanitarian protection from violence or persecution, citizen children, and children who have DACA or are undocumented. DACA, or Deferred Action for Childhood Arrivals, was a temporary status that allowed holders to work, but was not a step toward citizenship or any other permanent status (Gonzales et al., 2014). DACA was rescinded by the US administration in 2017 (Siemons et al., 2017), followed by legal challenges and legislative inaction. Even after the Supreme Court issued a ruling in summer 2020 that the rescission had not followed proper procedures, further lawsuits were necessary to restore the program to its previous form and allow new applications (Immigrant Legal Resource Center, n.d.). The 2020 election and change in federal administration may mean further changes to DACA, but the lack of a guarantee only underscores the difficult temporary status of DACA recipients.

Temporary Protected Status (TPS) was given to citizens from designated countries (like Syria, Somalia, Haiti, or Honduras) based on a catastrophe within their borders, but that has been rescinded for many of those individuals between 2016 and 2020 (Turner & Figueroa, 2019). Under certain circumstances, immigrants may apply for a status adjustment based on a qualifying situation (e.g., having a qualifying family member, being a victim of a crime), but those applications would be reviewed by whatever political administration was holding power. Finally, a green card is called "permanent legal status," but must be renewed, and thus is subject to the laws and policies that are in place at that time (American Immigration Council, n.d.). For example, changes to green card approval processes based on perception of being a public charge (i.e., utilizing social safety net programs such as subsidized housing, Medicaid, or nutritional assistance) were passed by the previous administration despite public outcry against them (USCIS, 2020).

Missing in this tangle of legal terms and power structures is the experience of a young person who remembers no country but the United States, who has almost all of their formative experiences here, who has worked and studied and contributed to this country in the hopes of belonging. Many of these youth, sometimes called "Dreamers," live in a household with an undocumented adult. The systemic implications of living in a mixed-status family become more powerful and obvious in adolescence and early adulthood, when limitations and constraints become harder to avoid. For example, the automatic access of K–12 schooling ends, and permission to drive, to work, to go to college, or to buy a home are all conditional (Gonzales, 2011).

As we think about immigrant hopefulness and the desire to self-actualize in the United States, we must also see the jarring contrast between the ideals of this country and the realities of policy and power (Chung et al., 2008; Gonzales, 2011). Part of the experience is the oppressive exclusion from the basic opportunities to become an autonomous and contributing adult (Perez, 2012). But part of the pain is the legalistic message "you do not belong," when the daily lived experiences of immigrants would attest that they are motivated to generate belonging. Indeed, even against a tide of discrimination, scapegoating, and backlash, immigrant youth who are undocumented are courageously asserting "I am here to stay" and advocating for their right to belong in the United States (Perez et al., 2009). These claims call us to a higher ethical standard, not one based on policy and paper, but one based on foundational ideals of this country and lived experiences in our communities.

The possibilities for belonging for individuals without permanent authorized legal status will be examined through the lens of critical humanism (Nemiroff, 1992; Tudor, 2015), which holds in tension both the power of individuals striving toward self-actualization and belonging and the structural barriers that may block or impede their progress. Humanism is consistent with a psychosocial viewpoint in that it brings together individual agency and the context; critical humanism attends to structures of power as well.

HUMANISM, LIBERATION PEDAGOGY, AND CRITICAL HUMANISM

Humanism in general can be defined as "a democratic and ethical lifestance which affirms that human beings have the right and responsibility to give meaning and shape to their own lives" (American Humanist Association, n.d.). Some key philosophical tenets of humanism include a holistic view of the needs and potential of people, an assumption of health rather than pathology, and (more recently) an acceptance of interdependence (Tudor, 2015). In this chapter, I have chosen to illustrate humanism through the writings of person-centered psychologist Carl Rogers, whose basic assertions are that humans are capable and healthy organisms who continually strive for self-actualization and the construction of a meaningful and full life.

In contrast to more psychoanalytic or behavioral views, the humanism expressed by Rogers (1961) took into account the whole being (thoughts, feelings, behaviors, aspirations) and focused more on present experiences and strivings than the past. Rogers thought that people developed a positive self-concept when their ideal image of self was congruent with their real self, which could be encouraged or promoted through experiencing unconditional positive regard (from family, from a therapist, and eventually from the self). In this theoretical view, an external condition (like legal documentation) would only matter for one's sense of self if a person valued it or relied upon it for meaning and experienced a lack of congruence between the ideal internal self and this external image. Certainly, the external barrier of legal documentation does create problems of access to resources and systems, as mentioned previously. In the psychological view of humanism, however, context is less important than individual agency and striving. Indeed, a critique of humanism has been that it maintains its roots in individual psychology and has been slower to embrace critical movements such as feminism or critical race theory (Tudor, 2015).

Although these critiques are fair, humanism does raise essential questions related to belonging: Where do people look for their meaning and value as they generate a self-concept? Can youth from immigrant families trust their own experiences (of belonging in the United States, for example) as they build a self-concept, and therefore move away from the burden of meeting the expectations and judgments of others? Can immigrants in the current sociopolitical climate choose their own goals and directions (albeit from a limited menu), move toward acceptance of self and others, trust in their inner compass and cultural values, and rely on their own worldview as they strive to fulfill their potential (Rogers, 1961)? Although it would be naïve to imagine that the legal and systemic barriers wrought by our hierarchical society can be wished away, it could be meaningful to work with immigrant youth to generate a sense of belonging guided by internal truths and not external condemnations. This is not the simple optimism of the privileged and lucky but the hard-won optimism of the survivors. In the words of Holocaust survivor Viktor Frankl (1992), "Even the helpless victim of a hopeless situation, facing a fate he [*sic*] cannot change, may rise above himself, may grow beyond himself, and by so doing change himself" (p. 147).

Critiques of such humanistic perspectives arise from the acknowledgment that unearned privilege and systemic discrimination do lift up some and cut down others in a way that is brutal, inequitable, and real. These omissions were addressed by Freire (1970) and others who wrote about and enacted liberation pedagogy. In this theoretical view, the focus is on the awakening of critical consciousness, wherein systemic oppression in the social context can be named, described, defined, and dismantled by the initiative and efforts of the oppressed. Thus, systems of privilege, power, and discrimination (such as a reliance on paperwork to divide people into the categories of "legal" and "illegal") are central to the analysis, and self-concept is secondary. Liberation cannot be achieved only by actualizing the self, but by disrupting the structures that perpetuate inequities. This point of view makes the important acknowledgment that belonging is structurally supported and more freely available in the cultural context for individuals with privileged identities, and harder to achieve for marginalized groups who must undertake conscious and significant effort to "write themselves into the story" (Gildersleeve, 2011, p. 74). It is easy to see evidence of structures that are oppressive to immigrants in contemporary United States; it is a complex task to find the tools to dismantle them.

However, critical humanism brings together these two philosophical strands in a way that honors both the ways that individuals seek to live up to their full potential and the need to address structural barriers to equity in the context (Nemiroff, 1992). In critical humanism, people are assumed to have aspirations, to be motivated and self-determining, and be capable of enacting behaviors to move themselves forward. However, critical humanism also acknowledges the structures that generate inequitable outcomes and impede this natural impulse toward self-actualization (Brady-Amoon, 2011). Thus, critical humanism attends to both the agency of individuals and the oppressive systems they live in, seeking empowerment efforts that are "intentionally aimed at nurturing people's innate developmental potential by eradicating oppressive systems and social injustices that restrict people's opportunities and lives" (Brady-Amoon, 2011, p. 141). The idea of belonging in a context where one's group is marginalized can create dissonance, but can also create an opportunity to generate new community, find allies, push back on stereotypes, and validate one's own "rightful presence" (per Faircloth in the current volume).

BELONGING AS FRAMED THROUGH CRITICAL HUMANISM

In this chapter, I will focus on belonging of children, youth, adolescents, and early adults in mixed-status immigrant families. These individuals increasingly use their voices to call us to see them not through the lens of paperwork but through the lens of agency, experience, and rightful presence. Certainly, the distinctions between having some kind of authorized status (e.g., DACA, TPS, a visa) or no authorized status create meaningful differences as individuals grow older and seek access to the systems that govern our daily lives (e.g., education beyond the K–12 system, legal workplaces, health care, voting). Outcomes for DACA recipients are better in terms of access to the systems that govern our social interactions (e.g., can have a driver's license, can receive a two-year work permit, can apply for a temporary social security number) (Gonzales et al., 2014). Youth with DACA were shown in one study to have a greater sense of belonging within their peer group and community, and less sense of shame, isolation, and stigma (Siemons et al., 2017). However, incorporation of immigrants with DACA into educational or work systems also depends to an extent on the local policies and context, and the willingness of other members of society to include them. Additionally, for many DACA recipients, the benefits of inclusion do not extend throughout their mixed-status families, and their sense of fear and tenuousness on behalf of their parents or siblings continues. Thus, we need to examine belonging in both individual and the systemic aspects.

Given the pernicious systemic challenges that are blocking immigrants without permanent legal status from full participation, one might reasonably ask how sense of belonging can make any difference. Drawing from the holistic definition of belonging offered in a previous section (I have thoughts that center me as part of my context, I have feelings that bolster my connection to the context, I can behave in a way that reinforces my membership in the context), I offer a list of possibilities to generate a critical humanist sense of belonging for individuals without permanent legal status. These suggestions incorporate the domains of cognitions, feelings, and behaviors, with additional implications for those in systems or positions of power. Pulling from a variety of social science and health-related fields, the following constructs will be offered for review: (a) shift and persist, (b) mattering, (c) coping and healing ethno-racial trauma, (d) substantive membership, (e) civic engagement, (f) critical validation, and (g) advocacy with. These frameworks will be discussed along a continuum of responses that are open to individuals and move to more systemic ideas that can be enacted by immigrant and nonimmigrant communities together.

Shift and Persist

One recent framework that can help answer the question "how do we thrive amidst individual and systemic discrimination?" is called shift and persist (Chen & Miller, 2012). Shift and persist relates to the cognitive and affective parts of holistic belonging. Rooted in public health scholarship, shift and persist describes a process of disengaging from overwhelming, chronic, and uncontrollable stressors (like discrimination or poverty) in order to protect oneself. In the first step, individuals intentionally shift their thinking or cognitively reframe stressors to be less threatening. This reappraisal is adaptive (when followed by the persist strategy) because it helps individuals better regulate their own emotions in the face of problems that are likely beyond their control. Importantly, shift must be followed by persist, which is a strategy of focusing on the ways that life can have purpose and cultivating the hope that the future may be better, despite current adversity. Sense of belonging is important to the ability to persist and maintain optimism, especially when stressors are systemic and unrelenting.

In one qualitative study with Latinx adults who had experienced ethnic discrimination (Torres et al., 2019), participants described the ways they attempted to thrive in spite of social hostilities. Themes included finding social support and encouragement, generating community involvement through civic participation, educating others about their cultural group, disproving racist stereotypes, and holding their ethnic identity up as central to their life experiences. Even though these strategies cannot be said to dismantle racial/ethnic discrimination, they do provide evidence of shifting one's interpretations and persisting by finding meaning and belonging in one's community, as exemplified in the following quote about an experience of discrimination:

> [My mother's] explanation more was ignorance of him saying that. And kind of like, I guess the way she wanted me to cope with it was to be, to feel more confident in my ethnic ties like demonstrations and the language and all the things that we do in our family . . . she wanted me to seek refuge in that. (Torres et al., 2019, p. 265)

Seeking refuge in one's identity and community are key aspects of belonging, growing out of that sense of connection.

Mattering

As defined by Schlossberg (1989), mattering includes feeling noticed, appreciated, valued/important, and needed. The opposite of mattering is marginality, where one does not feel connected or centrally involved in a community. Mattering encompasses both the cognitive appraisal and the affective response per our holistic definition of belonging. Importantly, mattering has a social aspect, where individuals, groups, and systems can leverage their power to notice, value, and appreciate a person (or not). Thus, mattering as a construct suggests a way to proactively promote a sense of belonging—by acting in a way that communicates to others "I see you, I know your worth, I appreciate your presence and your contributions." With intentional focus, we could generate mattering for mixed-status immigrant families by posting multilingual signs in schools, sharing resources that do not depend upon citizenship, learning about countries of origin that are unfamiliar to us, participating in civic action to uphold immigrants' rights, or any other act of appreciation. Although constructing a sense of mattering does not deconstruct systems of privilege, it could start movement toward self-valuing and self-actualization.

A recent study used focus groups to examine mental health and wellness for 61 DACA recipients who were in late adolescence or early adulthood (Siemens et al., 2017). Participants reported high levels of concern about their states of mental health, but reported mixed effects of DACA upon their feelings of wellness. In some ways, DACA had allowed them to access a supportive peer community where belonging could be generated and new opportunities were unearthed. However, DACA also thrust them into more adult-like roles in their families, taking responsibility for things that relatives without legal status could not safely do (like driving with a license or applying for food benefits). And while DACA conferred temporary relief from deportation to the individual recipient, it did not provide blanket protection for family members. Thus, DACA did send the message of visibility, temporary authorized presence, and valued contributions/mattering for young qualifying immigrants, but not in an all-encompassing way. This shows us a place to start, and also the work yet to be done within the systems that surround our daily lives. Individual mattering should ideally be paired with structural initiatives for equity.

Coping with Traumatic Environments

Living in a space that does not guarantee you any rights to safety or well-being is traumatic, and should be recognized as such. Belonging can possibly be promoted at the end of a process that addresses the trauma, but there is no shortcut to get there. A model of psychological coping that is grounded in liberatory theories is the HEART model (Healing Ethno and Racial Trauma; Chavez-Dueñas et al., 2019). This four-phase model begins with the recognition of traumatic experiences in the environment, and the need to first provide a reprieve or shelter from continued damaging attacks. Only after a zone of relative safety has been established can a family start to acknowledge and effectively process the after-effects of the trauma (phase II). The next step is to proactively engage in culturally consistent healing strategies (phase III), and the final step is to identify possibilities for collective social justice action to promote liberation (phase IV). Coping with the trauma of living with unauthorized legal status or mixed status is a collective task, characterized by relational coping with family and trusted friends, interdependence, and tapping into cultural strengths (Gonzalez et al., 2020). The sense of belonging embedded within the family and collective cultural tradition may be part of what confers some protection from the continuing trauma or provides space to process and heal.

However, having an increased sense of belonging with and commitment to one's ethnic group can also engender an increased awareness of microaggressions and outright discrimination against that group (Torres et al., 2019). In this sense, belonging also may create increased emotional vulnerability to bias as a stressor. This highlights, however, the vital importance of teaching coping skills to youth and adults who are very likely to experience the negative traumatic effects of ethno-racial discrimination. Belonging is a part of the answer but not sufficient on its own. Youth who are likely to be targeted for their legal status, ethnic group, or other marginalized characteristics must also learn strategies for disengaging and protecting themselves, as well as strategies for self-actualization in the midst of strife.

Substantive Membership

Immigrants come to the United States from all parts of the world and for many reasons. Some eventually become naturalized citizens, which is a powerful statement of commitment to an adopted land. In many naturalization ceremonies, there are quotes from famous Americans who have realized the gifts that newcomers to our country bring and the ways that their contributions make us stronger. In response to the question "Who belongs?" Perez (2012) raises the idea of "substantive membership," which is demonstrated through behaviors and experiences. Think of those who are working in the United States currently, obeying laws, participating and contributing, investing in this country and showing their dedication by their deeds. In the ways that mean the most, these individuals do belong to our communities. Substantive membership is thus an ethical claim, not a legal one, but certainly draws from the ideas of behavioral or experiential belonging and critical humanism (self-actualizing despite systemic barriers).

Turner and Figueroa (2019) have also emphasized "citizenship as process," which is not solely determined by official policy or paperwork. They highlighted opportunities that socially privileged practitioners and policymakers have for inclusion and engagement with immigrants (e.g., identifying ways to protect youth in schools such that immigration raids or deportations are not so impactful) and that immigrants have for negotiation of access and participation, using their collective voices to raise their concerns, shape the conversation, and engage with allies.

Together, these two ideas prompt us to consider the reasons why the formal and legalistic sense of citizenship has preempted the value of behavioral or attitudinal displays of belonging to a country. This is relevant because legalistic barriers to growth and development are real, and the power that keeps those barriers in place is not likely to be ceded easily. However, in the ethics of substantive membership, there is also a need to instill clear-eyed hope and agency. Mindsets, attitudes, and behaviors are sometimes the few places where individuals can exert control within systems of oppression, so they are not a luxury but a necessity. Mindsets can also be shared, such that substantive membership can become a more accepted lens on belonging than legalistic citizenship in the future.

Civic Engagement

Leaning into the critical consciousness angle of critical humanism, one natural avenue for action is civic engagement, or democratic leadership in public spheres. Civic engagement combines individual agency to make claims for justice and the collective voice to address systemic problems (Hope & Spencer, 2017). Civic engagement is not only a behavioral expression of belonging within a social system but also a form of "democratic therapy" where complaints can be poured into a constructive form of expression. The oppressive forces that ban undocumented students from official participation in education or work, for example, may catalyze them to engage in the public square, in civic dialogue, and protest (Borjian, 2018; Turner & Figueroa, 2019).

In his study of undocumented students, Perez (2012) lists "factors that facilitate positive academic engagement outcomes" (p. 2). One of these important factors was civic engagement as a way to channel frustrations with the system and feel empowered/agentic. While it is true that undocumented students are excluded from full membership as citizens (voting, working, advancing, etc.), there is evidence in the data from the study of persistence and growth as well. These youth have few incentives to continue along the trajectory toward academic or career achievement, and yet they have done so. In part, the student participants reflected on protective factors that helped them (personal sense of agency and motivation, a dual frame of reference as immigrants, family support, outreach programs). Of note, they also shared their deep-seated sense of belonging to the United States, their optimism for what was possible, and their feelings of duty and obligation to the families who had brought them here. As Perez wrote, "Students are motivated to get involved to expand their horizons, develop leadership skills, contribute to their communities, and ultimately, develop a sense of belonging" (2012, p. 135).

Torres et al. (2019) also documented a pull toward civic engagement, termed community involvement by the Latinx young adults in their qualitative study. These participants described a desire to engage in political or social causes, partly as a way to find a supportive community for themselves, but also in order to give back to their ethnic community, bring awareness to non-coethnic community members, and demonstrate a degree of agency and cultural pride. Civic engagement has the potential to move individuals toward self-actualization, and also push unjust institutions to redistribute power.

Critical Validation

The final two ideas offered in this chapter are directed toward both individuals and systems of power. The first is critical validation theory (Gildersleeve, 2011; Rendon, 1994), which is expressed in a way that parallels critical humanism. Critical validation acknowledges the importance of individual striving and self-actualization but also the legacy of oppression that has made belonging and affirmation hard to find in mainstream organizations. Critical validation theory holds that institutions must take responsibility for the type of welcome that they provide to marginalized individuals and groups. Rather than asking marginalized individuals to proactively look for spaces for belonging, validation places the onus for engagement on the school, the campus, the organization, and so on (Rendon, 1994). Individuals can use whatever power they hold within a system to create opportunities for groups to belong, and then hold the institution accountable for continuing that affirmative outreach.

If this task of critical validation is taken on by institutional actors, it has a better chance of programmatic longevity and embeddedness over time. One example could be the difference between a university stating that "DACA students can apply," but not providing any institutional resources, support, or communication, versus a university that proactively hosts an Undocu-ally program, posts information for DACA students openly on its website, creates mentoring programs and networks of DACA students, and helps students search for financial resources to maintain their enrollment. Programs, practices, and policies that bar cooperation with immigration enforcement, clarify the rights due to students without permanent legal status, and create a climate of trust and safety would be important components of critical validation by a campus community. These systemic efforts to be responsive then provide space for the self-actualization and agency of students who happen to be undocumented.

Advocacy With

Allies who do hold social privilege and power are important for their ability to convert their seat at the table into access and opportunity for a more fully representative group (Chen & Rhoads, 2016). This is similar to critical validation in its focus on what responsibility the institution holds, but advocacy will often focus on system actions or policies, whereas validation also attends to generating support and belonging. For example, cities, churches, or campuses that have declared themselves to be sanctuaries have both overtly welcomed undocumented immigrants and family members, and have stoutly declined to participate in the detention and deportation policies of the government (Turner & Figueroa, 2019). After the 2016 election and the rescission of DACA, over 600 college and university presidents signed a letter in support of the program and the students who were enrolled at their campuses (Fattal, 2017). Even though advocates and allies are often not in the position to grant citizenship status or rewrite federal policy, they are able to hear the concerns of individuals in mixed status families, find leverage points in their local contexts, and seek alternative and more humane practices (Turner & Figueroa, 2019).

Advocacy *with* also signifies the voice of affected parties is central to decisions and actions, and they are centered as the individuals with the most relevant life experience to the issue at hand. Advocacy *for* is often when those with social power act by themselves in a way that they hope is helpful, but does not incorporate the perspectives and agency of the most affected group.

There are individuals without legal status who prefer to maintain anonymity to protect themselves against deportation, but there are also individuals who speak out with courage on behalf of their community and are leaders of the effort (Gonzales, 2008).

CONCLUSION

This chapter has asked the simple question, "Is it a piece of paper that confers belonging, or is it human agency and experience?" Whereas much of the public discourse in this age would focus on the papers, the chapter has focused on human worth, an internalized sense of value, and the rightful presence of having generated one's belonging. Readers have been asked to consider citizenship privilege and to think about the legal environment for immigration that exists in the United States. Through the lens of critical humanism, this chapter has considered power, inequality, social justice, and personal agency.

The author's personal stance is that systems of power have created blockades and barriers to belonging where they don't need to be. Why would the United States deny further education or legal options for work to a young person who has studied hard and graduated from our high schools? Why would we remove adults from our communities who are working, contributing to the tax base, raising families, and abiding by laws (save crossing a border that has shifted over time). Why does the concept of illegality not extend to corporations that evade taxes, or wealthy individuals who can pay to shelter themselves from legal consequences? Systems of power have bent toward those with unearned privileges while they have berated and accused those who crossed a border in an attempt to escape danger and extortion, preserve family, and earn a living.

So how can we describe the pathway to belonging for those who have a just humanistic claim within an unjust system? We have noted the networks of undocumented youth building critical consciousness about their situation within the US policy environment and generating communities of liberation and empowerment (Hernandez et al., 2010; Morales et al., 2011; Perez et al., 2009, Sahay et al., 2016). These individuals work hard to maintain positive and tenacious outlooks despite a raft of systemic barriers that have been projected against them, and these agentic behaviors should be seen appropriately as expressions of rightful presence. Immigrants in mixed-status families have received few structural advantages and many have thrived in spite of the neglect. While we must certainly act to extinguish the neglect, the ability to thrive can be seen as powerful self-actualization as well as an irrefutable contribution to society. These motivated actions warrant an individual claim to rightful presence, which is the essence of belonging, and require those of us with unearned privilege to address the structural barriers that are within our purview.

This chapter has developed a critical humanist sense of what belonging could mean, with a view that includes both individual agency and responsibility for those within the systems of power. The strategies offered for consideration are based on lived experiences in generating belonging and community against difficult odds, and the power of resistance to unjust laws and oppressive systems. It is my hope that we all will reject the claim that one only "belongs" by receiving administrative approval and seek to deconstruct such barriers so that we can form the truest sense of community together.

REFERENCES

Abrego, L. J., & Gonzales, R. G. (2010). Blocked paths, uncertain futures: The post-secondary education and labor market prospects of undocumented Latino youth. *Journal of Education for Students Placed at Risk, 15*, 144–157.

American Humanist Association. (n.d.). Definition of humanism. https://america nhumanist.org/what-is-humanism/definition-of-humanism/

American Immigration Council. (n.d.). Why don't immigrants apply for citizenship? There is no line for many unauthorized immigrants. https://www.americanimmig rationcouncil.org/sites/ default/files/research/why_dont_immigrants_apply_for_ci tizenship.pdf

Baumeister, R. F., & Leary, M. (1995). The need to belong: Desire for interpersonal attachments as a fundamental human motivation. *Psychological Bulletin, 117*, 497–529. doi:10.1037/0033-2909.117.3.497

Borjian, A. (2018). Academically successful Latino undocumented students in college: Resilience and civic engagement. *Hispanic Journal of Behavioral Sciences, 40*(1), 22–36.

Brady-Amoon, P. (2011). Humanism, feminism, and multiculturalism: Essential elements of social justice in counseling, education, and advocacy. *The Journal of Humanistic Counseling, 50*, 135–148.

Chen, E., & Miller, G. E. (2012). "Shift-and-persist" strategies: Why low socioeconomic status isn't always bad for health. *Perspectives on Psychological Science, 7*, 135–158.

Chen, A. C. R., & Rhoads, R. A. (2016). Undocumented student allies and transformative resistance: An ethnographic case study. *Review of Higher Education, 39*, 515–542.

Chung, R. C. Y., Bemak, F., Ortiz, D. P., & Sandoval-Perez, P. A. (2008). Promoting the mental health of immigrants: A multicultural/social justice perspective. *Journal of Counseling & Development, 86*(3), 310–317.

Crenshaw, K. (1989). Demarginalizing the intersection of race and sex: A black feminist critique of antidiscrimination doctrine, feminist theory and antiracist politics. *University of Chicago Legal Forum*, 139–167.

Dueñas, M., & Gloria, A. M. (2020). Pertenecemos y tenemos importancia aquí! Exploring sense of belonging and mattering for first-generation and continuing-generation Latinx undergraduates. *Hispanic Journal of Behavioral Sciences, 42,* 95–116.

Fattal, I. (2017). How higher education leaders are fighting for DACA. The Atlantic. https://www.theatlantic.com/education/archive/2017/09/how-higher-education-leaders-are-fighting-for-daca/538740/

Frankl, V. E. (1992). *Man's Search for Meaning.* Beacon Press.

Freire, P. (1970). *Pedagogy of the Oppressed.* (M.B. Ramos, translator). Continuum.

Gee, G. C., Morey, B. N., Walsemann, K. M., Ro, A., & Takeuchi, D. T. (2016). Citizenship as privilege and social identity: Implications for psychological distress. *American Behavioral Scientist, 60*(5–6), 680–704.

Gildersleeve, R. E. (2011). Toward a neo-critical validation theory: Participatory action research and Mexican migrant student success. *Enrollment Management Journal, 5,* 72–96.

Gonzales, R. G. (2008). Left out but not shut down: Political activism and the undocumented student movement. *Northwest Journal of Law & Social Policy, 3,* 219–239.

Gonzales, R. G. (2010). On the wrong side of the tracks: Understanding the effects of school structure and social capital in the educational pursuits of undocumented immigrant students. *Peabody Journal of Education, 85,* 469–485.

Gonzales, R. G. (2011). Learning to be illegal: Undocumented youth and shifting legal contexts in the transition to adulthood. *American Sociological Review, 76*(4), 602–619.

Gonzales, R. G., Terriquez, V., & Ruszczyk, S. P. (2014). Becoming DACAmented: Assessing the short-term benefits of deferred action for childhood arrivals (DACA). *American Behavioral Scientist, 58,* 1852–1872.

Gonzalez, L. M., Mejia, Y., Kulish, A., Stein, G. L., Kiang, L., Fitzgerald, D., & Cavanaugh, A. (2020). Alternate approaches to coping in Latinx adolescents from immigrant families. *Journal of Adolescent Research.* doi:10.1177/0743558420914083

Hernandez, S., Hernandez, I., Gadson, R., Huftalin, D., Ortiz, A. M., White, M. C., & Yocum-Gaffney, D. (2010). Sharing their secrets: Undocumented students' personal stories of fear, drive, and survival. *New Directions for Student Services, 131,* 67–84.

Hope, E. C., & Spencer, M. B. (2017). Civic engagement as an adaptive coping response to conditions of inequality: An application of phenomenological variant of ecological systems theory (PVEST). In *Handbook on Positive Development of Minority Children and Youth* (pp. 421–435). Springer.

Hurtado, S., & Carter, D. F. (1997). Effects of college transition and perceptions of the campus racial climate on Latino college students' sense of belonging. *Sociology of Education, 70,* 324–345.

Immigrant Legal Resource Center. (n.d.). DACA: Frequently asked questions. https://www.ilrc.org/daca-frequently-asked-questions?gclid=CjwKCAiAudD_BRBX EiwAudakX70BZ3ruerYBIykjEX1limki6LNuJrzm5oGVj-E9d7s5VgC1iRbT AhoCbDIQAvD_BwE

McWhirter, E. H., Ramos, K., & Medina, C. (2013). ¿Y ahora qué? Anticipated immi-gration status barriers and Latina/o high school students' future expectations. *Cultural Diversity and Ethnic Minority Psychology, 19*, 288–297.

Morales, A., Herrera, S., & Murry, K. (2011). Navigating the waves of social and political capriciousness: Inspiring perspectives from DREAM-eligible immigrant students. *Journal of Hispanic Higher Education, 10*, 266–283.

Murdock-Perriera, L. A., Boucher, K. L., Carter, E. R., & Murphy, M. C. (2019). Places of belonging: Person-and place-focused interventions to support belonging in college. In M. Paulsen and L. Perna (eds.), *Higher Education: Handbook of Theory and Research* (pp. 291–323). Springer, Cham.

Nemiroff, G. H. (1992). *Reconstructing Education: Toward a Pedagogy of Critical Humanism.* Greenwood Publishing Group.

Pérez, P. A., & Rodríguez, J. L. (2012). Access and opportunity for Latina/o undocu-mented college students: Familial and institutional support factors. *Association of Mexican American Educators Journal, 5*(1), 14–21.

Pérez, W., Espinoza, R., Ramos, K., Coronado, H. M., & Cortés, R. (2009). Academic resilience among undocumented Latino students. *Hispanic Journal of Behavioral Sciences, 31*, 149–181.

Perez, W. (2012). *Americans by Heart: Undocumented Latino Students and the Promise of Higher Education.* Teachers College Press.

Portes, A., & Rumbaut, R. G. (2001). *Legacies: The Story of the Immigrant Second Generation.* University of California Press.

Rendon, L. I. (1994). Validating culturally diverse students: Toward a new model of learning and student development. *Innovative Higher Education, 19*, 33–51.

Rogers, C. R. (1961). *On Becoming a Person.* Boston: Houghton Mifflin.

Sahay, K. M., Thatcher, K., Núñez, C., & Lightfoot, A. (2016). "It's like we are legally, illegal": Latino/a youth emphasize barriers to higher education using photo- voice. *High School Journal, 100*(1), 45–65.

Schlossberg, N. K. (1989). Marginality and mattering: Key issues in building com-munity. *New Directions for Student Services, 48*, 5–15.

Siemons, R., Raymond-Flesh, M., Auerswald, C. L., & Brindis, C. D. (2017). Coming of age on the margins: Mental health and wellbeing among Latino immigrant young adults eligible for Deferred Action for Childhood Arrivals (DACA). *Journal of Immigrant and Minority Health, 19*, 543–551.

Strayhorn, T. L. (2018). *College Students' Sense of Belonging: A Key to Educational Success for All Students.* Routledge.

Suarez-Orozco, C., Yoshikawa, H., Teranishi, R., & Suarez-Orozco, M. (2011). Growing up in the shadows: The developmental implications of unauthorized sta-tus. *Harvard Educational Review, 81*, 438–473.

Torres, L., Morgan Consoli, M. L., Unzueta, E., Meza, D., Sanchez, A., & Najar, N. (2019). Thriving and ethnic discrimination: A mixed-methods study. *Journal of Multicultural Counseling and Development, 47*, 256–273.

Tudor, K. (2015). Humanist psychology: A critical counter culture. In I. Parker (ed.), *Handbook of Critical Psychology*, pp. 127–136. Routledge.

Turner, E. O., & Figueroa, A. M. (2019). Immigration policy and education in lived reality: A framework for researchers and educators. *Educational Researcher, 48*, 549–557.

USCIS (U.S. Customs and Immigration Services). (2020). Inadmissability on public charge grounds final rule. https://www.uscis.gov/green-card/green-card-proces ses-and-procedures/public-charge/inadmissibility-on-public-charge-grounds-final-rule-litigation

Walton, G. M., & Brady, S. T. (2020). The social-belonging intervention. *Handbook of Wise Interventions*. Guilford Press.

Yakushko, O. (2009). Xenophobia: Understanding the roots and consequences of negative attitudes toward immigrants. *The Counseling Psychologist, 37*(1), 36–66.

Chapter 5

Developing a Statewide Teacher Learning Community

Holt Wilson, Lauren Baucom, Emily Hare,
F. Paul Wonsavage, Arren Duggan, Jared Webb,
Allison W. McCulloch, Michelle Stephan,
Katherine J. Mawhinney, and Catherine Schwartz

Over the last two decades, learning scientists and critical theorists have transformed our understanding of how learning occurs, the kinds of environments that promote learning, and tools useful in supporting learning. Once understood to be primarily cognitive and governed by individual physiology and experience, learning is now widely regarded to be social, facilitated by positive and supportive relationships, and shaped by contexts and culture (National Academies of Science, Engineering, and Medicine, 2018). Though many aspects of formal learning contexts for PK–16 students and educators in the United States remain organized around individual cognition, conceptions of classrooms and schools as learning communities have emerged, signaling a growing appreciation and understanding of other dimensions of learning. In light of these advances, educational designers have increasingly attended to the social dimensions of learning by creating materials, activities, and contexts intended to foster a sense of community. For example, many contemporary PK–12 curricular programs offer explicit guidance and resources to assist teachers in developing a learning community in their classrooms, and most districts and schools have adopted Dufour and Eaker's (2004) notion of professional learning communities into their policies for ongoing professional learning.

For many teacher educators working in professional development settings, designing learning experiences in ways that build community has become a standard practice. Our hope is that over time, the teachers participating in the professional development will grow together, share experiences, feel as if they matter to one another, and eventually come to recognize the group as a collective unit, a community where they know they belong. In the short term, emotions like mattering and belonging are powerful motivators for learning and growth. In the long term, designing for a community to develop is believed to be a way to ensure that long after the professional development has concluded, the community will continue to support and sustain each other's learning. While such goals might be implicit, these emotional aspects of learning have rarely been an explicit focus of professional development designers and as a result, there is very little guidance for including emotional aspects of learning like belonging as a central feature of their innovations.

This chapter explores what designing for a sense of belonging might entail by examining the evolution of a large-scale professional development initiative created to foster a sense of community among mathematics teachers and leaders across our state. We begin by sharing our interest in belonging and community and why each is important to consider when creating professional learning contexts. Next, we describe the evolution of the initiative to illustrate how we aimed to foster a sense of community among participants. Using Raz et al.'s (2019) dimensions of belonging, we examine the iterations retrospectively and show how our focus on community also attended to belonging, but only partially. From this investigation, we identify and discuss three issues that arose during implementation that we conjecture have the potential to significantly moderate participants' sense of belonging. We conclude with a discussion of these observations and offer recommendations for professional development designers with goals of creating learning contexts that attend to both social and emotional aspects of teachers' learning.

BACKGROUND

Research on teacher learning and professional development points to learning communities as key drivers of educational reform (Cochran-Smith & Lytle, 1999; Darling-Hammond & Richardson, 2009). It is well-established that professional development leading to changes in teaching and improvements in student achievement engages groups of teachers in active collaboration to improve student learning over significant and extended periods of time (Darling-Hammond & Richardson, 2009; Yoon et al., 2007). Often, communities form as teachers establish norms of engagement and a collective identity, develop a shared responsibility for each other's growth, and learn to regard differences among them as sites for learning (Grossman et al., 2001). Researchers have shown that teachers who are members of these communities develop classroom cultures centered on collaboration, achievement, and agency (Berry et al., 2005; Supovitz, 2012) and use more learner-centered instructional practices (Dunne et al., 2000; Englert & Tarrant, 1995). Membership in a professional learning community has been repeatedly linked to increases in student achievement—sometimes with dramatic results (Berry et al., 2005; Dunne et al., 2000; Englert & Tarrant, 1995; Supovitz, 2012)—which is often associated with the strength of the relationships among community members (Bolam et al., 2005).

In our roles as professional development designers and facilitators, we create tools, activities, and contexts to support teachers in learning and improving their teaching. Over the last decade, we have worked on multiple professional development projects with mathematics teachers. In these projects, we typically join with a group of teachers from a school, several schools in a district, or teacher leaders from multiple districts and assist them in investigating student learning and their practice. As teachers engage in sustained inquiry and collective improvement, they share successes, setbacks, and insights with one another. Over time, the group becomes a community that supports and sustains their improvements after the professional development ends.

In 2016, we entered into a partnership with colleagues from our state education agency to design, facilitate, and research a statewide professional development effort focused on newly adopted state mathematics standards. The partnership developed tools and instructional resources, created and facilitated face-to-face and online professional learning, and established new structures for communicating, sharing resources, and locating expertise for mathematics teachers, coaches, and curriculum leaders in our state. During our first year, we began to notice differences in the ways some teachers were participating and how they engaged with the group. While some were eager to offer ideas and contribute, others were appreciative but reserved. Through conversations with one of the editors of this book, we began to make sense of our observations—some teachers were developing a sense of belonging to the emerging community, but not all.

This realization led to a number of questions about why some felt as if they belonged but not others, the similarities and differences between belonging and community, how one might promote a sense of belonging in synchronous and asynchronous virtual spaces, what aspects of our efforts were successful in developing community but not belonging, and how we might improve the design so that more teachers felt like they belonged? Guided by these questions, we used a lens of belonging to revisit our professional learning initiative with a goal of understanding how one might design professional learning environments that promote a sense of belonging.

SENSE OF COMMUNITY AND SENSE OF BELONGING

We use Wenger's (1998) notion of a community of practice as a working definition of community. He defines a community of practice as a group who uses a set of shared tools to engage in collective efforts around a shared and negotiated endeavor that is co-constructed over time with members of the community. Here, we focus more specifically on a sense of community, which describes a feeling that members of a community have about their relationship with the community itself (Mannarini & Fedi, 2009). Among the first to theorize about a sense of community, McMillan and Davis (1986) describe it as

> a feeling that the members of a community have in relation to their belonging to a community, a feeling that the members worry about each other and that the group is concerned about them, and a shared faith that the needs of the members will be satisfied through their commitment to being together. (p.9)

Their conception of a sense of community is built upon four elements which we have found useful in discussing how we design professional development. *Membership* refers to being recognized as a part of a group or network. It is facilitated by clear boundaries delineating who is and who is not a part of the community, emotional safety, personal investment, and visible markers of affiliation. *Influence* describes the feeling that one matters to the group. Mattering (Rosenburg & McCullough, 1981) is bidirectional as a member plays a part in both shaping community decisions and being shaped by the collective community. *Integration and fulfillment of needs* is the idea that members have needs that are met through being a part of the community and also that they contribute to meeting the needs of the community. Lastly, members have *shared emotional connections* grounded in meaningful experiences that have happened in the past or imagined in the future.

Whereas a sense of community describes a feeling shared among members about the group, a sense of belonging describes a feeling about one's relationship with the group and the extent to which they perceive themselves to be a part of it. First asserted by Maslow (1943, see also Baumeister & Leary, 1995) as a fundamental human need, researchers have conceptualized belonging in multiple ways and have shown that it is closely associated with emotional well-being, learning, and academic success (Immordino-Yang et al., 2018; Junoven, 2006). Faircloth and Hamm (2005) considered students' belonging to connect to relationships with peers and supervisors, involvement with extracurriculars, and their experiences with discrimination. Building on that, Faircloth (2009, 2011) identified students' cultures, their identities, and their sense of voice/agency as vital components of their ability to construct a sense of belonging in various contexts. Similarly, Shaalvik and Shaalvik (2011) posited that a teacher's sense of belonging is affected by the alignment between their belief and values and their current practice, administrative support, and collegial relationships. While researchers have explored its importance for learning, Raz et al. (2019) asked how one might design contexts where learners can develop a sense of belonging and identify four dimensions that can be fostered through social connection. *Inviting and Welcoming* describes how a person is invited into a community and the ways their identities are honored within it. *Knowing and Accepting* refers to the ways people are "embrac[ed] fully so they feel seen for who they are and known" by the community (p. 2). *Participating and Contributing* alludes to the ways one feels that their ideas and resources are valued and needed by the community. The final dimension, *Growing*, points to the ways one learns and changes through participating with and contributing to the community. They suggest that designing for belonging involves creating opportunities for participants to experience these dimensions in multiple features of a design, including ways of communicating, the spaces in which members of a community interact, and the tools of the community.

Using a sense of community and sense of belonging, we examine a large-scale professional learning initiative that was designed to expand teachers' community. First, we use McMillian and Davis's (1986) four elements of sense of community to highlight features of the learning contexts and resources created that reflect our community-focused goals. We then use Raz and colleagues' (2019) dimensions of belonging to identify aspects of belonging that are inherent when focusing on community and other aspects we conjecture require explicit attention.

THE NORTH CAROLINA COLLABORATIVE
FOR MATHEMATICS LEARNING

The North Carolina Collaborative for Mathematics Learning is a partnership of mathematics teachers, coaches, curriculum specialists, leaders from the state educational agency, mathematicians, and teacher educators. The partnership was formed in 2016 when our state began a process of adopting and implementing new mathematics standards. Five years earlier, the state agency had led the implementation of the Common Core State Standards using a traditional, top-down approach where individual districts were responsible for interpreting the standards, identifying and aligning instructional resources, and providing teachers with professional learning experiences. Despite their best efforts, most of the districts, especially those that were small or rural, did not have the capacity to fully support teachers with professional learning nor the funding to purchase aligned instructional materials. As a result, the state's mathematics educators felt underprepared and many were left to locate and adapt resources on their own.

When the state education agency announced a new standards initiative, all stakeholders were eager for a different plan that would draw on the expertise of teachers, district and state leaders, and university faculty for a more equitable, empowering implementation plan. Thus, the partnership was a collective response that challenged the status quo approach to implementing educational policy and featured collaboration, agency, and respect for the complementary expertise distributed across the state educational system. Our goal was for all teachers, regardless of their district's resources, to have access to the resources and professional learning opportunities needed for a successful implementation. To achieve this goal, the partnership had three main activities: (1) cocreating and promoting resources that embodied aspects of high-quality mathematics instruction (Munter, 2014); (2) developing and facilitating professional development; and (3) fostering a stronger sense of community among mathematics education stakeholders. Unlike the previous implementation plan, our focus on community was intended to promote agency, connect mathematics educators with different kinds of expertise, and transform the implementation process from one that provided teachers with no say in the process but total responsibility for student outcomes to one that centralized teachers' professional knowledge and prioritized their needs for implementation resources.

To achieve these goals, our design efforts were guided by a set of principles informed by the literature and our collective experiences (Wilson et al., 2017), several of which focus on developing community. One principle described the learning environments we sought to create as "providing access to safe and respectful opportunities to learn," focused on strengthening and expanding professional relationships, and regarded "teachers' and leaders' expertise, contexts, and histories as resources for learning" (p. 1433). Another aimed to balance meeting teachers' immediate needs for resources while also creating participation structures that would challenge teachers to examine their practice and commit to improving their teaching. Guided by these principles, we designed contexts that supported teachers in developing a sense of community by recognizing them as members of the statewide community with a difficult history of implementing standards, creating opportunities to expand their professional networks for advice and support, and meeting their needs for tools and resources.

We began by developing instructional resources and professional learning materials with our partners. In total, the partnership created or refined 15 grade level or course curriculum guidance documents, authored 55 research and practice briefs, awarded 732 certificates of completion across 25 professional learning modules, and facilitated over 250 hours of professional development. Over 300 educators from 80 school districts collaborated to produce these resources, with teachers from all 115 of the state's districts having accessed the partnership's resources by 2018. Approximately 57,000 North Carolinaians have visited our website more than once, and by 2019, downloads of partnership resources had exceeded 55,000. Taken together, we consider these numbers as evidence that the partnership made progress in creating spaces for mathematics teachers to identify with one another, have some of their professional needs met, and to share experiences of implementing standards. In the remaining sections, we focus on the evolution of professional learning contexts for the high school standards from 2016 to 2018 to examine what designing for belonging might entail.

NC HIGH SCHOOL MATHEMATICS STANDARDS, COMMUNITY, AND BELONGING

Beginning fall 2016, the partnership developed and refined a set of professional learning environments to support educators in making sense of the newly adopted high school standards. Using a curriculum guidance document initially developed by district leaders as an organizing framework for professional development, the partnership implemented and refined three major iterations of a design to share the resources and for teachers to use them to collectively make sense of the new standards. In this section, we describe each iteration and use McMilan and Davis's (1986) four elements to highlight the ways we designed for the group to form a learning community. We then reexamine each iteration using Raz et al.'s (2019) dimensions of belonging to identify the ways the design invited teachers and leaders to develop—or did not develop—a sense of belonging.

Iteration 1: Live Weekly Webinars

The new standards were adopted in early June and scheduled to be implemented at the beginning of the next school year. Teachers had little time to prepare and came back to school in August with two immediate needs—they wanted to make sure they understood the new standards so they could help students meet them and they needed instructional materials aligned with the new standards. To address these needs, the partnership hosted 15 weekly webinars for teachers, members of higher education institutions, and district-level mathematics leaders. An invitation email sent to the state education agency's email listserv for high school mathematics teachers provided access but also ensured that the sessions were closed to anyone who did not have the email link (e.g., principals, parents) to provide support for teachers in their learning process. Each webinar lasted approximately 60 minutes and was offered "just in time," focusing on the meaning of standards that were coming up soon. The design team and guest teacher(s)—who had recently taught a lesson addressing the new standards—led a discussion with attendees about the lesson content, the addressed standards, and examined student work samples from the guest teacher's classroom. Individual attendees or a small group (e.g., a PLC) could participate by watching the live feed and using the platform's interactive features, such as interactive polling, synchronous chat, or talk using the audio and video features.

The webinars were designed to develop and extend a sense of community among mathematics educators across the state by establishing a weekly forum to share their first teaching experiences with the standards. Attendees could freely share their questions and uncertainties about the standards, recognize that other districts were experiencing similar issues, and identify sources of expertise beyond their district. Using an interactive format, we offered teachers and leaders instructional materials and implementation support aligned with the new standards, many of which were created in response to previous webinar discussions. By creating a dedicated time each week to experience the implementation together, share and respond to one another's needs, and develop empathy for colleagues in different roles and from other districts, we hoped the webinars would be a space for teachers to know that their voices were heard and valued, that they were not alone in their struggles and frustrations, and that they mattered.

Although the webinars were intentionally designed to build community, aspects of them also promoted belonging. At the start of each webinar, hosts would welcome attendees by name and highlight groups of teachers participating together at a school or district. After welcoming attendees, hosts would spend a few minutes talking about the norms of the community we hoped to create, one of which was to value diverse perspectives from different teaching contexts as an opportunity to learn about the practice of teaching. Our commitments to dialogue and efforts to recognize multiple forms of participation in and around the webinars provided a variety of ways for attendees to participate and contribute (e.g., chat, audio only, and video platform tools, recordings of meetings, in person audience, guest teacher host). Though our focus at the time was on developing a sense of community, these features also provided opportunities for recognizing acceptance and extending it to others.

The webinars were successful in meeting the partnership's goals, but only for a relatively small number of teachers and leaders. Of the 4,500 high school mathematics teachers and leaders across the state, only 534 (12 percent) participated in one or more of the webinars. Low attendance, logistical challenges of planning and hosting a weekly live webinar, and community feedback ultimately led the partnership to pursue a second iteration of the professional development structure—an asynchronous online learning management system that the community could access regardless of geographic location.

Iteration 2: Virtual Learning Space

We designed this system to provide all 4,500 mathematics teachers, coaches, and leaders with resources (e.g., professional development modules, research briefs, videos, standards-aligned tasks) and support the implementation of new mathematics standards within a protected setting. We designed a total of 25 professional learning modules that attended to the standards content and practices of high-quality mathematics instruction. Each module was designed to take about an hour to complete and centered around a task that teachers could use in their classroom and included relevant research, student work, and videos on student thinking, along with discussion boards to actively participate in professional discussions.

Similar to the webinars, the online system was designed as a dedicated learning space for mathematics teachers, coaches, and leaders to share resources, facilitate access to collective expertise, and strengthen the emerging community. In the webinars, we consistently heard requests for a centralized location for accessing implementation resources, and we designed the space accordingly to meet their needs and as a demonstration of their influence on the emerging community. Other features of the space were also intended to foster a sense of community through influence and fulfillment of needs, including a variety of discussion boards for posting questions and sharing links to various resources. Much like teachers provide wait time for students in their classrooms, the asynchronous discussion boards allowed educators to share their needs and respond to the needs of others by reading the responses and reflecting before posting. Our hope was that the asynchronous nature of the discussions would encourage thoughtful discussion and engagement with others and thus communicate that the community valued their contributions.

The number of page views (n > 43,000) and discussion posts (n > 2,200) suggests that this platform met the needs of more teachers than the webinars. When examining the design with an eye for Raz at al.'s (2019) dimensions of belonging, there were a number of ways our attention to community also supported participants to construct belonging. Similar to the webinars, the space was exclusive, and only teachers and mathematics educators who were not direct supervisors of teachers in the community were invited. The space included multiple videos created by partners and collaborators to introduce and orient newcomers to the community. The space allowed for a range of ways to participate, from strictly reading and accessing resources to following and moderating a particular discussion by subscribing to email alerts when someone posts a new contribution. The professional learning modules allowed community members to grow in the profession and included numerous opportunities to respond to others' questions and ideas. Our overall goal of ensuring that all teachers had access to professional learning and instructional resources led us to investigate how teachers from different regions of the state were *participating in* and *contributing to* the space. Teachers from rural areas used the space more so than their suburban or urban counterparts (49.9 percent rural vs 26.7 percent suburban, 23.3 percent urban), suggesting that those teachers without a local mathematics learning community could have found a PLC to be a part of.

Over time, we received feedback from district leaders and PD facilitators that their *needs* for access to the resources were shifting. They found the linear format of the module logic cumbersome when needing to access specific videos or other resources for use in their work with teachers. We also were aware of the increasing access requests by educators outside of the community (e.g., educators from other states, principals, university faculty) the longer it remained closed. For these reasons, we created a third iteration to address the new needs of the community.

Iteration 3: Website with Social Media Presence

For our third iteration, we created a webpage repository for all implementation resources and began to use social media to alert the community when there were updates. Similar to the virtual space, the website was designed as a centralized location for resources and information but without the module logic that made accessing particular resources inconvenient. Because the space was no longer limited to our community, we made a decision to not include the existing discussion boards from the virtual space on the webpage, in part because the posts were made in a different space with a set of assumptions about who would be able to read their posts but also because the discussion boards would no longer be a representation of the community's knowledge and experience. Without moderation, the risk of creating distrust was too great. In addition to leaving the virtual space accessible, we began to use a networking tool to continue our lines of communication. The team designed several hashtags (e.g., #HQMI, #NC2ML) for educators to maintain connection to the community and to engage around specific ideas and emerging issues.

The move to public spaces with the web page and the social media platform was intended to connect the community with other communities that support high school mathematics teachers like principals and teacher educators and meet the needs of district leaders creating new professional learning experiences for teachers tailored to their specific contexts. By doing so, we considered our efforts to establish a state high school mathematics learning community a success. Thus in the design process, our attention shifted from fostering community to maintaining through social media. With respect to the community, we continued to assist members in having their *needs* met. The social media hashtags were new markers of membership, and the community continues to share experiences with one another about the work of teaching. Finally, the third iteration was a solution to a problem the community experienced. It provided a subset of members with a convenient way to adapt partnership resources and access to the resources to other communities.

In some ways, this current iteration of the design has proven useful. Approximately 8,800 individual users from North Carolina have viewed pages on the website dedicated exclusively to high school mathematics over 72,000 times since 2017. Though we do not know who these users are, we are confident that most community members and those who work to support them are among those users. On the other hand, there are only 714 people directly connected to the partnership's social media account. Though over 75 percent of these followers are mathematics educators from North Carolina, such a small number of community members using this aspect of the design suggests it did not function as we had hoped.

However, there was a significant trade-off with the move to an open space in the third iteration. Prior to this iteration, the community was well-defined, bounded, and exclusive by virtue of the space. Members could assume that anyone in the space shared many of their goals, concerns, needs, and experiences. Opening the space meant that not everyone observing or even participating in the community via social media was a member. Without a clear boundary of who was and was not a member of the community, the webpage and the social media platform provided no way for members to identify one another. As a result, participating in the community through the website was reduced to accessing resources or required other ways to communicate. Social media may have served this purpose, but because the forum is open and public, they did not use the tool to publicize their challenges and questions about their practice. And without a clear community to affirm membership, there was little in the design that would support one in developing a sense of belonging.

DISCUSSION

In this chapter, we discussed our effort to understand why some teachers and leaders participating in a professional development initiative designed to foster community-engaged with the emerging community while others did not. Using the idea of belonging, we retrospectively examined how the learning environment supported the group in forming a community plus how it invited individuals to develop a sense of belonging. The analysis suggested an explanation for why some teachers and leaders came to participate in new ways while others did not. All were a part of the statewide community of mathematics educators, and from our perspective, all belonged to the community. And though the professional development was designed to support the group in forming a learning community, and partnership leaders assured participants they belonged, it was not designed to support individuals in constructing a sense of belonging for themselves. Just as a group collectively creates a community, the individual members cocreate their own sense of belonging, within the affordances and constraints of the context. A community can no more bestow belonging on an individual than an individual in a group can proclaim it a community.

A lens of belonging not only offered an explanation for our observations about learning, it also highlighted various aspects of our design that had the potential to foster a sense of belonging or some that did not facilitate movement in that direction. We noted how some of our efforts to develop a sense of community also encouraged belonging. Inviting and welcoming teachers and providing clear ways for them to participate in and contribute to the work of the community were occasions for them to use their voice, have their needs fulfilled, and to be recognized as a part of the community. However, belonging was not always addressed when we attended to the community. Across the three iterations, there were at best *implicit* supports for participants to be authentic and accepted, and our efforts to meet the evolving needs of the group likely made it more difficult to feel as if one belonged. The increasing size and less defined boundaries of the community made it more difficult for individuals to share all of themselves, to feel known and accepted, and to support one another in learning the new standards. Because community implies a structure for members to feel a sense of belonging (Block, 2008), future revisions of the professional development could create opportunities for these more intimate dimensions of belonging. For example, designers of large-scale PD might encourage small groups organized around teachers' interests, goals, or concerns to form early and then provide time, space, and structure for those groups to meet throughout the professional development, allowing teachers to build authentic relationships and develop trust.

In addition to highlighting the distinctions between belonging and community, our analysis called into question whether attending exclusively for community is even possible. We have come to believe that when designing for community, one is also assuming the mantle of designing for belonging. The two ideas are codefined, and whether explicitly or unintentionally, learning environments that foster community also invite individuals to construct a sense of belonging. For those who want to include belonging in their work, we found Raz et al.'s (2019) framework useful for focusing on the ways each iteration was amenable (or not) to developing a sense of belonging and suspect it would be a helpful guide in similar work in the future. For others who may believe that belonging is beyond the scope of their project or that it would be addressed as a part of community, we suggest that a failure to attend to belonging will nonetheless most likely result in an environment that implicitly invites belonging. A decision about who to include in a community is also a decision about who is to be excluded; in a similar way, a design that extends belonging only to some is othering someone else. We encourage other educational designers to reflect on how their choices may be communicating a sense of belonging for some while erecting barriers to belonging for others.

For us, belonging proved to be a powerful tool for understanding teacher learning and for thinking about designs to support it. We began this chapter noting the ongoing evolution of what it means to know and to learn and how design plays a key role in introducing and integrating new forms of learning in schools. While this is true for children, parallel examples of professional development broadening understandings of teacher learning are rare. While schools embrace broader conceptions of student learning like identity development, belonging and agency, and social-emotional learning, what it means for teachers to learn in an era of accountability and reform remains mostly restricted to behavioral compliance, knowledge acquisition, and performance. Most formal opportunities to learn made available to teachers reflect these limited perspectives. Instead of promoting growth through belonging, agency, and voice, teachers are mandated to attend "training" that seldom acknowledges their expertise, addresses their goals, honors their identities, or recognizes their uniqueness as learners. Formal professional development too often positions teachers as permanently deficient and in perpetual need of remediation, and we must ask ourselves: Why would anyone want to belong in such settings? Why would anyone choose to be authentic and vulnerable so that they may grow? Why—in such settings—would anyone want to identify as a teacher?

For all of the explanations of how teachers learn and descriptions of effective professional development generated by the research community (Clarke & Hollingsworth, 2002; Darling-Hammond et al., 2009;

Desimone, 2009), there are few comparable explanations for why some teachers do not learn from PD beyond their backgrounds, content knowledge, effort to learn, or other characteristics of individual teachers. Broadening our conception of learning to include belonging offered an explanation for why some participants did not engage with the community as we had hoped. Rather than attributing nonparticipation to be the result of some inherent quality of teachers, a new perspective provided insights into how our design did not encourage a sense of belonging. While the former explanation would have left us with no recourse to improve their learning, the latter calls us to reexamine and improve our design. We encourage other teacher educators and professional development theorists and researchers to not only create contexts for teachers to collaborate and address their problems of practice as a community but also invite teachers to want to be a part of that community, that is, to belong.

Acknowledgment

The authors wish to thank Lisa Ashe, Jennifer Curtis, Joseph Reaper, Kitty Rutherford, Denise Schultz, and the mathematics educators of NC. The NC Dept of Public Instruction and the mathematics education group at UNC Greensboro provided support for the work reported in this chapter. Our opinions and ideas do not necessarily reflect those of NC DPI.

REFERENCES

Baumeister, R.F., & Leary, M.R. (1995). The need to belonging: Desire for interpersonal attachment as a fundamental human motivation. *Psychological Bulletin, 117*(3), 497–530.

Berry, B., Johnson, D., & Montgomery, D. (2005). The power of teacher leadership [electronic version]. *Educational Leadership, 62*(5), 56.

Block, P. (2008). *Community: The Structure of Belonging.* San Francisco: Berrett-Koehler.

Bolam, R., McMahon, A., Stoll, L., Thomas, S., & Wallace, M. (2005). Creating and sustaining professional learning communities. Research Report Number 637. London, England: General Teaching Council for England, Department for Education and Skills.

Clarke, D., & Hollingsworth, H. (2002). Elaborating a model of teacher professional growth. *Teaching and Teacher Education, 18*(8), 947–967.

Cochran-Smith, M., & Lytle, S. L. (1999). Chapter 8: Relationships of knowledge and practice: Teacher learning in communities. *Review of Research in Education, 24*(1), 249–305.

Darling-Hammond, L., Wei, R. C., Andree, A., Richardson, N., & Orphanos, S. (2009). *Professional Learning in the Learning Profession*. Washington, DC: National Staff Development Council, 12.

Darling-Hammond, L., & Richardson, N. (2009). Research review/teacher learning: What matters. *Educational leadership, 66*(5), 46–53.

Desimone, L. M. (2009). Improving impact studies of teachers' professional development: Toward better conceptualizations and measures. *Educational Researcher, 38*(3), 181–199.

DuFour, R., & Eaker, R. (2004). Professional learning communities. *Educational Leadership and Supervision, 31*, 40–44.

Dunne, F. Nave, B., & Lewis, A. (2000). Critical friends groups: Teachers helping teachers to improve student learning. [electronic version]. *Phi Delta Kappan, 28*(4), 31–37.

Englert, C. S., & Tarrant, K. (1995). Creating collaborative cultures for educational change. *Remedial Special Education, 16*, 325–336.

Faircloth, B. S. (2009). Making the most of adolescence: Harnessing the search for identity to understand classroom belonging. *Journal of Adolescent Research. 24*(3), 321–348.

Faircloth, B. S. (2012). "Wearing a mask" vs. connecting identity with learning. *Contemporary Educational Psychology, 37,* 1–9.

Faircloth, B. S., & Hamm, J. V. (2005). Sense of belonging among high school students representing 4 ethnic groups. *Journal of Youth and Adolescence, 34*(4), 293–309.

Grossman, P. L., Wineburg, S., & Woolworth, S. (2001). Toward a theory of teacher community. *Teachers College Record, 103*, 942–1012.

Immordino-Yang, M. H., Darling-Hammond, L., & Krone, C. (2018). *The Brain Basis for Integrated Social, Emotional, and Academic Development*. Washington, DC: National Commission on Social, Emotional, and Academic Development.

Junoven, J. (2006). Sense of belonging, social bonds, and school functioning. In P. Alexander and P. Winne (eds.), *Handbook of Educational Psychology* (pp. 655–674). Routledge.

Mannarini, T., & Fedi, A. (2009). Multiple senses of community: The experience and meaning of community. *Journal of Community Psychology, 37*(2), 211–227.

Maslow, A. H. (1943). A theory of human motivation. *Psychological Review, 50*(4), 370.

McMillan, D. W., & Chavis, D. M. (1986). Sense of community: A definition and theory. *Journal of Community Psychology, 14*(1), 6–23.

Munter, C. (2014). Developing visions of high-quality mathematics instruction. *Journal for Research in Mathematics Education, 45*(5), 585–636.

National Academies of Sciences, Engineering, and Medicine. (2018). *How People Learn II: Learners, Contexts, and Cultures*. National Academies Press.

National Commission on Social, Emotional, and Academic Development. (2019). *From a Nation at Risk, to a Nation at Hope: Recommendations from the National Commission on Social, Emotional, and Academic Development*. Washington, DC: The Aspen Institute.

Raz, A., Clifford, D., & Wise, S. (2019, April 30). Design for belonging. https://ds chool.stanford.edu/resources/design-for-belonging

Rosenberg, M., & McCullough, B. C. (1981). Mattering: Inferred significance and mental health among adolescents. *Research in Community & Mental Health. 2,* 163–182.

Skaalvik, E. M., & Skaalvik, S. (2011). Teacher job satisfaction and motivation to leave the teaching profession: Relations with school context, feeling of belonging, and emotional exhaustion. *Teaching and Teacher Education, 27,* 1029–1038.

Supovitz, J. (2012). Getting at student understanding: The key to teachers' use of test data. *Teachers College Record, 114*(11), 1–29.

Wenger, E. (1999). *Communities of Practice: Learning, Meaning, and Identity.* Cambridge, MA: Cambridge University Press.

Wilson. P. H., McCulloch, A., Webb, J., Stephan, M., Mawhinney, K., Hewitt, K., & Curtis, J. (2017). Partnering for professional development at scale. *Proceedings of the 39th annual meeting of the North American Chapter of the International Group for the Psychology of Mathematics Education* (pp. 1431–1434). Indianapolis, IN: Purdue University.

Yoon, K. S., Duncan, T., Lee, S. W. Y., Scarloss, B., & Shapley, K. (2007). Reviewing the evidence on how teacher professional development affects student achievement (Issues and Answers Report, REL 2007 No. 033). Washington, DC: U.S. Department of Education, Regional Educational Laboratory Southwest.

Chapter 6

Living as "In-Betweener" in Life and Work

Katherine Ramos

The great Maya Angelou has been the "theme soul" to my being. She has spoken words that I could never find that speak directly to my personal and professional experience. "I belong no place . . . I belong every place" is a phrase in which its very essence is one I continuously explore. I constantly reflect upon and wonder: What does it mean for a Latinx woman (like me) from a poor, underprivileged background, first-generation student, first-generation faculty to feel that they truly belong? What does it take? Who or what dictates my belonging? Me? And if it is, in fact, *I* who dictates my belonging, when do I know I have arrived?

MAYA ANGELOU: You only are free when you realize you belong no place—you
   belong every place—no place at all. The price is high. The reward is great
BILL MOYERS: Do you belong anywhere?
MAYA ANGELOU: I haven't yet.
BILL MOYERS: Do you belong to anyone?
MAYA ANGELOU: More and more . . . I belong to myself. I'm very proud of that.
   I am very concerned about how I look at Maya. I like Maya very much.

—A Conversation with Maya Angelou, November 21, 1973

Grappling with these questions means revisiting several times over my lived experiences to date. As a person whose norm is to live along the margins in my daily life, I often contemplate the meaning of *belonging* and what it signifies for someone who has felt "othered" their entire lives. Is it truly possible to find a space (*a rightful space?*) that is my own?

Several theories underscore the significance of belonging and its enhancement to psychological well-being (Sociometer Theory: Leary & Baumeister, 2000; De Silva et al. 2005). The feeling of belonging or belongingness is often contingent upon the power and social strata position one holds within a group, as well as aligned values and identifications to the majority status group (Roffey, 2013; Yuval-Davis, 2006). Among people from minority and underserved backgrounds, a sense of belonging and ethnic identity links to more significant psychological adjustment and positive identity formation. Although belonging is a fundamental core to our human experience (May 2016), it is often commonplace that individuals feel unwelcomed or often sidelined within and outside the social and cultural groups to which they belong. Such is true in the context of belonging across multiple intersecting domains that include one's personal and professional life. Despite the fact that the breadth and depth of belonging in life and at work has been widely studied, how the daily experiences of belonging are experienced and varied across these two domains has received limited attention.

This chapter will focus on the experiences of feeling as "other" and as an "in-betweener" in Latin culture and as a mental health clinician and academic in palliative and hospice care. Specifically, I discuss what it means to be a first-generation Latina achieving academic success and the tension of maintaining Hispanic cultural capital. I will share reflections of being a Latina woman in a predominantly majority status institution offering clinical care to those at the end of life. These two experiences will be examined in parallel while highlighting how achieving a sense of belonging and cultural capital is fraught with daily identity tensions. Domains of belonging in life and in the workplace are discussed using the following framework (guided by Filstad et al., 2019): (1) being part of something, (2) the process of becoming, and (3) the attempt to perform, engage, and participate in activities to belong.

AN INTRODUCTION

Early morning on March 12, 2016, I am sitting in my clinical supervisor's office following our weekly meetings of my rotation in palliative care. As we discuss my future in palliative care research, I am simultaneously distracted by earlier news from my family: Dad is ill, and he is getting worse. I spent the last 20 years of my young adulthood witnessing how Parkinson's disease took my father's mind and slowly deteriorated his body. At that moment of our meeting, I am trying my hardest to compartmentalize. My work expectation is that I "show up" for my older adult patients confronting their mortality in hospice. My family expectation is that as a Colombian Puerto Rican daughter, I "show up" to my family and to my father, who is dying. I cannot help but reflect on these experiences and how they trigger my own story of feeling somewhere in the middle of both my life and in my work.

Growing up, the responsibilities I feel toward my family while adhering to work obligations disclose my earliest anxieties of where I think that I truly belong. These feelings also bring about reflexive dilemmas. Every day, I experience the emergence of confronting my role as an in-betweener, a Latina woman, a researcher, and a provider navigating liminal space. Perhaps more importantly, I also discover how my role as an in-betweener serves as a source of strength to help those who I treat.

Belonging as Being Part of Something

I grew up with my mother, born and raised in Pereira, Colombia, and my father, born and raised in Ciales, Puerto Rico. Growing up in New York City, a mecca of diversity—if you will—there were always three critical household rules. Rule 1: We cannot speak English in our home, only Spanish. Rule 2: Never forget, dismiss, or dare to ignore where our family comes from. Rule 3: Always represent our family with respect and obedience. These rules or guiding principles became what anchored all my family members. They provided a foundation that made us feel we were a part of something, that all six of us (four siblings and our parents) belonged as a unit. And this unit provided us with a sense of identity, representation, and safety net. However, no one ever prepared us to negotiate our *belonging* across the different spaces we were to inhabit, starting with school.

Living in New York and attending public schools bring about great memories. But there were recurring moments where I noticed how I stood out, was different, and perhaps maybe did not belong. There was a brief period (one year to be exact) throughout my education when I attended a private school, in the first grade. My parents had worked hard and were hoping that placing my younger brother and me in a private school with a low student–teacher ratio would afford more opportunities for our education. I still recall starting my first day. While I have always been an introverted child and adult, I never shied from meeting new people. It was lunchtime, and no one wanted to sit next to me at lunch. I vividly recall looking at the sea of student's faces, all predominantly White, and having a pang of self-consciousness. No one offered me a seat, and no one seemed to notice me or care for my presence.

When I looked over to my left, a fellow six-year-old whose family emigrated from India, eating by herself, called me over. She noticed me; she gave me a space to feel welcomed. She also became my buddy when we were described as "too brown and dirty" to play red rover in the schoolyard, or when we were told our lunch meals "smelled funny," and we should keep to ourselves. These painful experiences made us feel ostracized and unwelcomed, but we had each other. Our differences from other students gave us a pocket to belong at least to each other. While that year was the only time spent in private school, it sure educated me. I learned that I was different. I also learned (even at such a young age) that I will not always belong. I also learned about the power of being seen, especially by someone who also was mistreated and dismissed.

This type of experience felt much less pronounced when I continued and finished my primary and secondary schooling in public schools. The diversity of students felt more welcoming. Yet, as I excelled in my education, I also realized that I was becoming more of a minority in my Advanced Placement and Honors courses, including attending college and graduate school. Upon entering my first graduate school (in a prestigious and affluent university in the south), I faced a predominantly White institution where all faculty were White. Many of these faculty members held several privileged identities, which I could not relate to or understand. This time felt quite isolating, frightening, and one that gave me my first taste of imposter syndrome. I was all by myself with no family to return to after a full day of classes and seminars. Everything I saw around me did not mirror my upbringing or lived experiences. In my struggle to belong, I turned inward and battled depression.

Although this time in my life was challenging, one where I did not feel as if I had a safe space or mentor to turn to, I realized I needed to make a different decision for my future. My decision to leave this graduate program was further solidified when seeking out help from a faculty member. When I sought help, I was invalidated, gaslighted, and told they simply "could not understand why attending graduate school was feeling hard for me, especially since they felt they did everything to help minority students." This message was then followed by being told they considered themselves as "Lady Liberty" in their role as a mentor to students of color. This last comment was so insulting and minimizing that the feeling of being a part of something (i.e., entering the world of academia) no longer felt like a possibility. My inability to belong was further reinforced by feeling like an "in-betweener," I had left my home in New York, left my Spanish family to follow individualistic pursuits, ones that they felt were "too American." And yet, during my time at this particular graduate program, I was too Spanish or too different from those I met in their Ivory Tower. I felt stuck, not belonging fully to any one place. However, I was lucky to reach out to my former high school teachers and undergraduate professors back at home to receive guidance.

Through the encouragement of past mentors, I became encouraged to find my "rightful place," a term beautifully captured by Dr. Beverly Faircloth on *Rightful Presence* in this volume. In relating to a larger idea of belonging (i.e., belonging to myself and my career dreams), I left my first graduate institution. I subsequently enrolled in a different graduate program that was responsive to all points of my diversity, contributions, and value. My story is not original or unique, as many black, Indigenous, and people of color (BIPOC) students and faculty can attest. Yet, I share my story to elucidate the nonlinear process of my journey to belonging. Belonging is an ever-evolving process. It comes with ebbs, flows, unexpected turns, and everything in between. My story also elucidates the struggle of finding a sense of belonging across the various spaces I live in. It is a reminder about how life experiences either anchor or disconnect us from finding spaces to connect.

Undoubtedly, we all share the human emotional need to be accepted. It is a primal, fundamental need to belong (Deci & Ryan, 2000; Maslow, 1954), be it with family, friends, coworkers, or a connection to something greater than ourselves. All of us as human beings (whether are aware of it or not) have an intrinsic desire to belong, and for others, this extends to being a part of something greater than themselves. The psychology of belonging tells us that much of meaning, identity, and sense of relevance is derived from our sense or state of belonging (Allen, 2021). As Dr. Kelly-Ann Allen succinctly and impactfully notes, "Our need to belong is like our need for water (p. 1)."

In academics, belonging predicts well-being, motivation, and reduced intentions for drop out (Suhlman et al., 2018). For students of color, the barrage of negative stereotypes encountered and feeling othered influence feelings of being an "in-betweener." The negative impacts of experienced stereotypes and of being dismissed include feeling unseen as individuals, in addition to feeling devalued and disrespected (Walton & Carr, 2012). The experiences like those that I share and experiences by those in academic and professional arenas are associated with increased vigilance for cues that communicate one does not belong (Inzlicht, & Schmader, 2012; Schmader et al., 2015; Taylor & Walton). While the literature on belonging is broad and diverse, perspectives and integrative frameworks of assessing belonging and targeting belonging remain understudied (Allen et al., 2021).

On Becoming: Mediation between Belonging at Work and Life

As I persisted in my journey of reducing my feelings of being an "in-betweener," I realized that my path to belonging would be one that I would continually seek to find and maintain. Following graduate school, internship, and then postdoctoral fellowship, I once again stepped into a new role: a first-generation faculty member at a prestigious and historically White institution.

My clinical and research expertise mainly promotes mental health and quality of life among individuals who are receiving palliative or hospice care services. In my work, I tend to care for individuals in the throes of facing their mortality as they cope and live with a serious, life-limiting disease (e.g., advanced cancer or heart failure, end-stage kidney disease, dementia). Part of my role is to bear witness to their struggles with mortality and what it means to exist in the face of impending death.

I still recall my first day of work. I was excited, nervous, simply happy that I had reached a point in my career that gave me an immense sense of pride, purpose, and accomplishment. It was also a bittersweet feeling. My father had recently died due to Parkinson's disease, and although he lived to see me graduate, I still carried a great deal of guilt over not being with him enough. Again, I felt like an "in-betweener," not fully being with my dad as he was in Florida and I in North Carolina. I resented my inability to practice my cultural value of *Familismo* while at that very same time needing to *show up* for my patients by holding their hand at the bedside in the hospice unit. It was a time in my life and career where I never knew where I fully landed. At that time, I did not feel enough of a daughter because I was not right next to my dad, and I feared that my guilt would impact my ability to be a present and compassionate health-care provider. Although I have processed that time in my life, there were two significant life lessons that I took with me and continue to parallel my work.

LESSON 1: BELONGING IS FLUID, A FLUX STATE THAT WILL REGULARLY REQUIRE REASSESSMENT AND REEVALUATION.

This lesson is reinforced by the patients I see in my work as a clinician and a researcher. As mentioned earlier, many of the patients I see face their mortality, are mourning past regrets, and are grieving the loss of future life events. My patients are also battling with internal struggles and fears of what it means to die. I would argue that these patients are in a constant flux of finding their belonging. Each patient is attempting to find connection not just in the world in which they are present but also in preparing themselves to say goodbye. In their own right, my patients also have to manage their feelings of an "in-betweener." They live their remaining days, not fully being in the present where they can engage with their daily lives in ways they used to but have yet to transition to the active stages of dying.

I often get asked what death will feel like or if there is such a thing as life after death. I find that these concerns are rooted in a strong desire to feel as if one belongs to either someone or something even after death. We address this in the therapy context by allowing patients to reflect and think about their value and what is of utmost importance. This process creates an exploration to understand personal values. It also creates opportunities to be more intentional in engaging in value-driven behavior. Our time in therapy focuses on creating a space to discuss further what it means to belong and how the patient can reorganize, redefine, and reassess their notions of belonging. During this time, as we continue to discuss values and belonging, patients open up in ways that they have not before. They discuss finding new opportunities, even at their deathbed, of how they will newly connect with themselves and with their loved ones before saying their final goodbyes.

Research suggests that those coping and living with serious and advanced disease seek activities that enhance meaning, purpose, and connection with others (Guerrero et al., 2017; Morgan et al., 2017; Peoples et al., 2018). Additionally, qualitative studies have shown that those with an advanced serious, life-limiting illness desire to belong (Håkanson & Öhlén, 2014; Morgan et al., 2017; Peoples et al., 2020), as they often feel excluded and isolated by their disease (Davies & Sque, 2002; Willig, 2015). Findings suggest that when patients can rethink or renegotiate their disrupted intersubjective world, patients experience a feeling of belonging and equality with others (Missel et al., 2019; Peoples et al., 2018, 2019).

LESSON 2: BELONGING IS PROFOUNDLY SUBJECTIVE AND REQUIRES US TO BE WHO WE ARE

Although I remain grateful for my work and what I have accomplished, being a BIPOC faculty is complex and, at times, downright exhausting. Every day I make conscious efforts of validating my feelings of belonging and countering my imposter syndrome. In my role as a researcher, a significant portion of my time is spent writing and submitting research grants to support my salary and research activities to improve the mental health of patients in palliative care. As a junior investigator, I have realized that there is difficulty in securing grants but that as a Latina woman, people who look like me are not well-represented in the world of research funding.

It is widely known that despite the recognized importance of diversity in the scientific community, pipeline issues remain among underrepresented minority faculty (URM), particularly in areas of securing grants and sustaining a history of funded research. For example, as a Latina in psychology, I comprise less than 4 percent of the Behavioral and Social Sciences Research (BSSR) workforce. Of psychologists engaged in BSSR, 88 percent of researchers who receive funding from the National Institute of Health (NIH) are White (Hur et al., 2017). There is a strong and growing research base suggesting faculty of color frequently experience various roadblocks and disadvantages in their career development while employed in predominantly White institutions. Women of color must commonly manage gendered, raced experiences in academe.

The more I become aware of the various and challenging struggles that someone like me will continue to face as a faculty member, I am also encouraged by recent efforts to focus on diversity, equity, and inclusion at my institution. I believe and hold hope that with the current sociopolitical and cultural climate pushing for change, there will be new open doors for those of us who have long-lived along the margins. Now more than ever, I am letting go of feeling as if I need to fit in my institution to be accepted and embracing that honoring who I am is all I need to own my power and place of belonging.

Performing, Engaging, and Participating in Activities to Belong

Living and surviving a global pandemic this past year has further reinforced the power and need for belonging. However, it is not just the reflections we make about belonging that matter; we must dig deep and pursue actions to find our rightful presence. These actions begin with how we address and take care of ourselves. It is clear to me that with the several challenges that all Americans (and people across the world) have had to face economically, culturally, socially, and politically during this past year, good mental health is vital.

As such, how can we feel as if we truly belong without first attuning specifically to our mental health and our mental health needs? We are now entering a special time in our lives. It is a time that is challenging us to rise to the occasion and meet our needs to belong and help others feel that they belong. In efforts to move toward a path of connection, taking an integrative framework for fostering belonging (see figure 6.1) is one approach worth considering. According to this framework, there are four key elements to belong. In Allen et al.,'s 2021 article, the four elements are

> (1) competencies for belonging (skills and abilities); (2) opportunities to belong (the availability of groups, people, places, times, and spaces that enable belonging to occur.); (3) motivations to belong (inner drive); and (4) perceptions of belonging (cognitions, attributions, and feedback mechanisms—positive or negative experiences when connecting). (p. 91)

Per Allen et al. (2021), "as a dynamic social system, these four components reinforce and influence one another over time" (p. 91). Finding strategies where these components interconnect carries the potential for consistently high belonging and positive life outcomes. Working from this model, as a mental health provider, I have been able to find my way to practical applications that one can follow to foster belonging:

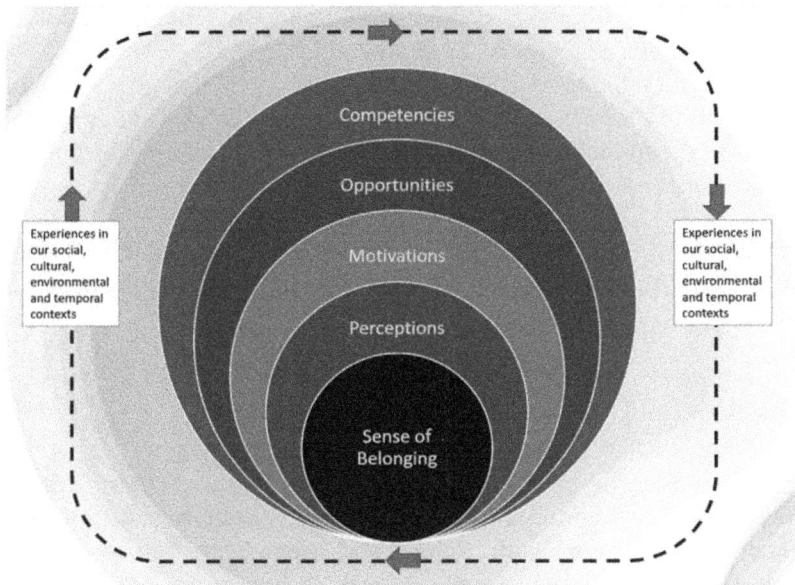

Figure 6.1 Integrative Framework Demonstrating How Belonging Can Be Examined, Assessed, and Understood. The competencies, opportunities, motivations, and experienced perception all inform and interact with one another, influencing how belonging is experienced across social, cultural, environmental, and temporal contexts. *Source:* This figure is guided by and adapted with permission: Allen, K. A., Kern, M. L., Rozek, C. S., McInerney, D. M., & Slavich, G. M. (2021). Belonging: A review of conceptual issues, an integrative framework, and directions for future research. *Australian Journal of Psychology*, 1–16.

1. Consider building competencies that connect you to your cultural values, heritage, and social circles. *Domain:* Competencies for Belonging.
2. Take the time (one-minute, three-minute, five-minute increments) to take a breath, pursue a mindfulness activity, and invest in relaxation using smartphone apps or enjoyable streaming services. Get into the practice of making time for yourself, and being consistent with self-care is more important than how much time you engage in that activity. DO SOMETHING different. It is the act and acknowledgment that taking time for yourself is what matters. *Domain:* Competencies for Belonging.
3. Find new ways to connect (ZOOM and other platforms have allowed for this): m movie sharing, watching free virtual music tours, attending live comedy shows (free or reduced rates). *Domain:* Opportunities to Belong.
• Volunteering your time remotely (e.g., Smithsonian, reading books to children) giving to others can be a mood booster. *Domain:* Motivations to Belong.

4. Offer gratitude, kindness, compassion—doing so provides perspective-taking. *Domain:* Perceptions of Belonging.
5. Evaluate your thoughts and behaviors—does this thought or behavior, or perspective move me toward what I value? Does it offer kindness, generosity, and inclusivity to myself and others? *Domain:* Perceptions of Belonging.

Adopting a framework like the one suggested here can support our efforts to claim our own rightful presence across the varied and changing contexts of our lives.

CONCLUSIONS

This chapter focused on the experiences of feeling as "other" and as an "in-betweener" in Latin culture. I provided my personal and professional experiences as a mental health clinician and researcher in palliative and hospice care. Throughout my accounts and path to find my sense of belonging, research literature was interwoven to support my lived experiences and represent the lived experiences of those who have been historically disenfranchised and undervalued in society. As I discussed domains of belonging in life and the workplace, I also brought forth an integrative framework to foster belonging and practical applications. In closing, I refer back to the wise words of Dr. Maya Angelou; I hold hope for those that read this chapter that *more and more [in time] may you find your path to belonging to yourself.*

REFERENCES

Allen, K. A., Kern, M. L., Rozek, C. S., McInerney, D. M., & Slavich, G. M. (2021). Belonging: A review of conceptual issues, an integrative framework, and directions for future research. *Australian Journal of Psychology, 73*, 87–102. doi: 10.1080/00049530.2021.1883409.

Deci, E. L., & Ryan, R. M. (2000). The "what" and "why" of goal pursuits: Human needs and the self-determination of behavior. *Psychological Inquiry, 11*(4), 227–268.

Filstad, C., Traavik, L.E.M., & Gorli, M. (2019). Belonging at work: the experiences, representations and meanings of belonging. *Journal of Workplace Learning, 31*, 116–142. https://doi.org/10.1108/JWL-06-2018-0081.

Guerrero-Torrelles, M., Monforte-Royo, C., Rodríguez-Prat, A., Porta-Sales, J., & Balaguer, A. (2017). Understanding meaning in life interventions in patients with advanced disease: A systematic review and realist synthesis. *Palliative medicine, 31*(9), 798–813.

Håkanson, C., & Öhlén, J. (2016). Connectedness at the end of life among people admitted to inpatient palliative care. *American Journal of Hospice and Palliative Medicine, 33*(1), 47–54.

Hur, H., Andalib, M. A., Maurer, J. A., Hawley, J. D., & Ghaffarzadegan, N. (2017). Recent trends in the US Behavioral and Social Sciences Research (BSSR) workforce. *PloS One, 12*(2), e0170887.

Inzlicht, M., & Schmader, T. (2012). *Stereotype Threat: Theory, Process, and Application.* Oxford University Press.

Leary, M. R., & Baumeister, R. F. (2000). The nature and function of self-esteem: Sociometer theory. In *Advances in Experimental Social Psychology* (Vol. 32, pp. 1–62). Academic Press.

Maslow, A. H. (1954). *Motivation and Personality.* Harper and Row.

May, V. (2016). What does the duration of belonging tell us about the temporal self?. *Time & Society, 25*(3), 634–651.

McKenzie, K., Harpham, T., & Huttly, S. R. (2005). Social capital and mental illness: A systematic review. *Journal of Epidemiology & Community Health, 59*(8), 619–627.

Missel, M., Borregaard, B., Schoenau, M. N., & Sommer, M. S. (2019). A sense of understanding and belonging when life is at stake—Operable lung cancer patients' lived experiences of participation in exercise. *European Journal of Cancer Care, 28*(5), e13126.

Morgan, D. D., Currow, D. C., Denehy, L., & Aranda, S. (2017). Living actively in the face of impending death: Constantly adjusting to bodily decline at the end of life. *BMJ Supportive & Palliative Care, 7*(2), 179–188. doi:10.1136/bmjspcare-2014-000744.

Peoples, H., Nissen, N., Brandt, Å., & la Cour, K. (2018). Belonging and quality of life as perceived by people with advanced cancer who live at home. *Journal of Occupational Science, 25*(2), 200–213.

Peoples, H., Nissen, N., Brandt, Å., & la Cour, K. (2019, August). Belonging as a dimension of quality of life. In *Occupational Science Europe Conference: Europe in Transitions: Impact on Occupation and Health.*

Peoples, H., Nissen, N., Brandt, Å., & la Cour, K. (2020). Perceptions of quality of life by people with advanced cancer who live at home. *British Journal of Occupational Therapy*, 0308022620976839.

Roffey, S. (2013). Inclusive and exclusive belonging: The impact on individual and community well-being. *Educational and Child Psychology, 30*(1), 38–49.

Schmader, T., Hall, W., & Croft, A. (2015). Stereotype threat in intergroup relations. In M. Mikulincer, P. R. Shaver, J. F. Dovidio, & J. A. Simpson (eds.), *APA Handbooks in Psychology®. APA Handbook of Personality and Social Psychology*, Vol. 2. *Group Processes* (pp. 447–471). American Psychological Association.

Suhlmann, M., Sassenberg, K., Nagengast, B., & Trautwein, U. (2018). Belonging mediates effects of student-university fit on well-being, motivation, and dropout intention. *Social Psychology, 49*, 16–28.

Taylor, V. J., & Walton, G. M. (2011). Stereotype threat undermines academic learning. *Personality and Social Psychology Bulletin, 37*(8), 1055–1067.

Walton, G. M., & Carr, P. B. (2012). Social belonging and the motivation and intellectual achievement of negatively stereotyped students. In M. Inzlicht & T. Schmader (eds.), *Stereotype Threat: Theory, Process, and Application* (pp. 89–106). Oxford University Press.

Yuval-Davis, N. (2006). Belonging and the politics of belonging. *Patterns of Prejudice*, *40*(3), 197–214.

Chapter 7

Promoting a Sense of Belonging

Black Girls and College and Career Readiness

Pamela N. Harris, Kaitlyn Ingram,
Marquita S. Hockaday, and Laura M. Gonzalez

The unique needs of Black males in K–12 settings have long been explored in the literature, ranging from overrepresentation in special education to underrepresentation in gifted education (Beljan, 2011; Sample, 2010). Whereas these issues are always of the utmost importance, it is just as critical to acknowledge that the voices and needs of Black females are constantly unheard. This disregard can be attributed to the assumption that Black female students are strong and more motivated, thus needing less specialized attention (Morris, 2007; Rollock, 2007). Moreover, when attention is granted, it's often for negative reasons. Black females are subjected to several negative stereotypes, such as being "angry" or "aggressive" (Smith-Evans & George, 2014). These stereotypes might lead to inordinate disciplinary actions, as Black females are more likely to be admonished for "loud and defiant" behaviors compared to their White and Latina peers (Annamma et al., 2019). Moreover, Black females are suspended at higher rates than their White female counterparts (Hing, 2014). The suspensions are often related to more subjective categories of student misbehavior, such as inappropriate dress or defiance instead of more serious infractions, such as fighting or bringing a weapon on school property (Bradshaw et al., 2010; Vavrus & Cole, 2002). As a whole, being ignored, stereotyped, or suspended are all instances which create distance between a Black girl and her school, and which make it less likely she will generate a sense of belonging there.

Numerous suspensions, as well as longstanding misperceptions of Black females being loud, aggressive, and strong (Evans-Winters, 2005, Smith-Evans & George, 2014) may also contribute to limited educational guidance and attention from key school personnel. For example, Black females are overlooked for advanced placement (AP) and honors courses, admission to science, technology, engineering, and math (STEM) programs, and inclusion in charter programs (Schott Foundation, 2016; Smith-Evans & George, 2014). When compared to their peers, Black female students are currently the least likely population to graduate from high school with college credit (Bryant, 2015; Sherwin et al., 2016; Smith-Evans & George, 2014). This can be attributed to a lack of access to AP and dual-enrollment courses. Current research has shown that even though Black students overall comprise about 14 percent of high school populations, only about 9 percent of these students are enrolled in AP courses (College Board, 2014). Black students, in general, are encouraged to take lower level courses as opposed to college preparatory classes (Bryant, 2015; Moore et al., 2010). Again, the underlying message of this exclusion is "you don't belong" in upper-level academic spaces or trajectories.

The aforementioned discrimination faced by Black females based on their intersectional identities can explain why this population is often underrepresented in advanced courses, unheard or unseen, and unacknowledged for their aspirations and potential. The authors of this chapter will explore what sense of belonging means to Black females in K–12 settings, and outline a group counseling model that addresses their college and career readiness (CCR) needs and, ultimately, kinship needs. Additionally, the authors will share how this sense of belonging threads between the counseling group members, group facilitator, and faculty supervisor—all of whom identify as Black females.

SENSE OF BELONGING IN SCHOOLS

Sense of belonging is used here to mean a psychological need for community, validation, and connection (Osterman, 2000), as opposed to simple membership. This psychological need is powerful, encompassing the need for safety, trust in others, and acceptance as you are. For students from minoritized social identities, certainly including Black girls, achieving a sense of belonging in school is complicated for several reasons (Harris et al., 2020). Depending on the racial-ethnic make-up of peers in the school, it might be hard to see examples of others who look like you being held up as valued, capable, and at great potential (Booker, 2007). Additionally, the racial-ethnic composition and attitudes of the adults in the school could contribute to stereotyping, bias, and inequitable treatment directed toward those who look like you (Morris, 2007). Even basic needs like trust and safety could be in short supply in the physical environment of the school (Osterman, 2000). Lack of belonging can bring with it negative outcomes like decreased motivation for school tasks, decreased engagement with classes and people, and lowered academic performance (Booker, 2007). Therefore, we should be thinking about the sense of belonging for various student populations across several domains (e.g., extracurricular involvement, student–teacher relationships, peer community, discrimination or mistreatment, opportunities for leadership or advancement) (Faircloth & Hamm, 2005).

How can school practitioners address this important dynamic? Scholars of critical race theory have pointed to the need for counterspaces in predominantly White institutions (Carter, 2007). Counterspaces can be formal or informal spaces where Black girls (for example) could (1) bond with each other in a way that affirms identities and pushes back on stereotypes, (2) express their frustrations and concerns among similar peers, and (3) share protective strategies for coping and resisting with each other. Students may intuitively create counterspaces with each other (e.g., sitting together in the cafeteria) for relief of the stress of confronting racism, sexism, classism, and other oppressive interactions. School leaders can also intentionally prepare a counterspace and invite students into it, with examples being student clubs, mentoring relationships, or counseling groups. The current chapter will share an example of a psychoeducational group for Black girls to support them along the journey toward CCR.

CCR is a specific task that is important to the developmental process of adolescence, as students try to discern future directions for postsecondary education or work (Harris et al., 2020). CCR is also embedded in the mission or purpose of most middle and high schools, going so far as to tie school funding or long-term viability to their success in promoting CCR among all students. Of great concern, CCR is often not generated in an equitable fashion among all student populations. A report from the ACT (2015) shows that 61 percent of African American students in the 2015 high school graduating class who took the ACT did not meet the four college readiness benchmarks. The intersection of the CCR task and the belongingness need suggests a possible response—a safe space where concerns can be raised honestly, identities can be affirmed genuinely, and meaningful strategies for identifying and moving toward goals can be implemented. Here, the authors describe a psychoeducational framework used for promoting CCR among a small group of Black female high school students.

THE SPARCK MODEL

The SPARCK Model for life design coaching (i.e., Story, Purpose, Aspirations, Reflection, Connection, Kick-Start) is a holistic and strength-based approach designed to engage students in a process to consider internal and external characteristics that may influence goals and goal-directed behavior (Johnson, 2017; Johnson & Delph, 2017). The example offered in this chapter is designed for ninth- and tenth-grade students engaged in CCR activities, but can be adapted appropriately for different age groups. The following section will discuss how the facilitator implemented the SPARCK model with a group of tenth-grade African American female students in a school district in the southeastern United States (for more details about the structure of the group, please see Harris et al., 2020). One of the primary goals of the psychoeducational group was to create a counterspace where safety and belonging could be generated, as a necessary precondition for any CCR activities. Additionally, we share process reflections as they relate to belongingness of the facilitator (who was a school counseling intern at the time), the group members, and the counselor educator overseeing the implementation of this group.

Parallel Experiences: Counseling Intern, Group Members, and Counselor Educator

School Counseling Intern Observations

I (second author) will organize my observations of the group chronologically, based on the journal I kept during the five sessions of the SPARCK group.

Session One: Story (Who Are You?)

Since the main purpose of the first session was to engage students in considering how contextual factors can influence postsecondary decision-making, I had students create an outline for a memoir of their life stories. Students had to title their memoir and think about four critical events in their lives that influenced them, or could possibly influence their future plans. One of the four chapters had to be titled "Transition to High School." Students struggled to get started with the activity at first, but providing examples such as Michelle Obama's memoir "Becoming" gave them a tangible model. Using self-disclosure to title my own memoir gave them the direction they needed.

In my experience, it is normal for students to be reluctant to share and engage within the first session, but to my surprise, this group was quite the opposite. The students openly shared and connected with each other. For example, one student discussed her sexual assault experience and struggles with being a teen mother, and another discussed her mother's death. They provided support to each other, and connected on the fact that their lives were changed, abruptly forcing them to take on different roles within their households. As the facilitator, I acknowledged and admired their bravery and resiliency through these difficult periods of grief and loss. This activity created a sense of safety and comfort with sharing each other's stories, and allowed them to connect with other young girls that looked like them. In that moment, I felt honored to be along this journey of empowerment, reflection, and finding their purpose.

Session Two: Purpose (What Are You Here to Do?)

I introduced the second session to the group as a "beginning step" to finding their best college or career fit. Students completed a values card sort with a list of 31 values on individual cards (see Osborn et al., 2015, for examples of sorting activities). The opportunity to review and understand our own values (e.g., achievement, cooperation, family, generosity, justice, self-knowledge) can shape our sense of purpose and happiness in a chosen field. We talked about ways to live our true and authentic selves by knowing and staying true to what is important to us in every area of our lives.

Due to limited session time, I allowed the students to choose their top five values and then write down how their values might influence their postsecondary choices. For example, my value "concern for others" influenced my future decision to go into counseling. I challenged students to consider how their past and present connect to their purpose. The group member that was a teenage parent had "family'" as her top value. She stated how she still wanted to go to college, and since her son was very important to her, she wanted to attend a college close by. There are a number of colleges and universities in the area, so she wanted to look into those. To conclude the session, students were given a chance to reflect on their experience for the day, and all agreed that sorting all value cards seemed overwhelming, so they appreciated the change of plans to choose five and found the time more productive.

Session Three: Aspirations (Where Do You Want to Go?)

I focused the third session by posing the question, "How can I find a college/career best suited for my strengths and interests?" I used the College Foundation of North Carolina's (CFNC.org) website and their resources for this activity. Each student had a different index card with the topics "Discovering Strengths and Interests," "Explore Careers," and "Explore Colleges." None of the students had explored the CFNC site before, so exposing them to resources such as the college search tool and career inventories proved to be helpful to them. For example, the student who had selected the task of exploring colleges picked three colleges that were all historically Black Colleges and Universities (HBCUs) and that were close to home, because she identified in previous sessions that her family and racial identity were two things that she valued. I noticed that this activity helped students think critically about the connection between their values and strengths and what they want to do after high school.

Session Four: Reflection and Connection (How Are You Doing? With Whom Can You Partner?)

Given all the activities in the previous sessions, taking time to slow down and reflect on how everyone was doing with this process was critical. As the facilitator, my goal was to give students an opportunity to process how they were feeling about college and career exploration, while also addressing how the intersectionality of their race and gender impacted the way they navigated these areas. Students felt a little more confident after learning about new resources like CFNC to help them, and seemed to appreciate the invitation to discuss how their identity might impact college and career decisions. The students were very focused and engaged on this topic, generating many questions and thinking carefully about how they could assess their belonging in various college and career spaces. For careers, students highlighted wanting to know the culture of the company, how managers support their employees, professional dress attire, the level of diversity among employees and many others. In addition, we applied these same questions to colleges (e.g., What would you look for while on a college tour?), and students again highlighted characteristics around diversity and inclusion, belonging, and campus/student life. I challenged the students to ask these questions on college tours and interviews so that they could find a good fit and feel this sense of belonging in other parts of their lives.

Acknowledging the possibility that future planning can feel stressful and overwhelming, I asked them to conclude the session by writing down their support systems and who they go to for guidance and motivation (e.g., family members, teachers, coaches, counselors). This served as a reminder of community and networks for belonging outside of the group setting. Especially for minoritized or underrepresented groups, the security of connection and belonging provides an important touchstone for future exploration.

Session Five: Kick-Start (What Will You Do Now?)

For the last session, students created a CCR pledge where they named three concrete steps they would commit to next on their college and career preparation journey. They discussed job shadowing, researching a job of interest, going on a college tour, and meeting with their school counselor as a few things they could do. To conclude our time together, I asked the group members to discuss their biggest takeaways from the group. One group member said that one of her biggest takeaways was being comfortable in sharing her story with other people. This was a big step for her that she hadn't done often, but being in a group with similar peers who seemed to have similar struggles helped her. This resonated with other students and they identified relating to the same feelings. Just having this time together created a sense of belonging that was an invaluable springboard into their futures.

EXPERIENCES OF THE GROUP MEMBERS

The SPARCK coaching model (Johnson & Delph, 2017) provided a structure for group members to not only share their stories but also process their thoughts and feelings about navigating the world as Black females. One student shared how her medical condition caused impulsivity such that she could not control blurting out things sometimes. She felt misunderstood at school and had got into trouble at school because of it. One student noted, "You know what I like about this group? I like that we're all Black. I can just be myself, unlike outside of here, I feel like I have to act a certain way." It is clear this group counterspace provided an avenue for students to feel they could be their true, authentic selves and demonstrated that developing strong kinship bonds with others who have similar identities can help affirm personal self-worth.

Throughout the course of this group, each student evolved in their comfort in engaging with each other and the session content. For example, it seemed one of the students felt isolated from the rest of the group in the beginning and did not speak much. However, every week she began to openly discuss more since she could relate to the other students' personal backgrounds and thoughts on CCR. She noted how the group made her feel more comfortable to openly discuss her concerns about college and career preparation. Another group member seemed to limit what colleges she could go to at the beginning of the group experience. However, learning about the college search option on CFNC broadened her scope to all of the colleges that might be a better fit for her. These shifts in the areas of college/careers, values, and interests really highlighted the importance of a space for belonging for Black girls, since they were empowered to explore their identities and what postsecondary options fit best for them.

In addition to these qualitative shifts in sense of belonging and agency, there was a preliminary indication of measurable change in the group participants. At the beginning and concluding portions of the group, the facilitator collected pre- and post-self-efficacy data (Gibbons & Borders, 2010) to measure the students' beliefs in their abilities to reach their college and career goals. Even though one student was absent from the data collection and the sample size was too small for analysis, overall, the scores seemed to indicate positive trends regarding students' self-efficacy about CCR (e.g., all students marked "very sure" they could get accepted to a college post-group, whereas only one student indicated "very sure" pre-group). Future groups with larger numbers could document this quantitative shift more definitively.

Sense of Belonging in the SPARCK Group

In this pilot psychoeducational group, sense of belonging was truly the foundational piece for the student participants, and without it, the information shared about CCR may not have found a space to germinate and grow. The availability of a formal group counterspace in high school to share frustrations and concerns was valued and needed by these young Black women. The ability to unburden first was an important precursor to the ability to dream about college and career, as noted in the case of the student who had initially limited her thinking about her future options, but then started to broaden her scope of thinking about college once she could feel safe and valued. The group together sorted through the topic of college/career environments, and how spaces that don't fit with a person's values and sense of self can result in unhappiness. The facilitator made it clear that the work of bringing one's genuine self to the fore in a caring and supportive environment was the precursor to stating goals and creating strategies for achieving them.

Facilitator Reflections

As the facilitator leading this group, I was very excited to lead a group for African American females, especially since being an African American female is such a huge part of my own identity. This group turned into one of my favorite parts of the week because I resonated with many of the group members' feelings of isolation and imposter syndrome from when I was a young student. Within the education system, there have not been many safe spaces that have affirmed my racial/cultural identity. Most spaces just did not provide the support that I needed. Thus, whenever I had these spaces for belonging, it made me feel more comfortable. Being able to create an avenue where students had this opportunity to feel they could be true to who they are in a school setting was amazing. I was impressed by their resiliency and the personal obstacles they had overcome at such a young age. I felt honored to be a part of this opportunity and extremely grateful for each student's vulnerability and willingness to share and ask questions.

Counselor Educator Reflections

I (first author) find it interesting to reflect on promoting sense of belonging for Black girls in K–12 settings when, working as a faculty member in the world of academia, I'm in a constant struggle to find my place. Though I can only think of one blatant, malicious act that occurred to me on a college campus in large part because I am a Black female, the subtle occurrences resonate as well. They range from not being offered proactive help and/or mentorship because I come across as "strong" and "self-sufficient" to being placed on committees and panels about diversity and equity issues because I seemed like I would be a "good fit." Though there were no harmful intentions in these latter instances, they did nothing to alleviate my feelings of imposter syndrome. I found myself wondering: Am I here to fulfill a need, or did I earn my right to be here?

When the opportunity arose to develop a CCR group model specifically for high school Black girls, I could not have been more thrilled to contribute. If I could plant the seed that they were valued and respected at an early age, perhaps these thoughts would reverberate for them throughout their postsecondary pursuits and beyond. Moreover, I wanted to provide an opportunity for these girls to connect with others with similar backgrounds. When one of my graduate students became available to facilitate this group, I became even more enthusiastic, in that these girls would have someone who "looked" like them to guide them throughout the experience. Little did I know that processing my graduate student's experience leading these CCR sessions for Black female high school students would influence my own sense of belonging as a counselor educator.

As I reviewed my graduate students' notes and reflections after each session, I could not help but be reminded about my own experiences in high school. I was one of those students who was fortunate enough to be in advanced classes, but unfortunate in that I seldom had a peer who looked like me to go through the experience alongside me. In fact, it wasn't until a Black female teacher took me under her wing and became my mentor that I started to feel somewhat comfortable in my accomplishments. Through her guidance, I applied for several scholarships and colleges, and had someone outside of my family to celebrate with when news of acceptance hit my mailbox. Whereas I would experience similar feelings of isolation as an undergraduate, graduate student, and now as a counselor educator, I fondly think about my high school mentor and her words of encouragement. Moreover, I actively seek opportunities to do the same for the next generation of Black females, which is why I wanted to support not only these high school students but my graduate students as well. Thus, reading their reflections about relationships and community warmed my heart and gave me hope that they all would remember these experiences of belonging as they pursued their goals—and eventually pay it forward as I have done.

DISCUSSION

Importantly, the sense of belonging that was forged among the Black girls participating in the SPARCK group was due in part to a common understanding of the painfulness of gender and race-based discrimination. Both the facilitator and the counselor educator reflected back on their adolescence and the lack of safe spaces to affirm their own identity or be supported in their developmental tasks. They both heard their own past isolation and lack of belonging echoed back to them in the group's stories, and thus connected in a very emotional way with the younger students. As summarized by the facilitator, almost all of the students had experiences of grief, loss, and trauma to share. The structures and systems that deny full belonging and personhood to Black women had impacted all of the members of this project, regardless of their age, educational attainment, or other identities. Being a Black woman in the United States had universality in the sense of confronting discrimination, resisting stereotypes, and trying to find space to express one's own genuine strengths and aspirations amidst hostile environments.

On the other hand, the joyfulness of the bonding that occurred among the young Black women in the group was emblematic of how meaningful counterspaces to generate a sense of belonging can be. The group quickly entered a space of willingness to share very personal material, and an excitement to hear their stories and core values shared and mirrored back to them. Students specifically mentioned the ability to "be myself in here, unlike outside where I have to act a certain way," and to find genuine camaraderie. When asked about their biggest takeaways, students did not mention the websites or resources, but instead the ability to share their stories together. Similarly, the graduate student intern who facilitated the group referred to it as "my favorite part of the week." Even the counselor educator reflected on how her aspirations as a young girl were always high, but her sense of belonging was low until she found a meaningful mentor with whom she could connect on several levels.

Because of the groundwork that was done to generate belonging, students were able to move into the advanced stage of sharing protective strategies with each other in the brief space of five weeks. The facilitator would model choices and actions from her own background and story when she felt the young women got stuck, giving the students trusted strategies that were culturally congruent for them. The students were able to actively connect their values for family, race/culture, and home with the possibility of applying to nearby HBCUs or maintaining connection throughout their college/career journeys. The group even brainstormed about how to navigate racism in workspaces or interviews, and how to assess campus environments on tours. Because of their shared understanding of the challenges of confronting racism and sexism simultaneously, the group members and facilitator could truly grasp the scope of the challenges and find meaningful and realistic pathways through them.

Finally, the counselor educator was able to see the generational impact of opening a space for belonging and aspirations, connecting her own experiences as a young Black girl in school to her current desire to mentor others who look like her. Although the additional labor of mentoring others can be daunting, through a mechanism like this group, the counselor educator was able to mentor a graduate student intern and indirectly impact the lives of the high school students. In this way, creative structures to generate belonging can have broader ripple effects as mentees grow up to pay it forward to others.

The importance of counterspaces for connection and belonging for marginalized or underrepresented groups cannot be overstated. Thus, one key takeaway from the tiered reflections about the group is that social identities do matter. From the counselor educator's memories about struggling to find a sense of belonging as a bright young Black girl to the facilitator's joyful participation in this counterspace and the member's growing confidence in themselves and each other, the solidarity and connection forged by their shared social identities was powerful. For educators or advocates who are not Black women, this may be a call to use any institutional power or resources to support the creation of counterspaces for and by Black women and girls as a primary goal. For educators or advocates who are Black women, this tool may be a helpful practice to encourage the creation of safe spaces to cultivate growth.

CONCLUSION

Filling the educational pipeline with a critical mass of young Black women can mean greater individual success or CCR but also greater group and community access to mentors and spaces of belonging. This broader ripple effect is an important aspect of the success of this project. It suggests the power of the potential reciprocal nature of belonging. The students, the intern, and the faculty member all genuinely learned from each other. The students not only constructed their own counterspace for belonging together with the facilitator but also catalyzed a new understanding of belonging as experienced upon reflection by the counselor educator and intern/facilitator. The potential ripple effects go backward, forward, and sideways. This example from the lived experiences of Black women reminds us that belonging cannot be bestowed—it is genuinely coconstructed within and across spaces of community.

Acknowledgment

We dedicate this chapter to Brooklyn Harris, with our deep wishes for her and the next generation of Black girls to have a sense of belonging.

REFERENCES

ACT. (2016). The condition of college and career readiness 2015: African American students. Retrieved from https://equityinlearning.act.org/wp-content/uploads/2016/06/2015-africanamerican.pdf

Annamma, S. A., Anyon, Y., Joseph, N. M., Farrar, J., Greer, E., Downing, B., & Simmons, J. (2019). Black girls and school discipline: The complexities of being overrepresented and understudied. *Urban Education*, 1–32.

Beljan, P. (2011). Misdiagnosis of culturally diverse students. In J. A. Castellano, A. Frazier, J. A. Castellano, A. Frazier (eds.), *Special Populations in Gifted Education: Understanding our Most Able Students from Diverse Backgrounds* (pp. 317–332). Waco, TX: Prufrock Press. Retrieved from EBSCOhost.

Booker, K.C. (2007). Likeness, comfort, and tolerance: Examining African American adolescents' sense of school belonging. *Urban Review 39,* 301–317. doi:10.1007/s11256-007-0053-y

Bradshaw, C. P., Mitchell, M. M., O'Brennan, L. M., & Leaf, P. J. (2010). Multilevel exploration of factors contributing to the overrepresentation of Black students in office disciplinary referrals. *Journal of Educational Psychology, 102*, 508–520.

Bryant, R. (2015). College preparation for African American students: Gaps in the high school educational experience. Retrieved from http://www.clasp.org/resources-and-publications/publication-1/College-readiness2-2.pdf

Carter, D. J. (2007). Why the Black kids sit together at the stairs: The role of identity-affirming counter-spaces in a predominantly White high school. *Journal of Negro Education,* 542–554.

College Board. (2014). The 10th annual AP report to the nation. Retrieved from http://media.collegeboard.com/digitalServices/pdf/ap/rtn/10th-annual/10th-annual-ap-report-to-the-nation-single-page.pdf

Evans-Winters, V. (2005). *Teaching Black Girls: Resiliency in Urban Classrooms.* New York: Peter Lang Publishing.

Faircloth, B. S., & Hamm, J. V. (2005). Sense of belonging among high school students representing 4 ethnic groups. *Journal of Youth and Adolescence, 34,* 293–309. doi:10.1007/s10964-005-5752-7

Frizell, S., & Nave, F. (2008). A preliminary analysis of factors affecting the persistence of African-American females in engineering degree programs. Paper presented at the American Society for Engineering Education Annual Conference, Pittsburgh, PA.

Gibbons, M. M., & Borders, L. D. (2010). A measure of college going self-efficacy for middle school students. *Professional School Counseling, 13*(4), 234–243.

Harris, P. N., Gonzalez, L. M., Kearney, B., & Ingram, K. (2020) Finding their SPARCK: College and career readiness groups for African American females. *The Journal for Specialists in Group Work, 45,* 40–55. doi:10.1080/01933922.2019.1702128

Hill, C., Corbett, C., & St. Rose, A. (2010). Why so few? Women in science, technology, engineering, and mathematics. Retrieved from http://www.aauw.org/resource/why-so-few-women-in-science-technology-engineering-mathematics/

Hing, J. (2014, September 25). New report detail barriers to Black girls' success [Blog post]. Retrieved from http://www.colorlines.com/articles/new-report-details-barriers-black-girls-success

Johnson, W. H. (2017, Oct). Revolutionizing advising and coaching with life design in mind. Presented at the National Academic Advising Association national conference, St. Louis, MO.

Johnson, W. H., & Delph, M. (2017). 8th Life Design Catalyst Coach Training Program. Unpublished training manual from the University of North Carolina at Greensboro.

Moore, G. W., Slate, J. R., Edmonson, S. L., Combs, J. P., Bustamante, R., & Onwuegbuzie, A. J. (2010). High school students and their lack of preparedness for college: A statewide study. *Education and Urban Society, 42*(7), 817–838.

Morris, E. W. (2007). "Ladies" or "loudies"? Perceptions and experiences of Black girls in classrooms. *Youth Society, 38*, 490–515.

National Coalition on Black Civic Participation. (2014). Black women in the United States, 2014: Progress and challenges. Retrieved from http://ncbcp.org/news/rel eases/bwr_report_release_2014_POST/

Osborn, D. S., Kronholz, J. F., & Finklea, J. T. (2015). Card sorts. In M. McMahon and M. Watson (eds.), *Career Assessment* (pp. 81–88). Brill Sense.

Osterman, K. F. (2000). Students' need for belonging in the school community. *Review of Educational Research, 70*(3), 323–367.

Reid, K. W., Jefferson, E., & Thomas, V. (2016). Bringing more Black girls and women into engineering. Retrieved from National Science Foundation: http://ste mrules.com/is-the-black-engineering-crisis-a-woman-problem/

Rollock, N. (2007). Why Black girls don't matter: Exploring how race and gender shape academic success in an inner city school. *Support for Learning, 22*, 197–202. doi:10.1111/j.1467-9604.2007.00471.x

Sample, R. A. (2010). A case of Black male: The overrepresentation of African American males in special education as emotionally disturbed. *Dissertation Abstracts International Section A: Humanities and Social Sciences, 70*(11-). (2010-99090-401)

Schott Foundation for Public Education. (2016 May). Shining a spotlight on Black girls. Retrieved from http://schottfoundation.org/infographic/shining-spotlight-bl ack-girls

Sherwin, G., Wedekind J., & Reynoso-Palley, A. (2016). Leaving girls behind: An analysis of Washington D.C.'s "Empowering Males of Color" initiative. Retrieved from https://www.aclu.org/sites/default/files/field_document/ aclu_emoc_report_5 -9-16_formatted_final.pdf

Smith-Evans, L., & George, J. (2014). Unlocking opportunity for African American girls: A call to action for educational equity. Retrieved from National Women's Law Center: http://www.nwlc.org/sites/default/files/pdfs/unlocking_opportunity _for_african_american_girls_final.pdf

The Sentencing Project. (2015). Incarcerated women and girls. Retrieved from http: //www.sentencingproject.org/wp-content/uploads/2016/02/Incarcerated-Women-a nd-Girls.pdf

United States Department of Education Office of Civil Rights. (2014). Gender equity in education: A data snapshot. Retrieved from http://www2.ed.gov/about/offices/li st/ocr/docs/gender-equity-in-education.pdf

Vavrus, F., & Cole, K. (2002). "I didn't do nothin'": The discursive construction of school suspension. *The Urban Review, 34*, 87–111.

Chapter 8

Allies, Advocates, and Agents of Change

Resisting Barriers to Belonging in Sixth Grade

Beverly S. Faircloth, Kia Barrett, and Jill L. McClanahan

In her 2017 TED Talk, Dena Simmons (director of Education at Yale Center for Emotional Intelligence) powerfully captured the barriers to learning often inflicted on youth at school:

> There is emotional damage done when young people can't be themselves, when they are forced to edit who they are in order to be acceptable. . . . Why, in the process of getting a better education, did I have to endure the trauma of erasing what made me, me? Youth pay a profound price when their schooling sends them the message that they . . . must leave their identities at home in order to be successful. Every child deserves an education that guarantees the safety to learn in the comfort of one's own skin.

Summarizing these insights, she claims that

> different things tell you that this environment wasn't created for people like you. . . . Constantly you're getting messages where your experience, or your identity, isn't present . . . is erased; it's invisible . . . You start to panic, to say <u>Do I belong here</u>? (Blad, 2020, p. 9).

Indeed, against the backdrop of the complex identity, ethnic and cultural intersectionalities that characterize most of life in the United States today, sense of belonging has recently been referred to as one of the premier social issues of our time (Allen & Boyle, 2016).

As one of the first and most enduring settings in which youth from disparate cultures encounter one another and diverse societal norms, learning spaces represent potentially significant contexts of belonging. Research and theory have consistently demonstrated that sense of belonging serves as a pivotal determinant of positive development (Anderman & Freeman, 2004; Author, 2005, 2018; Baumeister & Leary, 1995; Goodenow, 1993; Juvonen, 2006). Moreover, there is ample evidence that belonging mediates (i.e., is foundational to) motivation, achievement, and learning (Authors, 2005; Benner et al., 2008; Knifsend et al., 2018). Importantly though, research has also begun to reveal how learning contexts both foster *and impede* belonging (Faircloth, 2005, 2018; Berry et al., 2006; Kia-Keating & Ellis, 2007; Urdan, 2011). For example, school curricula and policies have persistently excluded the perspectives and histories of minority youth, seemingly operating under the assumption that the process of becoming educated is a race-neutral or colorblind experience (Cammorata, 2015; Dee & Penner, 2017; de los Rios et al., 2014; Paris & Alim, 2017). Until we embrace more culturally and critically informed approaches to understanding youth development, considering the impact of issues such as student ethnicity and culture, we are doomed to replicate this status quo instead of ameliorating the learning barriers (un) intentionally levied against many students.

Many threads of theory and research have identified culturally and critically informed perspectives regarding schooling. The bottom line is that understanding and validating the extremely varied perspectives and discourses of youth in our society, and recognizing and challenging barriers to that goal, are essential to the democratic project of schooling. Ethnic studies (Cammarota, 2015) stands as one primary example of praxis that attempts to accomplish this. An educational praxis used to provide students with tools for identifying, reflecting on, critiquing, and acting against systemic racism and other forms of marginalization, ethnic studies attempts to promote democratic principles of education (Dee & Penner, 2017; de los Rios et al., 2014; Jay, 2003).

It is therefore the goal of this chapter to further unpack how adolescents navigate connections between learning experiences and their developing awareness of their own ethnicity and culture, especially among nondominant groups. Specifically, the project explores the intersection between participation in an after-school ethnic studies club and the development of "critical consciousness" (CC) among sixth-grade students. It has been argued that such CC (Ladson Billings, 1995, 2004) would empower students with the kinds of understandings and skills that could contribute to their ability to establish an animating sense of belonging. Existing models of ethnic studies curricula provided frameworks from which to draw ideas, however, because many of these models are in place in high schools and beyond, and this project is based on the hope that such meaningful work can begin as early as middle school, the teachers and researchers involved in this study worked carefully to select/modify activities to be appropriate for middle-grade students.

Just as Gutierrez (2013) claimed that a quality multicultural curriculum functions both as a mirror (through which students can see themselves in the curriculum) and a window (through which they can imagine and create a new world), it was hoped that students in the project would recognize and validate their own cultural reference points and those of others, to recognize marginalization with its barriers to belonging, and identify and enact strategies to resist it.

SENSE OF BELONGING

Sense of belonging, that is, an enduring positive sense of authentic connection within one's primary contexts, has become well-established as an essential underlying element of positive development, motivation, engagement, and achievement (Faircloth, 2005; Baumeister & Leary, 1995; Benner et al., 2008; Goodenow, 1993; Knifsend et al., 2018; Urdan, 2011). The concept of belonging has traditionally been well-anchored in interpersonal relationships and extracurricular/participatory school experiences (Anderman & Freeman, 2004; Finn, 1989; Goodenow, 1993; Osterman, 2000). More recent theory and research however has recognized that the multiple intersectionalities between students' culture, identity, and voice and their learning experiences provide both supports *and barriers* to belonging (Author, 2009, 2011, 2018; Gonzalez et al., 2014; Urdan, 2011; Wong et al., 2003). The emerging notion of rightful presence (i.e., a sense of full respect, belonging, or voice within one's classroom or school) illustrates this new lens on belonging (Faircloth, chapter 1, this volume; Barnett, 2005; Squires & Darling, 2013). When students feel their identity, culture, race, background, or circumstances do not have full respect, such dispossession erects both large and small barriers to engagement or learning (referred to by Ahmed, 2014, as "atmospheric walls," para. 24) that intensify feelings that one does not fit in, potentially inhibiting one's participation. An animating sense of connection between context and culture (i.e., sense of belonging) easily deteriorates amidst such barriers or lack of rightful presence (Faircoth, 2009, 2012, 2017, 2018).

While acknowledging the complexity of culture as a construct that undergirds belonging we draw on Warikoo and Carter's (2009) explanation that culture is characterized by shared values, beliefs, behaviors, and styles, that is, "tool-kits of symbols, stories, rituals, and worldviews" (Swidler, 1986 p. 273).

This includes practices ranging from speech styles and language to specific kinds of physical interactions, to tastes in music, clothing, and food, and other ethnic cues. Research has consistently demonstrated that a strong connection with one's heritage culture, coupled with a strong connection with a host culture (e.g., school), consistently promotes psychological well-being for youth. For example, both the model of "biculturalism" set forth by LaFromboise, Coleman, and Gerton (1993, p. 395) and Garcia Coll and colleagues' (1996, p. 1891) "integrative model" of development among minority youth advocate for sociocultural supports that bridge an individual's culture of heritage and the host culture within which they find themselves. Ethnic discrimination serves as a classic case in point; it can convey to individuals that they are devalued because of their ethnic group membership, a depreciative experience that threatens their healthy psychological development likely to increase the probability of negative developmental outcomes, while a strong sense of belonging acts as a promotive and protective factor by both compensating for and buffering against the impact of perceived discrimination (Garcia Coll et al., 1996; Gonzalez et al., 2014; Urdan, 2012; Urdan & Munoz, 2012; Wong et al., 2003). Students' own explanations of their belonging highlight the importance of cultural sensitivity to different perceptions of belonging and how it is best supported (Aguinaga & Gloria, 2015; Author, 2018; Beaudrie et al., 2009; Hill, 2006; Urdan, 2011; Urdan & Munoz, 2012). It is essential therefore for teachers, school leaders, counselors, social workers, teacher educators, educational psychologists, learning scientists, and educational researchers to incorporate serious consideration of students' cultures into theories, research, practice, and measurement of belonging (Cartmell & Bond, 2015; Faircloth & Hamm, 2005).

Unfortunately, the instruments of society and schooling are not always adapted to the variety of students' cultural backgrounds, reinforcing instead dominant codes, artifacts, language, practices, interactions, and styles, and allocating resources based on the degree to which students possess dominant cultural capital (Bourdieu & Passeron, 1990; Farkas et al., 1990; Stanton-Salazar, 1997; Urrieta, 2009). This current state of affairs illustrates not only the importance of this issue but also the urgency of providing practical suggestions to the many individuals who are working to develop more culturally and critically informed practices. Unfortunately, as Wong et al. (2003) point out, ethnic or cultural differences in belonging have only been studied inconsistently, with mixed results, suggesting that more research in this area is warranted. We turned to an ethnic studies curriculum for potential solutions.

Ethnic Studies

Ethnic studies can trace its roots back to the push for multicultural education during the civil rights movement of the late 1960s (Dee & Penner, 2017; de los Rios et al., 2014; Sleeter 2011; Tintiangco-Cubales et al., 2015). Too often, traditional textbooks, curricula, district guidelines, and school practices adopted in the United States offered oversimplified, colorblind views of US history, culture, and learning (de los Rios et al., 2014; Hughes, 2007). Groups of people who had been historically marginalized by systemic inequalities based on race, ethnicity, language, culture, and other categories of difference challenged such discriminatory practices and demanded curricula and policies that were more representative of the US population and less dominated by Euro-American histories, perspectives, and experiences (Banks, 2012; Jay, 2003; Sleeter, 2011). Ethnic studies aimed to leverage authentic stories of marginalized groups to begin the necessary cognitive conflict to jar dysconscious racism among dominant and nondominant youth alike. The early roots of ethnic studies emerged from models such as "multicultural education" (Banks, 2006; Jay, 2003); "culturally relevant pedagogy" (Ladson-Billings, 1995, p. 74; see also Brown-Jeffy & Cooper, 2011; Dee & Penner, 2017; Tintiangco-Cubales et al., 2015); "culturally sustaining pedagogy" (Paris & Alim, 2017, p. 6; Paris, 2012); and "critical race theory" (Giroux, 2020, p. 175; see also Freire, 2000; Jay, 2003; Solorzano & Yosso, 2000). What all notable variations of ethnic studies have in common is their orientation toward "developing students who have the knowledge, skills, and attitudes needed to function in an ethnically and racially diverse world" (Banks, 2006, p. 137; Cammerota, 2016; Ladson-Billings, 2014; Sleeter, 2011), providing students and teachers with the opportunity to resist the barriers generated by educational models that have traditionally been predominantly "whitestream" (Urrieta, 2009, p. 47).

Ethnic studies programs in K–12 public schools have demonstrated evidence of positive student outcomes (de los Rios et al., 2014; Dee & Penner, 2017; Sleeter, 2011). For example, programs that allowed students to explore the lived experiences of Chicana/o young people in California (studying the history of immigration, civic engagement and critical literacies such as writing letters to local council members, and speaking publicly at community forums) (de los Rios, 2013; de los Rios et al., 2014) found that ninth graders increased their attendance (i.e., reduced unexcused absences), grade point average, and credits earned (Dee and Penner, 2017). Similarly, students in ethnic studies programs in Arizona reported increases in academic confidence in writing, identity development, critical literacies, higher student achievement (writing, reading, mathematics, and AIMS tests), and the highest graduation rates in their district despite having the lowest academic achievement during their freshman year (Cabrera et al., 2014; Tintiangco-Cubales et al., 2015).

Prior to endeavors such as ethnic studies, efforts to acculturate and assimilate ethnically minoritized groups had managed to produce what amounts to cultural and linguistic assault, which continues to have devastating effects on the access, achievement, and well-being of diverse students (Paris & Alim, 2017). Rather than measuring how closely students perform White middle-class norms, ethnic studies programs provide a pedagogy that explores, honors, and extends their own cultural practices, thus positioning students in respected, productive, agentic ways (Paris, 2012; Urietta, 2009; Vetter et al., 2010). Ladson-Billings (2014) suggests that simultaneously having students critically evaluate, offer solutions, and take action to challenge the status quo strengthens student awareness and problem-solving skills, potentially empowering them to learn to dismantle barriers erected by the status quo. It is just this sort of transformation that we hoped to harness with our middle grades students by exploring their belonging through the experience of ethnic studies.

"Club": An Exploration of Belonging

Given that racial and ethnic inequities, with their barriers to belonging, continue to persist, including in middle schools, the purpose of the current study was to engage sixth-grade students from an ethnically and culturally diverse urban middle school in content and activities that intentionally explored inequality and marginalization in their lived realities. This was designed to support their cultural competence and CC, with an eye to the impact on their sense of belonging. After examining various theoretical and practical models of ethnic studies and cultural competence/CC efforts and their impact, essential elements of such programs were selected:

1. Students explored their own identity as well as whether their identity was validated in learning settings, in order to center students' personal identities, cultures, and realities.
2. The work was centered on students' everyday lives in their homes, communities and schools, in order to make the club more culturally and historically relevant to them.
3. Club discussion included opportunities to explore taking action against marginalization for themselves and others.
4. Ethnic studies work was anchored in the traditional activities required of a sixth-grade English Language Arts class (e.g., reading, writing, presenting, discourse), thereby hopefully yielding cognitive as well as cultural and critical gains, as well as demonstrating how such gains can emerge within the required pedagogical practices.

For ease of syntax, the term "critical consciousness" will be used to capture the constellation of cultural and critical experiences and understandings that lie at the heart of this work and are essential for belonging. This is not meant to minimize the central role of cultural competence. Rather, both are viewed as inextricable elements of the experiences required for rightful presence, agency, and belonging.

While research increasingly asserts that such programs are beneficial and necessary for all students, the majority of reliable research draws from samples of high school and college students. This leaves explorations of their efficacy with middle-grade students almost nonexistent, resulting in a gap in our understanding of the efficacy or developmentally appropriate design of these models for younger adolescents. This is despite evidence that students inquire about issues of race and ethnicity as soon as early childhood (Paris & Alim, 2017) and that middle-school students can and do exhibit awareness, concern, and agency regarding the very issues at the heart of this chapter (Faircloth, 2017, 2018; Wong et al., 2013). Moreover, there is evidence that experiences of ethnic discrimination influence development during early adolescence and is a potential threat to socioemotional well-being (Wong, Eccles, & Sameroff, 2013). This is especially noteworthy because, at this age, adolescents are already at an increased risk for declining motivation, poorer self-perceptions, greater susceptibility to conforming to peers' negative influences, and involvement in problem behaviors, each with long-term implications (Authors, 2005; Eccles et al., 1997; Wong et al., 2013).

Context and Members

The school district where this inquiry took place is situated in an urban area in a southeastern state in the United States. The school is a Title 1 Middle School (grades 6–8) home to 716 students, including African American (49 percent), Latinx (20 percent), White (20 percent), Asian (4 percent), and Other/Mixed (5 percent). Students eligible for Free/Reduced Lunch based on families' gross annual income comprised 64 percent of the student body. In addition, 19 percent of enrolled students are identified as Students with Disabilities, and 6 percent are identified with Limited English Proficiency. The area is also host to one of the fastest growing Immigrant and Refugee populations in the United States.

Students given the opportunity to participate in this study were members of four classes (of 22–35 students each) taught by one sixth-grade English Language Arts teacher. This year, students reported challenges to their belonging or sense of emotional safety (which we referred to as rightful presence) in class, especially with regard to social and identity-based and culturally based bullying. About one month into the fall semester, the students were invited to participate in this hour-long, weekly ethnic studies club, immediately after school. Participants involved in this inquiry were students who returned assent and consent forms from among these four classrooms. On average, approximately 10 students attended each club meeting each week. These students represented various cultural and ethnic backgrounds including, African American, Asian American, Arab, Vietnamese, and Venezuelan.

Capturing Youth's Stories

Four sources were drawn on to understand students' stories. Every week, as students participated in the planned ethnic studies activities, the meetings were audio-recorded, transcribed, and coded. Every session was also followed by extensive field notes by the researcher which were coded by the researchers. All student written work (a small assortment of written responses to club activities) were collected and analyzed for themes related to their insights and reflections on club activities. Club members also participated in semi-structured, one-on-one interviews at the end of the year to explore their perceptions and attitudes toward their experience in the ethnic studies club and school in general. (Interviews were no longer than 45 minutes, were audio-recorded, and immediately transcribed for thorough analysis; interview protocol items are available upon written request.)

Club Design

A developmentally appropriate ethnic studies curriculum for a sixth-grade after school club, following the four principles outlined above and the models upon which this work is based, was designed by their sixth-grade English Language Arts teacher, a graduate student researcher from a local university, and a university faculty member. The graduate student researcher (an African American female) served as the facilitator for the club. She also assisted the students' teacher in her classroom two days a week during the fall semester and attended activities like the school's open house to meet students' parents and establish herself as a trusted presence in the classroom. In order to strongly center student perspectives (a tenet that lies at the heart of ethnic studies and CC) a variety of resources representative of the students' culture were incorporated, including spoken word, short films, video clips, and news articles to contribute to and draw upon their funds of knowledge. Club activities closely explored students' own identities, a crucial component of ethnic studies and a hot topic for students. Also, for these students, one of their most obvious and immediate experiences with power, oppression, and marginalization was school bullying and this became a focus of many discussions. Examples of these student-centric activities include the following.

Experiences with race and racism. Adapted from the Anti-Defamation League, this activity was used to provide an opportunity for students to explore a range of stories (through video and written pieces) of young people's first encounters with race and racism, as well as to reflect on their own early experiences. Students watched a four-minute video, titled "Being 12: 'People Think I'm Supposed to Talk Ghetto, Whatever That Is.'" In this video, 12-year-olds (the participants' age) share their ideas and experiences about race, ethnicity, and racism. After watching the video students were given the opportunity to share their reactions. They also read, "First Encounters with Racism," consisting of four short stories where US teens reflect on their first experience with racism. Students then engaged in discussion questions addressing how they could/would have responded in such situations.

"The Present" and living with a disability. Also from the Anti-Defamation League, this activity was used to provide an opportunity for students to watch and reflect upon an animated short film, learn more about people with disabilities, and the "othering" these individuals experienced. "The Present," a three-minute film is about a boy whose mom gifts him with a puppy. Initially the boy rejects the puppy after realizing it has a physical disability. It is later revealed that the boy, too, is living with a physical disability. After watching the video, students were able to share their reactions to the video and engage in discussions about ableism.

Identity-based bullying. Several activities required students to identify important aspects of their identity and how to deal with identity-based bullying. The goal was for the students to discover some similarities and differences they shared with one another, explore aspects of their identity that were important to them, discuss identity-based bullying, and brainstormed actions or solutions to bullying.

FINDINGS AND INTERPRETATIONS

The stories of the students' emerging CC in the ethnic studies club unveiled five overlapping and interconnected themes. Students' initial fledgling perceptions of their identity, and their claims that everything was "fine" (or there was nothing they could do regardless of how they were perceived or if they were bullied), transformed into a heartfelt cry to be validated and included by the end of the second semester. Similarly, their discomfort with, and the nascent nature of their understanding of (or readiness to discuss), racism early in the school year gave way to honest vulnerability about incidents that led to feelings of inferiority, rejection, and othering later in the year. Similarly, it was only later in the year that small steps in agency emerged among these students. For these sixth-grade students, this took shape around issues that tangibly emerged in their own worlds (e.g., microaggressions, school-based bullying) along with their burgeoning efforts to enact the identities of "ally, advocate, or agent of change" as explained below.

Elementary Perceptions of Identity

> I feel sad about my life. If I ever get a chance to [be] someone else, I will.
>
> —Abdul

Students in the club frequently participated in activities and discourses that required them to examine issues of how they perceive themselves, how they were perceived by others, and factors that influence their identities. Early in the year, the majority of students described and introduced themselves in terms of what they liked or didn't like about themselves and how others perceived them. It seemed difficult for students to describe who they were outside of concrete parameters. For instance, Shana wrote, "I love to cook and paint. . . . I love to dance and sing." Natasha shared, "I like to dance, play basketball, wrestle." When asked to tell the group about themselves this early in the school year, they did not focus on race, ethnicity, or culture. During one activity, for instance, Josh explained that he did not know his background. After thinking further, he shared that he considers himself to be African American but stated that he really didn't know what that meant, although he felt it was important to him in some way.

Most of the students made a point of saying that they were fine with how they were perceived by others. However, during a "four corners" activity later in the fall semester, many of them moved to the "strongly agree" corner in response to the statement, "My true identity is not the same as what others might perceive it to be." As the semester progressed, some of these same students also disclosed parts of their identity that contributed to a negative self-concept. For example, in response to a writing assignment, Deja wrote, "I don't really like the way my face looks, and I feel like nobody will like me when I get older." and Sarafina described disliking her body size and feeling judged because of it. Both girls described an obvious mismatch between how they wanted to be perceived and how they felt people perceived them. Abdul disclosed in his writing that "I feel sad about my life. If I ever get a chance to [be] someone else, I will." Likewise, Alexander explained that he is often misperceived because "they know that I am disabled, and they think I can't do anything, but I can." It is of note that these particular student comments came later in the fall semester, after students had been specifically asked to share a part of themselves that was unknown to many. Moreover, many of these more intimate insights were shared only with the club facilitator (primarily in writing), not the group, possibly illustrating students' focus on maintaining an acceptable image among their peers.

Confronting the Cost of Identity-Based Exclusion

> They hide who they are because they don't want to feel like they're worthless.
>
> —Kevin

Later in the school year, students shared stories about times when they did not feel as though they fit in. Most of these stories were related to school experiences with their peers, and were described through a deficit lens, as though students viewed themselves as lacking what was needed to be part of a group. When expanding on the topic of their lack of belonging, most students' experiences related to bullying were connected to aspects of their personal appearance that were made fun of (acne, height, body size, and image) or their skin color (e.g., being called African because of their darker complexion).

Other students described experiences of self-censorship. For example, Kevin wrote,

> When I was five, I watched "Team Umizoomi." I loved it, but my friends didn't. We had to watch the show in class, and I knew the whole song and my friends just booed it. So, I booed too and got in trouble. The next day we had to watch it again, but this time I was in this [other] group of kids and I sang the song and my friends did not hear me or see me.

When asked why he thought students would put on a masquerade in situations like this, he responded, "They hide who they are because they don't want to feel like they're worthless." When students were asked if they believed they could be their complete selves in school, all except one student responded, "Yes." However, data revealed a consistent pattern of students' self-censoring to avoid being excluded or seen as different.

Even as students were beginning to share the pain of exclusion in a vulnerable way in club, many described experiences of exclusion as if they were insignificant, insisting: "You aren't supposed to let what people say hurt you," "I really don't care what people think," and "I come to school to learn, I don't care about making friends." Somehow the students had come to believe that if they ignored their feelings they eventually went away, or perhaps that not caring represents some form of strength. Only one of the students seemed to feel free enough to reveal a lack of certainty on this stance. One day Kevin said:

Raul [a Puerto Rican character in a story who wanted to be an artist] is still following his dreams. I'm telling you the truth right now. It would be pretty hard
for me to keep on pushing like he is to do a dream if my brother or some other
kids were telling me 'you shouldn't paint.' I think that's pretty hard to keep it
in. And I would actually try to maybe quit and do the things that everyone else
does. If someone kept saying it, I would actually start believing it, till I finally
break.

Elementary Understandings of Racism

Everyone living in the hood is not bad, they just can't afford to live
somewhere else. . . . It's their fault cause they didn't make the right
decisions in life.

—Natasha

Because ethnic studies emphasizes the importance of centering issues
of race during our meetings together, the students were asked critical
questions that would center how they understood and experienced racism.
During the first week after receiving the book "Bronx Masquerade" at the
beginning of the club, students came to the club facilitator at school to say
that they believed the book was filled with racism. They asked, *Are we supposed to read books like this?* This could be because students did not typically discuss issues of race and racism in school as openly as was done in
the book, or perhaps it was a topic that they preferred to avoid. They were
encouraged to continue reading and assured that they would be given the
opportunity to voice their concerns during the next club meeting. During
the next meeting, it became clear that students were referring to particular
comments made by an African American character, Tyrone. For instance,
one of his comments read:

White folk! Who they think they kidding? They might as well go blow smoke
up somebody else's you-know-what, cause a Black man's got no chance in this
country. I be lucky if I make it to twenty-one with all these fools running "round
with AK-47s." (p. 8)

In these comments, Tyrone is expressing his thoughts after being told by
his White teachers that he needed to plan for his future. It came to light that
club members perceived anything that blatantly called attention to a person's
racial identity racist.

Quite naturally, the students' perceptions of racism initiated a critical dialogue regarding what they perceived racism to mean and whether
Tyrone's comments indicated he was racist. Questions like, "What is he

trying to say here?" "What is he trying to express"? and "Why do you think he feels this way?" were used to encourage their thinking. At first, students-related racism to any comment about a person's skin color, intent to do harm or cause offense, or critique someone's culture. For example, Kevin said, "To me, racism is if you're talking about someone else's color." and Lily considered Tyrone's comments to be racist because she believed they represented false judgments, arguing that a Black man does have a chance in this country. In contrast, India boldly proclaimed, "But he's black. It doesn't make any sense . . . but he's black so it's not being racist. He's talking about himself." Aliyah added a bit more nuance noting how tone and intent mattered, "I feel like it's the way you say it. Because sometimes you can just be talking in general, and sometimes you can be trying to be hurtful." After much debate regarding the context of the text, students began to develop an understanding of why Tyrone made his comments. Abdul reasoned that Tyrone felt like he had no chance with the Whites, while Sarafina added,

> In his head, he thinks that people favor whites over blacks more because, you know, racism is still around. Kevin added, I actually do remember in the book. I think he was talking about his dad got shot and blasted away and didn't make it to 30 or 31.

Such discussion supported students in developing an understanding of Tyrone's statements as a testament to his reality rather than racism toward Black men. When Natasha talked about growing up in the *hood*, she was asked what she meant by that term. She explained that it was a "bad neighborhood where people sell drugs." When asked what type of people typically live in the hood, she said, "Black people. Sometimes you see White people in the hood because they want to be like black people and start selling drugs or they are cops." When asked, "Is everyone living in the hood bad? she responded, Everyone living in the hood is not bad, they just can't afford to live somewhere else. . . . It's their fault 'cause they didn't make the right decisions in life."

As students revealed these emerging understandings of racism through the sharing of stories and engaging in debate, it appeared that they were aware of individual forms of racism that occurred within interpersonal relationships and could easily identify a racial prejudice or discrimination that was flagrant. However, most students were still relatively unaware of the role of daily or systemic racism in creating these dynamics in our culture. In fact, students were more likely to blame victims of systemic racism for their circumstances. They did not have concrete ideas about how to challenge racism other than to "be nice to people and treat people equally."

Confronting the Cost of Racism in Their Lives

> He [Kevin's younger brother] was telling me at home - because we are
> brothers and we do *brother secrets*. He only tells me. . . . When they
> would play tag or something he would never get tagged because no one
> wanted to touch him at all. . . . Yeah and he said this girl said he was
> *spider head* [because of his black hair]
>
> —Kevin

As the year progressed, students began to display a deeper level of vulnerability than they had previously by sharing experiences with racism they
admitted to be hurtful. Regardless of being born in the United States, some
students described experiences where they had been treated like a foreigner.
For instance, Aliyah shared:

> Well my dad's not fully Mexican because he was born here, but his parents are.
> Since I look like him, because he looks like a Mexican, I'm automatically seen
> as a Mexican. But I was born here. I am a US Citizen . . . [but] automatically
> everyone is always like, *why don't you go back to Mexico or something* and I'm
> like, *I'm not from Mexico. I'm from here.*

This experience was representative of many of the students' experiences, as
they all agreed that people commonly assume that if you speak Spanish or
look Hispanic that you are from Mexico. However, "not only do they assume
you are from Mexico, they assume *'you have no right to be in the US'*"
[emphasis added].

Kevin shared a similar experience when he was treated differently because
of his African American identity. He explained,

> I used to live in Virginia. And just saying, there were a lot of White kids in this
> one class. My only friend was Anthony. . . . He was my only friend because
> me and him were the only brown kids in the class. . . . I just saw him, and I
> saw everyone else. I was like [makes a face]. I didn't really understand what
> that was until people started picking [i.e., picking sides for games] . . . we were
> always the last picks. . . . I never knew what racism was or what democracy
> was but they would always do the "I'll pick her or I'll pick him" and whenever
> I would think they were gonna pick me, I was like [looks extremely excited]
> YAAAY!!!! but then it was like this [demonstrates being passed over]. I was
> like [demonstrates feeling let down].

Not only did Kevin and Anthony experience feeling like *the other*, but they
also experienced being perceived as *the inferior other*. When asked if any of
them had experienced prejudice or discrimination, Kevin also shared:

I remember, this is actually my little brother telling me at home—because we are brothers and we do *brother secrets* he only tells me. . . . He would never get, when they would play tag or something, he would never get tagged because no one wanted to touch him at all. . . . Yeah and he said this girl said he was *spider head* [referring to his black hair].

Both of Kevin's stories speak to feeling excluded and being made to feel like he possessed an inferior identity based on his ethnicity.

Students also described lost opportunities to share parts of their culture with others at school. For example, Alexander explained,

In elementary school, I was like eating the same thing that I ate like um I can't remember but it was a Venezuelan food, but I was like okay. Everybody was like, *what the heck is that?* I was like *As you can see that's food and I don't care what you say. As you can see it's something that people in my culture eat.*

This may seem to be a minor incident, but it becomes part of a collection of embedded memories that were hurtful and resulted in feelings of inferiority, rejection, otherness, and what Kevin referred to as worthlessness. Sharing these experiences among many group members during the second semester proved to be a bonding moment for students as most of them said they had never shared these types of experiences, or the emotions that result from them, with anyone.

Emerging Critical Consciousness: Ally, Advocate, or Agent of Change

If anyone's being bullied due to race or stuff like that, I will stand up!

—Aliyah

There was a consensus among these students that they seldom raised issues like those they shared in club with any adults. By giving students more opportunities to share, being transparent with them, and establishing a safe climate for vulnerability, they started using club time to "unload." They all admitted that they viewed club time together as a "safe place" that was helpful because they could "get things off our chest." Tracking their development over the course of the year, it became clear that it was extremely powerful for students to feel connected to the club as a safe place.

During the fall semester students had reported that they didn't care about what people thought of them, and they also had no solutions to the (often ethnic) bullying issues they perceived at their school. During the spring semester, students were able to became more honest with each other about their experiences. For instance, Kevin stated, "you just gotta say that it doesn't matter what you look like . . . but it still hurts." Moreover, in a one-on-one interview, Alexander explained that, "They [the Club] think that I'm normal . . . they don't see me as a disability." This statement bears witness to his intense desire to be seen as fully human and highlights a powerful development that had occurred across the year: the students had become *allies* (creating bridges between their experiences to create a safe space for all). Atalia affirmed the power of allies, reporting, "people that have a lot of friends" have more power because they "have their friends to back them up."

Through these discussions, students gradually began to transition from simply being allies to being *advocates* for one another (not only standing with each other but also speaking up for one another and with their peers). When Kevin was asked how he would like to see power used differently in his school he said, "If someone has power, and you have, you can stop someone from maybe bullying . . . you should at least tell them to stop." At that point, Aliyah said, "If anyone's being bullied due to race or stuff like that, I will stand up!" In addition, she reported, "I can now talk about it [racism, discrimination, bullying] to other people. I can start to talk about it with anyone who asks me how to deal with it." She also reported that she had begun to hold people accountable to the lessons learned in club and remind them to be cautious of what they say. It was rewarding to hear stories from their classroom teacher of club members actually standing up in these ways outside of club time, in genuine enactments of advocating for others.

At first, students were not convinced that they had any power, and progress was slow. For instance, when asked what he could do about the racism that concerned him at his school, Alexander responded, "I think nothing because I could tell them something, but I can't change . . . sometimes nobody can . . . like people can't change." When asked later in the school year for one small step that he could take, he explained that he would make a video game club that welcomed people from various cultures, ethnicities, and backgrounds. Alexander envisioned his club to simply be a safe place for people to hang out while sharing a common passion (creating videos), but it was a huge milestone in his sense of *agency* (the realization that they could actually engender change in the culture of their classroom and school). In another effort to take action against bullying, several of the students completed a peer mediation training to become certified peer mediators for their district. Similarly, Aliyah joined a second after-school club that directly addressed school bullying through designing and developing anti-bullying posters, videos, and public service announcements for the school. These students seemed to begin the school year believing that they could do absolutely nothing about the problems they faced and ended the year with ideas about how they could enact change regarding issues they thought were important. As *allies*, students shared one another's plights and provided a sense of safety for one another, as *advocates* they gained the courage to stand up for one another, and as *agents of change*, they took (and planned) action to make a difference in the culture of their classroom and school.

Intersection of Critical Consciousness and Belonging

Each of the themes that emerged throughout this analysis is infused with implications regarding the students' sense of belonging. The value of *rightful presence*, that is, when students feel their identity, culture, race, background, or circumstances are respected and included at school (Faircloth, chapter 1, this volume; Barnett, 2005; Squires & Darling, 2013; Calabrese Barton & Tan, 2019), was exemplified by the growth of these students. Rather than succumb to barriers to belonging, growth as allies, advocates, and agents of change encouraged their own sense of connection at school. Their growth also extended rightful presence to others at their school. For example, Aliyah stated that club had taught her that "everyone has a story," which motivated her to learn more about people and their experiences. Similarly, Atalia explained that learning about differences among people and cultures provided learning opportunities and developed communication skills which allow people to engage in authentic conversations, a powerful avenue to building and sustaining belonging. Students developed a deeper awareness that the world and people in the world are "capable of being known and understood. As Kevin shared, I've learned about how many people are the same- have gone through the same thing" [i.e., the same marginalizing experiences]. Each of these lessons are powerful lynch pins for belonging, cultural competence, and CC. They certainly allowed students to recognize and validate their own cultural reference points and those of others, to recognize marginalization with its barriers to belonging, and to begin to enact strategies to resist it.

DISCUSSION

The preceding analysis suggests that CC was slow to develop among these students, however, it did develop and in ways that were meaningful for this group of youth in their particular lived experiences. It resulted in advocacy and agency on the part of this group of students, and revealed significant lessons regarding their belonging. Three overarching themes inform and qualify these results.

Developmental Appropriateness

The fact that the students in this study were sixth graders—which was in fact a central element of this investigation—shaped the results in important ways. That is, understanding sixth graders' development of CC requires seeing these issues through sixth grade eyes. Although ethnic studies theorists argue for the centrality of systemic, societal issues, this was seen only in part among this group of students. Many of their insights into oppression or marginalization highlighted nonracial issues that plagued their existence at school, such as being bullied personally (often identity-, appearance- or culture-based). Moreover, applications related to racism were often anchored in their own intimate experiences rather than systemic issues (which is appropriate for their age).

At the start of the club, students were unable, perhaps unwilling or not ready, to interrogate their own personal experiences with racism and discrimination. This changed slowly yet dramatically across the school year as activities focused on counternarratives that more closely reflected their own lived experiences, and involved abundant time reflecting collectively on such experiences. This suggests that honoring students' developmental level and allowing development to unfold naturally appears critical for authentic growth of CC in students at this age.

These insights shed light on this early stage in the development of CC. Rather than minimizing the value of beginning this process as early as sixth grade, these early steps may serve as an important prelude to additional growth that ethnic studies and CC aim for.

Placing Students at the Center

Second, directly centering students' lived experiences in explicit and concrete ways was affirmed as crucial in this study. Rather than the common ethnic studies emphasis on empowering students to act as social agents of change by developing a project to address an issue in their community, after working with these students for a full school year, it seemed obvious that this original model of ethnic studies was not guided with the personal needs and interests younger students in mind; a project of that type may not have served them well at this point. Truthfully, students do not need to protest or engage in a major community activity to activate their CC. Students in this group saw CC manifest itself in authentic, personal, and concrete ways. One example is Kevin shared, "I've learned about how many people are the same—have gone through the same thing" (i.e., the same marginalizing experiences). For him and the other students, identifying common personally oppressive experiences was hugely important and resulted in an essential bond or rightful presence among the group that otherwise may not have occurred.

Fidelity to Ethnic Studies and Critical Consciousness Scholarship

A third important insight highlights the critical nature of each step in the development of CC, and therefore the wisdom of trusting the pace and process. Because the research group hoped to see rapid, significant change, we were discouraged when that did not happen. We were forced to return to ethnic studies and CC scholarship to be reminded of the complex nature of this development, support our persistence, and guide our thinking. For example, Cammarota (2015) describes the praxis of developing CC as a developmental cycle including (1) *reflection on a situation*, (2) plan of action to change the situation, (3) implementation of the plan, and (4) evaluation of the outcome. Time invested in reflection is vital in that it transforms our perception of situations, which is essential to knowing how to implement change. Not only does this cycle require much time and reflection in and of itself, extensive time was also required for students to gain one another's trust, in order to come to regard the club as a safe space to reveal themselves and abandon their social masquerades (again, central to their belonging).

Limitations

This project involved limitations that inform both interpretations and next steps. First, during this year-long study, the club began with reading and discussing two books. Although grade-level appropriate, engaging, representative of minoritized groups, and reflecting issues of identity and culture, the intense focus on students' own lived experiences that lies at the heart of ethnic studies and CC was hard to develop. It became obvious that in order to meet the actual goals of the club , the focus needed to be narrowed to be more centered on students' lives. The most skillful work of ethnic studies took place when the club more closely explored students' own identities, ethnicities, and cultures. For this reason, the time for most meaningful development was shorter in duration than one might have liked. Although much was learned from this group of students, it is possible that in future studies, when development of CC is given a longer runway, the possibilities and impacts might be even more significant.

Another possible addition that might enhance a future iteration of an ethnic studies club experience is the possibility of a *small* community-engaged project (e.g., possibly something in their own school, rather than protesting or larger acts of activism). The tool emerges often as a valuable piece of developing CC. Calibrating it carefully to the needs of middle-grade students is essential, however, there are strong research and theoretical suggestions that it could be a significant asset to student growth.

It has also become apparent that while important growth occurred in this study, working with young adolescents will, of necessity, redefine both ethnic studies and CC. Tenets that some believe to be vital elements of each must be recast when seen through the eyes of younger students. For example, both ethnic studies and CC literature place a heavy emphasis on challenging dominant groups in our society, thereby disrupting the status quo, which is ultimately the true goal. However, we would do well to meet young adolescents where they are, rather than imposing more complex expectations that they may not be ready for. Moreover, it is important to note that despite the limitations introduced by the young age of these participants, this project yielded important fruit, and potentially demonstrates a valuable early step in the CC cycle.

CONCLUSION

This research inquiry details a long process, full of mistakes, setbacks, personal doubt, and critical reflection. It highlights Martin's (2009) characterization of our current problematic educational research climate as a "solution on demand environment" (p. 299) wherein the scale of the problems we are taking on are minimized and project efforts are held to inappropriate expectations such that a singular project should be able to produce revolutionary impacts. Demanding immediate and simple solutions trivializes the complexities of issues of identity, equity, and marginalization. In fact, "deliberate change is laborious and involves the patient layering of practices and long-term visioning within the focal activity system" (Bang & Vossoughi, 2016, p. 189). For us, one powerful lesson from this study was to get out of the way, centering the students' instead of the teacher's or researchers' perspectives, and to trust the process and pace of this complex endeavor. If the club gave the students anything, we would argue that it empowered them to interrogate their experiences, to use their voices to share their experiences with others, and that everyone's story had a rightful and understandable place. These are central and powerful elements of the developmental trajectory of CC presented by Cammarotta (2015). It would be easy to bemoan such slow progress. However, the growth among these students has engendered in us great hope that they have come to see their lives through a different mirror, one that recognizes and honors their varied narratives (Takaki, 1993), providing them a way to see themselves as having a rightful presence (i.e., a sense that they do indeed belong) in the democratic project of schooling, and a window through which they can imagine and create a new world (Gutierrez, 2013).

REFERENCES

Aguinaga, A., & Gloria, A. M. (2015). The effects of generational status and university environment on Latina/o undergraduates' persistence decisions. *Journal of Diversity in Higher Education, 8*(1), 15–29. doi:10.1037/a0038465

Allen, K., & Boyle, C. (2016). Pathways to school belonging. *The Educational and Developmental Psychologist, 33(1)*, ii–iv.

Anderman, L. H., & Freeman, T. (2004). Students' sense of belonging in school. In M. L. Maehr & P. R. Pintrich (eds.), *Advances in Motivation and Achievement*, Vol. 13. *Motivating Students, Improving Schools: The Legacy of Carol Midgley* (pp. 27–63). Greenwich, CT: Elsevier.

Arellano, A., & Padilla, A. (1995). Academic invulnerability among a select group of Latino University students. *Hispanic Journal of Behavioral Sciences, 18*(4), 485–507.

Ahmed, Sara. 2014. "Atmospheric Walls." Feminist Killjoys. http://feministkilljoys.com/2014/09/15/atmospheric-walls/.

Ban on Ethnic Studies Curricula Act, H.R. 2281. Arizona House of Representatives. (2010).

Bang, M., & Vossoughi, S. (2016). Participatory design research and educational justice: Studying learning and relations within social change making, cognition and instruction. *34*(3), 173–193. doi:10.1080/07370008.2016.1181879

Banks, J. A. (2006). *Race, Culture, and Education: The Selected Works of James A. Banks*. London: Routledge.

Banks, J. A. (2012). Ethnic studies, citizenship education, and the public good. *Intercultural Education, 23*(6), 467–473.

Barnett, Clive. (2005). Ways of relating: Hospitality and the acknowledgement of otherness. *Progress in Human Geography, 29*(1), 5–21.

Baumeister, R. F., & Leary, M. R. (1995). The need to belonging: Desire for interpersonal attachment as a fundamental human motivation. *Psychological Bulletin, 117*(3), 497–530.

Benner, A., Graham, S., & Mistry, R. (2016). Discerning direct and mediated effects of ecological structures and processes on adolescents' educational outcomes. *Developmental Psychology, 44*(3), 840–854.

Berg, M., Coman, E., & Schensul, J. (2009). Youth action research for prevention: A multi-level intervention designed to increase efficacy and empowerment among urban youth. *American Journal of Community Psychology, 43*(3–4), 345–359.

Berry, J., Phinney, J., Sam, D., & Vedder, P. (2006). Immigrant youth: Acculturation, identity, and adaptation. *Applied Psychology, 55*(3), 303–332.

Blad, E. (2017). Teachers' Cues Shape students' sense of belonging. *Education Week, 36*(36), 9.

Bourdieu, P., & Passeron, J.-C. (1990). *Theory, Culture & Society. Reproduction in Education, Society and Culture* (2nd edition) (R. Nice, Trans.). Sage Publications, Inc.

Brown-Jeffy, S., & Cooper, J. E. (2011). Toward a conceptual framework of culturally relevant pedagogy: An overview of the conceptual and theoretical literature. *Teacher Education Quarterly, 38*(1), 65–84.

Cabrera, N. L., Milem, J. F., Jaquette, O., & Marx, R. W. (2014). Missing the (student achievement) forest for all the (political) trees: Empiricism and the Mexican American studies controversy in Tucson. *American Educational Research Journal, 51*(6), 1084–1118.

Cammarota, J. (2015). The praxis of ethnic studies: Transforming second sight into CC. *Race Ethnicity and Education, 19*(2), 233–251.

Cammarota, J., & Aguilera, M. (2012). 'By the time I get to Arizona': Race, language, and education in America's racist state. *Race Ethnicity and Education, 15*(4), 485–500. doi:10.1080/13613324.2012.674025

Campbell, C., & MacPhail, C. (2002). Peer education, gender and the development of critical consciousness: Participatory HIV prevention by South African youth. *Social Science & Medicine, 55*, 331–345.

Cartmell, H., & Bond. C. (2015). What does belonging mean for young people who are International New Arrivals? *Educational and Child Psychology, 32*(2), 89–101.

Chavez, L. (2010, May 24). Focus on US history, not ethnic studies. Dallas Morning News. http://www.dallasnews.com/opinion/latest-columns/20100514-Linda-Chavez-Focus-on-U-6265.ece (accessed July 14, 2017).

Chiseri-Strater, E., & Sunstein, B. S. (2006). *What Works? A Practical Guide for Teacher Research.* Portsmouth, NH: Heinemann.

De los Rios, C. (2013). A curriculum of the borderlands: High school Chicana/o-Latina/o studies as sitios y lengua. *Urban Review, 45*, 58–73.

de los Rios, C. V., Lopez, J., & Morrell, E. (2014). Toward a critical pedagogy of race: ES and literacies of power in high school classrooms. *Race and Social Problems, 7*(1), 84–96.

Dee, T. S., & Penner, E. K. (2017). The causal effects of cultural relevance: Evidence from an Ethnic Studies curriculum. *American Educational Research Journal, 54*(1), 127–166.

Diemer, M. A., Kauffman, A. L., Koenig, N. B., Trahan, E. B., & Hsieh, C. (2006). Challenging racism, sexism, and social injustice: Support for urban adolescents' critical consciousness development. *Cultural Diversity & Ethnic Minority Psychology, 12*, 444–460.

Eccles, J., Lord, S., Roeser, R., Barber, B., & Hernandez, Jozefowicz, D. (1997). The association of school transitions in early adolescence with developmental trajectories through high school. In J. Schulenberg, J. Maggs & K. Hurrelmann (eds.), *Health Risks and Developmental Transitions During Adolescence*, pp. 283–320. Cambridge, MA: Cambridge University Press.

Ellingson, L. (2011). Analysis and representation across the continuum. In N Denzin & Y Lincoln (eds.), *Sage Handbook of Qualitative Research*, 4th edition. Thousand Oaks, CA: Sage.

ESNow (ESN) (2016, May 4). Dr. Nolan Cabrera's Ethnic Studies presentation to LAUSD. [Video file]. Retrieved from https://www.youtube.com/watch?v=Vv41RtQRABA

Faircloth, B. S. (2009). Making the most of adolescence: Harnessing the search for identity to understand classroom belonging. *Journal of Adolescent Research, 24*(3), 321–348.

Faircloth, B. S. (2012). "Wearing a mask" vs. connecting identity with learning. *Contemporary Educational Psychology, 37*, 1–9.

Faircloth, B. S., & Hamm, J. V. (2005). Sense of belonging among high school students representing four ethnic groups. *Journal of Youth & Adolescence, 34*(4), 293–309.

Faircloth, B., McClanahan, J. & Barrett, K. (2018). "Rightful Presence" – The Heart of Belonging. Paper presented at the 2018 annual convention of the American Psychological Association, in San Francisco, CA.

Farkas, G., Grobe, R. P., Sheehan, D., & Shuan, Y. (1990). Cultural resources and school success: Gender, ethnicity, and poverty groups within an urban school district. *American Sociological Review, 55*(1), 127–142. doi:10.2307/2095708

First encounters with racism. (Aug. 2, 2017). New York Times.

Freire, P. (2000). *Pedagogy of the Oppressed.* New York: Continuum International Publishing Group.

Fuligni, A. J., Witkow, M., & Garcia, C. (2005). Ethnic identity and the academic adjustment of adolescents from Mexican, Chinese, and European backgrounds. *Developmental Psychology, 41*(5), 799–811. doi:10.1037/0012-1649.41.5.799

Giroux, Henry A. (2020). *On Critical Pedagogy*, Bloomsbury Publishing Plc.

Glesne, C. (2016). *Becoming Qualitative Researchers: An Introduction*, 5th edition. Pearson.

Goodenow, C. (1993). Classroom belonging among early adolescent students: Relationships to motivation and achievement. *Journal of Early Adolescence, 13*, 21–43.

Grimes, Nikki. (2002). *Bronx Masquerade.* New York: Dial Books.

Gude, O. (2014) You belong here. *Visual Arts Research, 40*(1), 61–63.

Gutiérrez, R. (2013). The sociopolitical turn in mathematics education. *Journal for Research in Mathematics Education, 44*(1), 37–68.

Hill, D. L. (2006). Sense of belonging as connectedness, American Indian worldview, and mental health. *Archives of Psychiatric Nursing, 20*(5), 210–216. doi:10.1016/j.apnu.2006.04.003

Hsu, J. (2015). *Being 12: 'People Think I'm Supposed to Talk Ghetto, Whatever That Is.* WNYC Public Radio. Jul 8, 2015.

Hughes, R. L. (2007). A hint of whiteness: History textbooks and social construction of race in the wake of the sixties. *Social Studies, 98*(5), 201–207.

Jay, M. (2003). Critical race theory, multicultural education, and the hidden curriculum of hegemony. *Multicultural Perspectives, 5*(4), 3–9.

Juvonen, J. (2006). Sense of belonging, social bonds, & school functioning. Alexander, P. & Winne, P. (eds.), *Handbook of Educational Psychology*, 2nd edition, pp. 655–674. Mahweh, NJ: Lawrence Erlbaum.

Kia-Keating, M., & Ellis, B. (2007). Belonging and connection to school in resettlement: Young refugees, school belonging, and psychosocial adjustment. *Clinical Child Psychology and Psychiatry, 12*, 29043.

Knifsend, C. A., Camacho-Thompson, D. E., Juvonen, J., Graham, S. (2018). Friends in activities, school-related affect, and academic outcomes in diverse middle schools. *Journal of Youth Adolescence, 47*(6), 1208–1220. doi:10.1007/s10964-018-0817-6

Ladson-Billings, G. (1995). Toward a theory of culturally relevant pedagogy. *American Educational Research Journal, 32*(3), 465–491.

Ladson-Billings, G. (2014). Culturally relevant pedagogy 2.0: A.k.a The remix. *Harvard Educational Review, 84*(1), 74–84.

Ladson-Billings, G., & Tate, W. (1995). Toward a critical race theory of education. The *Teachers College Record, 97*(1), 47–68.

LaFromboise, T., Coleman, H. L. K., & Gerton, J. (1993). Psychological impact of biculturalism: Evidence and theory. *Psychological Bulletin, 114*(3), 395–412.

Lincoln, Y., Lynham, S., & Guba, E. (2011). Paradigmnatic controversies, contradictions, and emerging confluences, revisited. In Denzin, N. & Lincoln, Y. (eds.), *The SAGE Handbook of Qualitative Research*, pp. 97–128. Los Angeles, CA: Sage.

Lowry, L. (1993). *The Giver*. Boston, MA: Houghton Mifflin.

Marshall, C., & Rossman, G. (2006). *Designing Qualitative Research*. Thousand Oaks, CA: Sage Publication.

Martin, D. (2009). Researching race in mathematics education. *The Teachers College Record, 111*(2), 295–338.

Nasir, N. S., & Hand, V. M. (2006). Exploring sociocultural perspectives on race, culture and learning. *Review of Educational Research, 76*, 449–475.

National Association for Multicultural Education (NAME). (2017). Ethnic studies or multicultural education? Retrieved from htmlhttps://www.nameorg.org/learn/ethnic_studies_or_multicultura.php

Nouri, A., & Sajjadi, S. (2014). Emancipatory pedagogy in practice: Aims, principles and curriculum orientation. *International Journal of Critical Pedagogy, 5*(2), 76–87.

O'Connor, C. (1997). Dispositions toward (collective) struggle and educational resilience in the inner city: A case analysis of six African-American high school students. *American Educational Research Journal, 34*, 593–632.

Osterman, K. (2020). Students' need for belonging in the school community. *Review of Educational Research, 70*(3), 323–367.

Paris, D. (2012). Culturally sustaining pedagogy: A needed change in stance, terminology, and practice. *Educational Researcher, 41*(3), 93–97.

Paris, D., & Alim, H. S. (2017). What is culturally sustaining pedagogy and why does it matter? In D. Paris & H. S. Alim (eds.), *Culturally Sustaining Pedagogies: Teaching and Learning for Justice in a Changing World*, pp. 1–21. New York: Teachers College Press.

Phelan, P., Davidson, A. L., & Yu, H. C. (1993). Students' multiple worlds: Negotiating the borders of family, peer, and school cultures. In P. Phelan & A. Locke Davidson (eds.), *Renegotiating Cultural Diversity in American Schools*, pp. 52–88. New York: Teachers College Press.

Pupil Instruction: Ethnic Studies Ban, Assembly Bill No. 2016, California State Assembly. (2016). https://leginfo.legislature.ca.gov/faces/billTextClient.xhtml?bill_id=201520160AB2016.

Ramos-Zayas, A. Y. (2003). *National Performances: The Politics of Race, Class and Space in Puerto Rican Chicago*. Chicago, IL: University of Chicago Press.

Sleeter, C. E. (2011). *The Academic and Social Value of Ethnic Studies: A Research Review*. Washington, DC: National Education Association Research Department.

Smith, W. A. (1975). Conscientizacao: An operational definition (Unpublished doctoral dissertation). University of Massachusetts, Amherst.

Solórzano, D., & Yosso, T. (2000). Towards a critical race theory of Chicano and Chicana education. In C. Tejada, C. Martinez, & Z. Leonardo (eds.), *Charting New Terrains in Chicana (o)/Latina(o) Education*, pp. 35–66. Cresskill, NJ: Hampton Press.

Squires, V. and Darling, J. (2013). The 'minor' politics of rightful presence: Justice and relationality in city of sanctuary. *International Political Sociology, 7*, 59–74.

Takaki, R. (1993). *A Different Mirror: A History of Multicultural America.* Boston, MA: Back Bay.

TED. (2020, January 17. How students of color confront impostor syndrome | Dena Simmons [Video]. YouTube. https://www.youtube.com/watch?v=8sQ2p89P0Us

The Present video (2014, 3 mins., Institute of Animation, Visual Effects & Digital Postproduction, Anti-Defamation League.

Tintiangco-Cubales, A., Kohli, R., Sacramento, J., Henning, N., Agarwal-Rangnath, R., & Sleeter, C. (2015). Toward an ethnic studies pedagogy: Implications for K–12 schools from the research. *The Urban Review, 47*(1), 104–125.

Urdan, T. (2012). Factors affecting the motivation and achievement of immigrant students. APA educational psychology handbook, Vol 2: Individual differences and cultural and contextual factors. 293–313.

Urdan, T., & Munoz, C. (2012). Multiple contexts, multiple methods: A study of academic and cultural identity among children of immigrant parents. *European Journal of Psychology of Education, 27*(2), 247–265.

Urrieta, L. (2009). *Working from Within: Chicana and Chicano Activist Educators in Whitestream Schools.* Tucson, AZ: University of Arizona Press.

Vetter, A. Fairbanks, C., and Arial, M. (2010). "Crazyghettosmart": A case study in Latina identities. *Qualitative Studies in Education, 24*(2), 185–207.

Warikoo, Natasha, & Carter, Prudence. (2009). Cultural explanations for racial and ethnic stratification in academic achievement: A call for a new and improved theory. *Review of Educational Research, 79*(1), 366–394.

Wong, C., Eccles, J., & Sameroff, A. (2003). The influence of ethnic discrimination and ethnic identification on African American adolescents' school and socioemotional adjustment. *Journal of Personality, 71*(6), 1197–1232.

Chapter 9

Challenges and Strength-Based Strategies for Cultivating a Sense of Belonging in a Heritage Language Program

Tierney B. Hinman, Ye He, Shameeka M. Wilson,
Adriana Abarca Paschal, and Jennifer Nelson

As a psychological construct, a sense of belonging is associated with academic and social indicators of learning success. Benefits include better attendance, increased prosocial behaviors, and more positive orientations toward learning (Allen & Bowles, 2012; Osterman, 2000). Research also suggests that belonging contributes to a broader sense of well-being defined by happiness, psychological functioning, adjustment, self-efficacy, and self-identity (Haslam et al., 2009; Holt-Lunstad et al., 2010). However, despite the amount of research that has been conducted on belonging, educational research provides limited insight into how learning environments might be constructed to develop and support this sense of belonging with culturally and linguistically diverse (CLD) learners. Specifically, Slaten et al. (2016) issued a call for more studies focusing on how traditionally marginalized populations experience belonging in comparison to their peers.

Attention to how CLD learners experience belonging becomes particularly important when considering societal and institutional pressures for Americanization (Jeon, 2008). For CLD families, these pressures limit accessibility to spaces that recognize their cultural and linguistic identities in support of an authentic sense of belonging. In this chapter, we describe a Spanish heritage language (HL) program engaging Latin*[1] (Salinas, 2020) students and their immigrant families, teachers, and teacher educators in an alternative learning space that supports and expands participants' sense of belonging. The HL program featured in this chapter provides a unique context from which a sense of belonging can be examined. Besides the program's commitment to serving heritage language learners (HLLs) and their families, who are rarely centered in literature on belonging, it also functions as a community-based school–university partnership. This intersection of home, school, university, and community addresses major facets significant in "creat[ing] a supportive atmosphere that emphasises the importance of school belonging, as each facet has relevance and importance to student well-being" (Allen et al., 2018, p. 28). Examining belonging through the HL program provides a novel perspective regarding how a sense of belonging might be shaped by the experiences, knowledges,[2] and strengths of a group of Latin* learners and families often given limited space for belonging in schools.

This chapter provides a general overview of HL programs and what is understood about the relationship between HL development and a sense of belonging. Here, *a sense of belonging* is defined using St-Amand et al.'s (2017) framework, which consists of four attributes—positive emotions, positive relationships, energy and willingness to get involved, and harmonization. We also describe challenges that Spanish HLLs and their families experience in the social, political, and economic contexts of schooling. Specific components addressing the four attributes of belonging in one HL program are shared, in addition to the strength-based instructional strategies the program implements to build upon the diverse capitals HLLs and their families leverage for learning. The chapter concludes by highlighting lessons learned about constructing spaces that encourage and support belonging for CLD participants in relation to the outcomes observed across 10 years of program implementation.

HERITAGE LANGUAGE PROGRAMS

Valdés (2001) defined an HLL as an individual "raised in a home where a non-English language is spoken, who speaks or . . . understands the heritage language, and who is to some degree bilingual in English and the heritage language" (p. 38). Hornberger and Wang (2008) extended this definition to highlight the agency of people with "familial or ancestral ties to a particular language that is not English . . . in determining whether or not they are HLLs of the HL (heritage language) and HC (heritage community)" (p. 27). Thus, individuals who identify as HLLs may possess a range of proficiency levels in the HL (He, 2012) and hold various ethnolinguistic affiliations with the heritage culture (Lee & Wright, 2014).

The US Census Bureau (2017) recorded more than 350 languages being spoken in homes across the United States. Languages other than English are spoken by more than 60 million individuals, or nearly 4 percent of the population. After English, Spanish remains the most common language, with Spanish speakers accounting for more than half of the individuals who have a home language other than English. In response, a number of HL programs have developed. According to the Center for Applied Linguistics (2020), these programs are designed to develop the linguistic abilities and cultural knowledges with the HL. To date, there are 878 HL program profiles registered in the Center's database of Heritage Languages in America, including those based in schools, communities, organizations, higher education departments, and summer programs.

Although these programs aim to enhance the linguistic abilities and cultural knowledges of HLLs, they do so through a variety of language ideologies. Program approaches range from those that teach language in isolation through decontextualized, skill-based instruction to those that position language as a socially and culturally situated practice (García, 2009; Pennycook, 2010). More monoglossic approaches to language instruction privilege monolingualism and treat language as an autonomous skill that functions independently from context. The HL is developed separate from instruction in English, often occurring at different times or in separate spaces (Lewis et al., 2012).

In contrast, heteroglossic approaches to language instruction privilege multilingualism and view languages as being inseparable, thus recognizing that the language practices of multilingual speakers are fluid and complex. More heteroglossic approaches to instruction leverage multilingual speakers' integrated language systems (i.e., translanguaging; García, 2007) and creative language blending and code-meshing (i.e., hybridization; Makoni & Pennycook, 2007). These moves promote the strategic use of multiple languages in the same spaces to allow for the use of complex semiotic processes in communication, positioning languages as complementary tools for meaning-making.

Despite their language ideology, HL programs aiming to develop linguistic and cultural knowledges generally share several central purposes: (1) strengthening the cultural identities of children of immigrants and their affiliations with their parents' homeland(s) (Blackledge & Creese, 2010); (2) enabling and facilitating intergenerational communication (Nordstrom, 2016) through the development and maintenance of the HL (Francis et al., 2010); and (3) developing career skills and knowledge to strengthen the prospective futures of HLLs (Cardona et al., 2008). These purposes are significant in terms of the relationships that exist among HL, identity (Little, 2020; Czubisnka, 2017), and belonging (Mills, 2001, Norton, 2013).

HERITAGE LANGUAGE AND BELONGING

Historically, belonging has been defined by measures of students' behavioral, cognitive, and affective engagement in schools. However, more recent studies on belonging have expanded to include an understanding of belonging as "political, performative, and interactional" (Saraví et al., 2020, p. 1110), specifically in terms of how a sense of belonging addresses who gets to feel at ease in social spaces; who is able to participate in the construction of spaces; and who gets marginalized, excluded, or subordinated (May, 2011).

For CLD students and families, this sociological perspective of belonging emphasizes the impact of power structures, established by a history of colonization (specifically of language), on the internalized norms of school settings, contributing to a common set of barriers to belonging. Barriers particular to HLLs include the subversion of language, which is directly associated with existing class structure and systems of gender and race, to account for the needs of those Freire (1972) termed *oppressors* (or those capable of systematically reproducing domination). Habermas (1971) described this oppression as including the manipulation of the words of the oppressed for the purpose of the oppressors, as well as the systematic distortion of communication through power structures that unequally distribute the ability to challenge the comprehensibility, truth, sincerity, and legitimacy of communication.

These barriers to learning are often constructed by and within institutionalized systems, including that of schooling. In a more general sense, Latin* families face the challenge of adjusting to a new set of cultural norms and political structures (including legal status and US immigration laws) while negotiating coexistence of their multiple identities. Competing identities, especially for those who experience discrimination related to identity as precipitated by larger economic, social, and political discourses, can lead to feelings of distress for Latin* individuals (Roche & Kuperminc, 2012).

Additional barriers created by these discourses and the systems that perpetuate them include the increased likelihood that Latin* families will live in a neighborhood of poverty and that their children will attend larger, more segregated, and more under-resourced schools (Pagan-Rivera, 2014; Sibley & Brabeck, 2017). In these schools, Latin* children are less likely to receive instruction that validates and leverages their ethnolinguistic identity (Beaudrie et al., 2014; Beaudrie et al., 2009) and more likely to have teachers who hold assumptions that individuals of Latin* descent have lower academic abilities than their White peers (Sibley & Brabeck, 2017). School personnel often lack essential cultural competencies to support students' integration of family, peer, and school experiences in ways that positively impact ethnic identity development (Gonzalez et al., 2017).

Often, this challenge of navigating different languages, cultural expectations, and educational systems between home and school can result in Latin* families feeling less connected to the school and their children's teachers and less confident about being involved in their children's schooling (Cha et al., 2017). These challenges contribute to the acculturative stress that defines part of the lived experiences of Latin* students and families in schooled contexts. A low sense of belonging, as Roche et al. (2012) indicated, may be a mechanism by which acculturative stress decreases Latin* youths' school performance.

St-Amand et al. (2017) used the concept analysis method (Walker & Avant, 2011) to identify and define four attributes of belonging. The first *positive emotions* encompasses feelings of attachment, intimacy, and usefulness and support, as well as a sense of pride. *Positive relations* with peers and teachers are defined by social relationships that incorporate encouragement, acceptance, support, respect, valorization, and warmth. Relations with teachers can contribute to an increased motivation to learn when support, caring, and respect are consistently given as learners are challenged to meet high expectations. The third attribute includes having the *energy and willingness to get involved* in a meaningful way within a group. *Harmonization*, the final attribute of belonging, is defined by an individual's adaptations and/or adjustments as needed to align with the situations or people within a group. This chapter extends the notion of harmonization as individual adaptation to include the ways in which learning spaces can disrupt systemic marginalization of HLLs to center their knowledges, experiences, and identities in school.

These four attributes of belonging are operationalized in the following sections of this chapter through the description of one specific HL program. We identify challenges to belonging that HLLs and their families experience in the US education system. By examining the particular HL program context that utilizes strategies for addressing these challenges, implications for creating spaces of belonging are drawn. Discussions are framed in terms of lessons learned and outcomes observed across 10 years of program implementation.

CHALLENGES FOR HERITAGE LANGUAGE LEARNERS

In this section, challenges facing Spanish HLLs and their families in terms of the four interconnected attributes of belonging are highlighted. These challenges consider the community cultural wealth (Yosso, 2005) that HLLs and their families possess—including aspirational, familial, linguistic, navigational, resistant, and social capital—that often goes unacknowledged in schools. Major challenges framing HLLs' experiences with belonging in schools include (1) subtractive schooling practices, (2) the privileging of vertical knowledge, (3) high social and cognitive demands, and (4) institutional resistance to change.

Subtractive schooling practices, in which HL development is neglected, devalued, or only encouraged to support learners' English language proficiency, negatively impact HLLs' ability to utilize their linguistic capital for learning (Menken, 2008; Menken & Kleyn, 2010; Nieto and Bode, 2008; Valenzuela, 1999). Additionally, when the HL is perceived as a liability that can disrupt English language learning, HLLs and their families may experience embarrassment, shame, and a sense of unease when using their home language (Coryell et al., 2010; Pavlenko, 2002). Ubiquitous privileging of English and associated acts of discrimination—including foreigner objectification, xenophobia, racism, and classism—that often occur when the HL is used may also be reflected in families' daily social interactions beyond schools, compounding the pressure to use English in both public and private spaces.

In addition, emphasis on vertical forms of expertise, which consider knowledge as a "coherent, explicit, systematically principled [and hierarchically organized] structure" (Bernstein, 1996, pp. 170–171), privileges competence and often fails to recognize the funds of knowledge families and communities possess as essential to learning (Gonzalez et al., 2005). This solidification and legitimization of school practices and knowledges minimize and eliminate opportunities for HLLs and their families to have their voices heard in the planning of curriculum and instruction (Valdez & Lugg, 2010). Additionally, this privileging contributes to rising tensions around HLLs' positionality; while families often value communication in the HL and continued growth and maintenance of the language, HLLs (particularly as adolescents) sometimes find less utility in doing so (Bell-Corales, 2006; Nesteruk, 2010).

HLLs also experience high levels of cognitive and social demands as they balance multiple linguistic and cultural norms and practices necessary for academic learning and language development (Belpoliti & Fairclough, 2016). These demands can often be overwhelming, and it becomes critical for learners to access and use capital to navigate unfamiliar institutional systems. Such navigational skills are key to being able to advocate for more inclusive policies and instructional practices that build and maintain communication between schools and HLL families while resisting inequalities. This resistance includes opportunities to pass on other dimensions of community cultural wealth.

The final challenge HLLs and their families face in terms of belonging is institutional resistance to change (Berkovich, 2011; Zimmerman, 2006). This resistance often encompasses schools, as well as the teachers who operate as a part of that institution (Vetter, 2012), and can create obstacles for collaborative, cohesive, and sustained movement toward pedagogies that are inclusive of all learners and the community cultural wealth they bring into the classroom. Traditional classroom curriculum and instruction are often focused on cognitive aspects of learning to the detriment of larger socioemotional aspects of learning (Allen et al., 2017) particularly essential to HLLs.

The major challenges faced by HLLs and their families impact their experiences with belonging in school spaces. Negative emotions often associated with the use of a language other than English in educational and social settings, in addition to the lack of recognition of families' and communities' ways of knowing, contribute to widening distance between home and school practices (Fairbanks et al., 2018). A generational distancing also often occurs between families who speak the HL and HLLs whose proficiency in the HL might be limited (Nesteruk, 2010). Consequently, social relationships at home and school often begin to form along a Spanish/English binary, creating additional obstacles to integrating language, knowledge, and experience for supporting multilingual and multicultural identity development. Without this ability, HLLs and their families are unable to shape learning, especially in ways that integrate individual and family aspirations. This limiting of voice and agency increases the challenges families experience when navigating systems of education, as well as legal, justice, health care, and employment systems, resulting in fewer opportunities to "become connected with others around common issues" and to realize that they are "not alone in dealing with their problems" (Delgado-Gaitan, 2001, p. 54). HLLs and their families, then, face additional barriers to building community networks that have the internal capacity and infrastructure to support and expand the capabilities of its individual and collective members (Leeman et al., 2011).

Heritage Language Academy Context and Strategies Promoting Belonging

In this section, we share specific program context and strength-based strategies that promote belonging to overcome the challenges identified in terms of positive emotions, positive social relations, involvement, and harmonization (table 9.1). We start with an introduction of the background of the Heritage Language Academy (HLA) and detail the HLA context and strategies regarding the four attributes of belonging.

Heritage Language Academy Background

The HLA is a Spanish HL program established as a partnership among the local Spanish-speaking community, the school district, and a university in the southeastern United States (Fairbanks, et al., 2017). As a rural school district, there are around 17 percent of K–12 students identified as English learners (Civil Rights Data Collection, 2015). Over 95 percent of the English learners are identified as Latin*. In the county, approximately 21 percent of the population five years and over speak Spanish (US Census Bureau, 2017).

Table 9.1 Summary of HLA Projects and Targeted Attributes of Belonging

Project		Targeted Attributes of Belonging			
Student	*Families*	*Emotions*	*Relations*	*Involvement*	*Harmonization*
Future career speeches	Letter to student about his/her strengths	X	X		
Solutions to community issues	Math tutoring video	X		X	
Family history narrative	Website on family communication	X	X	X	X
Financial literacy simulation	Family budget			X	

HLA was initiated by teachers and Latin* families in the local school district. Through discussion and by listening to needs from the local community, a Saturday HLA program model to support both students and families whose first language is Spanish was proposed. University teacher educators and teacher candidates were invited to support HLA program implementation through continued professional development and action research projects. In 2009, HLA was first launched in one elementary school with a small group of third-grade students and their families (He & Prater, 2011). The program has since been expanded to include students and families in the middle school (Hinman & He, 2017).

The structure of the HLA program was codesigned by teachers, families, and university teacher educators in response to the growing number of Latin* families moving into the district and an increasing awareness of the need to create a space where families felt a sense of belonging to collectively negotiate the social, cultural, and linguistic challenges they experienced in schools. Literacy and math instruction, in both English and Spanish, were integrated to provide students with opportunities to (1) develop content understanding through the use of their full linguistic repertoires (García, 2009) and (2) build upon their community cultural wealth (Yosso, 2005). Adult family members sought opportunities to enhance their use of technology through instruction in Spanish. In addition, families wanted to have a space to discuss issues regarding their children's learning and to develop strategies to support student learning at home.

Although instruction is often provided to students and families in separate spaces, HLA curriculum links instruction through project-based work (e.g., planning a family budget), which sometimes leads to shared instructional spaces. This codesigning of HLA extends to curriculum as teachers seek the input of students and families to inform the current year's work, as well as plans for subsequent years. University teacher educators are invited to participate in curriculum planning discussions and teacher candidates enrolled in one teaching methods course are offered opportunities to participate in action research projects through HLA. Research data have been collected throughout program planning and implementation. Teachers share research findings through conference presentations (He et al., 2017) and use research findings to inform their practice in both HLA and classroom instruction.

Cultivating Positive Emotions

In the HLA context, challenges related to the attribute of positive emotions contributing to a sense of belonging are addressed by planning and implementing lessons and projects that work to cultivate and sustain an intergenerational sense of cultural identity and pride despite anti-immigrant sentiments and institutional policies (e.g., deportation raids, the separation of children and families at the border, renewed efforts to construct the border wall) that devalue and stigmatize Latin* languages and cultures. HLA provides a space in which teachers and families can work together to express pride in their language and culture while simultaneously developing the sense that both have utility in the highly monolingual spaces of traditional schools and other institutionalized settings. This work has particularly focused on the HL, which has increasingly become a point of tension in HLA as students see less value in knowing and using their HL and parents and teachers express desire for students to build and maintain that HL.

For HLA teachers, communicating to students that their HL holds value and utility is essential. The bilingual teachers in HLA model this value and utility more naturally but the monolingual English-speaking teacher also seeks opportunities to (re)position the HL. This strategy entails the teacher positioning herself as a learner alongside students and families:

> Instead of me asking the questions and anticipating a certain answer, I am able to ask students questions with a different kind of genuine curiosity. In some cases, I am completely reliant on the students to translate, to show me where and what they are reading in Spanish. Through this experience, my role as a teacher has changed. The student-teacher relationship has become a partnership where both parties are reliant on the other to be the master of their craft and language. Not only has it changed my approach in teaching, it has given me a new appreciation for the students and families in HLA. (Jennifer, teacher anecdotes, 2020)

In this way, not only did the teacher develop her own positive emotions in terms of the families, their culture, and the HL, but her work to create a partnership with students and families communicated that she valued and was interested in the HL. She positioned bilingualism as an asset, creating a space in which the HLLs in the program could feel and express pride in their HL and develop a stronger sense of their linguistic assets as belonging in HLA.

By positioning bilingualism as a tool of empowerment in HLA, practices such as translanguaging (García, 2007) are legitimized and can be leveraged by agentive families in the production and implementation of projects situated in local community settings. One of the HLA projects engaged families in envisioning future career options with their children. This intergenerational work constructed a space for students to consider what role their HL knowledge and skills might play in pursuing their career.

In addition, HLA work is often conducted across the borders and boundaries (Anzaldúa, 2007) of traditional schooling spaces. That is, lessons and projects are planned to serve as a bridge between family activities and student learning, between the spaces in which English is spoken and the spaces in which Spanish is spoken, and between what it means to learn at home and what it means to learn at school. In HLA, families created a tutoring video in Spanish about a math strategy discussed in school and shared the video with other Spanish-speaking parents. Through this project, families and students worked collaboratively to use their HL and their knowledge about the math strategy to generate a shared understanding of the concepts in ways that crossed home and school boundaries.

These practices encourage a fluid shifting of the role of expert (Abbott et al., 2019). Parents are as likely to be positioned as knowledgeable experts as are teachers because all types of knowledge are legitimized. This was illustrated by one of the HLA's narrative-writing projects in which students were engaged in conducting interviews and writing narratives about their family history. Through this process, the teachers were positioned as experts in knowledge about narrative-writing strategies (e.g., narrative structure and the writing process) while parents were positioned as experts in cultural narrative practices and language. This shifting of expertise across participants is empowered by HLA's shared spaces and is essential to promoting positive emotions about the HL and culture and increases the sense of belonging participants experience.

Building Positive Social Relations

To overcome the challenges many CLD families experience in building positive relations, HLA works to contextualize academic learning by leveraging the sociolinguistic realities of HLLs and their families. The program itself provides opportunities for teachers to engage more extensively and in different contexts with HLLs and their families to surface these sociolinguistic realities. HLA teachers develop a deeper understanding of the students and their families by building positive social relations (Gonzalez, Eades, &

Supple, 2014) that inform teachers' visions of instruction and curriculum for constructing spaces of belonging.

The one monolingual English-speaking teacher in HLA was drawn to the program for this opportunity to build stronger relationships with students and families. Her assumptions that some of the Latin* students were "tough" with "high levels of disciplinary issues" were disrupted because of the act of relationship-building in the HLA context. She attributed her change in perception to the intentional construction of HLA as a place with "space to play, to chat, to get to know each other" (Jennifer, teacher anecdotes, 2020). This ability to play—an approach to teaching and learning that is free of the standardized pressures and traditional structures of school—is at the heart of what the teacher believed to be the power of relationship-building in HLA. Thus, she explained, what began as "Hey, Miss! Do a TikTok with us!" led to "Hey, Miss, if I'm having trouble in my other classes, can I come see you?" or "Hey, Miss, can I tell you about my family?" (Jennifer, teacher anecdotes, 2020). Even more importantly, as evidenced by these statements, the relationship-building in HLA spaces carries the potential for transferal into the more traditional spaces of Monday through Friday schooling so that HLLs and their families feel a stronger sense of belonging across all spaces.

HLA utilizes several strategies to contextualize academic learning by leveraging the sociolinguistic realities of HLLs and their families. First, lessons and projects intentionally target the leveraging of personal and familial strengths for learning in the building of relationships within the HLA context. To encourage intergenerational communication, particularly in the HL and between middle-school students and their parents, families were engaged in HLA in the visioning project about children's future careers by writing a letter to their children about what they considered to be their children's strengths and how they would support their children's aspirations. In their own writing about their future careers, students incorporated these strengths into imagining how they might accomplish the necessary goals to reach their dreams.

This work to link the sociolinguistic knowledges and experiences of home and family with students' formal learning expands traditional notions of what learning can look like and in what context learning can occur (Gutiérrez, 2008). The notion that learning only happens in schools and with expert teachers is subverted by stretching the borders and boundaries of formal and informal learning. This expansion of learning spaces empowers different types of knowledge to be leveraged across those spaces, communicating that all knowledges belong. By taking an asset-based approach that recognizes the wealth of knowledge and experience diverse students bring to learning (He et al., 2015), HLA empowers families to form inquiry groups about how home interactions might support their students' academic learning in school.

This work strengthens relationships between families and their children through interaction, between families and schools as parents' confidence in navigating the system of schooling grows, and between families and their larger sociocultural community as they develop a sense of agency and voice in the schooling of their children.

In addition, positive relations are also constructed through the process of decentralizing decision-making about content and pedagogy. Teachers, and thus the school, are not positioned as having the ultimate authority in making decisions about teaching and learning in HLA. Instead, teachers often elicit feedback from parents or leverage the informal work of the HLA classroom to inform the planning and implementation of future sessions. For example, when discussions in the family classroom began to frequently involve frustration about communication with their children at home, particularly in the HL, HLA teachers designed the narrative oral history project to engage children in interviewing their families and writing their narratives in Spanish. They also facilitated inquiry groups around the topic in the family classroom. Families often share that this strategy increases the positive interactions and sense of belonging they experience with their children in the home.

Promoting Meaningful Involvement

To overcome obstacles associated with involvement, HLA supports HLLs and their families by creating spaces in which they belong by envisioning how families could meaningfully participate and adapt or accommodate rather than assimilate (Portes et al., 2009). Their work toward this aspect of belonging challenges the notion that CLD families should aspire to "pass" as part of mainstream culture by participating in ways that defer to other people or selectively forget in order to feel as if they belong. To accomplish this, HLA centers families in their vision of teaching and learning, as well as in the implementation of instruction. That is, the program acknowledges and leverages families' agency and voice in shaping learning.

One of the bilingual teachers, who, as an immigrant from Mexico, shares some of the linguistic and cultural knowledges possessed by HLA families, explained how she thought about planning for involvement in terms of teaching the parent component of HLA:

> Before I took on the task of leading the parent component, I received an important lesson to follow: "I advise you to not lecture parents. They don't like it." This stayed in my head while I was planning for HLA sessions. Seven sessions was [*sic*] a challenge to start with because, to me, parents needed to take away meaningful experiences. I knew that parents would have a variety of knowledge

of English and computer skills. I knew parents in general were interested in their children having educational opportunities. (Adriana, teacher anecdotes, 2020)

The teacher plans for meaningful involvement by leveraging families' "wealth of information" (teacher anecdotes, 2020). Although families attend HLA to be better informed, she recognizes that they also have expertise. For many parents, hearing from other CLD families in HLA spaces motivates attendance and involvement in essential community-building that is a defining feature of HLA. She explained:

> The parents help each other with the diverse skills and information they possess. For example, one of HLA goals was for parents to create a presentation using technology. This made some of them uneasy because they would have to use a computer. Going step-by-step was not feasible because of time so having individuals with varying levels of knowledge about how to use computers was an issue at first. However, it turned out to be an opportunity for some to step in and others to feel comfortable and grateful. They all felt pride in what they were able to do. (Adriana, teacher anecdotes, 2020)

At the center of HLA's ability to construct these spaces of involvement for families is a shared background and understanding of cultural references, which create a sense of community, a sense of energy, and a willingness to share personal and cultural knowledges in collaborative learning tasks. Strategies incorporated to create this context include bringing together a group of like-minded people, including teachers who share beliefs about the value and utility of the HL and associated knowledge, and families who desire to build and sustain both in school and community spaces. This like-mindedness enables HLA to use culture and language as a binding experience, leveraging shared experience as a source of "moral, social, cultural, and economic support" for belonging (Rumbaut, 1997, p. 7). Incorporating projects, like the family history narratives, leverage both culture and language as a point of connectedness, increasing families' willingness to share their stories. The narratives allowed families to find the familiarity in the stories of others and to share in the emotions that this familiarity raised—an experience much less common for HLLs and their families in the context of more mainstream schooling.

Additionally, the work of HLA intentionally connects classroom experiences with the experiences of HLLs and their families to acknowledge and leverage background and knowledges that are not typically recognized in the traditional classroom. An example of this bridging involved a project that engaged students in identifying, researching, and developing solutions to issues in the local Latin* community. This project opened space for some affected families to address their legal status, a taboo topic in the traditional classroom, to collaboratively problem-solve issues like not being able to pick children up for school without an accepted form of identification. One student used Legos to build tiny homes (i.e., houses sized under 600 square feet) to imagine how housing might protect Latin* families by making them movable and dispersed so families could not be easily located in ICE raids. In this way, HLA adapts instruction to be inclusive of the experiences of HLLs and their families, providing spaces for them to feel a sense of belonging through meaningful participation.

This bridging of school knowledge with the knowledge of families contributes to the construction of spaces that help families feel comfortable coming to school and sharing their own stories and work. Incorporation of these family-oriented components of education supports their willingness and energy to be involved with HLA activities both within and beyond formal HLA spaces. An example includes the centering of families' informal knowledges and practices within a unit on financial literacy. An understanding of financial literacy practices (e.g., saving for college using 529 Plans, budgeting for routine family expenses within US contexts) was built upon what families already understood and did. This centering of informal knowledge encourages family participation by communicating the message that families already hold valuable expertise that belong in the learning space and contribute to the learning process.

Developing and Sustaining Harmonization

HLA addresses the challenges associated with harmonization by maintaining a flexible curriculum design supporting a sense of belonging that emphasizes the process of learning and sharing with consideration for standard-based content and language proficiency demands (Howard et al., 2018). Although more formal modes of learning are not dismissed, they are meaningfully integrated with the beliefs and practices that define learning in community and family settings. This space provides opportunities for HLLs and their families to construct new ways of learning that fulfill the requirements of formal school settings but still honor the informal knowledges that families and communities possess.

For example, in the construction of narrative histories, as students interviewed their families and collaboratively created initial transcripts with them, the teachers made the intentional decision not to provide any instruction about what languages the interviews and transcripts should use. Some families used English and some used Spanish, but there were also families that created the transcript using translanguaging practices. The provision of space for translanguaging practices enabled HLLs and their families to navigate the cognitive, metacognitive, and affective demands of constructing formal narratives about family histories by leveraging their varied linguistic repertoires.

Rather than placing demand on individuals in the HLA to accommodate school practices, the HLA employs specific strategies to disrupt traditional notions of instruction and create a sense of belonging through harmonization. First, curriculum and instruction welcome the introduction of knowledge and strategies not traditionally valued in mainstream classrooms in ways that allow for explicitly naming differences in linguistic and cultural norms and practices. By doing so, HLA spaces invite the flexible application of these multiple linguistic and cultural practices. In writing and revising narrative family histories in the HL, conversations arose around different linguistic practices originating from families' home countries. These differences were named, explored, and then leveraged in the telling of stories.

Based upon their experiences with HLA, the teachers also consistently engage in reflective practices and action research to adapt instruction and curriculum within and across HLA sessions. These reflective practices include debriefing as a team at the end of every instructional day and implementing ideas that arise through conversations for creation of both shorter-term and longer-term changes. Examples of action research include a focus on facilitating intergenerational communication (Kwon, 2017) through and beyond HLA activities. Findings from this teacher action research project were presented at a local conference (He et al., 2017) and were leveraged in planning for future HLA sessions by considering ways in which this intergenerational communication could be positioned as an asset in supporting students' development and achievement of future academic and career aspirations.

Finally, challenges in harmonization are addressed through the utilization of instructional strategies that target the three major aspects of learning—cognitive, metacognitive, and affective (Vermunt, 1996). Thus, HLLs and their families are provided with opportunities to explore and adapt to the learning context in multiple ways. The family history narrative project provides an example of the ways in which all three aspects of learning were targeted. Cognitive skills were addressed in terms of structuring narratives and examining how narratives are written both in the United States and in families' home countries. Metacognitively, families considered linguistic variations in the HL and made decisions about how to best communicate family stories in both English and the HL. And in terms of affective learning, multiple opportunities were provided for families to engage in project work, including whole group instruction, small group and one-on-one work, and during work time within family units. These opportunities incorporate instruction and discussion to create spaces of belonging across the English and Spanish languages. By engaging in learning through the integration of all three aspects of learning, the HLA context was adapted to give HLLs and their families' multiple opportunities to work collaboratively and develop their sense of belonging.

LESSONS LEARNED

In this section, we highlight the positive outcomes and summarize lessons learned in the last 10 years as we design and implement the HLA partnership program. Recommendations for other educators interested in initiating and sustaining similar partnerships are also provided.

HLA demonstrates positive outcomes and impact for a variety of stakeholders involved. First, the program offers a safe and welcoming space for students, families, and educators to use their full linguistic repertoires in navigating the teaching and learning process. Even though learners and teachers involved in this program are not all fully English–Spanish bilingual, the use of both languages offers the opportunity for everyone to develop their language competency and legitimize the use of a variety of forms of English and Spanish through heteroglossic practices (Blackledge & Creese, 2014). Students' speeches about academic and career goals and parents' letters to their children describing their strengths are good examples of how the multilingual space engaged all participants in discussing their values for education and their visions for academic success. Second, participants' completed projects highlighted their collective values and have generative impact in the community in terms of creating spaces for belonging. To promote positive parenting, for example, families who participated in HLA shared tips and resources for positive parenting and created a website to share this information with other community members. In addition, family members who participated in the HLA program have also been invited to serve on the parent advisory board at the school district. With their input and educators' support, the district launched its first Spanish–English dual language/immersion program at the elementary school in the 2016–2017 academic year. Third, the sustained partnership among the community, the school, and the university makes it possible to leverage human, financial, organizational, and community resources to support the implementation and continued improvement of the program.

At HLA, school administrators and teachers are actively engaged in designing and leading HLA instruction, while university teacher educators and teacher candidates support the action research efforts. Financially, the program benefits from various grant programs co-led by university and district personnel and the generous support from local private foundations. The organizational structure and existing collaboration between the university and the school district allow for shared responsibility in terms of facility use for HLA program offerings, including the graduation ceremony. Situating the program within the local community creates a network of support that enhances awareness of the benefits of the program and ensures continued participation of students and families because they feel a stronger sense of belonging in HLA.

The HLA context and specific strategies offer insights for educators and communities facing similar challenges along the four attributes of belonging detailed in this chapter. Table 9.2 provides a summary of the challenges, HLA context, and strategies.

For those who are interested in initiating or sustaining similar efforts for HLLs and their families, here are some specific lessons learned. First, it is critical to involve both families and students when designing programs targeting HLLs. Not only do families offer support, they are integral partners and experts in HL and culture learning. Meaningful involvement should start with the design of the program and be integrated throughout the implementation and continued improvement plan rather than as an addition to the established program curriculum. The evolved designs of the intergenerational projects in HLA are good examples of how to integrate the linguistic and cultural knowledges of CLD families.

Second, intentionally bridging and crossing the boundaries between learning practices within and beyond school settings enhances participants' sense of belonging. Educators and community leaders from diverse linguistic and cultural backgrounds with various educational experiences may be well-positioned to serve as the "broker" to initiate the boundary crossing. For example, teachers who are bilingual or HLLs themselves may be able to more readily connect with families who share similar backgrounds and experiences. Families who are cultural connectors (i.e., possess greater familiarity with the system of schooling) and cultural leaders (i.e., advocate to communicate the needs of immigrant families) may be positioned to take the leadership role in HL program design and implementation (Love & Han, 2015). In addition, a shared commitment to promote multilingual and multicultural development in ways that challenge traditional, standardized approaches to language instruction for the purpose of assessing language use can support boundary crossing. An underlying flexible and cooperative program structure encourages participation and lends value to the knowledges that may not be recognized or legitimized through traditional schooling.

Finally, localized professional capacity building to sustain and enhance the program needs to be taken into consideration through cooperative inquiry processes for the long-term impact of HL programs. Educators' critical reflections on language ideologies and engaged action research studying the HL program components and impact can further build both instructional and

Table 9.2   Summary of Challenges, HLA Context, and Strategies

Attributes of Belonging	*Challenges*	*HLA Context and Strategies*
Positive Emotions	• Subtractive schooling practices • Lack of recognition of linguistic/familial capital and funds of knowledge	• Position bilingualism as an asset, and multilingualism as a tool of empowerment • Cross borders and boundaries of traditional schooling spaces • Shift roles in teaching and learning
Positive Relationship	• Generational distance • Lack of recognition of social and familial capitals	• Recognize and leverage the sociolinguistic realities of HLLs and their families • Encourage intergenerational interactions and collaborations • Build teacher–student–family relationships in a safe space that encourages play • Decentralize decision-making about content and pedagogy
Meaningful Involvement	• Legitimization of school knowledges that constrain voice and agency • Lack of recognition of social and aspirational capitals	• Acknowledge and leverage families' agency and voice in shaping learning • Cultivate a sense of community based on shared background and understanding of cultural references and shared values of HL • Bridge school knowledge with the knowledge of families through project-based cooperative learning experiences
Harmonization	• Demand on learners to balance multilinguistic and multicultural norms and practices • Lack of recognition of resistant and navigational capital • Institutional resistance to change	• Maintain a flexible curriculum design to emphasize the process of learning and sharing • Engage in ongoing reflective practices and action research for program improvement • Target cognitive, metacognitive, and affective learning

research capacity in local settings to improve and sustain HL efforts. In addition, the sharing of outcomes from the various collaborative intergenerational projects also leads to better understanding of local community needs and resources. Such sustained capacity building in local schools and communities provides the foundation for shifts in schooling practices and boundary crossings in teaching and learning for constructing spaces of belonging.

CONCLUSION

Different from a fixed, predetermined, and one-way teaching and learning environment, HLA reflects a space where learning is a flexible, cooperative, and engaged inquiry process that engages all stakeholders to support their sense of belonging. The establishment of shared values of HL and the recognition of a heteroglossic language ideology provide the foundation for students, families, educators, and teacher educators to work together in such a learning space. In addition, the flexibility and shifting roles in the curriculum design, implementation, and improvement process empower all participants to contribute to learning based on their individual expertise, experiences, and passion.

Codesigning collaborative learning projects that not only focus on traditional cognitive learning outcomes (e.g., language proficiency) but that also target metacognitive and affective goals becomes possible. This engaged process (e.g., through projects that encourage intergenerational interactions) presents an example of considering family engagement as an integral aspect, rather than supplementary component, of teaching and learning. These projects also present evidence that the artificial boundaries between home and schooling experiences can be crossed to cultivate a more productive learning space that recognizes participants' funds of knowledge and community cultural wealth (Gonzalez et al., 2005; Yosso, 2005). Finally, continuous program improvement is achieved through action research conducted by practitioners and community partners through cooperative inquiry. The constructionist nature of the inquiry process generates localized expertise and knowledge that builds capacity within the program and sustains program development to support individual and community belonging.

Collaborative and reflective dialogues are at the center of the HLA design and implementation process. Participants' sense of belonging to the HLA space is constructed through extensive dialogue and storytelling using participants' full linguistic repertories and cultural knowledge. Such an engaged program design holds potential for supporting a sense of belonging for HLLs and their families. HL programs like HLA can expand opportunities that CLD families have, for achieving not only higher levels of academic learning but also higher levels of well-being. Commitment to centering language and knowledge as multidimensional and the impact of this commitment as illustrated by HLA outcomes thus far are indicative of the power of what Habermas (1999) called *communicative action* (p. ix). As Arendt (1958) claimed, narration possesses the power of action. By engaging in the telling of their stories and in sensemaking activities around those tellings, HLLs and their families gain access, in both understanding and action, to the political realm where their narrative actions hold potential for transforming teaching and learning processes for all CLD families to feel a sense of belonging in school.

NOTES

1. Pronounced Latin. Latin* is used as an all-inclusive term that considers the fluidity of social identities that currently exist (e.g., Latin*, Latiné, Latinu, Latino, Latina, Latina/o, Latin@, Latin, Latin American) and that may emerge in the future. Latin* opens space for Latin American peoples to self-identify and, thus, works to give voice to those who have been traditionally oppressed and whose identities have been framed by colonization.

2. We adopt the term *knowledges* to disrupt claims of a universal knowledge and recognize the multiple-situated knowledges possessed by culturally and linguistically diverse students and their families.

REFERENCES

Abbott, D. M., Pelc, N., & Mercier, C. (2019). Cultural humility and the teaching of psychology. *Scholarship of Teaching and Learning in Psychology, 5*(2), 169–181. doi:10.1037/stl0000144

Allen, K., & Bowles, T. (2012). Belonging as a guiding principle in the education of adolescents. *Australian Journal of Educational & Developmental Psychology, 12*, 108–119.

Allen, K., Kern, M., Vella-Brodrick, D., Hattie, J., & Waters, L. (2018). What schools need to know about fostering school belonging: A meta-analysis. *Educational Psychology Review, 30*(1), 1–34. doi:10.1007/s10648-016-9389-8

Allen, K., Vella-Brodrick, D., & Waters, L. (2017). School belonging and the role of social and emotional competencies in fostering an adolescent's sense of connectedness to their school. In E. Frydenberg, A. J. Martin, & R. J. Collie (Eds.), *Social and emotional learning in Australia and the Asia-Pacific: Perspectives, programs and approaches* (pp. 83–99). Springer.

Anant, S. S. (1967). Belongingness and mental health: Some research findings. *Acta Psychologica, 26*(4), 391–396. doi :10.1016/0001-6918(67)90035-2

Anzaldúa, G. (2007). *Borderlands/la frontera: The new mestiza.* Aunt Lute Books.

Arendt, H. (1958). *The human condition.* University of Chicago Press.

Beaudrie, S. M., Ducar, C., & Potowski, K. (2014). *Heritage language teaching: Research and practice.* Columbus, OH: McGraw-Hill.

Beaudrie, S. M., Ducar, C., & Relaño-Pastor, A. M. (2009). Curricular perspectives in the heritage language context: Assessing culture and identity. *Language, Culture and Curriculum, 22*, 157–174. doi:10.1080/07908310903067628

Bell-Corrales, M. (2006). The role of positive attitudes and motivation in minority language maintenance. *Journal of the Georgia Philological Association, 1*, 126–157.

Belpoliti, F., & Fairclough, M. (2016). Inquiry-based projects in the Spanish heritage language classroom: Connecting culture and community through research. *Hispania, 99*(2), 258–273. doi:10.1353/hpn.2016.0045

Berkovich, I. (2011). No we won't! Teachers' resistance to educational reform. *Journal of Educational Administration, 49*(5), 563–578. doi:10.1108/09578231111159548

Bernstein, B. (1996). *Pedagogy, symbolic control and identity.* Taylor & Francis.

Blackledge, A., & Creese, A. (2010). *Multilingualism: A critical perspective.* Continuum.

Blackledge, A., & Creese, A. (2014). Heteroglossia as practice and pedagogy. In A. Blackledge, & A. Creese (Eds.), *Heteroglossia as practice and pedagogy* (pp. 1–20). Springer.

Cardona, B., Noble, G., & Di Base, B. (2008). *Community languages matter: Challenges and opportunities facing the community language program in New South Wales.* Penrith.

Center for Applied Linguistics. (2020). *Heritage language program database.* Retrieved from http://www.cal.org/heritage

Cha, Y.-K., Ham, S.-H., & Yang, K. –E. (2017). Multicultural education policy in the global institutional context. In Y. –K. Cha, J. Gundara, S. –H. Ham, & M. Lee (Eds.), *Multicultural education in global perspectives* (pp. 11–21). Springer Nature.

Civil Rights Data Collection (2015). *English learner (EL) report.* Retrieved from: https://ocrdata.ed.gov/Page?t=d&eid=29088&syk=8&pid=2537

Coryell, J. E., Clark, M. C., & Pomerantz, A. (2010). Cultural fantasy narratives and heritage language learning: A case study of adult heritage learners of Spanish. *The Modern Language Journal, 94*(iii), 453–469. doi:10.1111/j.1540-4781.2010.01055.x

Czubinska, G. (2017). Migration as an unconscious search for identity: Some reflection on language, difference and belonging. *British Journal of Psychotherapy, 33*, 159–176. doi:10.1111/bjp.12286

Delgado-Gaitan, C. (2001). *The power of community: Mobilizing for family and schooling.* Rowman and Littlefield Publishers.

Demanet, J., & Van Houtte, M. (2012). School belonging and school misconduct; the differing role of teacher and peer attachment. *Journal of Youth Adolescence, 41*, 499–514. doi:10.1007/s10964-011-9674-2

Fairbanks, C. M., Faircloth, B., Gonzalez, L., He, Y., Tan, E. & Zoch, M. (2017). Beyond commodified knowledge: The possibilities of powerful community learning spaces. In S. Salas & P. R. Portes (Eds), *Latinization of K–12 communities: National perspectives on regional change* (pp.43–65). SUNY Press.

Francis, B., Archer, L., & Mau, A. (2010). Parents' and teachers' constructions of the purpose of Chinese complementary schooling: 'Culture,' identity, and power. *Race Ethnicity and Education, 13*, 101–117. doi:10.1080/13613320903550089

Freire, P. (1972). *Pedagogy of the oppressed.* Penguin Books.

García, O. (2007). Foreword. In S. Makoni & A. Pennycook (Eds.). *Disinventing and reconstructing languages* (pp. xi–xv). Multilingual Matters.

García, O. (2009). *Bilingual education in the 21st century: A global perspective.* John Wiley & Sons.

Gonzalez, L. M., Eades, M. P., & Supple, A. J. (2014). School community engaging with immigrant youth: Incorporating personal/social development and ethnic identity development. *School Community Journal, 24*, 99–117.

Gonzalez, N., Moll, L. C., & Amanti, C. (Eds.). (2005). *Funds of knowledge: Theorizing practice in households, communities, and classrooms.* Lawrence Erlbaum.

Gutiérrez, K. D. (2008). Developing a sociocritical literacy in the Third Space. *Reading Research Quarterly, 43*(2), 148–164. doi:10.1598/RRQ.43.2.3

Habermas, J. (1971). *Knowledge and human interests.* Beacon Press.

Habermas, J. (1998). *Moral consciousness and communicative action.* MIT Press.

Haslam, S. A., Jetten, J., Postmes, T., & Haslam, C. (2009). Social identity, health and well-being: An emerging agenda for applied psychology. *Applied Psychology: An International Review, 58*, 1–28. doi:10.1111/j.1464-0597.2008.00379.x

He, A. W. (2012). Heritage language socialization. In A. Duranti, E. Ochs, & B. B. Schieffelin (Eds.), *The handbook of language socialization* (pp. 587–609). Blackwell Publishing.

He, Y., Bettez, S. C., & Levin, B. B. (2015). Imagined community of education: Voices from refugees and immigrants. *Urban Education, 52*(8), 957–985.

He, Y., Hinman, T., Call, C., Harris, R., Paschal, A., Abercrombie, C., & Rodriguez, C. (2017, September). Heritage language academy: A university, school, and community collaboration. Coalition of Diverse Language Communities (CDLC) at UNCG, Greensboro, NC.

He, Y. & Prater, K. (2011). Collaboration in professional development for ELL content achievement. In C. J. Casteel & K. G. Ballantyne (Eds.), *Professional development in action: Improving teaching for English learners* (pp. 85–86). NCELA.

Hinman, T. & He, Y. (2017). Hybrid practices in the alternative learning spaces of community-based heritage language programs. *New Waves, 20*(1), 1–22.

Holt-Lunstad, J., Smith, T. B., & Layton, B. (2010). Social relationships and mortality risk: A meta-analytic review. *PloSMed 7*(7), 1–20. doi:10.1371/journal.pmed.1000316

Hornberger, N. H., & Wang, S. C. (2008). Who are our heritage language learners? Identity and biliteracy in heritage language education in the United States. In D. M. Brinton, O. Kagan, & S. Bauckus (Eds.), *Heritage language education: A new field emerging* (pp. 3–35). Routledge.

Howard, E. R., Lindholm-Leary, K. J., Rogers, D., Olague, N., Medina, J., Kennedy, B., Sugarman, J., & Christian, D. (2018). *Guiding principles for dual language education* (3rd ed.). Center for Applied Linguistics.

Jeon, M. (2008). Korean heritage language maintenance and language ideology. *Heritage Language Journal, 6*, 54–70.

Kwon, J. (2017). Immigrant mothers' beliefs and transnational strategies for their children's heritage language maintenance. *Language and Education, 31*(6), 495–508. doi:10.1080/09500782.2017.1349137

Lang, J. C. (2011). Epistemologies of situated knowledges: "Troubling" knowledge in philosophy of education. *Educational Theory, 61*(1), 75–96. doi:10.1111/j.1741-5446.2011.00392.x

Lee, J. S., & Wright, W. E. (2014). The rediscovery of heritage and community language education in the United States. *Review of Research in Education, 38*(1), 137–165. doi:10.3102/0091732X13507546

Leeman, J., Rabin, L., & Román-Mendoza, E. Identity and activism in heritage language education (2011). *The Modern Language Journal, 95*(4), 481–495. doi:10.1111/j.1540-4781.2011.01237.x

Lewis, G., Jones, B., & Baker, C. (2012). Translanguaging: Origins and development from school to street and beyond. *Educational Research and Evaluation: An International Journal on Theory and Practice, 18*(7), 641–654. doi:10.1080/13803611.2012.718488

Little, S. (2020). Whose heritage? What inheritance? Conceptualizing family language identities. *International Journal of Bilingual Education and Bilingualism, 23*(2), 198–212. doi:10.1080/13670050.2017.1348463

Love, J., & Han, Y. (2015). Stages of immigrant parent involvement – survivors to leaders. *Phi Delta Kappan, 97*(4), 21–25. doi:10.1177/0031721715619913

Makoni, S., & Pennycook, A. (2007). *Disinventing and reconstituting languages.* Multilingual Matters.

May, V. (2011). Self, belonging and social change. *Sociology, 45*, 363–378. doi:10.1177/0038038511399624

Menken, K. (2008). *English learners left behind: Standardized testing as language policy.* Multilingual Matters.

Menken, K., & Kleyn, T. (2010). The long-term impact of subtractive schooling in the educational experiences of secondary English language learners. *International Journal of Bilingual Education and Bilingualism, 13*(4), 399–417. doi:10.1080/13670050903370143

Mills, J. (2001). Being bilingual: Perspectives of third generation Asian children on language, culture and identity. *International Journal of Bilingual Education and Bilingualism, 4*, 383–402. doi:10.1080/13670050108667739

Nesteruk, O. (2010). Heritage language maintenance and loss among the children of Eastern European immigrants in the USA. *Journal of Multilingual and Multicultural Development, 31*(3), 271–286. doi:10.1080/01434630903582722

Nieto, S., & Bode, P. (2008). *Affirming diversity: The sociopolitical context of multicultural education* (5th ed.). Pearson.

Nordstrom, J. (2016). Parents' reasons for community language schools: Insight from a high-shift, non-visible, middle-class community. *Language and Education, 30*(6), 519–535. doi:10.1080/09500782.2016.1168431

Norton, B. (2013). *Identity and language learning: Extending the conversation* (2nd ed.). Multilingual Matters.

Osterman, K. F. (2000). Students' need for belonging in the school community. *Review of Educational Research, 70*(3), 323–367. doi:10.3102/00346543070003323

Pagan-Rivera, M. S. (2014). Risk and protective factors for depression in Mexican-American youth: The impact of generational status, family, and parental influences. *Social Work in Mental Health, 13*, 252–271. doi:10.1080/15332985.2014.896848

Pavlenko, A. (2002). "We have room for but one language here": Language and national identity in the U.S. at the turn of the 20th century. *Multilingua, 2*, 163–196. doi:10.1515/mult.2002.008

Pennycook, A. (2010). *Language and local practice.* Routledge.

Portes, A., Fernández-Kelly, P., & Haller, W. (2009). The adaptation of the immigrant second generation in America: A theoretical overview and recent evidence. *Journal of Ethnic and Migration Studies, 35*(7), 1077–1104. doi:10.1080/13691830903006127

Roche, C., & Kuperminc, G. P. (2012). *Multicultural counseling in the schools: A practical handbook.* Allyn and Bacon.

Rumbaut, R. (1997). Ties that bind: Immigration and immigrant families in the United States. In A. Booth, A. C. Crouter, & N. Landale (Eds.), *Immigration and the family: Research and policy on U.S. Immigrants* (pp. 3–46). Lawrence Erlbaum Associates, Inc.

Salinas, C. (2020). The Complexity of the "x" in Latin*: How Latin*/a/o Students Relate to, Identify With, and Understand the Term Latin*. *Journal of Hispanic Higher Education, 19*(2), 149–168. doi:10.1177/1538192719900382

Saraví, G. A., Bayón, M. C., & Azaola, M. C. (2020). Constructing school belonging(s) in disadvantaged urban spaces: Adolescents' experiences and narratives in Mexico City. *Youth and Society, 52*(7), 1107–1127. doi:10.1177/0044118X19838188

Sibley, E., & Brabeck, K. (2017). Latino immigrant students' school experiences in the United States: The importance of family-school-community collaborations. *School Community Journal, 27*, 137–157.

Slaten, C. D., Ferguson, J. K., Allen, K., Brodrick, D., & Waters, L. (2016). School belonging: A review of the history, current trends, and future directions. *The Educational and Developmental Psychologist, 33*, 1–15. doi:10.1017/edp.2016.6

St-Amand, J., Girard, S., & Smith, J. (2017). Sense of belonging at school: Defining attributes, determinants, and sustaining strategies. *IAFOR Journal of Education, 5*(2), 105–119. doi:10.22492/ije.5.2.05

U.S. Census Bureau (2017). Language spoken at home. *2013–2017 American Community Survey 5-year estimates.* Retrieved from: https://factfinder.census .gov/faces/tableservices/jsf/pages/productview.xhtml?pid=ACS_17_5YR_S1601 &prodType=table

Valdés, G. (2006). The foreign language teaching profession and the challenges of developing language resources. In G. Valdés, J. A. Fishman, R. Chávez, & W. Pérez (Eds.), *Developing minority language resources: The case of Spanish in California* (pp. 108–139). Multilingual Matters.

Valdez, T. M., & Lugg, C. Community cultural wealth and Chicano/Latino Students. *Journal of School Public Relations, 31*(3), 224–237. doi:10.3138/jspr.31.3.224

Valenzuela, A. (1999). *Subtractive schooling: U.S.-Mexican youth and the politics of caring.* State University of New York Press.

Vermunt, J. D. (1996). Metacognitive, cognitive and affective aspects of learning styles and strategies: A phenomenographic analysis. *Higher Education, 31*, 25–50. doi:10.1007/BF00129106

Vetter, A. (2012). Teachers as architects of transformation: The change process of an elementary-school teacher in a practitioner research group. *Teacher Education Quarterly, 39*(1), 27–49.

Walker, L., & Avant, K. C. (2011). *Strategies for theory construction* (5th ed.). New York: Prentice Hall.

Yosso, T. J. (2005). Whose culture has capital? A critical race theory discussion of community cultural wealth. *Race, Ethnicity, and Education, 8,* 69–91. doi:10.1080/1361332052000341006

Zimmerman, J. (2006). Why some teachers resist change and what principals can do about it. *NASSP Bulletin, 90*(3), 238–249. doi:10.1177/0192636506291521

Chapter 10

Community Voices

Belonging Narratives of Youth Recently Arrived in the United States

Beverly S. Faircloth, Tierney B. Hinman,
Pratigya Marhatta, Dominique McDaniel,
Amy Vetter, and Melody Zoch

INTRODUCTION

Against the backdrop of the complex transcultural and transnational inter-sectionalities that characterize American society (Crenshaw, 1993; Garcia Coll et al., 1996), sense of belonging has recently been referred to as one of the premier social issues of our time (Allen & Boyle, 2016). Research and theory have consistently demonstrated that belonging serves as a universal and pivotal determinant of positive development (Baumeister & Leary, 1995; Garcia Coll et al., 1996; Goodenow, 1993; Osterman, 2000). As under-scored by Ozer et al. (2008), however, immigrant and refugee individuals are likely to experience cultural and linguistic barriers to such connections due to the contrasts they negotiate as they move across the "multiple worlds" that constitute their school, family, and neighborhood settings. Nearly one in four Americans—70 million people—is an immigrant or the child of an immigrant(s)—some of whom are fleeing war, persecution, or environmental disaster as refugees—raising a raft of important considerations relative to supporting positive development among this group. Moreover, the percent of this population that is school age (under 18) is 40–50 percent (Homeland Security, 2019; Ryu & Tuvilla, 2018), underscoring the importance of atten-tion to the developmental needs for this age group in particular.

Research has made clear that such cultural contrasts—if not handled well—can seriously impede belonging and development (Faircloth, 2018; Berry et al., 2006; Cartmell & Bond, 2012; Garcia Coll et al., 1996; Kia-Keating &

Ellis, 2007; Urdan, 2011). For example, refugee resettlement communities often attempt to socialize new arrivals into ways of thinking and doing that reflect the cultural norms of the majority society (Asante, 2003; Banks, 1994; Vedder, 1994). As a key example, school curricula and policies have persistently excluded the perspectives and histories of marginalized youth, seemingly operating under the assumption that the process of becoming educated is a race-neutral or colorblind experience (Cammorata, 2015; Dee & Penner, 2017; de los Rios et al., 2014; Paris & Alim, 2017; Urrieta, 2009). This ignores the fact that "sustaining the cultural ways of being" of nondominant groups has been shown to serve a vital promotive and protective function, combatting the "dehumanization of marginalized communities by preserving and nurturing linguistic, literate, and cultural pluralism" (Coppola et al., 2019, p. 227). Informal learning settings (e.g., after-school clubs, summer camps, digital spaces) are somewhat more effective at supporting marginalized youth (Calabrese Barton & Tan, 2010; Rahm et al., 2005; He et al., 2015), but again, it is individuals who are able to develop a meaningful cultural connection to the host country while maintaining strong connections to their cultural, ethnic, historical, and linguistic heritage that appear to develop the most adaptive behavioral, motivational, and psychological profiles (Garcia Coll et al., 1996). Thus, an effective *pedagogy of belonging* requires practices that change a group of strangers into a successful, *transcultural community of practice* that supports academic, social, and cultural participation and development (Marlsbary, 2012, p. iii).

Given the complexity of belonging, against the backdrop of the rapid growth of new arrivals (e.g., immigrants, refugees) to many US communities, a detailed exploration of how belonging is instantiated in everyday cultural actions for immigrant and refugee youth is timely and necessary. In response to this need in our own community, a group of university professors and students, along with local school teachers, designed *Community Voices*, a two-week summer writing camp for self-identified immigrant and refugee middle- and high-school age youth. The camp experience was designed to (1) meet their writing and belonging needs, (2) respect their culture and identity (consciously building bridges between cultures), and (3) focus on multiliteracies (multiple modes of expression, including the invitation to write in their heritage language). This chapter attempts to unpack the culture and belonging experiences of immigrant and refugee youth participating during one summer of the *Community Voices* camp.

THE CASE FOR BELONGING AMONG IMMIGRANT AND REFUGEE YOUTH

Evolving Understandings of Belonging

Over the last three decades, a large body of work addressing belonging has emerged, which might be drawn upon to understand and support the transcultural and transnational needs of immigrant and refugee youth. Glick-Schiller et al. (1992) define transnationalism as "the process by which immigrants build social fields that link together their country of origin and their country of settlement" (p. 1). In order for immigrant youth to develop a sense of belonging within a transnational/transcultural social field, teachers need to draw upon students' transnational/transcultural funds of knowledge (Moll et al., 1992; Sánchez et al., 2005), suggesting distinct approaches to supporting belonging for immigrant and refugee youth.

Although definitions of belonging vary slightly, theorists and researchers from a wide range of fields agree that an enduring positive sense of meaningful and authentic place within their primary contexts is a nonnegotiable underlying experience for positive development (Faircloth & Hamm, 2005; Baumeister & Leary, 1995; Benner et al., 2008; Goodenow, 1993; Knifsend et al., 2018; Urdan, 2011). For example, in his hierarchy of basic human needs, Maslow (1943, 1999) laid the cornerstone for understanding the universal and essential nature of the need to belong. The seminal conceptual foundations of belonging research, published by Baumeister and Leary in 1995, also identified belonging as central among such needs, fundamental to human well-being and motivation. Aligned with this lens, Gray et al. (2018) describe belonging as a psychological hub that facilitates important outcomes—from motivation and achievement to health and well-being. Indeed research has consistently demonstrated that individuals have salient psychological needs that they are driven to fulfill within their various contexts (Eccles & Roeser, 2011). There is ample evidence that belonging is essential to motivation and learning in school settings in particular—which are often the first and most enduring settings in which youth from disparate cultures encounter one another and diverse societal norms (Benner et al., 2008; Goodenow, 1993; Knifsend et al., 2018). The informal, social, and sometimes community-based nature of outside-of-school and after-school clubs and camps can often help facilitate belonging as well (Calabrese Barton & Tan, 2010; Rahm et al., 2005; He et al., 2015).

Traditionally, explorations of belonging have been well-anchored primarily in interpersonal relationships and participatory experiences (Finn, 1989; Goodenow, 1993; Osterman, 2000). An important and burgeoning shift toward a more sociocultural and critical lens on belonging may be particularly relevant to immigrant and refugee youth by recognizing that the intersectionality between students' culture, identity, and voice, and the dominant culture within which they find themselves during resettlement, can provide important supports, *but also barriers*, to belonging (Faircloth, 2011, 2018; Garcia Coll et al., 1996; Urdan, 2011; Wong et al., 2003). Dominant community settings too often follow an assimilationist model for incorporation of culturally diverse students into a standardized American "whitestream" culture with its prescribed cultural norms (Urietta, 2009, p. 47; see also Asante, 1991;

Banks, 1994; Veder & Horencszk, 1994; Wong et al., 2003). Assimilationist views do not often promote true belonging, as they require individuals and groups to abandon their primary cultural perspectives in favor of others in order to be "accepted." Research has consistently demonstrated that a strong connection with one's heritage culture, *coupled* with a strong connection with a host culture, consistently promotes youth's psychological well-being. For example, Garcia Coll and colleagues' (1996, p. 1891) "integrative model" of development among minority youth and the model of "biculturalism" set forth by LaFromboise et al. (1993, p. 395; see also Valenzuela, 1999) advocate for sociocultural supports that form bridges between an individual's culture of heritage and the host cultures. Indeed, an integrative model, in which individuals are able to develop a meaningful cultural connection to a host community or country that honors and maintains strong connections to their cultural and linguistic heritage, appears to offer the most adaptive behavioral, motivational, and psychological profile (Berry et al., 2006; Coppola et al., 2019; Garcia Coll et al., 1996; LaFromboise et al., 1993; Phelan Davidson & Cao, 1991; Urdan, 2011; Veder & Horencyzk, 2006). These insights insist we look beyond traditional whitestream models of belonging, intentionally positioning positive development as at least a two-dimensional process, including preservation of one's heritage culture and meaningful adaptations to the host society, rather than being a linear process of change requiring giving up one's culture of origin and assimilating into a new culture (Berry, 1990, 1997; Paris & Alim, 2017; Urrieta, 2009).

Belonging Meets Resettlement

As a once leading resettlement country for refugees globally, the United States admitted 1,118,628 refugees during the first two decades of the twenty-first century (2000–2019) (Department of Homeland Security, 2019; US Department of State Refugee Processing Center, 2020). While an immigrant is someone who makes a conscious decision to leave his or her home and move to a foreign country with the intention of settling there, a refugee is a person who is unable or unwilling to return to his or her country of nationality because of persecution or a well-founded fear of serious harm (Section 101(a)(42) of the Immigration and Nationality Act). Although there are definitely distinct experiences between these groups, they have much in common as they both confront the resettlement process. While the project reported here focused primarily on refugee youth, drawing mainly from local refugee communities and the public school designated for first-year arrivals, not all self-reported as refugees, although all reported immigrant backgrounds. Moreover, the very limited research base addressing belonging specifically among refugees led to our adoption of research on belonging among immigrant youth as a proxy, while highlighting insights that were specific to refugees.

For many people, the process of resettlement creates a number of stressors, including moving away from family and friends in their native country, feeling pressure to learn different language or cultural norms, and adapting to a new community (Cervantes & Castro, 1985; Padilla, 2006). Williams and Butler (2003) provided a framework of concerns for new arrivals that includes typical adolescent developmental concerns, learning English, finding social support or networks of acceptance, acquiring new learning styles, coping with post-traumatic stress, and understanding different cultural scripts. Recent arrivals are also particularly vulnerable to anti-immigrant political rhetoric and the attendant media coverage, over the "dangers" of "illegal" immigration (Keogan, 2010, p. 4; Moradi & Hasan, 2004). Immigrant and refugee youth can also be ridiculed for their culture (e.g., religious practices) which may comprise a large core of their cultural identity that would have been highly valued and carefully nurtured in their home country (Kumar, 2015).

Refugees fleeing persecution often experience an additional layer of challenge in the form of a history of violence and trauma (McPherson, 2010). Existing status hierarchy based upon their country of origin is a challenge unique to some immigrant/refugee groups who find themselves rejected by students from other countries in the area of the world from which they come (Haddad, 2011). Youths' perceptions may differ according to immigrant generation as well, with a decline in social bonds, belief in the fairness and equity of school rules and punishments, and school bonding among second- and third-plus-generation youth (Bondy et al., 2015).

Issues of language and literacy further complicate the belonging experience of many immigrant and refugee youth. English Learners (ELs) tend to have the most favorable achievement outcomes when they feel a sense of belonging in school (Garcia Coll et al., 1996; Gonzalez et al., 2014; Valenzuela, 1999) and can relate positively to both their own ethnic/cultural group and the mainstream group (Altschul et al., 2008). Unfortunately, the common tendency to view native language as an impediment to academic success has been found to be an especially salient negative experience for ELs (Gonzalez & Ayala-Alcantar, 2008; Valencia & Black, 2002). Acquiring English language and literacy skills rapidly, as demanded for success in school and beyond, is challenged by instruction that is not culturally responsive or supportive of multilingual practices (Graham & Perin, 2006). Compounding this challenge, Urdan (2012) points out the lack of qualified teachers prepared to work with ELs.

Despite these challenges, it is important to note that belonging has been identified as a significant protective factor in the resettlement of refugee children in particular, a greater sense of belonging is being associated with lower depression and higher self-efficacy "regardless of the level of past exposure to adversities" (Kia-Keating & Ellis, 2007, p. 29). Among the largest- and fastest-growing immigrant category in US public schools, Latinx youth, González and Padilla (1997) found that the only variable that significantly predicted achievement was a sense of belonging, and the most significant factor in their belonging was a positive cultural climate for Latinx youth, that is, to simply feel represented and appreciated, and to have opportunity to participate in Latinx cultural groups or clubs (Aguinaga & Gloria, 2015; Hernández, 2017). Unfortunately, as Urdan (2012) and Valadez (2008) report, the dominant culture encountered in schools often holds cultural values and beliefs that are at odds with the values and beliefs of Latinx students, an experience referred to by Valenzuela (1999) as subtractive schooling.

Thus, understanding belonging among immigrant and refugee youth requires knowing that their developmental process is a function of the challenges of reconciling multiple cultural systems of reference (LaFramboise et al., 1993). It is therefore critically important for adults working with these youth to understand their complex and multilayered cultural reference points and intersections, and work to make sure these students know that they (and all that makes them who they are) belong.

Belonging While Learning

Schools and other educational settings (e.g., after-school, summer, and community-based programs) are major arenas for intergroup contact and acculturation for immigrant and refugee youth. Unfortunately, the instruments of schooling are rarely adapted to the variety of students' cultural backgrounds, allowing students' ethnic/cultural norms to potentially clash with the dominant culture of schools (Gonzalez et al., 2014). Traditionally, the United States has advocated the maintenance of American values and ideals, treating the cultural and discursive practices of nondominant groups as oppositional to an American ideal (Warikoo & Carter, 2009, p. 14). All too often, this reproduces hierarchies through the reinforcement of dominant codes, artifacts, language, practices, interactions, and styles (Alim & Paris, 2015; Bourdieu & Passeron, 1990; Farkas et al., 1990; Urrieta, 2009) despite the fact that such diminishing experiences at school are not conducive to healthy psychological development (Gonzalez et al., 2014; Urdan, 2012; Urdan & Munoz, 2012; Wong et al., 2003).

Refugee youth in particular invariably suffer disruption of formal schooling at various points during their flight from persecution in hostile home countries to neighboring border refugee camps to asylum-granting host countries (Dryden-Peterson, 2015). And while schools are supposed to provide security and aid in a return to a sense of normalcy, they are often not prepared to meet the particular needs of their refugee students (Lucas et al., 2008; MacNevin, 2012; Stewart, 2011). There is a lack of understanding about the processes of resettlement that support or oppress refugees (Ruiz-de-Velasco & Fix, 2000; Suárez-Orozco et al., 2008), and teachers often view students' behaviors from their own cultural frames of reference that may not be consonant with (immigrant/refugee) students' frames of reference (Kumar & Alvarado, 2013). Female students of Arab descent have reported that teachers ridiculed them for wearing *hijabs* (Abu El-Haj, 2007) and reminded them of the mainstream terrorist stereotype society holds about Arabs (Awad, 2010; Cristillo, 2008; Sirin & Fine, 2008).

In summary, it is hard to ignore the significant challenges faced by resettled youth in US schools. School practices and policies can force children to either assimilate and succeed, or identify ethnically and be silenced (Quiroz, 2001). Examples of such erasure are rampant and must be addressed if we hope to promote belonging and its attendant outcomes among this group of students.

Gutiérrez and Larson (2007) remind us that learning does not only occur in formal school settings; learning occurs in both vertical (within setting) and horizontal (across settings) sites, with each providing unique opportunities for learning and development. Indeed, informal learning settings (e.g., after-school clubs, summer camps) are somewhat more effective than formal school spaces in helping minority youth cultivate interest and belonging (Calabrese Barton & Tan, 2010; Rahm et al., 2005; He, Vetter & Fairbanks, 2015). For example, the principles and policies that drive writing instruction in school settings (e.g., Common Core State Standards) tend to emphasize the use of correct grammar and low-level writing tasks (Applebee & Langer, 2011). As a result, refugee and immigrant students can find it difficult to relate to the school material and wish teachers were more encouraging of and appreciative of diverse languages (Oikonomidoy, 2010). Informal writing spaces can provide the flexibility needed for strategies such as storytelling as a "meaningful context for literacy learning" that connects with cultural practices the youth were familiar with (Perry, 2008, p. 335), writing in the language of their choice, and with multimodal processes, with their cultural and linguistic identities engaged (Daniel & Eley, 2018).

A TRANSCULTURAL PEDAGOGY OF BELONGING FOR RESETTLED YOUTH

The vision for an effective pedagogy of belonging, as laid out by Marlsbary (2012), highlights the need to create a transcultural community of practice where youth are supported in their academic, social, and cultural participation and development (Marlsbary, 2012, p. iii). Much contemporary work provides helpful lenses through which to approach these goals. Work on *culturally sustaining pedagogy* highlights the notion that students must maintain links to first languages, values, and cultural practices of their heritage while accessing skills for competence in the dominant culture (Paris, 2014; Alim & Paris, 2017; Coppola et al., 2019). When students feel their identity, culture, race, background, or circumstances do not have full respect or welcome, such dispossession erects barriers to engagement or learning (referred to by Ahmed, 2014, as "atmospheric walls," para. 24).

Etzioni's (2000) concept of a *responsive community* is particularly helpful as well. He explains,

> *responsiveness* is the cardinal feature of authentic communities. If the values the community fosters do not reflect its members' needs, or only reflect the needs of some, the community's order will be ipso facto [i.e., merely assumed to be automatic] instead of truly supportive. (1996, p. 2)

Therefore, he argues, it is every community's task to find ways in which responsiveness can be authentically enhanced. Along these lines, Wenger argued that part of the social justice mission that schools need to embrace on behalf of diverse youth is the creation of space for their cultural knowledge, socio-familial histories and values; that is, teachers need to become *cultural brokers* (Wenger, 1998). Cultural brokers are individuals who are familiar with both the US culture and the ethnic culture of the immigrant and refugee students, who can translate, coordinate, and align between perspectives, address conflicting interests, and support belonging and learning by introducing elements of various cultures. For immigrant, and refugee youth, supporting belonging thus requires that teachers, administrators, and policymakers work to broaden their own understanding of their learners' cultural lives and shift individual understanding toward transcultural identities (He, Vetter & Fairbanks, 2014). This approach recognizes the rightful presence of multiple perspectives in any classroom (Squire & Darling, 2013), which is the heart of belonging.

Cumulatively, the research reviewed for this project provided four clear lines of approach toward these goals. We borrow from Yosso's notion of *Whose culture has capital?* (2005, p.69) to organize the specific sources and strategies that this group of youth drew upon to support their trajectory toward belonging. In this section, these sources are organized around the four sources of capital that emerged in literature specifically addressing belonging among immigrant and refugee youth (which mirror some of the dimensions of capital highlighted by Yosso without reproducing her entire theoretical model): *cultural capital*, *relational capital*, *linguistic capital*, and *voice*, as fruitful paths for immigrant and refugee youth.

Cultural Capital

A crucial place to begin is recognizing and honoring the various cultural identities in any classroom and the issues that arise as a result of the intersection of those identities. When teachers learn about and harness their students' cultural knowledge, the content and pedagogies they select *center* students by drawing upon their cultural, historical community and family heritage, harnessing rich funds of knowledge, rather than assuming they can simply fit in existing school cultures (Kia-Keating & Ellis, 2007; Matthews, 2008). This requires a two-way interaction that takes into account existing power relationships and ensures that refugee students can feel belonging on their own terms as well as those of the school (Paris & Alim, 2017; Matthews, 2008; Riggs & Due, 2011). This cultural perspective on belonging posits that school experiences (including curriculum and instruction) can provide students with opportunities to establish and maintain deep connections to their racial-ethnic-cultural-national background. Vedder and Horenczyk (2006) refer to this process as *enculturation*, the process of becoming skillful in using tools, learning behaviors, knowledge, and values that are *part of the culture of one's own group* (p. 420), drawing upon their transcultural and transnational funds of knowledge (Moll et al., 1992; Sánchez, 2007). Thus, enculturation (strengthening ties to one's own culture) and acculturation (becoming skilled in meaningful ways within a new culture) are both essential learning processes (Vedder, 1994).

Relational Capital

Although well-established as a traditional marker of belonging, social relationships take on additional importance among marginalized students. Teachers, administrators, and peers that value youth's cultural assets and work to build *confianza*, or trust, contribute substantially to students' sense of belonging (DeMartino, 2021, p. 246; Bartlett & García, 2011; Gonzalez et al., 2014). Belonging, in turn, plays a crucial role in establishing a sense of positive well-being for immigrant and refugee youth (Correa-Velez et al., 2010; de Heer et al., 2016). For example, in one study, immigrant and refugee youth appreciated, felt more *socially visible*, and improved their expectations about their future and their identity as a student when their teachers learned about them, respected them, affirmed their potential, and fought against discrimination against them (Urdan, 2012, p. 123). Bridging the divide between home and university cultures by including family, particularly caregivers, in education practices also draws on students' relational capital, increasing student adjustment and persistence (Gloria & Segua-Herra, 2004). Proximity to peers with similar immigration experiences is especially important for adolescents' psychological well-being (Moradi & Hasan, 2004; see also Sancho & Cline, 2012). Moreover, heterogeneous groupings and collaboration among students can be a means by which schools can foster social trust across ethnic, religious, and linguistic differences. Such connections within their community are crucial forms of relational wealth (Moll et al., 1992).

Linguistic Capital

Support and respect for their youths' native language, while they learn English, can be a crucial starting place for working with an immigrant and refugee population (Cartmell & Bond, 2015). Thus, it is important that teachers support students' *linguistic capital* while they work to acquire English (Yosso, 2005, p. 77). Immigrant and refugee youth frequently arrive at school with multiple language and communication skills and traditions, such as storytelling traditions that include listening to and recounting oral histories, parables, stories, and proverbs, supporting a repertoire of skills such as memorization, attention to detail, cross-cultural awareness, and real-world literacy skills (Gutierrez, 2002). Linguistic capital also refers to communicating via visual art, music, or poetry and drawing on different vocal and language registers or styles to communicate with different audiences (Anzaldúa, 2012; Gutierrez et al., 1995; Macedo & Bartolomé, 1999). This suggests the value of multilingual and multiliteracy opportunities to leverage what students know (Valenzuela, 1999; He et al., 2014; Yosso, 2005). Examples from Valenzuela's work (2015) include writing fan fiction, creating Japanese anime, developing J-Pop music, and the use of social networking sites to learn from others. Suarez-Orozco and Sattin (2005, p.2) refer to these learning spaces as "global classrooms" that operate through competing and contrasting cultural models and social practices, and privilege the ideas of transcultural communication, understanding, empathy, and collaboration.

Voice

In addition to echoing the need to support their linguistic capital, the need to incorporate students' *voices* into school experiences (e.g., incorporating student choice and ideas into planning) is imperative especially during this time of increased anti-immigrant sentiment and anti-bilingualism (see Beaudrie et al., 2009). Moreover, when educators collaborate with students and take actionable steps (i.e., exercising agency) toward eliminating structural barriers that devalue minoritized populations in the school and community, they attend to students' cultural needs, reassuring youth that they do belong (Cook et al., 2012). In a study of activism training that emphasized the value of students' voices in impacting positive change, researchers found that affiliations with others around civic engagement helped students develop a sense of agency in the classroom and in the community (Taines, 2012). Each of these opportunity structures is important for positioning students with agency at the center of their lives and learning (Walton & Brady, 2017).

COMMUNITY VOICES WRITERS' CAMP

Community Voices (the project addressed in this chapter) grew out of a larger mission from our university's School of Education to support refugee youth in our local area with their literacy development. We contribute to that effort by offering a two-week summer writing camp for resettled youth who are invited through our contacts with the local school district and a resettlement group. The metropolitan area our university receives the largest number of resettled individuals in our state, with an estimated 60,000 immigrants currently living in the area, representing 140 countries and 120 languages. The team coordinating the camp consists of three university faculty members in addition to graduate and undergraduate students.

The camp occurs for 3 hours each morning, for 2 weeks, with about 15–20 middle- or high-school-aged youth per class. So far, we have had between 30 and 45 youth attend camp each year, with their ages ranging from 12 to 19. The camp instructors include graduate students and local teachers. The youth had pen and paper available as well as laptops, and a wide variety of art supplies for creating maps and visual models of their identity and their stories. The youth were encouraged to compose in the language of their choice, although many chose to write in English, using the Internet to translate words and phrases.

The camp's primary focus is on writing; however, we emphasize an approach that resists traditional approaches students report experiencing in school. Our multiliteracy approach allows much latitude in the form and purpose of their writing, including maps, poetry, reports on their home country, artwork, and collaborative projects, among other things. One especially prominent aspect of the camp was the focus on community-building, including many activities that allowed campers to get to know each other, such as opening activities that centered the day and its agenda on the students, opportunities for expressing different aspects of their identities, instructor focus on getting to know students and their backgrounds, and respecting their students' perspectives and choices. Other time was structured around the use of quick writes, morning meetings, guided writing groups, mini-lessons, individual writing time, peer sharing, free (social) time, and a closing activity. Overall, it can be said that the adults involved in the camp were committed to confronting their own biases, building bridges across cultures, providing authentic social support, respecting students' linguistic capital, and enhancing student voice/agency.

To reflect the youth's authentic stories, graduate students, undergraduate research assistants, and one faculty member wrote daily observational field notes and analytic memos, conducted daily semi-structured interviews (which were transcribed), and audio-recorded class discussions (which were selectively transcribed). We also analyzed student work (written and visual) and documented what the youth are writing about, the languages they choose to write in, and what they said about their writing, as well as how the youth demonstrated, and talked about, their sense of belonging at camp and beyond. All three faculty members and the graduate students were involved with data analysis. One research question guided this work: *In what ways do refugee youth in the Community Voices writing camp speak to their experience of belonging in camp and beyond?*

NARRATIVES ON BELONGING

The stories that emerged from the lives and camp experiences of the youth reflect important lessons related to their culture, heritage, voice, and sense of belonging, among other things. The stories of three youth are drawn on here to illustrate the themes that emerged most clearly around belonging: cultural capital, relational capital, linguistic capital, and voice/agency. Challenges to belonging were a lived reality for these youth, as when one participant recounted with discouragement how peers at her American school criticized her use of her heritage language (which she used with peers from her home country), demanding that they speak English or "go back home." Nonetheless, campers made meaningful strides in harnessing their various forms of capital to stake a claim on belonging.

Cultural and Relational Capital: **Jesus's Story**

Jesus (all names are pseudonyms) began his story by sharing about his life in his home country and his transition from Thailand to the United States. He took a nostalgic approach when reflecting on living in the Mae La Refugee Camp. He described his love for the people and the environment while providing his audience with a description of the reality of Mae La Camp as well. He writes, "I grew up in a place in Mae La Camp. It is a poor place. It has a lot of trash all around the camp and the houses in the camp were old." He adds, "Some people do not have that much money, but we help each other out. Some people who never live there may not like it." He recounts what others have to say about the camp, such as "This is a poor place to live" or "It smells bad here."

Jesus repositions his story of his home country by focusing on the close relationships that people shared within the community, stating that, "people in the Mae La Camp don't care what other people say about it." His description of the bonds shared between those living in the camp downplays the negative physical attributes of the location. He described people in the camp as "survivors," stating "it is a poor place, but I love it there."

Jesus goes on to take the reader on the emotional roller coaster he experienced moving to the United States and the hardships he experienced attending an American school, making friends, and balancing the mixed emotions that accompanied those experiences. Recounting the memory of his arrival in the United States, Jesus's descriptive language allows his audience to visualize the physical reality of the experience and feel the emotional connection he makes to the moment.

> When I came here, I was 7-year-old. It was cold and it was snowing. It was my first-time seeing snow. I was so happy that day. It was beautiful to see the snow for the first time in my life. It was magical.

Going to school in a traditional American educational system, however, posed challenges. "I was scared to go to school because there are so many people there, but I have to and have no choice but to go. The day when I went to school, I was shy and scared." Then he describes the significance of making his first friend in America. "We had a lot of fun together; it was the best day of my life." Making more new friends, he shares, "We all became friends, but I like to think that we are really like family." "Going to school helped change me by helping me not be shy or scared anymore." He goes on to say, "Now I have been in American schools for 4 years. I learned so much about America and other places. I feel so happy." He offered a piece of advice to others: "Something I learned from my life is not to be scared or shy towards other people. My advice to you is never be shy because someone can be your friend."

In several short writing pieces, Jesus provides his audience with insights about the things he likes and his identity. In writing an "I am" poem, he reconnects with his culture and home country with claims like, "I am from Thailand." and "I am Asian, and I am proud of it." He goes on to draw on his cultural capital, sharing that he is "good at English, Burmese, Korean, Thai, and Karen" and a few lines later says, "I am still learning English." Through the poem, we also learn of his interest in music, specifically K-pop (Korean pop) and anime.

Reflecting his dreams through his writing, he shares, "My dream is to become a K-pop artist. I know it may not come true, but I want to become an artist anyway. If my dream does not come true, I have a second dream to become a doctor." Jesus knows that others may doubt him and shares how he plans to persevere:

I know my journey to become a K-pop artist may be hard, but I will follow my dream and make it come true. People might bring me down, but I will never give up and I will follow my dream. I want to join JYP Entertainment because it is one of the top four entertainment businesses in South Korea.

Through his writing about his dreams, he shared his passion for Korean culture. He writes, "I love everything about Korean culture. For example, the food stores, the style and fashion, and their music."

Linguistic and Relational Capital: Siti's Story

The Community Voices learning spaces were rich in linguistic diversity, with over a dozen languages and dialects spoken across camp participants. Siti, a 19-year-old from Egypt, attended the camp with her younger sister. Although she was a native Arabic speaker, her language repertoire also included some English, French, and Spanish. Her goals for attending the writing camp were predominantly focused on leveraging her linguistic assets, particularly by increasing her proficiency in English. She considered her multilingual knowledge a powerful tool for navigating a new country.

For Siti, attending the writing camp with linguistically diverse youth was also an opportunity to build new friendships. After being in the United States for just under a year, she felt that building and maintaining relationships with others, including in Egypt, was important for helping her feel comfortable and happy in a new country. She shared, "I want to know many friends . . . maybe friends in my country, in [the university where the camp was held]." Building upon her existing language repertoire made it easier to make new friends, including at the newcomer school she attended. Although she spoke English with her teachers, her friends spoke mostly French and Spanish. Her openness and skill for learning language expanded her perceptions of who could be called "friend" to include a diverse array of people across cultures, languages, and locations. At the same time, maintaining her proficiency in Arabic also sustained her sense of connection to Egypt, a place where she already felt she belonged.

During the writing camp, Siti chose to write a personal narrative in English. Unlike many of the other youth in the camp, who wrote about their experiences coming to the United States and starting school in a new country, Siti explored the possibilities of her future, writing:

I will go to college. I want to start to study about the Accountant in American banks and I want to have my business [degree] and be a businesswoman and do many important things. I have friends to make me very excited about it and push me to continue my work. I am very happy because I will continue in America and work here and push my life and forget all the bad things and start a good life with my work and make a good family.

When asked why she chose to write about her future in her personal narrative, Siti explained that her transition from Egypt to the United States had been challenging. Feeling excited and a little nervous when she first learned that she would be moving to the United States, Siti had sought advice from friends who had left Egypt. However, she said she found little support, unlike her younger sister. She shared, "I'm not like Fukayna, no one helped me. I was trying and trying." Instruction in Siti's classroom at the writing camp had emphasized selecting a purpose and audience for their compositions. Siti decided that she wanted to leverage her ability to write in multiple languages to widely disseminate her story to help others in similar circumstances, but she specifically wrote to an audience of friends in Egypt:

> I want to share with my friends in Egypt because I want to tell them that I will be successful anywhere, not only in Egypt. Because they told me you can't do the thing you want to do here [in the United States] because I'll have to start again. I want to tell them that I can do it.

For Siti, writing across languages was identity work that built her sense of belonging by providing her with an opportunity to consider her "last life and future and find a way to combine both" to tell her story.

However, although leveraging her linguistic assets to build relationships and find her voice was important to Siti, her goal for increasing her English proficiency in the writing camp extended beyond herself to spaces and places in which she could use language to advocate for others. During a camp activity in which small groups of youth had to work together to draw a representation of a writer, Siti's group included a pile of books in their image. In Arabic, Siti labeled the spine of one of the books with the name أحمد خالد توفيق (*Ahmed Khaled Tawfik*). She explained he was a well-known dystopian writer who wrote about what life was like for the Egyptian people and shared, "He makes hope for the people." Siti hoped to do the same, in her own way, using her knowledge of languages.

> [I want] to learn more English because some people in [the city] come from many countries and come to the newcomer school. My friends and me help the newcomers at the middle school to translate, to understand the teacher.

For Siti, who had found the transition into the United States so difficult and who had often had others question her ability to thrive in a new country, the writing camp was an opportunity to not just find her own voice by leveraging multiple languages, but to use that voice to advocate for a better experience for all newcomers and to participate in the actual creation of these spaces of belonging.

Voice: *Rekah's Story*

Many Community Voices campers positioned themselves as storytellers with important stories to be shared. In school, authorship was equated with writing correctly in English, with academic writing emphasized. This often situated the youth as nonwriters or unskilled at conveying their meaning in school. At camp, the youth were able to be storytellers of unique and passionate stories that often involved sharing difficult experiences and reflecting on how they changed or what they learned from these experiences. Thus, the youth repositioned themselves as authors who made connections to others through their storytelling.

Rekah was a native Nepali student, who wrote about her mixed feelings with regard to immigrating while navigating the transition to middle school in the United States illustrates this path to belonging. This was especially challenging for her because of being a shy individual. Working through these issues, we observe how Rekah repositions herself as an author of an important story, with something important to share. She starts off:

> Middle school was a whole new world for me. especially since I was the new kid again. I had just moved from North Dakota to North Carolina. I haven't made many friends my age. My first impression of North Carolina was there was a lot of trees. It reminded me of where I was from [in] Nepal and I thought to myself "maybe this is the reason my parents wanted to move here, it reminded them of their birthplace."

Although, conveying her identity as "the new kid" where she is having to start over yet again, Rekah also reconciles moving with understanding her parents' decision and how it might relate to their connection with Nepal, positioning herself as someone who is maturing in her understanding about the decisions adults make and their connection to their birthplace.

Rekah continued her writing by recounting how terrified she was to start school. She describes, "While walking to my class I had my head down the whole time and in class, I felt so awkward that I just kept staring right at my teacher, and nowhere else." But she ends her musings about beginning school with, "As I'm writing this today, I said to myself 'why was I so nervous?' To my past self I would say 'Don't be so nervous. You wouldn't learn anything if you hadn't taken a leap, you wouldn't have made new friends.'" To people reading this she would say, you can't go on in life being afraid of everything or being nervous–this might stop you from doing what you really want to do and you can't let fear get in the way. As I learned that day, I should have been more confident with myself, more confident with talking to others and not being so nervous. Although all first day is [*sic*] very nervous, I can tell you from experience that your second day and rest will get better.

Rekah used her writing to tell her story of transition but to also teach her readers a lesson that she learned. In this way, we see how Rekah adopted the identity of an author who has an important story and lesson to share. She shifted from writing about what she would tell her past self to speak directly to the reader when she says, "To people reading this." This shift in voice shows how Rekah took up the position as someone who has something meaningful to convey.

LEARNING FROM THE BELONGING NARRATIVES OF NEW ARRIVALS

The learning needs of newly resettled members of our communities—in particular immigrants and refugees—present important and urgent issues that deserve careful attention. Their needs are complex by any measure, but are made particularly problematic by a history of assimilationist and nationalist thought and practice that pervades attempts in US society to make sense of this growing demand. The growing body of work articulating a sociocultural and critical understanding of a sense of belonging—which is already demonstrably essential to positive development across all populations—has much to offer this work. It is the intersection of this new lens on belonging with the cultural realities of the process of resettlement that this chapter seeks to unpack. Findings from this chapter illustrate the belonging experiences of immigrant and refugee youth who participated in one summer's Community Voices summer writing camp. Through examples from their stories (written and otherwise), we illustrated important ways that these Community Voices youth effectively drew on cultural capital, relational capital, linguistic capital, and voice/agency to understand and support their experiences of belonging in camp and beyond. What, then, can educators and school leaders draw from these students' stories and experiences that can enhance sense of belonging (with its attendant benefits), and an authentic writer's identity (also anchored by belonging), thereby enhancing the development of newly resettled members of their classrooms?

First, the Community Voices camp provided an informal writing experience that was completely *intertwined* with the students' experience of belonging, demonstrating the natural reciprocal relationship between learning and belonging for these youth. Amid the belonging the campers experienced at camp, they situated themselves as writers, wrote about authentic experiences, made connections to others through storytelling, built relationships, and found their own voices. The writing they did opened spaces for the youth to engage in meaningful, literacy learning that connected with authentic personal experiences, familiar cultural practices, and multiple languages (Perry, 2008) further anchoring, while drawing on, their belonging.

Their experience of belonging did not end there however; they went on to describe ways in which they *leveraged* their belonging in service of others. For example, in the camp, Siti used her voice to write about how she helped newcomers in her school translate and understand their teacher as a way to provide a better experience for other students in her school. Rekah made sense of her belonging by talking directly to the reader (a newcomer) about her own increase in belonging and voice, and the lessons she had learned, reminding the reader to not be afraid. Both of these campers demonstrate an experience of rightful presence (i.e., belonging) as someone who believes their stories and insights were important to tell. By embracing this role, the campers became advocates who support the belonging of others, suggesting a hopefully self-sustaining cycle of belonging. Intertwining writing and belonging in this way, especially if done consistently, can foster powerful writing identities that open more opportunities for belonging in various contexts (Oikonomidoy, 2009).

These stories also conveyed the importance of adopting a *critical lens* toward belonging. For example, in Jesus's stories, he discussed how he was proud of being from Thailand and loved his original refugee camp, being "good at" multiple languages, and his interest in K-pop and anime, cultural artifacts that draw from his background. Siti discussed the importance of writing across languages and figuring out a way to make her dreams come true, despite the challenges of a new context. Thus, in their writings they drew from cultural, linguistic, and relational capital to maintain strong connections to their cultural and ethnic heritage (Berry et al., 2006; Urdan, 2011; Vedder & Horencyzk, 2006). Their writings illustrated how they resisted the idea of giving up one's culture of origin or one's dreams, in order to assimilate into a new culture (Berry, 1990, 1997; Alim & Paris, 2017; Urrieta, 2009), and instead focused on making connections in ways that could still made their dreams come true.

Regarding literacy education, the camp experience reflects several practices that opened opportunities for students to write in personal, authentic and informal ways, and in multiple languages and modalities, each of which anchored their learning in their personal belonging. Specifically, we recommend fostering a writing process approach that allows for multiple drafts, peer revision, and writing conferences with the teacher. We also recommend asking students to share their work in some way, such as reading it aloud or publishing it. Storytelling is one way to open space for, and build, belonging, and draw on linguistic capital (Cartmell & Bond, 2015), particularly when teachers work with students to learn how to listen and consider others' stories and languages. We also recommend inviting local or international authors to the classroom (which happened in camp, but could take place in-person or virtually) to discuss their experiences as writers. Each of these recommendations are valuable in their own right for learning to write; they also, however, animate the writing and learning process by leveraging belonging.

In summary, sharing this writing space with immigrant and refugee youth sheds important light on their belonging and writing experiences alike. The extant literature suggested four dimensions of capital that might be leveraged to construct spaces of belonging for this group, each of which was mirrored in the experiences and stories these students shared: Cultural, Relational and Linguistic Capital and Voice/Agency. The mechanisms of belonging were also illuminated in unique ways. Its cyclical possibilities, in which students experienced and made sense of their own belonging then leveraged their insights to scaffold the belonging of others suggests a promising pattern through which to build and sustain belonging. In addition, the reciprocal nature of belonging and authentic writing learning (each reinforcing the other) sheds light on the natural, constant interplay between belonging and learning, an insight that all teachers interested in supporting their refugee and immigrant youth can benefit from. With that said, we believe that writing spaces can be places in which educators practice effective pedagogies of belonging that can change a group of strangers into a successful transcultural community of practice (Marlsbary, 2012, p. iii).

REFERENCES

Aguinaga, A., & Gloria, A. M. (2015). The effects of generational status and university environment on Latina/o undergraduates' persistence decisions. *Journal of Diversity in Higher Education, 8*(1), 15–29. doi: 10.1037/a0038465

Ahmed, S. *Atmospheric Walls*. Feministkilljoys. https://feministkilljoys.com/2014/0 9/15/atmospheric-walls/

Allen, K. A., & Bowles, T. (2012). Belonging as a guiding principle in the education of adolescents. *Australian Journal of Educational & Developmental Psychology, 12*, 108–119.

Altschul, I., Oyserman, D., & Bybee, D. (2008a). Racial-ethnic self-schemas and segmented assimilation: Identity and the academic achievement of Hispanic youth. *Social Psychology Quarterly, 71*(3), 302–320. doi: 10.1177/019027250807100309

Anderman, L. H., & Anderman, E. M. (1999). Social predictors of changes in students' achievement goal orientations. *Contemporary Educational Psychology, 24*(1), 21–37. doi: 10.1006/ceps.1998.0978

Anzaldúa, G., Cantú, N., & Hurtado, A. (2012). *Borderlands / La Frontera: The New Mestiza* (4th ed.). Aunt Lute Books.

Asante, M. K. (2003). *Afrocentricity: The Theory of Social Change* (Revised and expanded 2nd edition). African American Images.

Awad, G. H. (2010). The impact of acculturation and religious identification on perceived discrimination for Arab/Middle Eastern Americans. *Cultural Diversity and Ethnic Minority Psychology, 16*(1), 59–67. doi: 10.1037/a0016675

Banks, J. A. (1994). *An Introduction to Multicultural Education.* Allyn and Bacon Inc.

Bartlett, L., & Garcia, O. (2011). *Additive Schooling in Subtractive Times: Bilingual Education and Dominican Immigrant Youth in the Heights.* Vanderbilt.

Baumeister, R. F., & Leary, M. R. (1995). The Need to belong: Desire for interpersonal attachments as a fundamental human motivation. *Psychological Bulletin, 117*(3), 497–529.

Beaudrie, S., Ducar, C., & Relaño-Pastor, A. (2009). Curricular perspectives in the heritage language context: Assessing culture and identity. *Language Culture and Curriculum, 22*, 157–174. doi: 10.1080/07908310903067628

Benner, A. D., Graham, S., & Mistry, R. S. (2008). Discerning direct and mediated effects of ecological structures and processes on adolescents' educational outcomes. *Developmental Psychology, 44*(3), 840–854. doi: 10.1037/0012-1649.44.3.840

Berry, J. W., Phinney, J. S., Sam, D. L., & Vedder, P. (2006). Immigrant youth: Acculturation, identity, and adaptation. *Applied Psychology, 55*(3), 303–332. doi: 10.1111/j.1464-0597.2006.00256.x

Bondy, J. M., Peguero, A. A., & Johnson, B. E. (2019). The children of immigrants' bonding to school: examining the roles of assimilation, gender, race, ethnicity, and social bonds. *Urban Education, 54*(4), 592–622. doi: 10.1177/0042085916628609

Bourdieu, P., & Passeron, J.-C. (1990). *Reproduction in Education, Society and Culture* (R. Nice, Trans.; 2nd ed.). Sage Publications.

Brown, T. A. (2015). *Confirmatory Factor Analysis for Applied Research* (2nd ed.). Guilford Publications. https://books.google.com/books?id=tTL2BQAAQBAJ

Calabrese Barton, A., & Tan, E. (2019). Designing for Rightful Presence in STEM: The Role of Making Present Practices. *Journal of the Learning Sciences, 28*(4–5), 616–658. doi: 10.1080/10508406.2019.1591411

Cammarota, J. (2016). The praxis of ethnic studies: Transforming second sight into critical consciousness. *Race Ethnicity and Education, 19*(2), 233–251. doi: 10.1080/13613324.2015.1041486

Cammarota, J. & Fine, M. (2008). Youth participatory action research. *Pedagogy for Transformational Resistance* (pp. 1–11); Revolutionizing Education: Youth Participatory Action Research in Motion, Revolutionizing Education. Routledge.

Cartmell, H., & Bond, C. (2015). What does belonging mean for young people who are International New Arrivals. *Educational and Child Psychology, 32*(2), 14.

Cook, J., Purdie-Vaughns, V., García, J., & Cohen, G. (2012). Chronic threat and contingent belonging: Protective benefits of values affirmation on identity development. *Journal of Personality and Social Psychology.* doi: 10.1037/a0026312

Coppola, R., Woodard, R., & Vaughan, A. (2019). And the students shall lead us: Putting culturally sustaining pedagogy in conversation with universal design for learning in a middle-school spoken word poetry unit. *Literacy Research: Theory, Method, and Practice, 68*(1), 226–249. doi: 10.1177/2381336919870219

Correa-Velez, I., Gifford, S. M., & Barnett, A. G. (2010). Longing to belong: Social inclusion and wellbeing among youth with refugee backgrounds in the first three years in Melbourne, Australia. *Social Science & Medicine, 71*(8), 1399–1408. doi: 10.1016/j.socscimed.2010.07.018

Daniel, S. (2019). Writing our identities for successful endeavors: Resettled refugee youth look to the future. *Journal of Research in Childhood Education, 33*, 71–83. doi: 10.1080/02568543.2018.1531448

de los Ríos, C. V. (2013). A Curriculum of the Borderlands: High School Chicana/o-Latina/o Studies as Sitios y Lengua. *The Urban Review, 45*(1), 58–73. doi: 10.1007/s11256-012-0224-3

Dee, T., & Penner, E. (2016). *The Causal Effects of Cultural Relevance: Evidence from an Ethnic Studies Curriculum* (No. w21865; p. w21865). National Bureau of Economic Research.

DeMartino, L. (2021). De-centering the deficit framework: Courageous refugee mentors in educational spaces. *Urban Review, 53*, 243–263. doi: 10.1007/s11256-020-00579-7

Dryden-Peterson, S. (2016). Refugee education: The crossroads of globalization. *Educational Researcher, 45*(9), 473–482. doi: 10.3102/0013189X16683398

Eccles, J. S., & Roeser, R. W. (2011). Schools as developmental contexts during adolescence. *Journal of Research on Adolescence, 21*(1), 225–241. doi: 10.1111/j.1532-7795.2010.00725.x

Etzioni, A. (2000). Creating good communities and good societies. *Contemporary Sociology, 29*(1), 188–195. doi: 10.2307/2654943

Faircloth, B. S., & Hamm, J. V. (2005). Sense of belonging among high school students representing four ethnic groups. *Journal of Youth and Adolescence, 34*(4), 293–309. doi: 10.1007/s10964-005-5752-7

Faircloth, B. S. & Hamm, J. V. (2011) The Dynamic reality of adolescent peer networks and sense of classroom belonging. *Merrill-Palmer Quarterly, 57* (1), 48–72.

Fine, M., & Sirin, S. R. (2008). *Muslim American Youth: Understanding Hyphenated Identities through Multiple Methods.* NYU Press.

Finn, J. (1989). Withdrawing from school. *Review of Educational Research, 59*(2), 117–142.

García Coll, C., Lamberty, G., Jenkins, R., McAdoo, H., Crnic, K., Wasik, B.& Vázquez García, h. (1996). An integrative model for the study of developmental competencies in minority children. *Child Development , 67* (5), 1891–1914.

Genishi, C., & Alvermann, D. E. (2017). *Culturally Sustaining Pedagogies: Teaching and Learning for Justice in a Changing World* (D. Paris & H. S. Alim, Eds.). Teachers College Press.

Gloria, A. M., & Segura-Herrera, T. A. (2004). Ambrocia and omar go to college: A psychosociocultural examination of Chicana/os in higher education. In *The handbook of Chicana/o Psychology and Mental Health* (pp. 401–425). Lawrence Erlbaum Associates Publishers.

Gonzalez, L. M., Eades, M. P., & Supple, A. J. (2014). School community engaging with immigrant youth: Incorporating personal/social development and ethnic identity development. *School Community Journal, 24*(1), 99–117.

Gonzalez, L. M., Stein, G. L., Kiang, L., & Cupito, A. M. (2014). The impact of discrimination and support on developmental competencies in Latino adolescents. *Journal of Latina/o Psychology, 2*(2), 79–91. doi: 10.1037/lat0000014

Gonzalez, R., & Ayala-Alcantar, C. U. (2008). Critical caring: Dispelling latino stereotypes among preservice teachers. *Journal of Latinos and Education, 7*(2), 129–143. doi: 10.1080/15348430701828699

Gonzalez, R., & Padilla, A. (1997). The academic resilience of Mexican American high school students. *Hispanic Journal of Behavioral Sciences, 19*, 301–317. doi: 10.1177/07399863970193004

Goodenow, C. (1993). Classroom belonging among early adolescent students: Relationships to motivation and achievement. *The Journal of Early Adolescence, 13*(1), 21–43. doi: 10.1177/0272431693013001002

Graham, S., & Perin, D. (2007). *Writing Next: Effective Strategies to Improve Writing of Adolescents in Middle and High Schools.* A Report to Carnegie Corporation of New York.

Gray, D. L., Hope, E. C., & Matthews, J. S. (2018). Black and belonging at school: A case for interpersonal, instructional, and institutional opportunity structures. *Educational Psychologist, 53*(2), 97–113. doi: 10.1080/00461520.2017.1421466

Guidotti-Hernández, N. M. (2017). Affective communities and millennial desires: Latinx, or why my computer won't recognize Latina/o. *Cultural Dynamics, 29*(3), 141–159. doi: 10.1177/0921374017727853

Gutiérrez, K. D., & Larson, J. (2007). Discussing expanded spaces for learning. *Language Arts, 85*(1), 69–77.

Haddad, Y. Y. (2012). *Becoming American?: The Forging of Arab and Muslim Identity in Pluralist America.* Baylor University Press.

He, Y., Vetter, A., & Fairbanks, C. (2014). Extending the conversation. *English Education, 46*, 327–344.

Heer, N. de, Due, C., Riggs, D. W., & Augoustinos, M. (2016). "It will be hard because I will have to learn lots of English": Experiences of education for children newly arrived in Australia. *International Journal of Qualitative Studies in Education, 29*(3), 297–319. doi: 10.1080/09518398.2015.1023232

Keddie, A. (2012). Refugee education and justice issues of representation, redistribution and recognition. *Cambridge Journal of Education, 42*(2), 197–212. doi: 10.1080/0305764X.2012.676624

Keogan, K. (2010). *Immigrants and the Cultural Politics of Place: A Comparative Study of New York and Los Angeles.* LFB Scholarly Publishing LLC.

Kia-Keating, M., & Ellis, B. H. (2007). Belonging and connection to school in resettlement: young refugees, school belonging, and psychosocial adjustment. *Clinical Child Psychology and Psychiatry, 12*(1), 29–43. doi: 10.1177/1359104507071052

Knifsend, C. A., Camacho-Thompson, D. E., Juvonen, J., & Graham, S. (2018). Friends in activities, school-related affect, and academic outcomes in diverse middle schools. *Journal of Youth and Adolescence, 47*(6), 1208–1220. doi: 10.1007/s10964-018-0817-6

Kumar, R., & Alvarado, L. (2013). Teachers' cultural and professional identities and student outcomes. In J. Hattie & E. M. Anderman (Eds.), *International Guide to Student Achievement* (pp. 250–253). Routledge/Taylor & Francis Group.

Kumar, R., Seay, N., & Karabenick, S. A. (2015). Immigrant Arab adolescents in ethnic enclaves: Physical and phenomenological contexts of identity negotiation. *Cultural Diversity and Ethnic Minority Psychology, 21*(2), 201–212. doi: 10.1037/a0037748

LaFromboise, T., Coleman, H. L. K., & Gerton, J. (1993). Psychological impact of biculturalism: Evidence and Theory. *Psychological Bulletin, 114*(3), 395–412.

Lucas, T., Villegas, A., & Freedson-Gonzalez, M. (2008). Linguistically responsive teacher education: preparing classroom teachers to teach English language learners. *Journal of Teacher Education, 59,* 361–373. doi: 10.1177/0022487108322110

MacNevin, J. (2012). Learning the way: Teaching and learning with and for youth from refugee backgrounds on Prince Edward Island. *Canadian Journal of Education, 35*(3), 48–63.

Malsbary, C. B. (2012). *The Pedagogy of Belonging: The Social, Cultural, and Academic Lives of Recently-Arrived Immigrant Youth in a Multiethnic, Multilingual High School* [UCLA]. https://escholarship.org/uc/item/5sp7r6fg

Maslow, A. H. (1998). *Toward a Psychology of Being* (3rd ed.). Wiley.

Maslow, A. H. (1943). A theory of human motivation. *Psychological Review, 50,* 370–396.

Matthews, J. (2008). Schooling and settlement: Refugee education in Australia. International *Studies in Sociology of Education, 18*(1), 31–45. doi: 10.1080/09620210802195947

McPherson, M. (2010). "I Integrate, Therefore I Am": Contesting the normalizing discourse of integrationism through conversations with refugee women. *Journal of Refugee Studies, 23*(4), 546–570. doi: 10.1093/jrs/feq040

Moll, L. C., Amanti, C., Neff, D., & Gonzalez, N. (1992). Funds of knowledge for teaching: Using a qualitative approach to connect homes and classrooms. *Theory Into Practice, 31*(2), 132–141. doi: 10.1080/00405849209543534

Moradi, B., & Hasan, N. T. (2004). Arab American persons' reported experiences of discrimination and mental health: The mediating role of personal control. *Journal of Counseling Psychology, 51*(4), 418–428. doi: 10.1037/0022-0167.51.4.418

Mosley, D. V., Hargons, C. N., Meiller, C., Angyal, B., Wheeler, P., Davis, C., & Stevens-Watkins, D. (2020). Critical consciousness of anti-Black racism:

A practical model to prevent and resist racial trauma. *Journal of Counseling Psychology, 68*(1), 1–16. doi: 10.1037/cou0000430

Na, N., Macedo, D., & Bartolomé, L. I. (1999). *Dancing With Bigotry: Beyond the Politics of Tolerance.* Palgrave Macmillan US.

Nasir, N. S., & Hand, V. M. (2006). Exploring sociocultural perspectives on race, culture, and learning. *Review of Educational Research, 76*(4), 449–475.

Niyozov, S., & Pluim, G. (2009). Teachers' perspectives on the education of Muslim students: A missing voice in Muslim education research. *Curriculum Inquiry, 39*(5), 637–677.

Oikonomidoy, E. (2010). Zooming into the school narratives of refugee students. *Multicultural Perspectives, 12*, 74–80. doi: 10.1080/15210960.2010.481186

Osterman, K. (2020). Students' need for belonging in the school community. *Review of Educational Research, 70*(3), 323–367.

Ozer, E. J., Wolf, J. P., & Kong, C. (2008). Sources of perceived school connection among ethnically-diverse urban adolescents. *Journal of Adolescent Research, 23*(4), 438–470. doi: 10.1177/0743558408316725

Padilla, A. M. (2006). Bicultural social development. *Hispanic Journal of Behavioral Sciences, 28*(4), 467–497. doi: 10.1177/0739986306294255

Paris, D., & Alim, H. S. (2017). *Culturally Sustaining Pedagogies: Teaching and Learning for Justice in a Changing World.* Teachers College Press.

Perry, K. H. (2008). From storytelling to writing: Transforming literacy practices among sudanese refugees. *Journal of Literacy Research, 40*(3), 317–358. doi: 10.1080/10862960802502196

Phelan, P., Davidson, A. L., & Cao, H. T. (1991). Students' multiple worlds: Negotiating the boundaries of family, peer, and school cultures. *Anthropology & Education Quarterly, 22*(3), 224–250. doi: 10.1525/aeq.1991.22.3.05x1051k

Phinney, J. S., Horenczyk, G., Liebkind, K., & Vedder, P. (2001). Ethnic identity, immigration, and well-being: An interactional perspective. *Journal of Social Issues, 57*(3), 493–510. doi: 10.1111/0022-4537.00225

Quiroz, P. (2001). The silencing of Latino student "voice": Puerto Rican and Mexican narratives in eighth grade and high school. *Anthropology & Education Quarterly, 32*, 326–349. doi: 10.1525/aeq.2001.32.3.326

Rahm, J., Martel-Reny, M.-P., & Moore, J. (2005). The role of afterschool and community science programs in the lives of urban youth. *School Science and Mathematics, 105*, 283–291. doi: 10.1111/j.1949-8594.2005.tb18129.x

Ramos-Sánchez, L. (2007). Language switching and Mexican Americans' emotional expression. *Journal of Multicultural Counseling and Development, 35*(3), 154–168. doi: 10.1002/j.2161-1912.2007.tb00057.x

Riggs, D., & Due, C. (2011). (Un)Common ground?: English language acquisition and experiences of exclusion amongst new arrival students in south Australian primary schools. *Identities: Global Studies in Culture and Power, 18*, 273–290. doi: 10.1080/1070289X.2011.635373

Ruiz-de-Velasco, J., Fix, M., & Clewell, B. C. (2000). *Overlooked and Underserved: Immigrant Students in U.S. Secondary Schools.* American Psychological Association.

Ryu, M., & Tuvilla, M. R. S. (2018). Resettled refugee youths' stories of migration, schooling, and future: Challenging dominant narratives about refugees. *The Urban Review, 50*(4), 539–558. doi: 10.1007/s11256-018-0455-z

Sánchez, B., Colón, Y., & Esparza, P. (2005). The role of sense of school belonging and gender in the academic adjustment of Latino adolescents. *Journal of Youth and Adolescence, 34*(6), 619–628. doi: 10.1007/s10964-005-8950-4

Sancho, M., & Cline, T. (2012). Fostering a sense of belonging and community as children start a new school. *Educational and Child Psychology, 29*, 64–74.

Schiller, N. G., Basch, L., & Blanc-Szanton, C. (1992). Towards a definition of transnationalism: Introductory remarks and research questions. *Annals of the New York Academy of Sciences, 645*(1), ix–xiv.doi: 10.1111/j.1749-6632.1992. tb33482.x

Squire, V., & Darling, J. (2013). The "minor" politics of rightful presence: Justice and relationality in city of sanctuary. *International Political Sociology, 7*(1), 59–74. doi: 10.1111/ips.12009

Suárez-Orozco, C., Suárez-Orozco, M. M., & Todorova, I. (2008). *Learning a new land: Immigrant students in American society.* Belknap Press/Harvard University Press.

Suárez-Orozco, M., & Sattin, C. (2007). *Wanted: Global Citizens.* Educational Leadership: Journal of the Department of Supervision and Curriculum Development, N.E.A, 64.

Taines, C. (2012). Intervening in alienation: The outcomes for urban youth of participating in school activism. *American Educational Research Journal, 49*(1), 53–86. doi: 10.3102/0002831211411079

Trickett, E. J., & Birman, D. (2005). Acculturation, school context, and school outcomes: Adaptation of refugee adolescents from the former Soviet Union. *Psychology in the Schools, 42*(1), 27–38. doi: 10.1002/pits.20024

Urdan, T. (2012). Factors affecting the motivation and achievement of immigrant students. In K. R. Harris, S. Graham, T. Urdan, S. Graham, J. M. Royer, & M. Zeidner (Eds.), *APA Educational Psychology Handbook*, Vol 2: Individual differences and cultural and contextual factors. (pp. 293–313). American Psychological Association.

Urdan, T., & Munoz, C. (2012). Multiple contexts, multiple methods: A study of academic and cultural identity among children of immigrant parents. *European Journal of Psychology of Education, 27*(2), 247–265.

Urietta, L. (2010). *Working from Within: Chicana and Chicano Activist Educators in Whitestream Schools* (3rd ed.). University of Arizona Press.

Valadez, J. R. (2008). Shaping the educational decisions of Mexican immigrant high school students. *American Educational Research Journal, 45*(4), 834–860. doi: 10.3102/0002831208320244

Valencia, R. R. (2002). "Mexican Americans Don't Value Education!" On the basis of the myth, mythmaking, and debunking. *Journal of Latinos and Education, 1*(2), 81–103. doi: 10.1207/S1532771XJLE0102_2

Valenzuela, A. (1999). *Subtractive Schooling: U.S.-Mexican Youth and the Politics of Caring.* SUNY Series, The Social Context of Education. State University of New York Press, c/o CUP Services, Box 6525, Ithaca, NY 14851 ($21.

Van Ryzin, M. J., Gravely, A. A., & Roseth, C. J. (2009). Autonomy, belongingness, and engagement in school as contributors to adolescent psychological well-being. *Journal of Youth and Adolescence, 38*(1), 1–12. doi: 10.1007/s10964-007-9257-4

Vedder, P. (1994). Global measurement of the quality of education: A help to developing countries? *International Review of Education, 40*(1), 5–17. doi: 10.1007/BF01103001

Vedder, P. H., & Horenczyk, G. (2006). Acculturation and the school. In *The Cambridge Handbook of Acculturation Psychology* (pp. 419–438). Cambridge University Press.

Velásquez, R., Arellano, L. M., & McNeill, B. (Eds.). (2004). *The Handbook of Chicana/o Psychology and Mental Health*. Lawrence Erlbaum.

Walton, G. M., & Brady, S. T. (2017). The many questions of belonging. In A. J. Elliot, C. S. Dweck & D. S. Yeager (Eds.), *Handbook of Competence and Motivation: Theory and Application* (2nd ed., pp. 272–293). The Guilford Press.

Warikoo, N., & Carter, P. (2009). Cultural explanations for racial and ethnic stratification in academic achievement: A call for a new and improved theory. *Review of Educational Research, 79*(1), 366–394. doi: 10.3102/0034654308326162

Wearmouth, J., & Berryman, M. (2012). Viewing restorative approaches to addressing challenging behaviour of minority ethnic students through a community of practice lens. *Cambridge Journal of Education, 42*(2), 253–268. doi: 10.1080/0305764X.2012.676626

Wenger, E. (1998). *Communities of Practice: Learning, Meaning, and Identity*. Cambridge University Press.

Wong, C. A., Eccles, J. S., & Sameroff, A. (2003). The influence of ethnic discrimination and ethnic identification on African American adolescents' school and socioemotional adjustment. *Journal of Personality, 71*(6), 1197–1232. doi: 10.1111/1467-6494.7106012

Yosso, T. J. (2005). Whose culture has capital? A critical race theory discussion of community cultural wealth. *Race Ethnicity and Education, 8*(1), 69–91. doi: 10.1080/1361332052000341006

Chapter 11

The Project for Critical Research, Pedagogy, and Praxis

An Educational Pipeline Model for Social Justice Teacher Education in Times of Division and Authoritarianism

Benjamin "Benji" Chang, Shynar Baimaganbetova, Mel Hyeri Yang, Iris Man Wai Cheung, Catherine Marie Galang Pun, and Benjamin Wai San Yip

INTRODUCTION

Hong Kong is a city-state of 7.4 million people on the southern tip of China, positioned at intersections of East and Southeast Asia. Officially named the Hong Kong Special Administrative Region (HKSAR) of the People's Republic of China (PRC), Hong Kong was one of the British Empire's most prized territories until it returned control to the PRC (aka Mainland China) in 1997. Despite officially being under the rule of Mainland China, Hong Kong was given the status of "1 nation, 2 systems" and allowed to maintain a separate political, economic, and educational system. Along with Macau (also a SAR), independent Taiwan, and Mainland China, Hong Kong is categorized as part of Greater China. Emerging from the Cold War, Hong Kong came to be known as one of the world's great metropolises. Not only was it the pop culture mecca of Chinese peoples, and the portal city to China and much of Asia, it also consistently ranked among the Top Five in the world on international education exams (e.g., PISA, TIMSS) and is a global financial center after New York and London (Chang & McLaren, 2018; Ip, 2017; Lowe & Tsang, 2018). In 2014 and 2019, students in Hong Kong caught the world's attention and imagination in a different way. This occurred through massive long-term protests for democratic elections and socioeconomic reforms while under the PRC's de facto rule. Following both waves of social movements that numbered from the thousands to 2 million, heightened sociopolitical repression was brought down upon students, other activists, and much of mainstream society. This repression was observed in numerous forms, including police brutality, retaliation in courts of law, and conservatism and censorship in the schooling system and academia. Under such conditions, students, teachers, and teacher educators struggled to develop a sense of agency, belonging, and community. It is within these contexts that the Project for Critical Research, Pedagogy and Praxis (PCRP) emerged in 2015.

Cowritten by the student and teacher members of PCRP, this chapter discusses PCRP's collective efforts at building an educational pipeline from the undergraduate to PhD level, across university campuses and K–12 schools. Utilizing theories of sociocultural learning and critical pedagogy, this pipeline's focus was on developing more engaging and rigorous teacher education praxes at research universities, linking student teachers, in-service teachers, teacher educators, and researchers. Particularly concerned with equity issues, the PCRP pipeline was based at a research-intensive campus that also largely serves working-class students, or those who are the first in their family to attend a university. The pipeline was loosely organized under Chang's approach of an iterative process of recognition, solidarity, and collaboration toward building a community of learners, educators, and scholars (Chang, 2015). Utilizing this and other social justice–oriented theories originally promoted in the Global North, this chapter presents insights and considerations to teacher education and educational pipeline work in Asia, and how they can be sustained as spaces of greater agency, belonging, and community. Toward these ends, this chapter is organized around addressing three research questions, and their implications for teachers and researchers in North America and elsewhere:

1. How might a teacher education pipeline using critical pedagogy and sociocultural learning approaches be effectively implemented within the context of Greater China?
2. How might such a pipeline help address issues of equity and community for new teachers, especially those from minoritized backgrounds?
3. What do the pipeline's pre and in-service teachers think are the most important experiences they gained from such an approach?

CONCEPTUAL FRAMEWORK

Both PCRP and this study use a framework of sociocultural learning and critical pedagogy, in trying to better understand how to collectively build community and create a space of belonging within schools and teacher education programs. Critical pedagogy aids in analyzing broader issues of social justice, agency, and resistance (Au, 2011; Bartólome, 1994), but while it offers significant grounds for addressing key problems in education, conceptualizations of learning and culture within this literature are not always robustly addressed. To bridge learning and culture more dynamically, and see learning community members as capable and mutually participating agents in their own development, we also adopt a sociocultural learning lens (D'warte, 2016; Dyson, 2000). This combination of critical pedagogy and sociocultural learning theory helps to cultivate a more humanizing, collaborative, and community-based approach to teacher education in Hong Kong.

Critical Pedagogy

With roots in works of Paulo Freire, critical theory, and decolonizing theory, critical pedagogy seeks to build social justice and liberation via critical consciousness and praxis, especially with marginalized groups. Despite foundational works generated by mostly White men and those trained in the Global North, critical pedagogy has been challenged and grown to engage a far greater diversity, including across lines of gender, ethnicity, sexual orientation, class, and nation-state, while disrupting Eurocentric standpoints and White savior narratives (Chang, 2019; Grande, 2015). Such developments have enabled the scholarship to become more intersectional and inclusive of the narratives, experiences, and practices of disenfranchised populations. Critical pedagogy in Hong Kong has evolved over some 15 years in its efforts to disrupt divisions and stratification within and between dominant and marginalized communities. Focal areas of research have gravitated toward policy and curricula, and incorporated diverse frameworks such as postcolonial theory, poststructural feminism, and culturally relevant pedagogy (Lin, 2004; Pérez-Milans & Soto, 2016).

Among its analysis of contexts such as curriculum, testing, and teacher education, critical pedagogy includes looking at how schooling systems engage in social reproduction and perpetuate socioeconomic hierarchy (Kincheloe, 2004). A commonly applied concept is Freire's critique of the banking model of education, which takes the form of *one-size-fits-all* factory models of teaching, with top-down, teacher-centered, direct-instruction lessons that generally do not consider student diversity and maintain teachers as keepers of knowledge and power. In addition, students and other schooling community members who do not exhibit forms of culture and knowledge modeled after the dominant hegemonic group (typically elite White and Han Chinese men in Hong Kong) are branded with labels like "culturally deficient," "poor motivation," and "low achievement" (Chang, 2019). This banking model helps maintain hierarchies between dominant and minoritized groups, including between students and teachers, and diminished opportunities for belonging in community. Critical pedagogy critiques schooling systems for reproducing passive and uninformed students/citizens, and seeks to challenge this system via dialogical teaching (Shor & Freire, 1987), which can include problem-posing, inquiry-based learning, and embracing students' communities. This approach promotes a more equitable relationship among educational community members in an organic process that builds multiple forms of agency (e.g., civic, educational). In Hong Kong, despite the current dominance of curricula and assessments like the DSE (Diploma in Secondary Education) exam, various school stakeholders have emerged to challenge the ideological status quo of neoliberal and/or colonizing schooling (Bhowmik et al., 2017; Leung, 2020; Woo, 2013), such as the standardization of White Europeans in textbooks, and deficit views of South Asian linguistic and cultural practices. At this juncture, the critical pedagogy literature informing PCRP's teaching and research begins to connect with recent developments in critical approaches to belonging and rightful presence theory (Calabrese Barton & Tan, 2020), which our team first came across toward the end of our write-ups on PCRP. As we did not apply this theory during the implementation of PCRP's pipeline or our research studies of it, we more deeply delve into rightful presence in this chapter's implications section.

From early childhood to university levels in Hong Kong, scholarship has emerged that deploys lenses or practices of critical pedagogy to improve teacher and student agency (Koh, 2015; Moorhouse, 2014; Yuen, 2017), with many studies tending to be in the subjects of Liberal Studies and English. In addition, there has been equity-oriented research that engages with gender, creativity, civic education, and human rights (Chan, 2004; Leung, 2008; Mui, 2010), although they do not always explicitly name critical pedagogy as their sole framework. With research that looks at K–16 and teacher education classrooms using critical pedagogy (Chan & Lo, 2016; Chang, 2018; Soto, 2019), these works often focus more on student backgrounds that are working-class or "ethnic minority," which in Hong Kong typically means students of South or Southeast Asian heritage (e.g., Nepal, the Philippines). Within this scholarship on teaching and teacher preparation, emphases on building community, resilience, and multiple literacies (e.g., traditional academic, critical) are emphasized in the efforts to challenge the didactic, neoliberal, and patriarchal ideologies embedded within Hong Kong's official curricula and assessments.

Sociocultural Learning

Despite its strengths, critical pedagogy may have oversights regarding notions of culture, especially with regards to culture ascribed to dominant versus minoritized communities, and culture's interplay with learning. It is at this juncture that sociocultural learning theory presents a more nuanced conceptualization of culture and helps to address some gaps in critical pedagogy. This work is heavily rooted in approaches initiated by Lev Vygotsky (Gan & Lee, 2016), which have been in turn refined and applied over various fields and disciplines (Nasir & Hand, 2006). A sociocultural lens identifies influences of social and cultural processes that may occur across diverse ecologies, such as organizations, homes, and neighborhoods. A tenet is that human activity, mediated by language, takes place in local cultural contexts. These settings cannot be studied in isolation from the distinctive historical and political context of the activity's development and the meaning ascribed to it by activity participants. In schooling, sociocultural learning highlights the interplay between teacher/student interactions, students' lived experiences, and their learning ecologies. This highlight is instructive given the twenty-first-century reforms that were adopted to steer Hong Kong toward learner-centered curricula, and enhance local pedagogies (Tong, 2010; Walker, 2004).

In schooling systems like those of Hong Kong and the United States, there are two common ways of conceptualizing culture (Nasir & Hand, 2006). One way, which is critiqued by sociocultural learning theory, is understanding culture via an essentializing perspective. This boils down to attributing beliefs, behaviors, and rituals to different cultural groups. Common within these approaches is the interchangeable use of "culture" and "cultural groups" with "race" and/or "ethnicity." This cultural essentialism attempts to draw distinct lines between groups of people in order to categorize and assign them to "cultural groups" despite often arbitrary definitions of what constitutes a culture, a group, and what makes them "different" from each other. This static approach to defining culture and cultural groups risks generating simplistic binary constructions (e.g., "East vs. West," "Hongkongers vs. Mainlanders"), and blanketly ascribing schooling behaviors to a cultural group (e.g., Pakistani boys are aggressive, Chinese girls are more studious, "Eurasian" kids are natural leaders). These essentializations of "groups" and "their culture" can lead to problematic research, policies, and pedagogies. Outcomes may include framing students as "passive vessels" assigned one culture once and forever (D'warte, 2016; Ryan & Louie, 2007), which deprives them of their respective diversity and agency, overlooks individual and collective hopes and challenges, and exaggerates dissimilarities between the "cultural groups."

An alternative approach examines culture through a sociocultural lens where culture is not defined by a fixed set of traits, but is socially embedded, situated, and fluid (Carter & Bolden, 2012; Chan & Lo, 2016). This means that culture is something that is constructed, interpreted, and negotiated through ongoing social interaction in local contexts. The sociocultural understanding helps us to untangle the conflations between culture, race, and ethnicity, thereby encouraging us to notice unique and divergent stories, the peoples behind them, and how they think about and practice culture. This approach offers insights for thinking of culture as a repertoire of practices (Vossoughi & Gutiérrez, 2016), encouraging the humanization of teaching and learning because it helps diverse participants to acknowledge each other's simultaneous differences and similarities. Moreover, it instructs us that learning is more beneficial in experiential and collaborative environments as participants are capable of changing culture. Valuable in-and-of-themselves with sustaining students and their communities' practices in schooling, culture as a repertoire of practices is helpful for students and educators to localize, (re)negotiate, and (re)construct classroom contexts to promote more equitable belonging (Bang et al., 2017).

Aligned with critical pedagogy, sociocultural learning facilitates a pedagogy where cultural, linguistic, and literacy practices are not something that students and teachers are born or stuck with (Vossoughi & Gutiérrez, 2016), but develop and change over time in relation to the individual and their interactions with their communities and broader environment. Attuned to recent asset-based pedagogies literature (Paris & Alim, 2014), the sociocultural and critical approach deployed here practices active *recognition of* learners' capacities to be resistant to difficult circumstances, demonstrates *solidarity* with the learner community's perspectives and practices, and builds *collaboration* with the learners' community in challenging and transforming situational difficulties and structural inequities (Chang, 2015; Wong, 2017). In addition to congruence with asset-based pedagogies, our framework is aligned with grassroots social movements of working-class people of color in the United States and Global South, such as womanist and abolitionist contingents of the Civil Rights and Third World Liberation movements from the past half-century (Collins, 2000; Horton & Freire, 1990). In aligning these approaches of educators, organizers, and communities, this chapter's framework focuses on a learners' potential to reimagine and reshape their practices and lives toward hope and change. It is this framework that PCRP used to build students' sense of community, belonging, and agency.

METHODOLOGY

University Context

PCRP is a teaching and research project directed by Dr. Benji Chang (hereafter referred to as Benji to reduce hierarchy between PCRP members), whose goal is to develop approaches in addressing international standards and educating Hong Kong university students to become teachers and research-ers. PCRP commenced in 2015 when the Education University of Hong Kong (EdUHK) was transitioning from an institute which trained the majority of teachers in Hong Kong, to a comprehensive university with research objec-tives and capacities resembling a Research-1 institution (R1). In the late 2010s, EdUHK quickly rose in international standings, such as consistently coming within the Top Three for QS educational research rankings in Asia. Over the past four years, EdUHK has continued to serve a majority of stu-dents who are of ethnically Chinese heritage and residents of Hong Kong (approximately 85 percent). In looking at specific statistics for Benji's B.Ed. and teacher certification courses of approximately 850 students (2015–2019), it can be observed that a majority of EdUHK undergraduates are either from working-class backgrounds or the first in their family to attend a four-year institution. Ten percent of students are of ethnically Chinese heritage from Mainland China, 1 percent are international students (e.g., Burma, Finland, Japan, USA), and 3 percent are from "ethnic minority" backgrounds. "Ethnic minority" is a label commonly given to those whose family origins are non-ethnically Chinese from South or Southeast Asian countries, regardless of Hong Kong residency or citizenship, and whether or not the student is of "mixed" race or ethnicity. Often replaced by the terms "non-local" or "non-Chinese speaking," the usage of the term "ethnic minority" in Hong Kong is viewed by numerous researchers as part of the minoritization and discrimina-tion of "Brown" communities (Gube & Gao, 2019; Thapa, 2017).

At EdUHK, tensions between "Local" Hong Kongers and "Mainlanders" are not as tense as they have been portrayed in some media since the 2019 protests began. However, if one visits the campus it can be observed that students who grew up in Mainland China, ethnic minority students who grew up in Hong Kong, and ethnically Chinese students who grew up in Hong Kong, mostly associate with those of "their background" (e.g., in classes, library, resident halls). Despite Hong Kong's official recognition of three language varieties in public schooling (Cantonese, English, Putonghua), some two decades of international-multicultural policies, and the university officially teaching 70 percent of courses in English, Cantonese remains the campus lingua franca. This has been divisive in various situations, such as professors teaching English Mode of Instruction courses in Cantonese despite having students who do not speak it, most dormitory and student societies conducting their activities in Cantonese, and jobs, prestigious programs, and other opportunities conducting applicant interviews in Cantonese. Some decry these practices as exclusive or xenophobic. Others support them as an affirmation or survival tactic of Cantonese and Hong Kong culture amid the PRC's local and global economic dominance and the proliferation of Putonghua as Chinese lingua franca. In general, there remain frustrations among many Hong Kongers toward Mainland Chinese and the PRC for their real or perceived involvement in the deterioration of Hong Kong's afford-able housing path to the middle-class (Ip, 2017; Ng, 2018), the withering of its once-dominant cultural industries in pop entertainment and martial arts (Lowe & Tsang, 2018; Yang, 2016), and the hegemony of pro-mainland corporate interests in the government (Chan & Pun, 2020; Morris & Vickers, 2015).

The 2014 Umbrella Movement erupted over issues related to the above, and used occupation, civil disobedience, and other nonviolent methods that were supported by many in Hong Kong and abroad (Partaken, 2017; Walsh, 2017). Unfortunately, these protests were met by a level of police violence that had largely been unseen for decades. Identifiable leaders, including pro-fessors and secondary/university students, were imprisoned for "sedition" long after the demonstrations had peacefully ended, with no policy conces-sions made. Repercussions were also felt in schools and universities (Poon & Leung, 2018), as discourse on democracy and human rights were discour-aged or rejected on school exams required for university admission, and on government grants that are prerequisites for advising graduate students, job promotion, and tenure. This level of censorship and oppression increased dis-satisfaction and disassociation with the PRC, which in turn heightened senses of desperation and the localist Hong Konger identity, and exacerbated divi-sions between ethnolinguistic communities in Hong Kong (Lowe & Tsang, 2018; Walsh, 2017). At EdUHK, these sentiments presented challenges to promoting students' senses of agency, belonging, and community, in addition to preexisting challenges in their teacher preparation where students struggled to understand and practice more democratic, constructivist, and culturally relevant pedagogy. It was under these conditions that PCRP began, in the semester after the Umbrella Movement occupations were dismantled. From the start, PCRP was not solely focused on the training of pre-service teach-ers but also the historical moment that included significant discord among student communities and how we could get various stakeholders to work together.

PCRP Context

PCRP's efforts began within B.Ed. courses which were required for Hong Kong teaching certification programs. Compulsory courses were *Curriculum & Assessment*, *Teaching & Classroom Management*, and *Honors Project Research Methods*. Elective courses included *Citizenship, Equality & Schooling, Creativity in Teaching, School-Based Curriculum*, and *Curriculum & Assessment in International Schooling*. Within these courses, strategies of critical pedagogy and sociocultural learning were employed which included building on intersubjectivity, pop culture, formative assessments, theatre of the oppressed, small-group dialogue, reflective writing, visual arts, and project-based learning (Dyson, 2000; Morrell & Duncan-Andrade, 2005). For example, students had weekly check-in "quick-writes" (or drawings) at the start of class, to access prior knowledge and be discussed in small groups. Another activity included making memes to poke fun at and theoretically critique examples of government, schooling, and success in Hong Kong and US social media. These strategies were used to promote a classroom culture of mutual respect and a sense of humor, which did not shy away from "sensitive" topics such as patriarchy, Chinese Hong Konger elitism over other ethnic groups, and democratic schooling and government. From these courses, several students showing interest and promise in equity education were identified, whether or not they earned As. These students were invited to apply for the PCRP team where they would gain mentorship and practice as a teacher and researcher, in addition to the standard pay for undergraduate student helpers. PCRP members worked a few hours a week in the office, and attended team meetings each month. The office hours and meetings heavily employed elements of apprenticeship, communities of practice, and funds of knowledge in an overall approach that sought to build recognition, solidarity, and collaboration between the professor and team members at different stages of their studies and career (Chang, 2015). Over the years in the pipeline, team members engaged in a range of activities that have been shown to raise academic achievement and various forms of agency and literacy (Irizarry & Donaldson, 2012; Tintiangco-Cubales et al., 2010). These activities included sharing readings, helping coordinate B.Ed. coursework, planning and conducting research projects, visiting schools, mentoring peers, coordinating events, and attending lectures and seminars around Hong Kong. Aside from these activities, a few times a semester PCRP members would get together for social events.

Most of PCRP's research took place in Hong Kong, the Philippines, and the United States, with methodology that utilized critical and feminist approaches to action research (Esposito & Evans-Winters, 2007; Vaughan & Burnaford, 2016). The projects looked at pop culture, curriculum, teacher preparation, and multicultural education, within broader themes of equity and social justice. Participants included university students, pre-/in-service teachers, artists, activists, and school leaders from various ethnolinguistic backgrounds, although the data was communicated and collected in English. These projects sought a triangulated approach to data collection and analysis, making use of surveys, interviews, and focus groups and analyzing them via critical approaches to grounded theory. Through the iterative process of training and engaging in action research, the team had to regularly engage in discussions about culture, privilege, positionality, and oppression in their lives and those of the participants, and the implications of such teaching-research for promoting belonging and agency within schooling.

By the end of the first year, the undergraduate PCRP team began running the annual *Critical Issues in Education Symposia Series* (CIESS) which hosted international and local scholars who worked on issues of educational equity in contexts of teacher education, Greater China, and/or literacy studies. Participating scholars came from Canada, the United States, and Mainland China, whose works we read collectively (Au, 2011; Chan & Lo, 2016; Chang & McLaren, 2018; Du, 2016; Goodwin, 2010; Guo & Guo, 2016; Kang, 2014; Lau, 2013; Lin, 2004; Low & Sarkar, 2014). Many of these scholars also served as Scholar-Mentors for PCRP team members, advising them on their studies and teaching, and continuing to be resources before and after each CIESS. By PCRP's third year, the team began copresenting with Benji at local and international conferences in cultural studies, multicultural education, and literacy, including for the International Society for Language Studies (ISLS). Without Benji, the team flew to Seoul and presented at the Korean Association of Multicultural Education (KAME) conference. Aside from these activities, PCRP members also occasionally worked with non-profit organizations that sought to address inequities within Hong Kong schooling and ethnic minority communities. In their senior years, most completed their Honors Projects on educational equity issues under the supervision of Benji and aligned faculty.

Participants

Aside from the aforementioned studies, PCRP has done three participatory action research (PAR) studies on its efforts (Chang, 2017). Data drawn from these studies provide the bulk of what is examined in this chapter's remaining sections. The PCRP participants were made up of 10 diverse members (four undergraduates, six graduates), with three currently earning a graduate degree, and five who are teachers in Hong Kong or South Korea. While the majority are of Chinese ethnic background and grew up in Hong Kong, the team has a diverse background including various nationalities (e.g., British, Kazakhstani, South Korean), ethnic groups (e.g., Hong Kong Chinese, Punjabi, Mainland Chinese, Filipino, and Chinese), home languages, disciplines, sexual orientations, and schooling (i.e., instruction in English or Taiwanese Mandarin). Most members joined PCRP in the second or third year of their B.Ed. studies (e.g., English Language, Physical Education, General Studies, Chinese Language), with the exceptions of a Korean undergraduate exchange student and a PhD student from Kazakhstan.

Participatory Action Research Method

As mentioned in the previous section, PCRP has utilized critical and feminist approaches to action research as its primary methodology. For this chapter, data is drawn from PAR projects (Fox et al., 2010; Lau, 2013) conducted by the PCRP team on its members, which were carried out in two segments: once during the span of about two months in 2018, and the other during the span of about two months in 2019. Data was collected through an online survey on the participants' demographic information and a reflection of PCRP's influence on their studies and teaching. A critical grounded theory approach (Malagón et al., 2009) was applied to data reduction and analysis of thematic coding which was done by hand and entered into spreadsheet software. The constant comparative method to coding continued to be used in pairs and then small groups during weekly analysis sessions, and later, with the whole team and the principal investigator during several meetings that occurred every three weeks.

FINDINGS

So what were the findings for students who engaged with various efforts of PCRP? Was it able to help students develop a more equitable teaching pedagogy, and promote a greater sense of agency and community with peers? In going over the data, three themes emerged, which were (1) *Exploring Diversity in Experiences and Perspectives*, (2) *Addressing "Within Group" Diversity in Members' Classrooms*, and (3) *Applying Sociocultural and Critical Theories to Practice*.

THEME 1: EXPLORING DIVERSITY IN EXPERIENCES AND PERSPECTIVES

For this chapter, we focus on 2018–2019 data collected. As it was a PAR project, the members themselves had the chance to examine the data we collected on our team. The first major theme discovered was *Exploring Diversity in Experiences and Perspectives*. While local teacher education training in Hong Kong has typically focused on delivering "objective" content knowledge and theories of instruction (Clark & Gieve, 2006; Soto, 2019), PCRP provided a space for members to individually and collectively develop their own understandings and agency when it came to language and culture issues, whether in their personal experiences or among Hong Kong and Asian societies. This was helpful in fleshing out their understanding of diversity beyond foods, festivals, heroes, and holidays.

Beginning with the individual in relation to the team, PCRP members wrote about the significance of five meeting practices, including (1) speaking their personal Check-Ins at the start, (2) freewriting on various topics concerning equity and justice, and (3) composing "I Am From" poems (Christensen, 2000). Building upon this foundation of sharing personal experiences and views, PCRP would read academic articles, often via (4) shared/guided reading activities and (5) key terms emphasized at each meeting and their relevance to everyone's work in teaching and research. These activities at the meetings and office hours would help make connections between the often international contexts of the articles, and educational issues in Hong Kong and Asia. For example, Monica explained how PCRP facilitated critical explorations of each other's experiences and perspectives when she shared, "When we discuss topics and issues in the readings, our members see things from different perspectives, and this dialogue is benefited by the diversity of PCRP members." Brenda added, "This is a skill I got from PCRP because in our meetings, we critique different research papers that are presented to us and have fruitful discussions on how those notions can reflect bigger social and cultural issues." Brenda's statement corroborates with comments she made on diversity and reflexivity two-and-a-half years earlier when she said she was able to "reflect on my own experiences and think deeply about the issues that affected me as a student," and improve on her ability to work with people of diverse backgrounds. From Benji's notes he observed how the team was also able to mutually engage in meeting and office dialogue about typically sensitive topics (e.g., democracy, mainland/Hong Kong forms of elitism) without sweeping essentializations and accusations that were known to take place in spaces like student societies, social media, and classrooms.

Through the diversity brought out of our team in the previously named activities, members were able to come up with divergent analyses and suggestions when navigating EdUHK as students, and as future teachers and/or researchers. This gave members a broader scope when tackling various educational issues. But this theme of *Exploring Diversity in Experiences and Perspectives* was also promoted externally, through dialogue, partnerships, and collaborations in and out of Hong Kong. Three examples of these include (1) dialogue with Visiting Scholar-Mentors, (2) participation in off-campus seminars/events (e.g., schools, university, NGOs), and (3) an apprenticeship model to learn and practice research methodology with PCRP's projects locally and abroad. For example, Brenda stated, "There are things I wouldn't come across in courses or from textbooks, but through engaging in seminars and listening to different people during roundtable discussions and after talks from the international scholars." In discussing more about the content and the progression of ideas in PCRP, Beth writes,

This integral theoretical picture was particularly valuable for my research, as no other professor really addressed it in a way it was explained and discussed in PCRP meetings. Through those discussions emerged issues of false binaries in theory, research and practice, e.g. East vs West . . . that might affect our practices and thinking not only in research and teaching, but also in daily lives.

These statements about making connections between research, teaching, and daily lives is congruent with those made about developing agency in our previous study (Chang, 2017), such as when Claire shared, "I discuss more complicated issues and concepts with others now. . . . I'm more able to react to different issues. I sometimes think of solutions to social problems that seem feasible." In going through the data, it became clear that these collective experiences and activities contributed to members first developing greater sensitivity, reflexivity, belonging, and agency in the PCRP space. They then extended these experiences into their work in schools as teachers and/or researchers.

Theme 2: Addressing "Within Group" Diversity in Members' Classrooms

A second major theme that emerged from the PAR project was *Addressing "Within Group" Diversity in Members' Classrooms*, which in Greater China can look rather different from diversity as it is addressed in United States–based scholarship. Throughout the PCRP pipeline, members shared that they were able to build on their sociocultural and critical understandings of diversity, and apply it to their school observations and teaching practica. This was important because although Hong Kong is known to be multicultural and promoted as "Asia's World City" (Law & Lee, 2012), its student populations are often grouped together under the monolithic category of "Chinese" and within-group differences such as sexual orientation, class, language variety, residential status, and length of time in Hong Kong are rarely addressed or prioritized. For example, Hong Kong's high averages on international exams are often explained through learning-style essentializations like "The Chinese Learner" and "Confucian Heritage Culture" (Chang, 2019; Clark & Gieve, 2006), but when students do not do well the issues are framed as individual lack of motivation. What is left out of this discourse are the many different communities lumped under the "Chinese" umbrella category, as well as "non-Chinese" populations. If classroom diversity is addressed, it is often framed as differences among "Non-Chinese" aka "ethnic minority" students (e.g., class, language, religion), and individual and subgroup differences across the many Chinese communities are not addressed. These oversights were significant for PCRP as most students were from working-class, or first-in-the-family to college backgrounds. Chelsea, who has taught at both local government schools and international schools, stated, "I noticed that even though a student (newly arrived from Mainland) might have a similar ethnicity as a local Hong Kong student, she might have developed different cultural practices due to her family's background." Building on this sociocultural analysis is Claire, whose current classroom contains all but one student of Chinese heritage. She shared:

> Sometimes it's easy to assume that within the hegemonic group, students have the same cultures, linguistic backgrounds, practices, and behaviors. With activities like allowing them to bring in their cultural practices to the classroom, they learn more as they make connections between themselves and developing multiliteracies.

These insights also contributed in important ways to the development of greater sensitivity, reflexivity, belonging, and agency in the PCRP space.

Theme 3: Applying Sociocultural and Critical Theories to Practice

A third theme that the team uncovered was applying theories to practice as teachers of their own classrooms. As mentioned earlier, a major concern that EdUHK's student teachers and teacher educators share with peers around the globe (Chan & Lo, 2016; Harris & de Bruin, 2018) is how to connect equity theory to real-world teaching in public schools. While notions like critical pedagogy's problem-posing and sociocultural learning's funds of knowledge are attractive to new teachers in Hong Kong who aim to make a difference, both practitioners and researchers have often framed these approaches as impractical when attempted in the scripted curricula and high-stakes exam system that permeates the HKSAR's schooling system (Walker, 2004; Woo, 2013). Despite these struggles, PCRP members reported that they were more comfortable and able to apply theory to practice, given their significant engagement with the concepts and scholars who develop them. For example, Charlie, who is of Chinese heritage but taught many students from South Asian families and Chinese backgrounds, stated, "The curriculum and textbooks in Hong Kong are often ethnocentric. For ethnically minoritized students, these curriculum and textbooks often alienate them to a greater extent from the marginalizing education system." To tackle this issue, Charlie connected students' cultural backgrounds with the official curriculum and textbooks via providing culturally responsive materials (e.g., documentary clips, personalized worksheets, pop culture), which enabled students to better relate their personal and cultural experiences to their classroom, which can be tied to elements of rightful presence. For Brenda, whose family is of South Asian background but mostly teaches students of Chinese heritage, she often emphasized the skill of critical textual analysis. She shared, "I try to guide them to read between the lines and ask if they can identify social problems or cultural issues from those texts . . . to guide students in seeing how different social texts can convey underlying meanings and reflect issues in societies that we live in."

Altogether the team's analysis of the PCRP pipeline found the most data on Theme #1 *Exploring Diversity in Experiences and Perspectives*, which entailed various mentions of developing each member's analysis through reflexivity on their own lives, and then connecting them with educational theories and local contexts and abroad. In further discussion among members, the emphasis on Theme #1 was a bit expected given the project's focus on critical and sociocultural learning approaches that promoted recognition, solidarity, and collaboration (Chang, 2015) across our team's members. These approaches were facilitated by a "small batch" approach, where a few students were added on to the pipeline each year, and mentored by a specific professor. Instead of larger teams, PCRP's smaller personalized approach allowed for deeper understanding and flexibility for members in their learning process.

A Note on Schooling and University Institutions

While this chapter mostly focuses on PCRP's pipeline with students/teachers/researchers, we close with a note about implications for schooling and university institutions. Despite it being a major global research methodology, PCRP's core praxis of PAR was discouraged by many Hong Kong faculty and administration. The research methodology, and the pedagogy it focused on, were often deemed incongruent with government grant competitions, faculty performance indicators, school curriculum, high-stakes testing, and so on. Some faculty openly mocked the endeavor, and PCRP professors and classroom teachers were advised to step away from its work in order to keep their jobs. PCRP was not awarded grant funding to initiate its efforts, which were thus run-on volunteer hours and a small start-up fund to operate its annual programming with international scholars, mentoring, student assistant wages, and school/NGO collaborations.

However, within a few years, PCRP's approach and outputs came to be known within the region. PCRP students earned individual accolades such as government scholarships and Honors Project distinctions. Courses within the PCRP pipeline received high teaching evaluations by students across ages and majors (n = 458). As instructor-of-record, Benji was given the *Outstanding Teaching Performance* award for all five years the courses were taught. Off-campus faculty at Hong Kong's most elite universities praised its implications for grassroots and transformative approaches to building student/teacher/researcher capacity. This praise materialized into collaborations with scholars around Greater China and winning two of Hong Kong's most prestigious government grants. As we close this *Findings and Implications* section, we make note of these developments not to pat ourselves on the back, but to indicate how difficult it can be to implement such approaches to place and belonging in certain global contexts, but also how transformative it can be if educators and researchers can weather the storm of these uphill battles.

CONCLUDING THOUGHTS AND IMPLICATIONS

In addressing this chapter's three research questions, we have discussed a five-year educational pipeline program that sought to build students' senses of community and agency as teachers and researchers, through critical and sociocultural approaches that emphasized processes of recognition, solidarity, and collaboration. Via quantitative data from over 400 student surveys, and qualitative data with 10 PCRP members, it can be noted that PCRP's pipeline approaches were deemed effective within the Hong Kong context, thus answering Question 1. Concerning Question 2's emphasis on equity and community for new teachers from minoritized backgrounds, we see less direct discussion as participant responses were more about preservice and new in-service teachers. But Questions 2 and 3 are addressed via the major themes of *Exploring Diversity in Experiences and Perspectives*, *Addressing "Within Group" Diversity in Members' Classrooms* and *Applying Sociocultural and Critical Theories to Practice*. Across the data for this study, we could see that the students, who were at various stages of their training and careers, repeatedly emphasized two practices that benefited their sense of agency:

1. Dialogical teaching and mentoring methods of PCRP.
2. Engagement with issues, theories, and pedagogies addressing equity, primarily through interactions with peers and scholars in education.

What did not emerge as much as expected in the data were statements that specifically named community and belonging as themes. While practices that built community were mentioned numerous times, especially under Theme #1 (*Exploring Diversity in Experiences and Perspectives*), the actual terms community and belonging were rarely mentioned. Instead, terms like "team," "teamwork," "safe space," and "third space" were used to describe the efficacy of PCRP's approaches, which we now feel can all be associated with equitable practices of belonging. At the time of data collection it is understandable that not every goal of PCRP was emphasized by students. Nevertheless, lack of use of the term "community and belonging" warrants attention in teacher education scholarship given the emphases on related themes within traditions of critical, sociocultural, and asset-based pedagogies, suggesting a future deeper dive into these themes. Upon initial analysis, some tentative points can be raised about teacher/researcher positionality and social versus academic paradigms.

Insider/Outsider Positionality

In attempting to build community and belonging in academic settings, the negotiation of difference and positionality is crucial in the process of building a shared community among its stakeholders. Over the past 20 years, critical pedagogy and sociocultural learning research have demanded reflexivity and self-critique by the teacher-researcher. Informed by a variety of traditions, including indigenous ways of knowing and poststructural feminism (Grande, 2015; Lin, 2004), this literature often calls out the teacher-researcher to address their positionality, biases, and privileges in how they view the world and thus carry out their methodology and pedagogy. This was a somewhat new process for PCRP members, especially those who grew up being framed as part of their society's dominant groups. For Benji this was an ongoing process as the PI and coordinator for PCRP, and something he had been working on for many years over his personal trajectory. For example, he was aware that in the United States, he was minoritized in the sense of being the child of immigrants, a person of color, and an "English Language Learner." However, he was also privileged in the sense of being an able-bodied, straight, cis-gender man who grew up middle-class, and was of the dominant Chinese subgroup within the preferred Asian American minority: such as those who are "lighter-skinned" (Ramkellawan-Arteaga, 2020). With reflexivity on his positionality in these overlapping and contradictory categorizations, Benji crossed the Pacific, in the reverse direction of his migrant ancestors, into the most capitalistic and "Westernized" part of China. In simply flying back to Hong Kong, Benji became part of the society's hegemonic "Han Chinese" group, despite not having familial roots there, not knowing its Cantonese lingua franca, or being fluent in cultural practices of the "local" middle-class, or the elite. In many instances being marked as Chinese granted Benji various privileges and normalized him as an insider, but at the same time due to his politics, pedagogy, language fluencies, methodology, and so on he was marked as an outsider.

In the tradition of other insider–outsider scholars (Chow, 1993; Hall, 1999; Luke, 2018), Benji actively worked on developing insights on issues of diversity and power, and addressed these in theory and practice via PCRP.

As outlined earlier, these efforts were well-recognized by students, including those from "non-local," working-class, and "ethnic minority" backgrounds. However, there were subtle and not-so-subtle "hiccups" as well, which included a time in the early years when Benji was enthusiastically telling Brenda (whose family is Punjabi, but has been in Hong Kong for generations), that his only Asian neighbors as child were Punjabi Sikh and that they grew up together and got into much mischief as kids. When Brenda had little reaction, Benji reflected on it and asked Brenda about it later when they got to know each other better. Benji asked, "Was that like my 'I have Black friends too' moment?" and Brenda said "Yeahh." While it was embarrassing, Benji came to better understand how his whiteness as a Han Chinese in Hong Kong was the most pertinent positionality in that exchange. Regardless of his individual history with racist violence from White peoples, being childhood best friends with South Asian youth, and going through the trenches of years of volunteer activism in the streets with pro-Brown and Black organizations, he was still constructed as "White" within Hong Kong society. Thus his pedagogy and methodology needed to be more humble and mindful of shifting positionality, and revise its approach to assume less and listen more in building community and each team member's belonging.

Another potential barrier to building community within PCRP classrooms, meetings, and office hours was the PI/teacher's lack of familiarity and insider positionality with local language varieties, pop culture (e.g., Cantopop, Bollywood films), and progressive community of color organizations. Throughout Benji's work as a researcher, organizer, and educator in California and New York, he had made use of this capital but did not have them in Hong Kong. In order to build connections and relationships with students and community groups, Benji drew upon critical, sociocultural, and grassroots organizing pedagogies in approaching the various stakeholders as a learner himself, trying to show genuine interest and solidarity. While these strategies were not often discussed in the data, these were explicitly utilized by Benji when navigating the new and unexpected terrain with diverse stakeholders. Negotiating these webs of relationships and cultural-linguistic practices allowed for PCRP's pipeline to have a range of participants and supporters on and off campus, despite its democracy and social justice orientations, but their specific impact is not completely clear.

Academic vs. Social Goals

In reflecting on PCRP's development of belonging and community, it can be said that the pipeline was more explicitly successful in achieving traditional academic goals, with less clarity on its more "social"-oriented goals. For goals like building the academic skills of members and affiliated students, it was clear that writing, research, speaking, and analysis were improved and helped bolster the student–teachers' pedagogies. This helped earn them teaching jobs, as well as fellowships, internships, and master's program admissions, all of which can be aligned with following neoliberal market ideology. But with less traditional academic or career-oriented goals, such as becoming activists in their local school communities, or developing friendships and community with racialized and gendered "others" in their everyday lives, it was less clear what the outcomes were. While these outcomes and factors leading to them are beyond our current study's scope, we are interested to learn more about:

- To what degree would students have been invested in critical and socio-cultural perspectives if it did not help them earn higher grades, jobs, and accolades?
- Would participants view the perspectives and pedagogies differently if they were presented by educators/researchers who were not from the Global North or elite educational backgrounds?
- Have participants' views shifted concerning Hong Kong-Mainland China tensions and who "belongs" in the HKSAR? If so, how has this affected their everyday interactions with various stakeholders as they navigate their rightful presence?

Rightful Presence

Over our years in working together, we consistently discussed building team and community as vital to PCRP's pedagogical, methodological, and political projects toward equity. We approached these projects through a critical and sociocultural framework grounded in feminist and intersectional lenses. Thus we workshopped practices of resistance, critical consciousness, working-class youth and grassroots activism, third space, community organizing, mentorship, apprenticeship, communities of practice, educational pipelines, and PAR. Our goal was to embody a more inclusive and sustainable praxis of students, teachers, teacher educators, and researchers working together to challenge schooling oppression. Given our trajectory, we did not come across belonging and rightful presence theory that aligned with our efforts until late in our work together, following this study's data collection. Prior to this, belonging scholarship we had access to largely operated within positivist paradigms that had few challenges to neoliberal ideology, White and Han Chinese supremacy, "post"-colonial conditions, and other systemic inequities (Gray et al., 2018; Macartney, 2012; Núñez, 2014).

As we proceeded to write about our efforts, we found that the notion of rightful presence in education (Calabrese Barton & Tan, 2020), which can be highly tied to critical models of belonging (see Faircloth, this volume), was a generative path to explore for future work. An example of this path would be rightful presence's first tenet of challenging equity as de jure policies of migrant and refugee inclusion in schooling (i.e., non-Chinese Southeast Asians in Hong Kong teacher training), through allied sociopolitical struggle. While PCRP pipeline data showed that coursework was helpful in theory to this end, it also required standing up to institutional norms and potential job repercussions to clear space for student–teachers to practice the pedagogies they were learning about, and for minoritized students to garner leadership roles. Another example of rightful presence's connection would be its third tenet of collective disruption of guest/host classroom relationalities. For PCRP, this meant being strategic in collaborating with local and international scholars, who had different politics and networks, but were all willing to help disrupt some of the guest/host power dynamics at the university, and legitimize these counter-hegemonic efforts as the teacher-researchers sought careers, advocacy, and leadership off campus.

While rightful presence has generative implications for pipeline work, we note that there may be differences between Greater China and some of the contexts in which the theory has been developed (Squire & Darling, 2013). Although Hong Kong was colonized by the British, the dynamics of the city-state vary greatly from many other Commonwealth states (e.g., Australia, Canada). For one, Hong Kong's current "colonizer" in the PRC is dominated by the same racialized group as the majority of citizens in the HKSAR. In addition, Hong Kong has different histories of oppression compared to other states studied in rightful presence theory (e.g., genocide, slavery, military industrial complex) (Chang & McLaren, 2018). Relatedly, cultural-linguistic disparities of voice, silence, visibility, and other issues of agency can materialize quite differently in Hong Kong and the region. Thus as we step forward in applying belonging and rightful presence concepts to our work, we seek to contribute to the theory via our shared critical and sociocultural foundations and diverse contexts in Asia.

As we look back as a team toward the past five years of PCRP, we are still working on our pipeline's implications. Challenges still exist for our student–teachers and graduates as they go on to face teaching practica, job placements, and careers in a system dominated by neoliberal, behaviorist, and positivist schooling institutions, and where critical pedagogies, sociocultural learning, and action research are disparaged as utopian pseudoscience. Yet we are confident in our deliberations on PCRP's efficacy over the years from undergraduates, to preservice teachers, to early career teachers, and to postgraduate researchers. While we have much to learn about long-term effects on our relationships, belonging, pedagogies, and activism within our professional and everyday lives, we believe that PCRP has helped address gaps between well-researched pedagogies that build on learner diversity, and

Hong Kong's dominant teaching paradigms. Finally, we believe that over the short- and long-term, PCRP's pipeline approach is an uncommon but generative example for teacher education programs in the Greater China region and abroad in the United States, especially in our current times of mass societal divisions and authoritarianism.

Acknowledgments

We would like to thank PCRP members Michelle Chang, Renu Kaur, Hugo Liu, Sibyl Jiayi Min, Sarah Cheung, and Pratigya Marhatta for their fellowship toward the success of this writing. We would also like to thank our editors, Beverly Faircloth, Laura Gonzalez, and Katherine Ramos, for their support within this volume.

REFERENCES

Au, W. (2011). *Critical curriculum studies: education, consciousness, and the politics of knowing*. Routledge.

Bang, M., Brown, B., Calabrese Barton, A., Rosebery, A., & Warren, B. (2017). Toward more equitable learning in science: Expanding relationships among students, teachers, and science practices. In C. Schwarz, C. Passmore, & B. Reiser (Eds.), *Helping students make sense of the world using next generation science engineering practices* (pp. 33–58). NSTA Press.

Bartólome, L. (1994). Beyond the methods fetish: Toward a humanizing pedagogy. *Harvard Educational Review*, *64*(2), 173–194.

Bhowmik, M., Kennedy, K., & Hue, M. (2017). Education for all – but not Hong Kong's ethnic minority students. *Race Ethnicity and Education*, *21*(5), 661–679. doi: 10.1080/13613324.2017.1294573

Calabrese Barton, A., & Tan, E. (2020). Beyond equity as inclusion: A framework of "rightful presence" for guiding justice-oriented studies in teaching and learning. *Educational Researcher*, *49*(6), 433–440. doi: 10.3102/0013189X20927363

Carter, S., & Bolden, C. (2012). Culture work in the research interview. In J. Gubrium, J. Holstein, A. Marvasti, & K. McKinney (Eds.), *The SAGE handbook of interview research: The complexity of the craft* (pp. 255–268). SAGE.

Chan, A. (2004). Gender, school management and educational reforms: A case study of a primary school in Hong Kong. *Gender and Education*, *16*(4), 491–510. doi: 10.1080/0954025004200300394

Chan, C., & Lo, M. (2016). Exploring inclusive pedagogical practices in Hong Kong primary EFL classrooms. *International Journal of Inclusive Education*, *21*(7), 714–729. doi: 10.1080/13603116.2016.1252798

Chan, D., & Pun, N. (2020). Economic power of the political powerless in the 2019 Hong Kong pro-democracy movement. *Critical Asian Studies*, *52*(1), 33–43. doi: 10.1080/14672715.2019.1708019

Chang, B. (2015). In the service of self-determination: Teacher education, service-learning, and community reorganizing. *Theory Into Practice, 54*(1), 29–38. doi: 10.1080/00405841.2015.977659

Chang, B. (2017). Building a higher education pipeline: Sociocultural and critical approaches to "internationalisation" in teaching and research. *The Hong Kong Teachers' Centre Journal, 16*(1), 1–25.

Chang, B. (2018). Issues of educational equity, curriculum, and pedagogy in Hong Kong. In K. Kennedy & J. Lee (Eds.), *The Routledge handbook on schools and schooling in Asia* (pp. 110–122). Routledge.

Chang, B. (2019). Two more takes on the critical: Intersectional and interdisciplinary scholarship grounded in family histories and the Asia-Pacific. *Curriculum Inquiry, 49*(2), 156–172. doi: 10.1080/03626784.2019.1595537

Chang, B., & McLaren, P. (2018). Emerging issues of teaching and social justice in Greater China: Neoliberalism and critical pedagogy in Hong Kong. *Policy Futures in Education, 16*(6), 781–803. doi: 10.1177/1478210318767735

Chow, R. (1993). *Writing diaspora: Tactics of intervention in contemporary cultural studies.* Indiana University.

Clark, R., & Gieve, S. (2006). On the discursive construction of "The Chinese Learner." *Language, Culture and Curriculum, 19*(1), 54–73. doi: 10.1080/07908310608668754

Collins, P.H. (2000). *Black Feminist thought: Knowledge, consciousness, and the politics of empowerment.* Routledge.

D'warte, J. (2016). Students as linguistic ethnographers: Super-diversity in the classroom context. In D. R. Cole & C. Woodrow (Eds.), *Super dimensions in globalisation and education* (pp. 19–35). Springer. doi: 10.1007/978-981-10-0312-7_2

Du, L. (2016). Education, social stratification and class in China. In Y. Guo (Ed.), *Handbook on class and social stratification in China* (pp. 161–176). Elgar.

Dyson, A.H. (2000). Linking writing and community development through the Children's Forum. In C.D. Lee & P. Smagorinsky (Eds.), *Vygotskian perspectives on literacy research: Constructing meaning through collaborative inquiry* (pp. 127–149). Cambridge University

Esposito, J., & Evans-Winters, V. (2007). Contextualizing critical action research: Lessons from urban educators. *Educational Action Research, 15*(2), 221–237. http://www.informaworld.com/10.1080/09650790701314775

Fox, M., Mediratta, K., Ruglis, J., Stoudt, B., Shah, S., & Fine, M. (2010). Critical youth engagement: Participatory action research and organizing. In L. Sherrod, J. Torney-Purta, & C. Flanagan (Eds.), *Handbook of research on civic engagement in youth* (pp. 621–650). Wiley.

Gan, Z., & Lee, F. (2016). Understanding ESL student teachers' learning of classroom practices in the practicum: A case study in Hong Kong. *The Asia-Pacific Education Researcher, 25*(2), 251–266. doi: 10.1007/s40299-015-0258-x

Goodwin, A.L. (2010). Curriculum as colonizer: (Asian) American education in the current U.S. context. *Teachers College Record, 112*(12), 3102–3138.

Grande, S. (2015). *Red pedagogy: Native American social and political thought* (2nd ed.). Rowman & Littlefield.

Gray, D. L., Hope, E., & Matthews, J. (2018). Black and belonging at school: A case for interpersonal, instructional, and institutional opportunity structures. *Educational Psychologist, 53*(2), 97–113. doi: 10.1080/00461520.2017.1421466

Gube, J., & Gao, F. (2019). *Education, ethnicity and equity in the multilingual Asian context.* Springer.

Guo, S., & Guo, Y. (Eds.). (2016). *Spotlight on China: Changes in education under China's market economy.* Sense.

Hall, S. (1999). Thinking the diaspora: Home-thoughts from abroad. *Small Axe, 6,* 1–18.

Harris, A., & deBruin, L. (2018). Secondary school creativity, teacher practice and STEAM education: An international study. *Journal of Educational Change, 19*(2), 153–179. doi: 10.1007/s10833-017-9311-2

Horton, M., & Freire, P. (Eds.). (1990). *We make the road by walking: Conversations on education and social change.* Temple University.

Ip, I.-c. (2017). State, class and capital: Gentrification and new urban developmentalism in Hong Kong. *Critical Sociology, 0*(0), 0896920517719487. doi: 10.1177/0896920517719487

Irizarry, J., & Donaldson, M. (2012). Teach for América: The Latinization of U.S. schools and the critical shortage of Latina/o teachers. *American Educational Research Journal, 49*(1), 155–194. doi: 10.3102/0002831211434764

Kang, M.-O. (2014). *Multicultural education in South Korea: Language, ideology, and culture in Korean language arts education.* Routledge.

Kincheloe, J. (2004). *Critical pedagogy primer.* Peter Lang.

Koh, A. (2015). Popular culture goes to school in Hong Kong: A language arts curriculum on revolutionary road? *Oxford Review of Education, 41*(6), 691–710. doi: 10.1080/03054985.2015.1110130

Lau, S.M.-C. (2013). A study of critical literacy work with beginning English Language Learners: An integrated approach. *Critical Inquiry in Language Studies, 10*(1), 1–30. doi: 10.1080/15427587.2013.753841

Law, K.-Y., & Lee, K.-M. (2012). The myth of multiculturalism in "Asia's world city": Incomprehensive policies for ethnic minorities in Hong Kong. *Journal of Asian Public Policy, 5*(1), 117–134. doi: 10.1080/17516234.2012.662353

Leung, W.-T. (2020). *Applying critical pedagogy in the senior secondary Liberal Studies curriculum: An action research study in Hong Kong.* The Education University of Hong Kong.

Leung, Y.-W. (2008). An "action-poor" human rights education: A critical review of the development of human rights education in the context of civic education in Hong Kong. *Intercultural Education, 19*(3), 231–242. doi: 10.1080/14675980802078590

Lin, A.M.-Y. (2004). Introducing a critical pedagogical curriculum: A feminist reflexive account. In B. Norton & K. Toohey (Eds.), *Critical pedagogies and language learning* (pp. 271–290). Cambridge University.

Low, B., & Sarkar, M. (2014). Translanguaging in the multilingual Montreal hip-hop community: Everyday poetics as counter to the myths of the monolingual classroom. In A. Blackledge & A. Creese (Eds.), *Heteroglossia as practice and pedagogy* (pp. 99–118). Springer.

Lowe, J., & Tsang, E. (2018). Securing Hong Kong's identity in the colonial past: Strategic essentialism and the Umbrella Movement. *Critical Asian Studies*, *50*(4), 556–571. doi: 10.1080/14672715.2018.1503550

Luke, A. (2018). No grand narrative in sight: On double consciousness and critical literacy. In A. Luke (Ed.), *Critical literacy, schooling, and social justice: The selected works of Allan Luke* (pp. 1–27). Routledge.

Macartney, B.C. (2012). Teaching through an ethics of belonging, care and obligation as a critical approach to transforming education. *International Journal of Inclusive Education*, *16*(2), 171–183. doi: 10.1080/13603111003686218

Malagón, M.C., Huber, L.P., & Velez, V.N. (2009). Our experiences, our methods: Using grounded theory to inform a critical race theory methodology. *Seattle Journal for Social Justice*, *8*(1), 253–272.

Moorhouse, B. (2014). Using critical pedagogies with young EFL learners in a Hong Kong primary school. *International Journal of Bilingual & Multilingual Teachers of English*, *2*(2), 79–90.

Morrell, E., & Duncan-Andrade, J. (2005). Popular culture and critical media pedagogy in secondary literacy classrooms. *International Journal of Learning*, *12*(1), 1–10.

Morris, P., & Vickers, E. (2015). Schooling, politics and the construction of identity in Hong Kong: The 2012 "Moral and National Education" crisis in historical context. *Comparative Education*, *51*(3), 305–326. doi: 10.1080/03050068.2015.1033169

Mui, M.-S. (2010). Identity and the visual arts curriculum in colonial and postcolonial Hong Kong. *Visual Arts Research*, *36*(1), 1–11.

Nasir, N., & Hand, V. (2006). Exploring sociocultural perspectives on race, culture, and learning. *Review of Educational Research*, *76*(4), 449–475. doi: 10.3102/00346543076004449

Ng, M.-K. (2018). Transformative urbanism and reproblematising land scarcity in Hong Kong. *Urban Studies*, *57*(7), 1452–1468. doi: 10.1177/0042098018800399

Núñez, A.-M. (2014). Advancing an intersectionality framework in higher education: Power and Latino postsecondary opportunity. In M. Paulsen (Ed.), *Higher education: Handbook of theory and research* (Vol. 29, pp. 33–92). Springer.

Paris, D., & Alim, H. (2014). What are we seeking to sustain through culturally sustaining pedagogy? A loving critique forward. *Harvard Educational Review*, *84*(1), 85–100.

Partaken, J. (2017). Listening to students about the Umbrella Movement of Hong Kong. *Educational Philosophy and Theory*, *51*(2), 212–222. doi: 10.1080/00131857.2017.1318045

Pérez-Milans, M., & Soto, C. (2016). Reflexive language and ethnic minority activism in Hong Kong. *AILA Review*, *29*, 48–82.

Poon, Y.-h., & Leung, Y.-w. (2018). Making of patriotic: Experimenting with China's sharp power in Hong Kong's education. In B. Tai (Ed.), *China's sharp power in Hong Kong* (pp. 63–78). Hong Kong Civil Hub.

Ramkellawan-Arteaga, R. (2020). Just because we look alike doesn't mean we are the same: Using an examination of Indo-Caribbean identity to inform a third space lens. *Review of Education, Pedagogy, and Cultural Studies*, 1–16. doi: 10.1080/10714413.2020.1757958

The Project for Critical Research, Pedagogy, and Praxis 249

Ryan, J., & Louie, K. (2007). False dichotomy? "Western" and "Confucian" concepts of scholarship and learning. *Educational Philosophy and Theory, 39*(4), 404–417. doi: 10.1111/j.1469-5812.2007.00347.x

Shor, I., & Freire, P. (1987). What is the "dialogical method" of teaching? *Journal of Education, 169*(3), 11–31. doi: 10.1177/002205748716900303

Soto, C. (2019). *Critical Pedagogy in Hong Kong: Classroom stories of struggle and hope.* Routledge.

Squire, V., & Darling, J. (2013). The "minor" politics of rightful presence: Justice and relationality in City of Sanctuary. *International Political Sociology, 7*(1), 59–74.

Thapa, C. B. (2017, February 1). Who, really, are Hong Kong's ethnic minorities? No policy can work without understanding. *South China Morning Post.*

Tintiangco-Cubales, A., Daus-Magbual, R., & Daus-Magbual, A. (2010). Pin@y Educational Partnerships A counter-pipeline to create critical educators. *AAPI Nexus: Asian Americans & Pacific Islanders Policy, Practice and Community, 8*(1), 75–102.

Tong, S. Y. A. (2010). Lessons learned? School leadership and curriculum reform in Hong Kong. *Asia Pacific Journal of Education, 30*(2), 231–242. doi: 10.1080/02188791003722000

Vaughan, M., & Burnaford, G. (2016). Action research in graduate teacher education: A review of the literature 2000–2015. *Educational Action Research, 24*(2), 280–299. doi: 10.1080/09650792.2015.1062408

Vossoughi, S., & Gutiérrez, K.D. (2016). Critical pedagogy and sociocultural theory. In I. Esmonde & A. Booker (Eds.), *Power and privilege in the learning sciences: Critical and sociocultural theories of learning* (pp. 157–179). Routledge.

Walker, A. (2004). Constitution and culture: Exploring the deep leadership structures of Hong Kong schools. *Discourse: Studies in the Cultural Politics of Education, 25*(1), 75–94. doi: 10.1080/0159630042000178491

Walsh, S. (2017). Under the Umbrella: Pedagogy, knowledge production, and video from the margins of the movement. *Educational Philosophy and Theory, 51*(2), 200–211. doi: 10.1080/00131857.2017.1310018

Wong, N.-W.A. (2017). *Opening doors: Community centers connecting working-class immigrant families and schools.* Peter Lang.

Woo, D. (2013). Neoliberalism in two Hong Kong school categories. *Current Issues in Comparative Education, 16*(1), 37–48.

Yang, C. (2016, August 22). Exit the dragon? Kung fu, once central to Hong Kong life, is waning. *New York Times.* http://www.nytimes.com/2016/08/23/world/asia/hong-kong-kung-fu.html?_r=2

Yuen, G. (2017). Ready for ethical and critically reflective practice in supercomplex times? Discourses, knowledge and values in the postmodern society of Hong Kong. In M. Li, J. Fox, & S. Grieshaber (Eds.), *Contemporary issues and challenge in early childhood education in the Asia-Pacific region* (pp. 293–308). Springer.

Conclusion

Belonging—An Invitation to Action

Laura M. Gonzalez, Beverly S. Faircloth, and Katherine Ramos

As you approach the end of this book, we invite you to spend a moment reflecting with us. Are there voices that stick with you? What do you notice as far as new learning or new perspectives are concerned? What systems that were previously invisible to you are now coming into focus? What roles or responsibilities in this discourse are emerging on your own personal radar? We have directly heard the voices of those who have been marginalized and told they do not belong by the systems and structures of our society, so that we as readers with varying points of privilege can correct our mistaken impressions about their presence in our world. Even those of us with intersecting identities that situate us with unearned social benefits coupled with barriers to access and power can still find ways to think about belonging and marginalization as they have been expressed throughout this book. We have also heard accounts of transformation, agency, and an emerging right to belong. This part of "Resisting Barriers to Belonging" is an invitation to engage in your own "noticing, naming, and interrupting" practices, a space in which to reconceptualize belonging and barriers to belonging in a way that is holistic, critical, and actionable. It is our opportunity to ask ourselves hard questions about our role in both contributing to barriers to belonging and resisting them.

We would like to return to the words Dr. Rendón offered in the Preface as we reflect back on this book. First, we want to honor her as a foremother in this work, as a scholar-practitioner-activist upon whose shoulders we stand. This book and we ourselves are stronger because of her. Second, her words serve as an essential reminder that "we exist not just as individuals, but also as a part of the greater social collective." We therefore invite you to reflect deeply, with openness and receptivity to the voices you have heard in these pages. If we are to define ourselves as members of "the great family of the world," as Dr. Rendón suggests, we must think carefully about our stance regarding learning and living, accommodating our world view to include the perspectives shared by others. If we are able to internalize the messages carried by those voices and connect with them in some way, we may also notice a call to action that begins to grow in our hearts and minds, compelling us to not sit idle while our brothers and sisters are killed, dispossessed, shamed, deported, left behind, demeaned, silenced, erased, punished, or devalued. For we are indeed wrapped in a single garment of destiny, belonging together to a just community of peers. Whatever social capital we have earned, or unearned benefits we have received, can be wielded to resist the barriers to belonging in our world and to hold each other accountable.

NOTICING/NAMING/INTERRUPTING

We invite us all to clear our vision and reflect on our own experiences (whether beginning or advanced) of noticing and naming. There are aspects of noticing/naming that we do reflectively by ourselves, especially as it relates to removing our blinders and taking a hard look at our privilege. However, it would be hard to fully grasp a socially embedded concept like belonging without the next step of engaging with our communities. One way we might work on this task together is the process of "calling in," which involves "making meaning together, finding a mutual sense of understanding across differences, and taking the opportunity to explore deeply" (Haslam, 2018, pp. 1–2). Calling in makes space for multiple perspectives to be heard, based on the willingness of people who are most affected by a problem to share their perspectives, an act made possible in a just community where we are also invested in shifting our mental paradigms in order to manifest different outcomes for all.

Taken as a whole, the pages of this book help us notice and name the many ways that social power has been used to tokenize and dispossess. This oppressive and exclusionary social power may come in the guise of immigration laws and policies, of disproportionate disciplinary decisions, of hostile climates and closed doors, of gatekeeping to let in a few brave souls but no more, of stereotyping and low expectations. These dominant frames of seeing, interpreting, and acting give very explicit messages about who belongs and who does not. Social power may also surface more insidiously in the form of colorblind statements of shared humanity, of expecting assimilation into a preselected set of words and values, or in the language of scarcity and hoarding of privilege. It can be easy to stay in our comfort zones and assume that we are not participating in these barriers to belonging, but we would like to humbly encourage our readers with social privilege to resist that tendency.

We are not advocating for blame and shame, and have no right or intention to prescribe next steps. We do, however, invite all of us to take inventory of the spaces we inhabit, the spaces that make us feel that we belong and those that do not. If we can offer ourselves the grace to explore, grow, and sit with the potential distress of our own privilege, we may begin to open new doors for ourselves and others that ultimately welcome connection, community, and dare we say belonging.

This is likely to be hard work, a long-term and collective process, one that requires us as members of a community to work together, engaging consistently and persistently. There may be a willingness to connect—a need to strive for belonging—required by the very process of learning to do this work. Each of us will have access to different levers of power in our lives and can gather our own ideas. We challenge each reader to consider where they can create structural counterspaces for inclusion and belonging in their life and work, where they can channel the voices of the most affected into the problem-solving process to envision more just ways to acknowledge rightful presence, where they can push back on deficit narratives and celebrate, value, and honor the strengths of each group. This book is an invitation to begin that endeavor.

Toward a Unifying Message of Belonging: Emerging Themes

With the goal of learning and growing in mind, we hope that the experience of reading these authors' truths related to the inherent right to belong fosters newfound appreciation and perspective. Unique considerations have surfaced in these chapters related to various social identities and positions, with some common themes that we may find actionable.

Calling In

Several chapters deftly identified potential points of leverage within established systems that historically and politically undermine individuals' ability to belong. For example, Hope, Smith, Griffin, and Briggs' chapter rightfully demands a shift in the view that it is the responsibility of Black students to "fit in" or feel like they belong, to a view in which it is the responsibility of educators and policymakers to create spaces where belonging is possible for Black students. Similarly, Antonicci, Killion, and Johnson document pervasive barriers to belonging, and strategies to combat them, for members of the LGBTQ+ community on college campuses. Following that, Gonzalez calls us to think about individuals without permanent, authorized legal status in the United States. She describes the "jarring contrast" between the ideals of our country and the realities of policy and power, identifying both the need for, and strategies for, a higher ethical standard when dealing with new arrivals to your country. These chapters, and others, call us in. They help us make meaning anew, and then leave us with an invitation to greater responsibility or accountability. Specific approaches and programs for disrupting barriers to belonging are highlighted in the second half of the book.

Addressing Narratives and Counternarratives

As illustrated in Hinman et al.'s work (chapter 9), powerful potential can be found even in tasks as simple as

> engaging in the telling of one's story, and sensemaking activities around those tell-ings, marginalized students and their families gain access, in both understanding and action, to the political realm where their narrative actions hold potential for transforming teaching and learning processes for all CDL [culturally & linguisti-cally diverse] students and their families to feel a sense of belonging in school.

This practice of storytelling (or counterstory/counternarrative) as a "making present practice" as showcased in Faircloth et al.'s Community Voices sum-mer writing camp for immigrant and refugee youth, where campers leveraged their various funds of knowledge to claim a right to belong (chapter 10). By embracing the narratives, or counternarratives, of individuals who have been previously positioned as outsiders, invisible, or "missing" (Edkins, 2011; Tedesco & Bagelman, 2017), we acknowledge and honor their roles as con-tributing members of the social contexts they inhabit.

Repairing Belongingness

Other chapters describe programs that not only allow students to share their sto-ries but to also purposefully process their thoughts and feelings as part of navigat-ing the world as marginalized youth. Examples include Harris et al.'s chapter on a College and Career Readiness group for Black females high school students and the ethnic studies club designed to support the critical consciousness of margin-alized middle school students in Faircloth, Barrett, and McClanahan's chapter, both of which prompt students to reflect on and challenge the ways society has positioned them. Such practices recognize existing strengths and cultural capital, building back the rightful belonging and agency of people in marginalized com-munities, while also illuminating the systemic barriers that need to be tackled by those of us with some social capital in those spaces.

Counting on Hope

Finding and leveraging *hope* also emerges as a tool for belonging as we attempt to map our diverse paths. Ramos, for example, rather than interpreting challenging life experiences as unavoidable detours to belonging, evidences an ability to hold belonging in a fluid, nuanced, resilient way. In so doing, she comes to embrace the value of her life as an *in-betweener*, recognizing that her fluid reflective handling of the concept of belonging allows her to "see the role of in-betweener as a source of strength" especially in the space where her own experiences with belonging intersect with her professional experience with others struggling with belonging at the end of life (chapter 6). Hope is also reflected in the narratives of so many in these chapters who recognize a path forward to belonging, such as the middle-grade student who realizes at last that "everyone has a story and is capable of being known and understood; I've learned about how many people are the same- have gone through the same thing"—a powerful lesson for a sixth grader (Faircloth et al., chapter 8).

A Reinforcing Cycle of Belonging

Lastly, Laura Rendón's gift of the term "withness" resonated throughout the narratives in this book as a *tool* for belonging, while simultaneously being the very definition of belonging. Consider the experience of a Black, female high school student in a College and Career Readiness group designed specifically for her, who claims, "You know what I like about this group? I like that we're all Black. I can just be myself, unlike outside of here, [where] I feel like I have to act a certain way" (Harris et al., chapter 7). This suggests that seeing herself in the CCR group (i.e., a concrete moment of withness) helped generate connection/belonging (i.e., a growing sense of withness), suggesting a potential path to belonging that holds much promise. This cycle is also demonstrated by the community of math educators and state leaders, who enlarged their circle to include others (belonging scholars) who could think *with* them about building community, not as something that can be levied but that must be cocreated (Wilson et al., chapter 5). These examples suggest that the cycle of belonging is ever evolving, creating and recreating itself in our own efforts to negotiate our belonging in spaces where people look and feel like us or come alongside us in a spirit of withness, while also navigating our feelings and choices in unwelcoming spaces or challenging endeavors.

These voices—and others that we have yet to surface from the rich depths of these works—offer signposts for our paths to belonging. In sculpting our understandings using their diverse insights, these authors guide our hands, their ideas sitting with us (if we allow those moments) to help us find the levers of change that are within our grasp and the courage to use them.

AN INVITATION TO ENGAGE

We have titled this concluding chapter "Belonging—An Invitation to Action" because we are especially interested in how the time invested in reading and learning may prompt us to action. How do we enact these ideas to return to the original withness that was acknowledged by our ancestors as the true nature of things (Preface), or interrupt dominant frames that pose barriers to belonging in our work spaces, our home and community spaces, our civic and political spaces? In considering potential paths forward, we once again want to recognize our own privilege that comes with our education, being academicians and having the opportunity to reflect, turn-inward and put together a collection of work that offers an invitation to belong. This is a luxury that is not equally available to all. We acknowledge that every person who reads or comes across this book will themselves be on their own respective journey of belonging. As such, the intent of this book and all that it offers is to be open, welcoming, and thoughtful about how people engage in their own reflective process. Because the truth is, if we cannot model for ourselves how we can belong, how can we open ourselves up to help others feel the same? The work begins with us, and it is our hope that this book is one that will be of service in that journey.

Empathy for the lived experiences of others seems a reasonable starting place, especially for those of us whose lives allow us to stay in a "bubble" of homogeneity. However, empathy and insight that allow us to remain untroubled by barriers to belonging is not the goal of this book. In addition to new insights, are there new commitments? Can we move past the initial steps of inviting individual participation or creating small zones of hospitality for some to models of belonging that create greater accountability for belonging within structures and systems? This may include some early steps, such as noticing barriers to belonging or structures that cause harm, and creating more inclusive spaces to encourage and defend the right of participation of groups that have been historically left out. Taking the ideas shared in this book seriously suggests moving beyond a hospitality model, possibly ceding some of the social space and power we have, so that historically excluded groups can affirm and honor their own histories, traditions, and cultures. As Faircloth stated in chapter 1, a critical understanding of belonging would require us to "promote social change by altering institutional processes that contribute to marginalization. It is this agency that lies at the heart of the criticality that must now undergird our considerations of belonging." As Dr. Rendón has pointed out, we can choose from a menu of restorative practices, acknowledging what has been taken from some groups, and dedicating ourselves to cocreating a process that starts to right the wrongs and make amends to individuals and groups. And as our eyes look further down the road, it is safe to anticipate needing to continue addressing power and privilege when it inevitably shows up in the systems and structures we (especially as those with some unearned privilege and power) inhabit currently.

If we attend to the chapter authors and their perspectives carefully, there is an approach to belonging that begins with a series of questions. For example, we can start or expand the process by noticing who is absent or excluded from our systems, and where the gatekeeping is happening. What assumptions are hidden in our work and life systems, and do they affirm the agency, value, and possibility of each member equitably? If we intend to disrupt the status quo in our workplaces, which voices need to be elevated, heard, and believed, and which voices have been given more than their fair share of space and need to step back? Do our systems provide *each* member the tools they need in order to manifest their true selves and move into the future living at their fullest potential? Or, which systems need to be reconfigured in a way that moves beyond providing access and support to those who already have privilege and power. When we view the outcomes that our system produces, is there a pattern of disproportionality who embodies them and who does not? Which tools that we use every day in our work are, in the words of Audre Lorde (2018), "the master's tools," and reflect whitestream cultural values and traditions to the exclusion or dehumanization of others?

We encourage readers to consider questions like these to conduct an audit of their work (and other spaces they inhabit) to see where there are barriers to true and inclusive belonging, and to move closer to those who are most impacted by the barriers in order to start cocreating transformed and just systems in those places. To invite the systems in which we participate to take responsibility for creating spaces where belonging is not only possible, but rightful. Resisting barriers to belonging will mean deconstructing and divesting from the harmful practices that have been named in these chapters and many others. In the words of Vrasti and Dayal (2016), "Rightful presence is not about pursuing inclusion into an already established order; rather, it seeks to assert a new measure of justice even if that means undoing the order we currently exist in and benefit from" (p. 999).

In addition to the charge to those of us with unearned power and privilege to engage in serious examination, we also want to lift up and to speak life into the idea that historically marginalized communities have agency, have tools, have wisdom. As the chapters have clearly modeled, critical consciousness exists in communities that do not have access to the tools of dominant social power but have developed strategies for surviving and thriving in spite of the oppressive barriers to belonging they have faced. Authors in this book have demonstrated this right to belong in the counterspaces they have created, in their experiences of mediating across boundaries and barriers to find spaces for shared practices and engagement, in naming their cultural assets and developing sense of identity, and in creating communities for voice, expression, agency, and solidarity. Across wide-ranging marginalizations, places where people are dismissed and endangered by our society's insistence on a whitestream dominant lens, the authors of this book have spoken and pushed back, providing cultural brokering that has forged new realities of belonging.

Importantly, these voices remind us that their strengths exist even if the contexts created by the whitestream majority have "made them missing" or refused to acknowledge them. Those of us who have lived at the center can choose to stop believing that we deserve our historical placements in the nexus of power, and to vigorously reconsider the idea that people who have been purposefully placed in the social margins are less deserving in any way. To harken back to the metaphor of moving into a room in a house that was shared in the introductory chapter, to support belonging is to encourage and empower everyone in a space to move the furniture around to suit their purposes. Even more, belonging as a right requires us to commit "not only to moving the furniture, but also remodeling the entire structure if necessary" (Watt, 2015, p. 19). These new arrangements will accommodate more people, generate more opportunity, and reduce the chances of harm. As stated another way by Chang et al. in this volume (chapter 11), the sociocultural and critical approach deployed here practices active recognition of learners' capacities to be resistant to difficult circumstances, demonstrates *solidarity* with the learner community's perspectives and practices, and builds collaboration with the learners' community in challenging and transforming situational difficulties and structural inequities.

The right to belong, withness, and solidarity are all ways of saying that each human being is intrinsically valuable, and that inequitable circumstances have altered our trajectories in a manner that is not normal, just, or inevitable in any way. To create a just and beloved community we must ensure equity and accountability—that everyone has what they need to survive and flourish, and that harmful structures and barriers are removed. Belonging as a fundamental right says that circumstance should not be destiny, that I/we/you belong just as we are. Let's dedicate ourselves to the work of making it so.

NOTE

1. Please note that chapter-related article or book references mentioned in this Conclusion are cited in the reference list for that respective chapter.

REFERENCES

Haslam, RE. (2018, August). *Interrupting Bias: Calling Out vs. Calling In*. Seed the Way. http://www.seedtheway.com/

Lorde, A. (2018). *The Master's Tools Will Never Dismantle the Master's House*. Penguin Classics.

Vrasti, W., & Dayal, S. (2016). Cityzenship: Rightful presence and the urban commons. *Citizenship Studies, 20*(8), 994–1011. doi:10.1080/13621025.2016.1229196

Watt, S. (2015). *Designing Transformative Multicultural Initiatives: Theoretical Foundations, Practical Applications and Facilitator Considerations*. Stylus Publishing.

Index

About the Editors and Contributors

EDITORS

Beverly S. Faircloth, PhD, is associate professor of educational psychology at the University of North Carolina Greensboro. Her research explores how minoritized youth can experience an empowering sense of belonging through honoring their identities, cultures, communities, and voices. The Belonging Project (a 15-year partnership with diverse, middle/high schools), the Community Voices summer writing camp for immigrant and refugee youth, and a community partnership with a refugee neighborhood each serve as spaces of discourse, advocacy, and learning, for this work.

Laura M. Gonzalez, PhD, is associate professor in the higher education program at the University of North Carolina Greensboro. She has degrees in Women's Studies (Colgate University), College Counseling and Student Development (University of Delaware), and Counselor Education (North Carolina State University). Her research interests are in diminishing barriers and promoting supports to college access for youth from Latinx immigrant families, which is but one strand in the larger tapestry of human belonging.

Katherine Ramos, PhD, is assistant professor in the Department of Psychiatry and Behavioral Sciences at Duke University School of Medicine. She also has secondary faculty appointments with the Department of Medicine, Geriatrics Division, and with the Department of Population Health Sciences. Katherine has specialized in mental health with older adults and those suffering from medical complexity receiving palliative and/or hospice care. A bulk of this work is facilitating her client's own sense of resilience, belonging, and purpose. For the past seven years, she has been involved in direct clinical care, research, teaching, and mentoring.

CONTRIBUTORS

Nicholas Antonicci, MA, is the director of the Center of Sexual and Gender Diversity at Duke University and currently pursuing a PhD in Educational Studies, Higher Education at the University of North Carolina Greensboro. His research interests include the intersections of critical whiteness studies and LGBTQIA+ communities in higher education.

Shynar Baimaganbetova is a PhD student in the Department of Education Policy and Leadership at the Education University of Hong Kong. She has over four years of research and seven years of practical experience as an English language teacher. Shynar's research interests center around diversity, multiculturalism, sociocultural studies, international student mobility, and life transitions.

Kia Barrett is a graduate of the University of North Carolina Greensboro with a master's degree in education. She is currently a practicing attorney.

Lauren Baucom is a doctoral student and graduate research assistant at the University of North Carolina at Greensboro. A former high school mathematics teacher of 11 years, Baucom has devoted her time to teaching students from both rural and urban areas, and her research primarily focuses on disrupting power structures in the educational system by seeking justice for students and teachers of marginalized populations in the content area of mathematics and statistics. Baucom hopes to continue her passion in mathematics education as she focuses her research on attending to students' and teachers' identities through the learning of critical statistical literacy.

Alexis S. Briggs is a doctoral student at NC State University who is studying pathways of liberation for Black youth.

Benjamin "Benji" Chang is associate professor of Equity Education in the School of Education and International & Global Studies at the University of North Carolina Greensboro, and Adjunct Faculty at the Education University of Hong Kong. His work focuses on teacher education, community engagement, literacy, and culture, particularly with minoritized communities. He has published in books like *Theory Into Practice and Curriculum Inquiry* and is coeditor of *Critical Inquiry in Language Studies*.

Iris Man Wai Cheung is a graduate student at the Hong Kong University, and an international school classroom teacher in Hong Kong. Her research interests include comparative and international education with emphasis on cross-cultural and multicultural contexts.

Arren Duggan is currently a PhD candidate in Teacher Education with a focus on mathematics education in the School of Education at the University of North Carolina Greensboro. Interests include multiple stakeholder group collaboration, mathematics teacher learning, and professional development.

Charity Brown Griffin is assistant professor in the Department of Psychological Sciences at Winston-Salem State University. She earned a BA in Psychology from the University of North Carolina, Chapel Hill and a MA and PhD in School Psychology from the University of South Carolina. Dr. Griffin's research program examines cultural and contextual factors that contribute to Black youths' development including racial identity, racial socialization, racial discrimination, school racial climate, and school engagement.

Emily Hare is currently a PhD candidate in Teacher Education with a focus on mathematics education in the School of Education at the University of North Carolina at Greensboro. Interests include anticipating students' mathematics and professional development.

Pamela N. Harris is a clinical assistant professor for the Online Counseling Program at William and Mary. A former school counselor, her research interests falls under the umbrella of culturally responsive counselor preparation, including cultivating school–family partnerships with families of color, and postsecondary planning for Black female students.

Ye He is professor in the Department of Teacher Education and Higher Education at the University of North Carolina at Greensboro. Her research focuses on the promotion of strength-based, community-engaged, and diverse language and culture-centered teaching and learning practices.

Tierney B. Hinman is assistant professor of Reading Education at Auburn University. Her work focuses on the construction of culturally and linguistically responsive spaces for literacy learning. She is an active participant in community-engaged learning spaces with students and families.

Marquita S. Hockaday is adjunct lecturer of Education at The University of North Carolina at Greensboro and Pfeiffer University. She teaches courses on diversity in education and cultural awareness. Her research interests include culturally responsive curriculum and instruction in the K–12 setting.

Elan C. Hope is associate professor of Applied Social and Community Psychology at North Carolina State University and director of the Hope Lab. Her research focuses on critical consciousness, racism, racial identity, racial socialization, civic engagement, academic achievement, and mental health. She uses qualitative and quantitative approaches to examine these phenomena among racially marginalized adolescents and emerging adults.

Kaitlyn Ingram is a licensed school counselor and clinical mental health counselor associate (LCMHCA) in North Carolina. She has experience working with at-risk high school students and drop-out prevention. She is passionate about diversity and inclusion, and supporting youth and young adults, particularly those in underrepresented populations.

R. Bradley Johnson (he/him) is clinical associate professor of Higher Education and Program Coordinator/Graduate Program Director of the MEd in Higher Education program at UNC Greensboro. He has worked in higher education/student affairs as an administrator and faculty member for over 25 years. His research focuses primarily on LGBTQ+ issues in higher education and students' experiences in residence hall environments.

Louis Killion (MEd) is a recent graduate of UNC Greensboro where he studied higher education with a concentration in student affairs administration. He led Q+: The Queer Graduate Student Association and worked in the postsecondary education office as an instructor of life skills courses.

Pratigya Marhatta is a doctoral student at University of North Carolina at Greensboro, with research interests in teacher education that focuses on interdisciplinary social studies as a conduit for social justice education. She teaches undergraduate methods classes and works with teachers in a local charter school and civil rights museum.

Katherine J. Mawhinney is professor of mathematics at Appalachian State University. Her interests include undergraduate mathematics education and K–12 mathematics teacher professional development. She is currently the assistant chair of the Department of Mathematical Sciences.

Jill L. McClanahan holds a Master of Education from the University of North Carolina Greensboro where she currently teaches Child and Adolescent Development/Learning, Student Engagement in the Classroom, and Teaching

English Learners with Diverse Abilities. She is also an English Language Arts Instructional Coach for Guilford County Schools at Western Guilford Middle School. Mrs. McClanahan is National Board Certified and has more than 23 years of classroom teaching experience.

Allison W. McCulloch is associate professor of Mathematics Education in the Department of Mathematics and Statistics at the University of North Carolina at Charlotte. Her research focuses on practicing and prospective teacher learning, cross-organizational collaborations, and teaching and learning in technology-mediated learning environments.

Dominique McDaniel is a doctoral candidate and graduate assistant in the Teacher Education and Higher Education Department at the University of North Carolina at Greensboro. Her research interests include the identity work of minoritized youth, marginalized youth's experiences in literacy contexts, specifically in and out of school, and the literacies Black and Brown youth engage in within online contexts, such as social media platforms. Dominique taught for ten years, most recently in middle grades language arts, and holds licensure certifications in Elementary Education K–6, Middle Grades Language Arts 6–9, High School English 9–12, and Reading K–12.

Jennifer Nelson graduated from The University of North Carolina at Greensboro with a degree in English. She currently teaches middle school in Asheboro, North Carolina.

Adriana Abarca Paschal, as an immigrant herself, likes to keep in touch with other immigrants that may not know how to navigate the educational system. She assigned herself the task of becoming a teacher to follow the path of service and to advocate for heritage language education of young students.

Catherine Marie Galang Pun is a final-year student at The Education University of Hong Kong. With her biracial background, she strives to work on issues involving ethnic minority youth in Hong Kong. In addition, she is passionate about social justice within education, which she tries to achieve through her role in the Project of Critical Research, Pedagogy & Praxis (PCRP).

Laura I. Rendón is professor emerita at the University of Texas at San Antonio. Rendón is a student advocate and contemplative educator. She developed validation theory and authored the book *Sentipensante*

(Sensing/Thinking Pedagogy): Educating for Wholeness, Social Justice and Liberation.

Catherine Schwartz is associate professor of Mathematics Education. She researches the role teachers' instructional vision and agency play in the enactment of elementary grades mathematics instruction.

Chauncey D. Smith is a community psychologist of education who examines the sociopolitical development of Black youth at intersections of race, class, and gender. In his current role as an assistant professor of Education at the University of Virginia School of Education and Human Development, he examines Black boys' meaning-making of school in an after-school youth participatory action research program.

Michelle Stephan is professor of Mathematics Education at the University of North Carolina at Charlotte with a joint appointment in the Cato College of Education and the Department of Mathematical & Statistics. Her work focuses on engaging middle school teachers in classroom design-based research to create and test student-centered mathematics materials. Recently, she has incorporated a critical mathematics education perspective into designing for ethical and critical mathematics reasoning.

Amy Vetter is professor in English Education at the University of North Carolina Greensboro. Her areas of research interest are the writing identities of youth, critical conversations, and equity and justice in education.

Jared Webb is assistant professor of Mathematics Education at the North Carolina Agricultural & Technical State University. His work focuses on racial equity in mathematics teaching and learning, designs for professional learning, and STEM education.

Holt Wilson is associate professor of Mathematics Education and serves as codirector of the Institute for Partnerships in Education at the University of North Carolina at Greensboro. His work focuses on mathematics teacher learning, designs for professional learning, and cross-organizational collaborations and includes research, professional development, and advocacy.

Shameeka M. Wilson is a former elementary special education teacher and alumna ('18, '20) of The University of North Carolina at Greensboro. She is currently pursuing her PhD in Race, Inequality, and Language in Education (RILE) at Stanford University. Using critical qualitative methodologies, her research focuses on students at the intersection of Emergent Bilingual (EB) and Exceptional Children (EC) enrolled in Dual Language Immersion (DL/I) programs within public K–12 spaces.

F. Paul Wonsavage is currently a PhD candidate in Curriculum and Instruction with a focus on mathematics education in the School of Education at the University of North Carolina at Greensboro. His interests include building the capacity of practitioners to use research and working with mathematics pre-service and in-service teachers.

Mel Hyeri Yang has served as a classroom teacher for four years in South Korea. She is currently continuing her graduate study at the University of Michigan – Ann Arbor as a Fulbright fellow. Her research interest comprises developing a curriculum for marginalized students and investigating the intersection between technology and K–12 education, focusing on racial and gender equity.

Benjamin Wai San Yip is a final-year undergraduate in The Education University of Hong Kong. He is also a pre-service English teacher in secondary schools.

Melody Zoch is associate professor of Literacy Education at the University of North Carolina Greensboro. Her research focuses on how teachers respond to their educational contexts in their literacy teaching, including teachers' responsiveness to culturally and linguistically diverse students and communities. Her work has been published in journals such as *Journal of Literacy Research, Anthropology and Education Quarterly, Urban Education*, and *The Teacher Educator.*

www.ingramcontent.com/pod-product-compliance
Lightning Source LLC
Chambersburg PA
CBHW031351290326
41932CB00044B/972